For 2,500 years, since the time of Herodotus and Thucydides, historians have sought to record the truth about the past. Today, however, the discipline is suffering a potentially lethal attack from the rise to prominence of an array of French-inspired literary and social theories, each of which denies that truth and knowledge about the past are possible. These theories claim the central point on which history was founded no longer holds: there is no fundamental distinction between history and myth or between history and fiction.

Historians in classrooms from Berkeley to Paris have embraced these views, and an increasing number of literary critics and social theorists now feel free to define their own work as history and to call themselves historians. The result is revolutionary: historians have not only changed how history is taught, they are also increasingly obscuring the very facts on which the truth must be built. In *The Killing of History*, Keith Windschuttle offers both a devastating exposé of the absurdity of these developments and a defense of the integrity of Western intellectual traditions which are now so widely attacked.

Windschuttle examines exactly what is being taught about Columbus' discovery of the New World; the history of asylums and prisons in Europe; the fall of Communism in 1989; and the Battle of Quebec in 1759. He offers a much needed defense of traditional history as a properly scientific endeavor and argues that the great works of history should still be regarded as among the finest forms of Western literature.

KEITH WINDSCHUTTLE

THE KILLING
OF HISTORY

HOW LITERARY CRITICS AND SOCIAL THEORISTS
ARE MURDERING OUR PAST

THE FREE PRESS
New York

THE FREE PRESS
A Division of Simon & Schuster Inc.
1230 Avenue of the Americas
New York, NY 10020

First Free Press Edition 1997
First published in Australia

THE FREE PRESS and colophon are trademarks
of Simon & Schuster Inc.

Manufactured in the United States of America

10   9   8   7   6   5   4

Library of Congress Cataloging-in-Publication Data

Windschuttle, Keith
     The killing of history : how literary critics and social theorists
are murdering our past / Keith Windschuttle. — 1st Free Press ed.
          p.   cm.
     Originally published: Paddington, NSW, Australia : Macleay Press,
1996. Rev. and expanded international ed.
     Includes bibliographical references (p.) and index.
     ISBN 0-684-84445-1
     1. Historiography.   2. Historicism.   I. Title
D13.W624   1997
907′.2—dc21   97-18957
                                                                    CIP

For Elizabeth

CONTENTS

PREFACE

History is an intellectual discipline that is more than 2400 years old. It ranks with philosophy and mathematics as among the most profound and enduring contributions that ancient Greece made, not only to European civilisation, but to the human species as a whole. Instead of the mythical tales which all human cultures had used to affirm their sense of self-worth and their place in the cosmos, the Greek historians decided to try to record the truth about the past. They did this even though they knew their stories would expose how fragile was their existence, how their heroes could not guarantee their victories, how their oracles could not foretell their future and how their gods could not ensure their fortunes. The greatest of them, Thucydides, revealed how the fate of people was entirely contingent upon human actions and social organisation. Myth had been comforting, but history was bracing. For most of the last 2400 years, the essence of history has continued to be that it should try to tell the truth, to describe as best as possible what really happened. Over this time, of course, many historians have been exposed as mistaken, opinionated and often completely wrong, but their critics have usually felt obliged to show they were wrong about real things, that their claims about the past were different from the things that had actually happened. In other words, the critics still operated on the assumption that the truth was within the historian's grasp.

Today, these assumptions are widely rejected, even among some people employed as historians themselves. In the 1990s, the newly dominant theorists within the humanities and social sciences assert that it is impossible to tell the truth about the past or to use history to produce knowledge in any objective sense at all. They claim we can only see the past through the perspective of our own culture and, hence, what we see in history are our own interests and concerns reflected back at us. The central point upon which history was founded no longer holds: there is no fundamental distinction any more between history and myth. This view is not itself new. It was forcefully argued more than one hundred years ago by the German philosopher Friedrich Nietzsche, and has been nurtured by his followers ever since. What is new is the success these ideas have had among English-speaking universities and academic publishers in the last ten years. I have long agreed with E. P. Thompson's assessment that history is the 'Queen of the Humanities'[1] and, indeed, is the proper study of humankind. Sociology, anthropology and psychology have always been prey to fashionable and sometimes bizarre theories, but, while history remained intact, the humanities and social sciences had some claim to being intellectually respectable. It is amazing how quickly this has changed.

The traditional practice of history is now suffering a potentially mortal attack from the rise to academic prominence of a relatively new array of literary and social theories. As well as making a general frontal assault on the principles for which the discipline has traditionally stood, these theories have entrenched themselves behind the lines in three specific ways. First, we are now witnessing a breed of literary critics, literary theorists and theoretical sociologists who have moved in and begun writing their own versions of history. To create the room for this manoeuvre they have proclaimed the traditional discipline to be fatally flawed. Second, some of those who trained as historians and spent most of their working lives in the field have accepted the validity of the critics' arguments and have written works from what would once have been regarded as an alien perspective. In doing so, they have been applauded not only by their new allies but by many who might have been expected to have defended the other side. Third, there are a small number of very good historians who, though still upholding the discipline's traditional methodology, have recently incorporated into their work ideas and practices that a decade ago they would not have countenanced. The representatives of this last group are embracing assumptions that have the capacity to demolish everything they stand for.

The structure of the book is designed to examine how both the general and the specific versions of these theories have been applied to the writing of history. The principal targets of the investigation and the places where they are discussed are:

Cultural relativism: Chapters Two and Nine
Semiotics: Chapter Two
Structuralist theory: Chapters Two, Three and Nine
Poststructuralist theory: Chapters Four and Five
Anti-humanism, genealogy and discourse theory: Chapter Five
Hegelian and Marxist philosophy of history: Chapter Six
Postmodernist philosophy of history: Chapter Six
Radical scepticism and scientific relativism: Chapter Seven
Hermeneutics: Chapter Seven
Historical fiction and theory of poetics: Chapter Eight.

These chapters discuss the attempts at writing history made by some of the most influential literary and social theorists and critically examine their views about historical methodology, especially their rejection of empiricism and induction. In discussing their works, I have tried to present summaries of their views that are detailed, clear and fair; characteristics that are conspicuously absent from their own critiques of traditional historiography. The final two chapters of the book are intended, respectively, to defend the integrity of history as a properly scientific endeavour, and to canvass the nature of history as a form of literature. Ultimately, the book is offered as a positive contribution to debate, rather than as simply a negative critique of the current fashions. Its aim is to show that, despite all the present claims to the contrary, history can be studied in an objective way and that there are no philosophical obstacles to the pursuit of truth and knowledge about the human world.

I want to emphasise, though, that the last thing I wanted to do was publish yet another boring book about theory. There are enough works critical of the current vogue for theory on the market already. Most of these have been written for people with interests in literary criticism or philosophy and many, I am afraid, are just as unreadable as their targets. In addressing this book to readers who are interested primarily in history itself, I have tried to make a case through a discussion of actual historical topics and subject matter. Most of the theories the book discusses are approached not in an abstract way but through examples of their application to the events of the past. These include:

- the European discovery of America and the Spanish conquest of Mexico
- the British discovery and exploration of the Pacific islands, the death of Captain James Cook, and the mutiny on the HMS *Bounty*
- the foundation of European settlement in Australia, including British exploration, the convict system and relations with the Aborigines
- the history of mental asylums and penal policy in Europe
- the expansion of the aristocracy of Western Europe in the Middle Ages
- the fall of Communism in 1989
- the Battle of Quebec in 1759.

The most positive way to defend the traditional practices of history, I decided, was to use the work of real historians to combat their theoretical opponents. So I have relied upon the evidence provided in a number of recent works of empirical history about the events listed above to question the adequacy of those theory-dependent works that have discussed the same topics. Apart from the first, introductory chapter of this book, each of the others can be regarded as a road test of one or more of the latest season's theoretical models to see, first, how it handles the rougher terrain of actual historical subject matter, and, second, how it stands up to competition over the same ground from those empirical jalopies that the new crew wants to consign to the junk yard.

Obviously, if there is enough recent work by genuine historians to assist in this task, the traditional discipline of history could hardly be pronounced dead yet. This is true, but I have used the word 'killing' in this book's title to signal that there is a lethal process well underway. The examples provided in this book are, hopefully, enough evidence of this but those who still have doubts about the extent of the demise should consult the latest editions of what were once the more respected of the academic journals of the discipline. There they will now find page after page of essays deferring to the views of one or more of the French theorists who are now so much in vogue. What is particularly disturbing is that the authors of these essays are either unaware or unconcerned that it is these same theorists who insist the traditional methodology of the discipline is so defective that it should be jettisoned completely. The killing of history is being perpetrated to some extent by the theoretical naivety of historians themselves.

The institutional prospects of the discipline are also cause for alarm. In the last six years, Australia has gone through a period of rapid expansion of the higher education system. The former vocationally oriented colleges of advanced education have all been upgraded so that the number of universities has almost doubled. Not one of these newly elevated institutions has established a department or school in which history is taught as a proper discipline in its own right. This is in notable contrast to the previous period of university expansion in the 1960s when no self-respecting university would establish a faculty of humanities or social sciences without including a department of history staffed by people trained as historians. Instead, Australia's newest institutions have established any number of schools and appointed dozens of professors to teach cultural studies, communications studies and media studies. There are a few new offerings euphemistically named 'historical studies', but, in every case, these are dominated by sociological and literary approaches to the past, rather than anything deserving the name of history. Precisely the same patterns are evident in Britain where the former polytechnics are now being converted into universities, with similar results. A mere two decades ago most English-speaking countries regarded the study of history as essential to any liberal arts education worthy of the name. Today, only about half the institutions offering arts degrees bother to teach it at all.

One of the risks one runs today in defending anything traditional is to be seen simply as a knee-jerk reactionary. Indeed, one of the assertions sometimes made about responses like this one is that they primarily represent a generational conflict. Hence, some might argue this book signifies little more than a middle-aged academic defending the remnants of his own intellectual capital while trying to stem a tide of fresh and invigorating ideas from the younger generation. In convening a 1991 conference on these new literary and social theories, one senior academic, Ken Ruthven, Professor of English at the University of Melbourne, said none of the members of his own generation could afford to be dismissive of this new movement. 'Faced by mounting evidence of one's own intellectual obsolescence', Ruthven said, 'the options are either to retire gracefully or to become a student again'.[2] Nothing, however, could be more misleading. This movement, which Ruthven dignifies with the label 'the new humanities', is not the work of any younger generation at all. By far the majority of the academics in Australia, the United States and Britain who are pushing these ideas are either well into their forties or have recently turned fifty. The Continental gurus who initiated the movement are now either in their sixties and even their seventies or, like Michel Foucault, Roland Barthes and Michel de Certeau, are already dead. In other words, the movers and shakers of this movement are the old New Left crowd from the 1960s, my own generation, obviously not so new these days but just as addicted to the latest fashions as they were in the days of hippy beads and flared trousers.

One of the reasons the humanities and social sciences have been taken over so quickly by the sophistry described in this book is because too few of those who might have been expected to resist the putsch understood what its instigators were saying. The uninitiated reader who opens a typical book on postmodernism, hermeneutics, poststructuralism et al must think he or she has stumbled onto a new foreign language, so obscure and dense is the prose. Now, this happens to be a very effective tactic to adopt in academic circles where there is always an expectation that things are never simple and that anyone who writes clearly is thereby being shallow. Obscurity is often assumed to equal profundity, a quality that signals a superiority over the thinking of the uneducated herd. Moreover, those students who put in all the work needed to comprehend a dialogue of this kind very often become converts, partly to protect their investment in the large amount of time already committed, and partly because they are bound to feel they have thereby earned a ticket into an elite. Obscurity is thus a clever way to generate a following. As Luc Ferry and Alain Renaut, the two wittiest and most devastating critics of the French philosophy behind this movement, have observed:

The 'philosophists' of the '68 period gained their greatest success through accustoming their readers and listeners to the belief that incomprehensibility is a sign of greatness and that the thinker's silence before the incongruous demand for meaning was not proof of weakness but the indication of endurance in the presence of the Unsayable.[3]

The opposite, unfashionable, but nonetheless egalitarian view is that writing of any kind should be simple, direct and accessible,[4] and that the content of any academic debate can be presented without compromise in language that can be readily understood by all intelligent people. Sometimes specialist disciplines adopt their own words, terms and phrases because they are dealing with concepts that are exclusive to their own field or that are genuinely new. This is fair enough, but anyone writing for a wider audience who is forced to adopt uncommon terminology of this kind should accept the onus of clearly explaining what it means whenever it crops up. At the grave risk of producing a work that is too easy to understand for its own good, I have tried to present my case in a clear and comprehensible manner, even for those who are completely new to the debates that are entered into here. No doubt, I have not always succeeded, but the attempt is still better than adopting the alternative, wilfully obscurantist approach that is so characteristic of the theoretical works discussed in these pages.

THE FIRST EDITION of this book was published in Australia in November 1994. This revised edition is being distributed internationally and I have taken the opportunity to make some corrections and to add Chapter Nine, The Return of Tribalism, written specifically for this edition.

Keith Windschuttle, February 1996

---

1   E. P. Thompson, *The Poverty of Theory and other essays,* Merlin, London, 1978, p 262
2   K. K. Ruthven, 'Introduction', in K. K. Ruthven (ed.), *Beyond the Disciplines: The New Humanities,* Australian Academy of the Humanities, Canberra, 1992, p ix
3   Luc Ferry and Alain Renaut, *French Philosophy of the Sixties: An Essay on Antihumanism,* (French edn 1985), trans. Mary S. Cattani, University of Massachusetts Press, Amherst, 1990, p 14
4   Typically, one follower of the French poststructuralist philosopher, Jacques Derrida, claims that clear writing is the sign of a reactionary. Mas'd Zavarzadeh has dismissed a critic of Derrida because of 'his unproblematic prose and the clarity of his presentation, which are the conceptual tools of conservatism', *Journal of Aesthetics and Art Criticism,* 40, 1982, pp 329–33, cited by John M. Ellis, *Against Deconstruction,* Princeton University Press, Princeton, 1989, p 10

1

PARIS LABELS AND DESIGNER CONCEPTS

THE ASCENSION OF CULTURAL STUDIES AND THE DELUGE OF SOCIAL THEORY

Almost every week, the book review pages of the newspapers and magazines in most of the world's large English-speaking cities repeat a message that is rapidly becoming one of the intellectual axioms of our era: there is no longer any clear distinction between works of fiction and non-fiction. Hence, academics are only deluding themselves if they think that when they undertake research and write about society they are engaged in the pursuit of truth and knowledge. A recent Sydney newspaper review of a novel set in the French Revolution flags most of the currently fashionable terms and serves to indicate those views that are now in and out of favour.

In this age of postmodernist literary criticism, we are more than ever aware of the ways in which historical writing resembles the novel as one individual's reconstruction of an imagined past. Historians may seek to be as 'objective' as possible, but they are no longer under positivist illusions about the scientific pretensions of their discipline.[1]

Behind the confidence with which such statements are made lies a movement that has been gathering momentum over the last decade. Over this period, academic circles throughout the West have become as permeated by Parisian labels as the fashion industry. In English-speaking countries the movement can trace its theoretical origins back to the mid-1970s when a number of academics discovered French theory. In the United States, the most influential was the 'Yale School' of literary criticism, which embraced the poststructuralist theories of the French philosopher Jacques Derrida. In Britain, much of the early momentum came from the Birmingham Centre for Contemporary Cultural Studies, which housed the most enthusiastic English adherents of the structuralist Marxism of another Parisian, Louis Althusser. By the early 1980s both groups were in the ascendancy in their own areas but remained confined to a fairly narrow range of subjects: literary theory, communications theory and media studies, all places where practitioners could make a lot of noise but do little damage to anything further afield.

By the middle of the decade, however, the situation had changed very quickly. One of the early primers of the movement, *The Return of Grand Theory in the Human Sciences*, was published in 1985 by Cambridge University Press. This was a collection of essays edited by Quentin Skinner that was designed to both record and celebrate what it championed as an iconoclastic group of theories and methods for the study of human society. Several of these theories were not new, the editor noted. Some had their origins in the nineteenth and early twentieth centuries. By the 1950s and 1960s, he said, they had been rejected by prevailing academic opinion in most English-speaking countries and had then been 'consigned to the dustbin of history'. However, in the 1970s and 1980s, new theorists breathed life into them once more and they re-emerged to 'restructure' the human sciences. Although in 1985, Skinner wrote, they had not yet toppled the main enemy—'piecemeal empirical research'—they were nonetheless well on the way.

During the past generation, Utopian social philosophies have once again been practised as well as preached; Marxism has revived and flourished in an almost bewildering variety of forms; psychoanalysis has gained a new theoretical orientation with the work of Lacan and his followers; Habermas and other members of the Frankfurt School have continued to reflect on the parallels between the theories of Marx and Freud; the Women's Movement has added a whole range of previously neglected insights and arguments; and amidst all this turmoil the empiricist and positivist citadels of English-speaking social philosophy have been threatened and undermined by successive waves of hermeneuticists, structuralists, post-empiricists, deconstructionists and other invading hordes.[2]

The stance adopted by Skinner was that of the outsider trying to break in but, even as he wrote, some of the key citadels had already fallen. Skinner himself at the time held one of Britain's most prestigious social science posts as Professor of Political Science at Cambridge University. Similarly, one of his contributors, Anthony Giddens, was Professor of Sociology at the same university and one of Britain's most influential sociologists. Other contributors were well-known American academics who held chairs of anthropology, philosophy and politics at such distinguished institutions as Cornell, Princeton and the University of California. Skinner's metaphor of invading hordes storming in from the outside was misplaced. It was more like a coup by dissident courtiers from within the palace itself.

Since 1985, the dissidents have expanded their territory enormously. Although they still like to portray themselves as embattled outsiders, they are today the ones making all the running—devising the new courses, contracting the publishers, filling the new jobs, attracting the postgraduate students. The humanities and social science departments of universities in most English-speaking countries still employ a considerable number of old-style empiricists, but they are either too busy, too tired or too bemused to come to terms with what they see as a wave of alien concepts and terminology. The 'restructuring' celebrated by Skinner has proceeded apace and has now spread to all corners of the globe. It has found its most fertile soil in the American university system, where the speed of its growth has elicited comments of both amazement and envy from foreign supporters. For instance, at a conference that attracted nine hundred people, including a bevy of Australians, to the University of Illinois in 1990 to deliberate on one of these newly defined fields, cultural studies, the Professor of Sociology at Britain's Open University, Stuart Hall, remarked upon the 'explosion' of cultural studies and cultural theory that he had witnessed in the United States.

I am completely dumbfounded by it. I think of the struggles to get cultural studies into the institution in the British context, to squeeze three or four jobs for anybody under some heavy disguise, compared with the rapid institutionalisation which is going on in the US.[3]

In Australia, the academic strongholds have also been successfully stormed, and, as in America, the dissidents no longer feel the need to cover the appointment of like-thinking colleagues with 'heavy disguise'. The new movements have now captured much of the intellectual high ground in the humanities, according to the University of Melbourne's former Professor of English, Stephen Knight. In 1990 he described the position they had won.

In recent years the area of research that has been most prominent, attention earning and intellectually prestigious in the arts and social sciences area has been what is being called the New Humanities. Literary studies has linked up with aspects of linguistics, usually called semiotics, and together they have explored the social relations of culture, bringing in aspects of philosophy, psychology and history. Important work was being done in France; Gallic names like Foucault, Lacan, Macherey, Derrida, flow like great wine brands around the lips of serious staff and students these days.[4]

The Australian Academy of the Humanities, the body that represents all Australian university humanities schools, devoted its 1991 symposium to these 'new humanities' and to their call for the dissolution of the existing divisions between academic disciplines. The convenor of the symposium, Professor Ken Ruthven of the Department of English at the University of Melbourne, asserted that the organisation and its members must now take on board the ideas of this movement. 'The credibility of any academy which claims to represent the humanities is dependent nowadays on its willingness and ability to engage critically with the new humanities.'[5]

Down at the level of day-to-day undergraduate teaching in Australia, the story is similar. One could point to a proliferation of examples in the new universities created since 1988, but it is more revealing to show how the traditional institutions have succumbed. The once-conservative Department of History at the University of Sydney in 1991 introduced a new seminar in those theoretical developments that it said had transformed the traditional concept of the discipline. The seminar was compulsory for all students taking the honours stream, and was introduced as follows:

The old-fashioned concept of the historian's task was that he (rarely she) 'described what really happened in the past'. This notion, though still widely held, has been exploded by theoretical developments which have occurred largely outside the field of history itself. The work of social philosophers, anthropologists, linguists, scientists, political, literary and feminist theorists, have, from a variety of directions and with increasing momentum, exploded the old concept of history. It is no longer possible for historians to work in isolation from these developments.[6]

Despite flattering endorsements of this kind, the 'new humanities' have not had it all their own way. A small number of critics have argued that, rather than intellectual prestige, these trends amount to intellectual catastrophe. The most prominent of these critics was the American philosopher, the late Allan Bloom, whose book, *The Closing of the American Mind,* argued in 1987 that radical theory had captured the entire agenda about how we in the West study human society and how we understand human beings as individuals. The results were that humanities and social science departments within universities had abandoned objectivity and truth and become hopelessly politicised. Most young people today were taught to scorn the traditional values of Western culture—equality, freedom, democracy, human rights—as hollow rhetoric used to mask the self-interest of the wealthy and powerful. This teaching, Bloom argued, had bred a cynical, amoral, self-centred younger generation who lacked any sense of inherited wisdom from the past. 'The crisis of liberal education', Bloom wrote, 'is a reflection of a crisis at the peaks of learning, an incoherence and incompatibility among the first principles with which we interpret the world, an intellectual crisis of the greatest magnitude, which constitutes the crisis of our civilisation'.[7]

In 1990, another American critic, Roger Kimball, wrote a book called *Tenured Radicals* with a similar theme to Bloom's in which he underlined with more recent detail both how rapid and how extensive had been the process of politicisation of American university life in the late 1980s. He focused particular attention on the influence of the French theorist Jacques Derrida and his 'deconstructionist' approach to literature and language, and on how these ideas had infiltrated the teaching of literature, art, architecture and law. Like Bloom, Kimball saw these developments as 'ideologically motivated assaults on the intellectual and moral substance of our culture'.[8] Another celebrated response was Dinesh D'Souza's 1991 book *Illiberal Education: The Politics of Race and Sex on Campus,* a critique of the political correctness movement in American universities.[9] Indian-born D'Souza provided an incriminating analysis of ethnically biased admission policies and of the 'multiculturalist' movement. The latter concept has been adopted by feminist studies and black studies in the United States to label the whole body of Western learning as nothing but the ideology of dead, white males. Multiculturalists want the curriculum of higher education to be rewritten from a 'gender specific' or 'Afrocentric' perspective. The central issue that concerned all three of these authors, Bloom, Kimball and D'Souza, was the preservation of the canon of Western learning; that is, the generally recognised body of great works that have stood the test of time and that, until recently, were acknowledged as central to a complete education.

In Britain, the influence of deconstruction also became a matter of bitter public debate in May 1992 when Cambridge University proposed to confer an honorary doctorate of literature on Jacques Derrida. In an unprecedented move against the bestowing of an honour that is normally done without question, a group of Cambridge professors challenged the decision. The issue eventually went to a vote of academic staff. The majority supported Derrida, but not before one of the forty per cent who dissented, Howard Erskine-Hill, called the decision a 'symbolic suicide for a university'.

In France, there have also been signs of resistance. The main critics have been the philosophers Luc Ferry and Alain Renaut, who caused a sensation in Parisian intellectual circles in 1985 with their critique of what they called 'French Philosophy of the Sixties'.[10] They focused on the 'anti-humanism' of four of the most fashionable French writers—Michel Foucault, Jacques Derrida, Pierre Bourdieu and Jacques Lacan, who emerged as celebrities in the wake of the student radical movement of 1968. Among the central claims of anti-humanist philosophy were the impotence of human reason and the impossibility of universal moral judgements. It thereby rejected the concept of universal human rights and traditional notions of freedom and equality. Ferry and Renaut argued that the main project of the philosophy of the Sixties, 'the total critique of the modern world', was permeated by internal inconsistencies and was both logically vacuous and politically irresponsible. In

1987, another French publication, by Victor Farías, cost Foucault, Derrida and Lacan many of their supporters by showing that the intellectual mentor to whom all three were indebted, the German existentialist philosopher Martin Heidegger, had been an anti-Semite, a Nazi informer on academic colleagues in the 1930s, and a financial member of the Nazi party from 1933 to 1945. While Foucault and Derrida thought his work pointed in radical directions, Heidegger himself continued to believe until his death in 1976 that his philosophy confirmed the 'inner truth and greatness' of the Nazi movement.[11] While the political career of the founder of a school of thought is obviously insufficient to refute the theories of his disciples, it raised embarrassing questions about the political judgement of the disciples when they themselves proclaimed that all thought was charged with politics. In their home country, if not yet abroad, some of the 'great wine brands' of France are now on the nose.

There is one thing that all the so-called 'new humanities' have in common, despite the considerable differences among the gurus who inspire them. All share a similar set of views about the concepts of knowledge, truth and science and about the way that academic study has been organised into disciplines. On each of these concepts, they insist, the Western tradition has got it wrong. Let me outline the principles endorsed by the 'new humanities' to emphasise just how radical is the challenge that is underway.

Knowledge: These theories are united in the view that inductive reasoning and empirical research cannot provide a basis for knowledge. They challenge the concepts of objectivity and certainty in knowledge, arguing that different intellectual and political movements create their own forms of relative 'knowledge'.

Truth: They believe that truth is also a relative rather than an absolute concept. The pursuit of unconditional truth is impossible, they argue. What is 'true', they claim, depends on who is speaking to whom and in what context.

Science: They claim that science cannot be value-free or objective. They also agree that neither the human sciences nor natural science provide us with what could be called knowledge. We invent scientific theories rather than make scientific discoveries.

Disciplines: Most believe that the traditional divisions of academic disciplines, especially in the humanities and social sciences, are inappropriate. The established disciplines should all become far more multi- and cross-disciplinary. The adoption of the term 'studies' reflects the new emphasis. Supporters of the movement advocate that, instead of being organised into disciplines such as history, law and English, teaching and research be reorganised into new, cross-bred fields such as 'cultural studies', 'textual studies', 'women's studies', 'peace studies' and 'media studies'. Some of these give the appearance of retaining a traditional discipline—'historical studies' and 'legal studies', for example—but turn out on closer examination to bear only a marginal resemblance to the original, to which they are often strongly opposed.

Although they are beyond the scope of this book, it is important to recognise that there are other academic fields outside the humanities and social sciences that are affected. Several other areas have been just as extensively colonised, especially in professional education, where this is probably more damaging because of the greater practical consequences. Architectural schools, for instance, have now been influenced by these movements to the extent that architectural firms today see many graduates as 'deconstructivist clones', very well versed in postmodernist theory but poorly educated in structure, construction and budgeting and, as a result, barely fit for practice.[12] In Australia, law schools including those at Monash University, Melbourne, and the University of Wollongong, have recently introduced courses in literary and cultural studies to address such issues as 'legal fictions' and 'legal poetics', while academic legal conferences now attract papers with such titles as: 'Metalanguage and the Crisis of Representation: Some Thoughts on the Law of Genre, the Discourse on Language and the Re-Writing of Law as Postmodern Fiction'.[13] In the United States, professors of English literature, such as Stanley Fish of Duke University, have been appointed heads of law schools on the grounds that the basis of legal education is expertise in hermeneutics or textual interpretation.[14] In a growing number of Australian art schools, students complain they spend most of their time on the theories of fashionable Parisians such as Jean Lyotard and Jean Baudrillard, but are not taught how to draw properly.[15] Poststructuralist theory is even making headway in the unlikely fields of business management and accounting. No, I am not joking. In the United Kingdom and the United States, poststructuralist theories have formed part of the academic literature in accounting for at least five years.[16] In Australia, Michel Foucault's methodologies are now taken seriously enough to be taught to graduate students in accounting at the University of New South Wales. The newest field to be colonised is health and medicine, where a recent author, who lectures in an English medical school, assures us that our concepts of 'the patient' and 'illness' are 'sociological fictions' which can be expunged by 'elements of feminist theory and Derridean concepts of *différance* and intertextuality'.[17]

THE ASCENDANCY OF CULTURAL STUDIES

Without a doubt, cultural studies is the fastest growing area in the humanities and social sciences. The editors of a recent book of essays on the subject talk of its 'unprecedented international boom'.[18] Moreover, the growth of this field is not only a matter of intellectual fashion; it has also caused a dramatic redistribution of educational resources, as its supporters readily attest:

At the same time, it is undoubtedly cultural studies' material and economic promise that contributes, as much as its intellectual achievement, to its current vogue. In the United States, where the boom is especially strong, many academic institutions—presses, journals, hiring committees, conferences, university curricula—have created significant investment opportunities in cultural studies.[19]

Cultural studies is one of the more prominent of the fields to emerge from the French-indebted literary theory and media studies of the 1970s. Unlike the traditional discipline of English literary criticism, cultural studies does not confine itself to high culture. It is even more interested in popular culture, especially film and television. Overall, its adherents consider its domain to be 'the entire range of a society's arts, beliefs, institutions, and communicative practices'.[20] Although the majority of its practitioners are former literary critics, the field is not confined to literary studies. In the United States, academics from cultural studies are leading a charge across almost every territory of the humanities: 'media criticism, education, history, feminism, African–American studies, Latino studies, studies of indigenous and aboriginal cultures.'[21] In other words, this relatively new field is attempting to stake out for itself a terrain that includes the study of just about everything in human society. Though they sometimes admit they might be making a tall order, the advocates of cultural studies emphasise that there are very few limits to what they hope to accomplish.

Continually engaging with the political, economic, erotic, social and ideological, cultural studies entails the study of all the relations between all the elements in a whole way of life.[22]

Moreover, enthusiasts for the field see its growth accompanying either the transformation or the destruction of existing disciplines within the humanities. Despite being employed as Professor of English at the University of Queensland, John Frow has for some years expressed his dissatisfaction with the restriction of the study of English to high culture and has put on record 'my pleasure that the discipline, in this form, has been falling apart for some time now'. Frow much prefers cultural studies, which he defines in the following terms:

Cultural Studies takes as its theoretical object the culture of everyday life, where the concept of culture is understood in a broadly anthropological sense, as the full range of practices and representations in which meanings and personal group identities are formed. Cultural Studies is concerned as much with the social relations of representations as it is with self-contained texts.[23]

When the proponents of cultural studies write about the past they now have

few reservations about calling their practise 'history'. However, they are usually careful to distinguish this from the discipline of traditional history, in
which very few of them have trained. They normally claim that they are
engaging in a new kind of interdisciplinary activity which redefines history as
a version of cultural studies. The American literary critic, Professor Annabel
Patterson of Duke University, North Carolina, described a recent collection
of her theory-laden analyses of sixteenth and seventeenth century texts by
authors such as Shakespeare, Milton, Spenser and Donne as 'an experiment in
the new interdiscipline, cultural history'.[24] She regards this work as a form of
history because, as well as conventional literary works such as poetry and
drama, she includes within her ambit a number of pamphlets, tracts and ser-
mons written at the same time. Like the other literary critics discussed below
who now define themselves as historians, Patterson believes that the study of
the past is best done by approaching social practices and relations through
textual analysis.

Part of the appeal of the focus of cultural studies on social practices and
relations has been the opportunity this has provided its practitioners to take up
political positions. The field has always been heavily politicised and the more
successful it has become, the wider its political spectrum has grown. Indeed,
some practitioners now complain that the politics of a number of their colleagues amounts to little more than personal opportunism. 'Too many people
simply rename what they were already doing to take advantage of the cultural
studies boom.'[25] Broad though its political appeal might now be, cultural
studies had its origins among academic radicals, and it still draws the overwhelming majority of its practitioners from the Left side of politics. Moreover, as Marxism has grown both intellectually unfashionable and politically
untenable, leftists in English departments have been increasingly drawn to this
new flame. 'Certainly, within the fragmented institutional configuration of
the academic left', the editors cited above observe, 'cultural studies holds
special intellectual promise because it explicitly attempts to cut across diverse
social and political interests and address many of the struggles within the current scene'.[26] One American literary critic, Catherine Gallagher, has argued
that cultural studies has worked with both Marxism and feminism to achieve
the goals of 'making students of literature more aware of the history and
significance of such phenomena as imperialism, slavery and gender differentiation'. Though it rejects some of the doctrines of 1960s Marxism, she says
that much of this work 'can be said to possess a remarkable continuity with
certain cultural assumptions of the New Left'.[27]

No discussion of the politics of this field should omit the impact of feminism. As academic feminists themselves never seem to tire of pointing out,
discussion of the origins of cultural studies too often assumes that feminist

theorists are 'the dependent heirs of male intellectual capital'. In reality, we should acknowledge that feminists have made an independent contribution to the key assumptions. The American Marxist–feminist Judith Lowder Newton says that these have been:

... partly generated by the theoretical breaks of the second wave of the women's movement, by feminist criticism of male-centred knowledges for their assumption of 'objectivity', by feminist assertion of the political and historically specific nature of knowledge itself, and by feminist analyses of their cultural construction of female identity. Since the late sixties, moreover, feminist work has emphasised the role of 'ideas', or symbolic systems in the construction not only of identities but social institutions and social relations as a whole.[28]

Hence, whatever view we take about cultural studies, we should certainly go along with the demand of academic feminists that they share the responsibility for what is happening to the humanities and social sciences.

THE RESURRECTION OF HISTORICISM

Although cultural studies originated in Britain, it has produced in the United States a number of indigenous variations, which have made their own contribution to its development. One of the movements that became prominent in the United States in the 1980s is known as 'new historicism'.

The term 'historicism' originated in the nineteenth century to describe an approach to history writing and literary criticism that emphasised that each era of the past should be interpreted in terms of its own values, perspectives and context, rather than by those of the present. However, the term was taken over in the 1950s by Karl Popper and given a different meaning. In his book *The Poverty of Historicism*, Popper used it to describe belief in large-scale laws of historical development, especially those which predicted the future and saw history heading towards some ultimate objective. His particular targets were the works of Hegel and Marx whom he held responsible for providing the intellectual foundations of twentieth century totalitarianism. 'New historicism' is a term first used in the 1980s by a group of American literary critics who revived the original meaning and applied it initially to the study of the literature of the past. They chose the term partly to differentiate themselves from the literary orthodoxy of the 1950s and 1960s, which held that critics should ignore the context of the times and focus exclusively on the internal workings of the text. They also wanted to distance themselves from the Yale School, which, in the 1970s and early 1980s, had used the poststructuralist theories of Jacques Derrida to make a radical assault on the older criticism by arguing that the internal working of the text contained little more than ambiguities and 'deferred' meanings. The revival of historicism aimed at providing a more socially oriented or contextual type of criticism. As such, it fitted fairly readily into the broad framework of the emerging cultural studies movement.

New historicism is of particular interest because it produced the first group of literary critics to bring their techniques to the writing of history. Of all the different perspectives now gathered under the umbrella of cultural studies, new historicism has gone furthest in the aim of breaking away from the discipline of English and colonising other territory. Coinciding with the five hundredth anniversary in 1992 of the discovery of America by Christopher Columbus, the critic Stephen Greenblatt, who had coined the movement's name, published a history of the contact in 1492 between Europeans and natives entitled *Marvellous Possessions: The Wonder of the New World*. At the same time he edited a collection of essays, *New World Encounters*, written mostly by members of the new historicist group, about the European exploration and conquest of Mexico, Central America, Brazil and Peru in the fifteenth century.[29] Other practitioners of new historicism have ranged fairly freely across the fields of literature, history and social theory, from study of the works of ancient Greek historians such as Thucydides, to Enlightenment thinkers such as Giambattista Vico, and poststructuralist historians such as Michel Foucault. The editor of one collection of their works, H. Aram Veeser, has emphasised that their approach is taking them well outside the old confines of literary criticism and into almost every area of the humanities and social sciences. 'New Historicism', he has written, 'has given scholars new opportunities to cross the boundaries separating history, anthropology, art, politics, literature, and economics'.[30]

Despite their origins in a movement distinct from poststructuralist approaches to literature, new historicists have not engaged in any major intellectual critique of that theory. Instead, despite their hankering for social context, they have perpetuated virtually all the anti-realist assumptions that were already entrenched within American poststructuralist criticism. When they discuss their methodology, they insist that they do not regard the historical context of a work of culture to be something that is *external* to that work. They accept that we cannot speak of a social or material world being distinct or separate from the culture of the same period of history. Human beings, they tell us, experience the 'world' only through language. All our representations of this world are grounded in the values and politics of the time, that is, they are dominated by the prevailing culture or ideology. In one of the collections of new historicist essays, Louis Montrose, Professor of English at the University of California, San Diego, has insisted that we should not see culture and language as a joint category located at one pole, with history and society forming a separate category located at another, opposite pole.

The prevailing tendency across cultural studies is to emphasise their reciprocity and mutual constitution: On the one hand, the social is understood to be discursively constructed; and on the other, language-use is understood to be always and necessarily dialogical, to be socially and materially determined and constrained.[31]

To translate this into English, Montrose is rejecting the view that we can distinguish between a work of culture and its social context. The social context is always 'discursively constructed', that is, it is formed by culture (or discourse) and is not separate from it. And language-use or culture is always 'dialogical', that is, it is a product of the social context since it is formed by the verbal interaction between people. Montrose says his view is compatible with the work of Jacques Derrida, which has always been concerned with the 'ideological force of discourse'. Hence, despite its origins, new historicism should not be regarded as a *critique* of poststructuralism but rather as an *extension* of this movement into the ideology, history writing and social theory of the past. When they talk about the social context of these expressions of culture, new historicists are referring to the non-literary 'discourses' of the past, that is, ideas about politics, law, medicine, science and so on. They see the world of human beings as one based entirely on language-use or culture. Hence, in their view, cultural studies becomes the proper method for the study of society.

Two of the key assumptions of new historicism, according to Aram Veeser, are 'that literary and non-literary "texts" circulate inseparably' and 'that no discourse, imaginative or archival, gives access to unchanging truths nor expresses inalterable human nature'.[32] He is arguing that we do not have access to any such thing as a real world, only to texts about the world. Moreover, when we study the past we can never discover any certainties, any 'unchanging truths', which we might once have called knowledge. The term 'archival discourse', we should note, is an attempt to define the archival research done by historians as simply another form of literature, that is, a text. The overall claim that Veeser is making is that literary critics and theorists are, in effect, no different from historians, and the work the former produce is not merely analysis of the literature of past eras, but history proper.

By discarding what they view as monologic and myopic historiography, by demonstrating that social and cultural events commingle messily, by rigorously exposing the innumerable trade-offs, the competing bids and exchanges of culture, New Historicists can make a valid claim to have established new ways of studying history, and a new awareness of how history and culture define each other.[33]

This is a very audacious claim. It is not simply arguing that works of literary criticism that focus on the past add an extra dimension to our conventional view of what should be contained within the discipline of history. Rather, the denunciation of traditional history writing as 'monologic' and 'myopic' and the insistence that culture *defines* history, constitute an attempt to over-turn the traditional concept of the discipline and replace it with another. Society is no longer a place in which material events occur but is redefined as a 'cultural system'. Literature is no longer something autonomous, nor is it able to transcend its time by telling us about the universal predicaments of humanity. Instead, it is bound within the ideology of the prevailing cultural system. Works of history are defined as 'texts' and thereby accorded similar status to works of literature. Overall, written history is reduced to a text that is nothing but the ideological expression of the prevailing cultural system. Debates about what happened in the past no longer need to be conducted by one historian discovering 'facts' that counter or contradict the views of an-other. The belief that there are 'facts' about history is no longer accepted as the starting point for debate, but is itself seen merely as one ideological posi-tion among several, hence the 'monologic' and 'myopic' tags. We are told we do not have access to 'facts' in any objective or permanent sense. Thus, facts become tainted offerings. Historical debate is reduced to conflicts within the ambit of literary and cultural studies, that is, to conflicts between different approaches to the study of texts.

Behind the assumptions described here, that all we have access to are texts and that there are no unchanging truths, lie a range of arguments derived from a number of theories and philosophies that have risen to prominence at the same time as cultural studies. All have fed upon and fattened one another. The following sections examine these developments.

A DELUGE OF SOCIAL THEORY

What annoys the critics of history most is its lack of dependence on theory. The structure of most histories is narrative and the explanations usually made by historians are inductive. That is, historical explanations are based on the movement of events over time and their conclusions come from the evidence the historian finds during research into the subject. This is the opposite of a theoretical approach in which large-scale generalisations about human society or human conduct are taken as given before either research or writing starts. These generalisations or laws then provide a framework from which deductions about the subject can be drawn. Any evidence that might be brought into play is used to confirm the theory that has already been chosen. Traditional historians usually make some deductions in the course of a work, especially when they deduce the cause of an event from the range of possibilities provided by the evidence. But to draw findings from large generalisations or from anything resembling scientific laws is not part of the historical approach.

Historians have long been chided for this by sociologists and social theorists, who cannot accept that such a thing is possible. One of the chief functions of this book is to study a number of cases where both historians and social theorists have examined the same subject matter and to see which approach is the more successful. In Chapter Seven, I also offer a defence of the scientific integrity of historical explanations as they have traditionally been practised. At this point, however, let us take the theorists' argument seriously and put the case for their side in the strongest terms possible.

The really significant development of the past twenty years has been the publication of a solid body of theoretically self-conscious historical work which has progressively made nonsense of earlier conceptions of history as somehow, in principle, not engaged in the theoretical world of the social sciences. Social change is made by people doing new things. As the acknowledged masterpieces of the discipline of history become increasingly theoretically explicit, and as the unity of theoretical method between history and sociology becomes thereby steadily more obvious, the continued insistence of a rump of professional historians that theory is not part of their trade becomes steadily less firmly the effective basis of the 'institution' of history and steadily more plainly an ineffectual nostalgia.[34]

When he wrote this in 1982, the theories that Philip Abrams had most, though not exclusively, in mind were the variants of the predominantly Marxist-inspired explanations that were then in vogue. A decade later, however, the choice of theory is far wider and the decision for the historian who would follow Abrams's advice is consequently much more difficult. The rest of this chapter provides a quick review of the most heavily promoted of the theories that are currently on the market. If historians should become more theoretically conscious, what follows is the range of offerings from which they can choose. One problem, though, which becomes clear from the following outlines, is that every one of the latest crop is quite hostile to most of the traditional assumptions and practices of historians. Indeed, the adoption of any of these theories into the trade of mainstream history would change the discipline in ways that would render it unrecognisable.

STRUCTURALISM AND SEMIOTICS

Historians have sometimes revealed themselves to be confused about the distinction between structuralism and poststructuralism. For instance, in the recently published history of the Department of History at the University of Sydney, there is a chapter entitled 'Poststructuralism at Sydney'.[35] Most of the discussion in the chapter—about theses and courses on heresy in medieval times, suicide in the seventeenth century, radical political cartoons in the nineteenth century, Ronald Reagan's presidency and, wait for it, American rap music in the 1980s—is about work that is more properly described as structuralist than poststructuralist. Structuralism derives from the linguistic theories of the nineteenth century Swiss academic Ferdinand de Saussure. Poststructuralism shares some of its assumptions but has different philosophical origins and premisses, which are discussed in the section that follows.

Structuralism initially had appeal among literary critics because it provided them with something they had long felt they lacked; a theory of literature. Instead of being confined forever to studying nothing but particular works of literature, literary theory became an attempt to study literature as a whole, a means of studying what all forms of literature had in common. Saussure's structuralist linguistics provided the initial model. Literary critics believed that, in structuralism, they had found a theory, or a poetics, that stood in relation to literature as linguistics did to language. Art critics were similarly enthusiastic for similar reasons. A theory of art at last appeared within their grasp.

In structuralist theory, a structure is a collection of laws or rules that governs the behaviour of any system. These laws themselves remain stable but they control individual components that are in a state of constant change within the system. For example, an economic *system* stays intact even though the economic *acts* that it enables and controls are all unique occurrences. Thus a structuralist would argue that the laws that govern capitalist society remain constant but the actions and decisions of individual businesses, corporations, executives and workers are always unique and changeable. Though they are all discrete, these actions and decisions will always be expressions of the underlying rules. Even though the rules cannot be said to exist unless there are players who abide by them, the players are all nonetheless governed by the rules.

In the same way, the rules of language provide the system within which individual acts of speech are made. Saussure called this structure *langue* (corresponding roughly to the English word 'language'), which is a system of signs in which the only essential thing is the union of meaning and acoustic images.[36] He contrasted this with *parole* (roughly 'speech' or 'utterances'), which is the executive side of language. The rules of *langue*, or of any structuralist system, cannot be said to exist in time. Their presence can be detected only though *parole*, that is, when they are expressed or uttered. Structuralism thus conceives of language as an idealised system, much like the abstractions of 'beauty' or 'justice'. It is inferred from, but nonetheless thought to be independent of, the particular instances in which it is found.

There are at least four aspects of structuralist theory that challenge the traditional assumptions of historians.

The ahistorical character of structuralism. Saussure distinguished between the 'diachronic' (or historical) dimension of speech, and the 'synchronic' (or timeless) dimension of language. Because his theories dealt with language rather than speech, his linguistics was a form of study that omitted the dimension of time. For structuralists, the historic or diachronic dimension is merely incidental. The deepest understandings can only come from the study of the timeless or synchronic field.

The self-enclosed system. One of the main points upon which Saussure insisted was that language is a self-enclosed system. The meaning of a word, he claimed, is not the object to which that word refers. The idea of a 'tree' (the signified) has no direct connection with the word 'tree' (the signifier). Words or signs are arbitrary. They gain their meaning not from any connection with the real world but from the relationships that words have with one another, or more precisely, from words' differences from one another. It is language, rather than any 'real' world, that structures thoughts, and thought that 'signifies', or gives meaning to, our sense of reality. Hence the 'real' world can never be reflected in our minds and we cannot know things in themselves. We are locked within a closed circuit of signs or 'texts'. From this perspective, it is naive to think that historians can accurately re-create what has happened in the world.

The critique of induction. The practice of induction, of looking at the records of the past, accumulating facts, and then using these facts to construct an explanation of what happened and why, is also rejected by structuralists. They claim there are no facts that are independent, so historians cannot be engaged in a process of induction; all they are really doing is *deducing* conclusions from within their own pre-existing theoretical framework. Nor can the historian claim that the discipline has its own methods of explanation and its own logic of enquiry. All of these involve making a clear distinction between the evidence used and the explanation provided, which structuralists claim is impossible.

The rejection of human agency. The anti-humanism of structuralism—or, in the jargon, the 'de-centring of the subject'—also challenges the historian's traditional practice. Structuralism does not regard as important for the study of human kind the decisions taken by people, no matter whether, on the one hand, they are individual authority figures such as Napoleon, Lincoln or Stalin, or whether, on the other hand, they are collections of people such as political parties, military factions, trade unions or lobby groups of various kinds. Instead of the autonomous human subject, structuralism emphasises the languages and codes, and the consequent culture and ideology, that men and women bear within themselves, irrespective of their conscious wishes. In other words, human agency is ineffective; structure is all.

It should be clear from this why literary critics and others in cultural studies have embraced structuralism so readily. If all we can know is a set of linguistic conventions and products, literary theory and literary criticism become the most effective tools for the study of humankind. Moreover, in a period when Marxism had failed to account for the fact that its supposed agents of revolution, the workers, seemed happy to accept the capitalist status quo, structuralism's emphasis on people being unconsciously dominated by the vast impersonal forces of ideology and culture came to appear more plausible to many radical academics. The French anthropologist Claude Levi-Strauss took the question one step further. He claimed structuralist linguistics could provide modes of analysis that were applicable to the study of *all* aspects of human culture and, ultimately, to the nature of the human mind. Linguists and social scientists 'do not merely apply the same methods', Levi-Strauss said, 'but are studying the same thing'.[37]

SEMIOTICS. The field of semiotics is usually regarded as a sub-category within structuralist theory. Semiotics is the study of meaning in human communications in all its varieties—spoken and written language, art, poetry, advertisements, gestures, facial expressions—which are all treated as 'signs'. There are 'formalist' versions of semiotics, which have tried, unsuccessfully, to make the field into a rigorous philosophy or science, and 'culturalist' versions, which see semiotics more as a tool through which to approach literary and media studies. The most celebrated writer on semiotics has been the Parisian Roland Barthes, who analysed the political or ideological content of signs such as advertisements, magazine covers, fashion garments and motor car bodies and of activities such as serving food and wrestling. There are some Marxist structuralists, notably the followers of Louis Althusser, who have tried to use semiotics to show how signs impose meanings that constitute the underlying ideology of the capitalist system. This work was influential in media studies in the late 1970s and early 1980s. The term semiotics is not used as frequently today as it was a decade ago but Barthes's methodology and interests (though not the formalist aspects of this theories) remain part of the mainstay of cultural studies.

TWO VERSIONS OF POSTSTRUCTURALISM

The term 'post-structuralist' originated in American literary and philosophical circles to describe some varieties of French writings that became influential in the late 1970s and early 1980s. In its original adjectival form it was a compound that bore a hyphen, but it has now passed into such common academic usage that both it and the noun 'poststructuralism' have become words in their own right. There are two French theorists usually identified with separate tendencies within poststructuralist thought. One is Jacques Derrida, who holds a radical, textualist approach to the notion of 'meaning'. Derrida's version of poststructuralism is not a form of anti-structuralism. Derrida's work shares some of the assumptions of Saussure but it derives principally from the existentialist philosophy of Martin Heidegger. Derrida follows Heidegger's critique of the foundation of modern philosophy, that is, the philosophy developed in the Enlightenment of the eighteenth century. Because we are locked within a system of language, Derrida argues, we have no grounds for knowing anything that exists outside this system. 'What one calls real life', according to Derrida, is itself a text. Hence, it follows that all we have access to are texts. 'There is nothing outside the text', he has claimed in a famous aphorism. Whereas structuralist linguistics holds that language is not about the relationship between words and objects but between words and meanings, Derrida goes on to argue that there is no such thing as a fixed meaning.

The methodology most identified with poststructuralism is that of deconstruction, a term established by Derrida. Deconstruction is a way of reading texts and acts as a critique of both philosophy and traditional literary criticism. To deconstruct a text is to expose or demystify it. Derrida's method is to analyse the ambiguity in some selected philosophical and literary works. From this, he purports to show that a text never says just what the writer consciously intended. He then goes on to claim that no text ever says only one thing, but, rather, creates many different meanings. Meaning is always relative since it is produced by its difference from other meanings. The meaning of a word is never stable; rather, it is always 'deferred'. Therefore, he argues, there can be no reference from a text to any specific meaning inherent within the text. This approach has been used to undermine the assumptions of older literary critics that the job of criticism was to apply close reading and careful analysis to bring out 'the' meaning of a work of literature. It is also intended to undermine the practice of philosophy, which, Derrida claims, can no longer be based on a naively rationalist theory of meaning. Philosophy is essentially a literary genre and is best conducted not by rational argument but by aphoristic or poetic writing.[38]

The other poststructuralist camp is represented by Michel Foucault, whose work is far more comprehensible to anyone educated in history than are the theories of Derrida. The histories written by Foucault about socially marginalised groups, including the insane, the sick and the criminal, are a less textual and a more worldly kind of poststructuralism. Foucault was also an historian of ideas. As Chapter Five discusses in more detail,[39] Foucault followed the critique of the nineteenth century German philosopher Friedrich Nietzsche of the humanism of the eighteenth century Enlightenment, especially Nietzsche's rejection of the view that history is made by the reason and will of the autonomous human subject. In this, Foucault's 'anti-humanism' takes the same position as structuralism about the dominance of human agency by the structures of language, ideology and culture. Foucault was also a critic of the scientific method devised in the Enlightenment. Science is not something with universal application but, rather, is no more than a product of the ideology of its era. In the late twentieth century, he claims, there are no absolute concepts of knowledge that can be derived from science or any other 'discourse'. No classification devised by either natural or social scientists, he says, can bear any direct relationship to an outside world.

One of Foucault's central concepts is that of 'power/knowledge'. The power of those in authority determines what is to count as 'knowledge' or acceptable discourse. He argues that the role of the historian should be to demystify the claims to knowledge made by the powerful and to support those who are oppressed by it. In arguing against any absolute concept of knowledge, Foucault adopts a poststructuralist position to claim that all classifications are arbitrary products of language, that there is no hierarchy of meanings, and that all we can do with language is engage in a kind of interpretive play. He acknowledged that the 'histories' he had written were not exempt from this critique and that they should consequently be regarded as novels or fiction.

THE VARIETIES OF POSTMODERNISM

The term postmodernism is used by a wide range of writers in ways that are often varied and, indeed, inconsistent. There are several authors who, while generally sympathetic, argue that postmodernism is not really 'post' at all, but is rather a variety of modernism itself.[40] Others claim that postmodernism is part of the poststructuralist matrix,[41] or vice versa. On the other hand, there are some poststructuralists, such as the English literary critic Christopher Norris, who are well known for their hostility to postmodernism.[42] To try to make some sense of these competing claims we can divide them into six separate versions.

Nietzsche and Heidegger version. These two German philosophers are often regarded as the most profound critics of modernism. They identified modernism not as something born in the twentieth century but as a project of eighteenth century Enlightenment philosophy, which saw history as the triumph of the rational mind over nature. Modernism regarded history as a story of 'progress' due to the accumulation of knowledge provided by scientific thought. Nietzsche rejected not only the idea that knowledge was accumulating but the very idea that the conclusions we draw from science or history could be grounded in any kind of certainty. He wanted to replace the whole of Western philosophy with a position that held there are no facts, only interpretations, and no objective truths, only the perspectives of various individuals and groups.

Heidegger rejected humanism and the rational domination of nature and called for a new mode of thinking that rejected Western philosophy and returned to premodern modes of thought and experience. Both philosophers adopted more of an *anti*-modernist than a *post*modernist position, but most surveys of the field identify them as either the founders or the precursors of postmodernism. Certainly, their categorical rejection of Western learning is characteristic of most postmodern tracts.

Paris 1980s version. The French theorist Jean François Lyotard defines postmodernism as 'an incredulity toward metanarratives', by which he means a rejection of any explanation which sees history or society in its totality, especially the works of Marx and Hegel. Lyotard follows Nietzsche in this because the latter claimed 'metanarratives' were all products of Enlightenment or modernist belief in rational progress. Lyotard's writings were attractive to many former Marxists like himself who saw Marxism go out of fashion in the 1980s and who wanted to find an alternative position that remained critical of modern society.[43] Another former Marxist, Jean Baudrillard, argues that the radical intellectual must abandon the quest for rational explanation of society or anything else since 'there is no longer any critical and speculative distance between the real and the irrational'. As I explain in more detail in Chapter Six, Baudrillard agrees with Lyotard about the end of metanarratives and subscribes to a thesis that holds that the Western world has now arrived at the end of history.

Art and architecture version. There are a number of versions of postmodernism found in art and architecture circles that are far less politicised and theoretical than the above two versions. In art criticism, postmodernism looks at a work of art not to discern a meaning that lies beneath it but rather to enjoy it for what it is, with no intention to be discovered, only the play of the work itself. *Blue Poles* is nothing but *Blue Poles*. In the practice of art, postmodernist works are usually based on a Nietzschean rejection of reason and progress, and exhibit qualities such as pastiche, parody and eclecticism. Postmodernist art rejects the signed 'masterpiece', the originality of the author, museum display, and commodification through galleries. It prefers mixed media and mass media. One of its favourite forms is the pop music video clip. In architecture, postmodernism has moved away from twentieth century modernist functionalism towards what it regards as 'colourful play' and 'eclectic quotation'; that is, borrowing from several architectural styles and periods of the past, and assembling them at random in new buildings as a kind of joke at the expense of the untutored client.[44]

Literary version. Postmodernist literary critics often condemn their discipline's focus on the objects of high culture because this defines other works as low or inferior culture. Postmodernist literary criticism eschews the old elitism of a canon of great books and, as in art criticism, approves works that display parody, eclecticism, playfulness and the deferral of meaning. Despite its egalitarian protestations, most postmodernist criticism is couched within arcane language and concepts and, moreover, most of it is concerned either with literary theory or with works of literature that sell only to an educated elite.

Popular culture version. This reflects a revival of interest in popular culture by some literary critics who want to incorporate its study within their field. Some practitioners of this version have used semiotics to deconstruct the representations and signs of popular culture to expose their underlying ideology. Some value the cultural expression of television advertisements and soap operas. Others agree with the Russian critic Mikhail Bakhtin that popular culture is a continuation of the ethos of the medieval carnival and should be appreciated because it is subversive of official institutions and hierarchies.

Marxist version. This is largely the product of the American literary critic Fredric Jameson, Professor of Comparative Literature at Duke University who believes that the current period is best understood as 'late capitalism'. Jameson says that postmodernist culture's amoral, uncommitted, though often attractive, eclecticism, is an apt expression of our current 'social confusion' because we are now in a 'transitional period' of capitalist development. However, this confusion will soon change, he claims, because the extension of capitalism into the developing world is now causing 'proletarianisation on a global scale'. This will transform postmodernist culture into 'class consciousness of a new and hitherto undreamed of kind'. In other words, for Jameson, the socialist revolution is still on the agenda. Though he has written a huge tome on the subject, Jameson appears to have generated few supporters, since postmodernists generally regard Marxism as the most audacious of the metanarratives produced by modernism itself.[45]

There are, as may be apparent, weak and strong versions of postmodernism. The weak versions are those usually advanced by art and literary critics and popular culture analysts, who often have considerable difficulty in establishing any significant difference between postmodernism and the modernist culture it is supposed to have replaced. Like the Australian critic John Frow, they normally speak in the vaguest terms of postmodernism originating from the current 'proliferation of information', from a 'crisis' among intellectuals in the 1980s and 1990s, and from the blurring of the distinction between high and low culture.[46] Most of these claims are supported solely by reference to other postmodernist writers and very few are backed by anything so crass as empirical evidence. Hence there is little on which to assess their merit, an outcome perhaps not unintended. There are a number of American critics in the same vein, such as Professor E. Ann Kaplan, who is employed to teach English literature to undergraduates at the State University of New York, but who produces postmodernist, feminist and 'oedipal' analyses of such towering works of art as the rock videos of Madonna and the rebel yells of Billy Idol on MTV.[47]

The stronger versions of postmodernism are those that stick more closely to philosophy and social theory and see it as a phenomenon closely allied to French poststructuralism. This perspective would include within postmodernism Michel Foucault's critique of modernity, the Nietzschean philosophy of Giles Deleuze, the end-of-history thesis of Baudrillard and the critique of metanarratives by Lyotard, plus some contributions by French Freudian feminists.[48] This is the only intellectually coherent version of postmodernism on offer.

MARXISM AND CRITICAL THEORY

While other social theories have been advancing over the past decade, the appeal of Marxism within academic circles has gone in the opposite direction. Most of those who still remain faithful are middle-aged or older and, since the fall of communism in 1989, it has been almost impossible to recruit followers from among the younger generation. This is in contrast to the late 1960s and 1970s, when the leading Marxists had celebrity status among intellectually oriented youth. As the other theories described above gained support, some Marxists recognised how out of date they had become and, like the French postmodernists Lyotard and Baudrillard, threw off their old garb. Others have responded by adapting to the new fashions and incorporating what they would once have regarded as alien styles. For example, in the late 1970s, a combination of structuralism and Marxism offered by Louis Althusser was very much in vogue. In the 1980s, while there were some prominent Marxists—such as the former editor of *New Left Review* Perry Anderson—who were trenchantly critical of the poststructuralist movement, there were other even more celebrated Marxists—such as Terry Eagleton, Professor of English at Oxford University and one-time advocate of Althusserian theory—who defended poststructuralism and deconstruction from these attacks.[49] As I noted above, we have even seen the unlikely merger, in the work of Fredric Jameson, of postmodernism and Marxism.

The version of academic Marxism to which most members of the ageing congregation now defer is called 'critical theory'. This euphemism reflects how great has been the fall. It is like the Church dropping the name Christianity and calling its faith 'religious theory'. Nonetheless, critical theory retains enough support to be ranked among the contenders. Those historians who are looking, as they have been urged, to make their own work more theoretically self-conscious and more theoretically explicit should at least consider it as one of the still-viable choices on offer.

Though it is sometimes used today, misleadingly, to encompass all of the new literary theory, the term 'critical theory' has been most closely associated with the version of German Marxism produced by the Frankfurt School, which has been a shifting but identifiable group since the 1930s. This is a school that has abandoned a number of the central tenets of the Marxism written by Marx. Instead of a capitalism riven by class conflict, the school sees a stable, self-reproducing system with no significant revolutionary opposition. The working class is no longer seen as the prime agent of history. Socialism has become a utopian ideal rather than the imminent outcome of revolutionary praxis. The economic base of society, or the relations of production, no longer determine what happens in the social superstructure and so government, law, culture and intellectualism are all held to operate with relative autonomy. Yet, on the other hand, members of the Frankfurt School still accept a number of Marxist principles about the nature of the social structure and social relations. The targets of their criticism are those familiar to generations of Marxists: capitalism, commodification, consumerism, the media, commercial culture, imperialism, liberalism, positivism, patriarchy and the bourgeois family. They believe the capitalist system and the state have merged to form a great overarching system of domination and exploitation. They claim that once-independent institutions of civil society, including the education system, the Church, the media and trade unions, have been subsumed beneath this edifice while the formerly distinct social classes have been reduced to a homogeneous and largely mindless mass.

The leading figure in contemporary critical theory is Jürgen Habermas, who has spent much of the last decade arguing against the same target as the poststructuralists and postmodernists—that is, Enlightenment philosophy and social investigation—while also arguing against poststructuralism and postmodernism themselves. He is a defender of what he considers the progressive elements of modernism and, in contrast to the French theories, he believes it is possible to develop 'objective science, universal morality and law, and autonomous art, according to their inner logic'.[50] On the other hand, he shares some of the 'anti-humanist' assumptions of poststructuralism, especially its critique of Enlightenment rationality, which he thinks is too centred on the individual reasoning subject. Habermas sees his big project as establishing an alternative conception of rationality based on what he calls 'communicative action'.

Habermas wants to create a 'paradigm shift' from the philosophy of the Enlightenment, which he calls the 'philosophy of consciousness', to his own project of a 'philosophy of communication'. The distinction he is making is

actually a very old one. He is arguing against philosophies based on individualism and the self, and is supporting philosophies based on social interaction
and the group. The philosophy of consciousness, he says, derives from instrumental rationality grounded in the drive for self-preservation. Instrumental
rationality is the relating of means to ends without reflection on the rationality
or justness of the ends themselves. He argues that this rationality, which had
once been a weapon against superstition and tyranny, has today become a
force that supports the rigid bureaucratic organisation of industrial society and
that no longer fulfils an emancipatory role. So he calls for Enlightenment
rationalism, with its focus on subjectivity and individual interests, to be replaced by a more socially aware mode of thought. His philosophy of communication is aimed to generate action oriented towards understanding and agreement. As its name suggests, it is grounded in social togetherness and the bind-
ing power of language. Whereas the philosophy of consciousness fosters the
individual's domination of both man and nature, Habermas believes his philosophy of communication will lead to mutual understanding and will forge
uncoerced consensus.[51]

One of the consequences of the Habermas philosophy of communication is
the production of his own version of the status of truth. Although he is a critic
of the relativism of those poststructuralists and postmodernists who say that
what is 'true' depends on the context and the speaker, a number of commentators have pointed out that his own theory leads also to a relativist position
on truth. Habermas's philosophy of communication commits him to the view
that truth is not a relationship between an individual and the world. Truth is
rather a form of agreement reached by rational discussion. What is true, in
Habermas's theory, is determined by 'rational consensus'. However, this proposition is fraught with difficulties. How is a 'rational' consensus to be distinguished from a consensus derived from custom, authority, money or mob
rule? The reply that Habermas has given is that a rational consensus is one
reached 'by the force of the better argument'; that is, anyone weighing the
same evidence would reach the same conclusion. But this is hardly satisfactory. If truth is nothing more than consensus we can well ask what happens
when, after weighing the same evidence, one consensus disagrees with another, as it so often has done in science, not to mention in far more problematic areas such as politics and religion? One of the principles of Enlightenment
rationality that Habermas would thus overthrow, along with individualism
and subjectivity, is the idea that the truth is something that cannot be altered
by subsequent human influence. The Enlightenment believed that truth was
something we discovered, not something we decided.

For historians, the debate over truth and relativism is obviously important.
Most historians over the last two hundred years have accepted the view that

the truth about the past is something independent of themselves. However, the current generation of social theorists, and quite a few historians today as well, believe that the past is not something we discover but something that each age invents for its own purposes. This position is taken not only by critical theorists but also by the movement called 'postcolonialism', described in the next section.

POSTCOLONIALISM AND HETEROLOGY

Postcolonialism is another term that began as a hyphenated compound but is now accepted within academic parlance so extensively that the hyphen is increasingly being dropped. The first examples of what are now regarded as postcolonial writing were a number of West Indian and African novels that were published in the 1960s and that, at the time, were labelled 'Commonwealth literature'. The novels of the Trinidad-born author V.S. Naipaul are probably the best-known. Other works include non-fiction denunciations of European imperialism and racism such as *The Wretched of the Earth,* written by the Algerian author Frantz Fanon in 1961. Most of these works were published by Third World authors either just before or shortly after their countries had gained their independence from the European imperial powers. The term 'postcolonialism' was taken up in the 1980s by a number of postmodernist literary critics who welcomed this form of writing as an ally in their own rejection of the values of the European literary tradition. In the most influential collection of essays of this kind, Bill Ashcroft, Gareth Griffiths and Helen Tiffin's 1989 anthology, *The Empire Writes Back: Theory and Practice in Post-colonial Literature,* the term is expanded to encompass a range of authors who, while not living in or writing from Third World countries, are still regarded as offering perspectives that differ radically from the literary traditions borne by the main nineteenth century imperial powers, Britain and France. These writers include Salman Rushdie, author of the novels *Midnight's Children* and *The Satanic Verses*. The same editors also argue for a radical interpretation of the prefix 'post' to include writing that starts at the beginning as well as at the end of a colonial era.

We use the term 'post-colonial', however, to cover all the culture affected by the imperial process from the moment of colonisation to the present day. This is because there is a continuity of preoccupations throughout the historical process initiated by European imperial aggression.[52]

Hence, even some eighteenth century Indian poems are placed within the ambit.

In the hands of some interpreters, postcolonialism is defined so widely that it goes well beyond writing by indigenes and people descended from the former slaves of the colonies. It can also include those European–descended authors in the white settler dominions of Australia and Canada who can be regarded as literary 'outsiders' or as writers identifying not with the mainstream but with the 'other' within their own societies, especially homosexuals, feminists and postmodernists.[53] Postcolonialism is a term obviously in some danger of becoming all things to all its interpreters.

Given that there has been a powerful tendency within the literary criticism of the past decade for the critics to regard not the novelists, poets and dramatists but *themselves* as the true bearers of contemporary culture, those who have written about postcolonialism have similarly come to assume the high ground of the genre. This is despite the fact that most were born and bred in, and hold tenured academic positions within, such metropolitan centres as Los Angeles, Paris and Melbourne. The most celebrated of the postcolonialist critics is Edward Said, a New Yorker of Palestinian descent who has written two of the seminal texts, *Orientalism* (1978) and *Culture and Imperialism* (1993). In *Orientalism*, Said argues that European writings about the Orient, especially travel writing, literature and history, 'had systematically disclaimed the insights of the people it claimed to tell the truth about'. The 'other' of the colonies were never permitted to speak for themselves. Much of the so-called objective knowledge about colonial peoples was nothing more than Eurocentric stereotypes that helped perpetuate Western dominance.[54] In *Culture and Imperialism*, Said argues that the whole of Western culture of the past three hundred years has been moulded by the fact of European world dominance and settlement. He argues that the two principal cultural forms of this period, the novel and the historical narrative, have both been tools that were complicit in the imperialist project. He denounces a number of canonical works as culpable including, rather astonishingly, Jane Austen's *Mansfield Park*, Thomas Mann's *Death in Venice* and David Hume's *History of England*.[55]

One of the main problems raised by commentators on this movement is the fact that large segments of postcolonialist work have been produced within both the language and the cultural forms of the imperial powers they are supposed to have been rejecting. Rushdie, Naipaul and other authors from India, Pakistan, the Caribbean and Africa have not only written in English but have produced their ideas in the form of the novel, the quintessential cultural vehicle of imperialism itself, according to Edward Said. Similarly, the anti-imperialist writings of Frantz Fanon were written in French and derived their theory largely from Karl Marx and Sigmund Freud, two representatives of the German philosophic tradition. The Australian Aboriginal novelist and critic Mudrooroo Narogin acknowledges that his own postcolonial work is written in English, is read by a largely white audience and is couched within not Aboriginal but European cultural traditions.[56]

One of those who tries to avoid this dilemma by making a total critique of the products of imperial culture, especially history, is the French author Michel de Certeau. Of all the French theorists who have been recently taken up in the English-speaking academic scene, de Certeau is the most radical. He is critical of the poststructuralist Foucault for his use of documentary evidence and of Derrida for the way he privileges the practice of writing. For de Certeau, writing is a form of oppression. Indeed, he argues that the practice of writing itself constitutes the act of colonisation. The principal form of writing through which he makes this charge is that of history. He has written a general methodological critique of the practice of history as well as his own versions of the nature of the first cultural contact between European explorers and the natives of Brazil and Central America. He has also written a theoretical account of the relations between people who possess writing and those who do not, as well as an analysis of everyday life in the contemporary world. His three main works written in France in the 1970s have been translated into English. They are *The Practice of Everyday Life* (translated 1984), *Heterologies: Discourse on the Other* (1986) and *The Writing of History* (1988).[57] In other words, for someone who thinks writing is a form of oppression, he has done a lot of writing. While the breadth of his interests makes it somewhat equivocal to categorise him here simply as part of the postcolonialist movement, it is de Certeau's theories that some recent postcolonial literary theorists have recommended to their colleagues as providing the most fruitful theoretical and political perspective for the field.[58] The foray into history by the new historicist literary theorists discussed above has been partly inspired by de Certeau's work. In 1991 his new historicist admirers dedicated to him an issue of the journal *Representations*.[59] A collection of their historical essays on the European encounter with the New World includes some of de Certeau's own writing as well as an appreciation of his work.[60]

Like both structuralist and poststructuralist theorists, de Certeau subscribes to the thesis that we have access only to our language and not to any real, outside world. From this perspective, speaking and writing are the vehicles through which we produce the only 'world' we can know. Of the two, writing is the more powerful. Writing, he claims, is a means of imposing a rational order. Writing produces a world, he says, that is consistent with its own grammar. Hence the only vehicle through which this world is intelligible is writing itself. Those people who lack writing lack the power to define their own world in the way that is possible to those cultures that possess writing. Outsiders never understand these non-literate peoples directly, only through the writings of others. Thus, he argues, the first writings by Amerigo Vespucci and others describing the people of the New World constituted the act of colonisation through the 'discourse of power'.

This is *writing that conquers*. It will use the New World as if it were a blank, 'savage' page on which Western desire will be written. It will transform the space of the other into a field of expansion for a system of production.[61]

Because it sees things only through its own perspective, de Certeau claims that writing can never be objective. Its status is no different from that of fiction. So, because history is a form of writing, all history is also fiction. 'The past is the fiction of the present', he says.[62] When historians write, they are not recording history; rather, they are manufacturing history. From de Certeau's point of view, the whole enterprise of writing history as it has been practised for the last several hundred years is fatally flawed because of the ways in which it handles chronology. The first problem arises in the attempt to separate present time from the past. The second problem is the convention of dividing the past into periods, such as the Middle Ages and the Renaissance. In making these divisions, de Certeau says, historians create a period in which they judge whatever preceded it to be dead. There is a 'breakage' involved in this kind of historical interpretation. 'In the past from which it is distinguished, it promotes a selection between what can be *understood* and what must be *forgotten* in order to obtain the representation of a present intelligibility.'[63] Rather than being a simple and objective methodological device to promote clarity, de Certeau sees these divisions into periods as an ideological tool peculiar to Western imperialism. He gives some examples of the attitude to the past held in India, Madagascar and Dahomey to show that in these non-Western societies the past remains alive within the present and that new forms never drive out the old. In separating the past from the present and dividing the past into periods, de Certeau says, historians perform an act of oppression. They do this because they thereby define some peoples and some human practices as irrelevant, outdated or inferior.

De Certeau includes among those who perpetuate this kind of oppression a number of French radicals who had thought themselves to be on the same side as the oppressed. He accuses Michel Foucault, through the act of selecting documents about the imprisoned and the insane for his histories of prisons and mental asylums, to have turned the meaning of the documents to his own ends rather than to those of the incarcerated.[64] He accuses the structuralist anthropologist Claude Levi-Strauss of climbing to academic prominence on the backs of the tribes he studied. 'The Bororos of Brazil sink slowly into their collective death, and Levi-Strauss takes his seat in the French Academy. Even if this injustice disturbs him, the facts remain unchanged.'[65] De Certeau uses the terms 'heterologies', 'discourses on the other' and 'discourses of separation' to describe the practices of virtually all historians and anthropologists, as well as those of academics in the fields of psychiatry, pedagogy and modern medicine. All these heterologies are 'built upon a division between the body of knowledge that utters a discourse and the mute body that nourishes it'.[66] However, despite all the academic oppression of the non-literate 'other' of the colonies, de Certeau maintains that their alternative understandings can never be completely eliminated.

But whatever this new understanding of the past holds to be irrelevant—shards created by the selection of material, remainders left aside by an explication— comes back, despite everything, on the edges of discourse or in its rifts and crannies: 'resistances', 'survivals', or delays discreetly perturb the pretty order of a line of 'progress' or a system of interpretation.[67]

He describes this phenomenon as 'the return of the repressed'. He believes it is impossible to completely repress since the repressed will always find a way through which to 'return'. He maintains that the critic of history can assist this by an examination of the processes of historical writing. By questioning the theoretical basis of the text, the auspices under which was it written, the status of the documents it consults and its relation to other books in its field, and by generally showing how histories are produced, their weaknesses can be exposed. Careful examination of the texts, especially the 'shards' they create and the remainders they leave aside, can allow the critic to find the holes through which the forgotten voices can 'return' to right the wrongs of history.

De Certeau's work is couched in the typical obscurantism, linguistic idealism and inept metaphor of much recent French theory, but there is nonetheless a legitimate point buried beneath it all. This is that a great deal of the history of European expansion in the past two hundred years has been written from a strictly European perspective. For example, until 1970 almost all Australian historiography was written in terms of the 'settlement' and 'development' of the country by Europeans. Even those left-wing historians who criticised the process did so on the grounds that the local white working class had not got a fair share of the spoils. The Aboriginal perspective, and the often shocking and disgraceful story of how Aborigines were treated, was omitted entirely. Since 1970, however, there has been a great deal of history writing done to correct this and to try to see Australian history through Aboriginal eyes. So, today, the question is not one of whether the views of this repressed 'other' should return or be revived. It is more an issue of whether this return can be legitimately accomplished through the tools of traditional historiography, or whether the historical methodology nurtured by the imperial power is so hopelessly compromised that it is useless for the task. A further question is whether there could be a postcolonial methodology consistent with de Certeau's theories that would offer a more fruitful and valid alternative.

An Australian example of something along the latter line of which de Certeau might have approved is the work of Paul Carter on the origins of European settlement in Australia. Carter's writings are examined in Chapter Four of this book where they are compared with approaches to the same subject matter made by the 'imperial history' to which he, like de Certeau, is so opposed. While the verdict reached in Chapter Four is flattering to neither Carter nor, by implication, de Certeau, it is nonetheless clear that this is hardly likely to dent the enthusiasm of the postcolonial writing movement. It has now reached the stage where its adherents are certain to continue to offer critiques of existing historiography as well as works of their own that repudiate the practices of the traditional discipline.

ALL THE THEORIES described here have been applied to the production of historical works over the past decade. The next five chapters provide a number of highly celebrated and, in some cases, powerful examples of this. I am not giving anything away by reporting here that the conclusion I reach in every one of these chapters is that the result is deplorable in terms of the traditional practice of history. While there are specific reasons for this in each case, the summaries of the theories provided above should be enough to indicate that there are three common qualities that all, or nearly all, of them share which make them jointly culpable. First, they reject those aspects of the scientific method of the Enlightenment that were based on observation and inductive argument. They consequently reject works of history that are based on the same principles. Second, they all hold a relativist view of the concepts of truth and knowledge. Most deny that we can know anything with certainty, and believe that different cultures create their own truths. Third, most deny the ability of human beings to gain any direct contact with or access to reality. Instead, they support a form of linguistic idealism that holds that we are locked within a closed system of language and culture, which refers not beyond our minds to an outside world but only inwardly to itself.

Despite the urgings of those who claim that greater adoption of theory would enrich history, the widespread acceptance of any one of these last three points would be enough to kill off the discipline, as it has been practised, for good. The first undermines the methodology of historical research; the second destroys the distinction between history and fiction; the third means not only that it is impossible to access the past but that we have no proper grounds for believing that a past independent of ourselves ever took place. In other words, if historians allow themselves to be prodded all the way to this theoretical abyss, they will be rendering themselves and their discipline extinct.

---

1   Peter McPhee, 'Lunatic Liberty', *Sydney Morning Herald,* 17 October 1992, p 45

2   Quentin Skinner (ed.), *The Return of Grand Theory in the Human Sciences,* Cambridge University Press, Cambridge, (1st edn 1985), Canto edn 1990, pp 5–6

3   Stuart Hall, 'Cultural Studies and its Theoretical Legacies', in Lawrence Grossberg, Cary Nelson and Paula Treichler (eds), *Cultural Studies,* Routledge, New York, 1992, p 285

4   Stephen Knight, *The Selling of the Australian Mind,* William Heinemann Australia, Melbourne, 1990, p 181

5   K. K. Ruthven, 'Introduction' in K. K. Ruthven (ed.), *Beyond the Disciplines: The New Humanities,* Australian Academy of the Humanities, Canberra, 1992, p ix

6   'Introduction', History and Theory 1991, course notes produced for the Department of History, University of Sydney, Sydney, March 1991

7   Allan Bloom, *The Closing of the American Mind: How Higher Education has Failed Democracy and Impoverished the Souls of Today's Students,* Penguin Books edn, Harmondsworth, 1988, p 346

8   Roger Kimball, *Tenured Radicals: How Politics Has Corrupted Our Higher Education,* Harper and Row, New York, 1991 edn, p xviii

9   Dinesh D'Souza, *Illiberal Education: The Politics of Race and Sex on Campus,* Random House, New York, 1991

10   Luc Ferry and Alain Renaut, *French Philosophy of the Sixties: An Essay on Antihumanism,* (French edn 1985), trans. Mary S. Cattani, University of Massachusetts Press, Amherst, 1990

11   Victor Farías, *Heidegger and Nazism,* (French edn 1987) English edn trans. Paul Burrell, eds Joseph Margolis and Rom Rockmore, Temple University Press, Philadelphia, 1989; Luc Ferry and Alain Renaut, *Heidegger and Modernity,* trans. Franklin Philip, University of Chicago Press, Chicago, 1990. I discuss the Heidegger case in more detail in Chapter Six

12   Michael Ostwald, *Architecture Bulletin,* 1992, republished in *Sydney Morning Herald,* 28 April 1992, p 32. See also chapter 'Deconstruction Comes to Architecture', in Roger Kimball, *Tenured Radicals,* pp 116–41

13   Paper by Associate Professor Terry Threadgold, University of Sydney, to Law and Literature Association of Australia's second annual conference, Monash University, Melbourne, September 1991

14   Stanley Fish, *Doing What Comes Naturally: Change, Rhetoric and the Practice of Theory in Literary and Legal Studies,* Duke University Press, Durham, 1989; Hilary Charlesworth, 'The New Jurisprudences', in K. K. Ruthven (ed.) *Beyond the Disciplines,* pp 121–34

15   John McDonald, 'The Failure of Art Schools', *The Independent Monthly,* Sydney, March 1991, pp 37–8

16   For one of the seminal discussions of the application of Foucault's theory to accounting, standard costing and budgeting see Peter Miller and Ted O'Leary, 'Accounting and the Construction of the Governable Person', *Accounting, Organisations and Society,* 12, 3, 1987, pp 235–65

17   Nicholas Fox, *Postmodernism, Sociology and Health,* Open University Press, Buckingham, 1993

18   Cary Nelson, Paula A. Treichler and Lawrence Grossberg, 'Cultural Studies: An Introduction', in Lawrence Grossberg, Cary Nelson and Paula A. Treichler (eds), *Cultural Studies,* p 1

19   Cary Nelson, Paula A. Treichler and Lawrence Grossberg, *Cultural Studies,* p 1

20   Cary Nelson, Paula A. Treichler and Lawrence Grossberg, *Cultural Studies,* p 4

21   Cary Nelson, Paula A. Treichler and Lawrence Grossberg, *Cultural Studies,* p 15

22   Cary Nelson, Paula A. Treichler and Lawrence Grossberg, *Cultural Studies,* p 14

23   John Frow, 'Beyond the Disciplines: Cultural Studies', in K. K. Ruthven (ed.), *Beyond the Disciplines,* pp 23, 25

24   'Introduction' to Annabel Patterson, *Reading Between the Lines,* University of Wisconsin Press, Madison, 1994

25   Cary Nelson, Paula A. Treichler and Lawrence Grossberg, *Cultural Studies,* pp 10–11

26   Cary Nelson, Paula A. Treichler and Lawrence Grossberg, *Cultural Studies,* p 1

27 Catherine Gallagher, 'Marxism and the New Historicism', in H. Aram Veeser (ed.), *The New Historicism,* Routledge, New York, 1989, pp 43

28 Judith Lowder Newton, 'History as Usual? Feminism and the "New Historicism" ', in H. Aram Veeser (ed.), *The New Historicism,* p 153

29 Stephen Greenblatt, *Marvellous Possessions: The Wonder of the New World,* Clarendon Press, Oxford, 1991; Stephen Greenblatt (ed.), *New World Encounters,* University of California Press, Berkeley, 1993

30 H. Aram Veeser, 'Introduction', in H. Aram Veeser (ed.), *The New Historicism,* p ix

31 Louis A. Montrose, 'Professing the Renaissance: The Poetics and Politics of Culture', in H. Aram Veeser (ed.), *The New Historicism,* op cit, p 15

32 H. Aram Veeser, 'Introduction' p xi

33 H. Aram Veeser, 'Introduction' p xiii

34 Philip Abrams, *Historical Sociology,* Open Books, London, 1982, p 300

35 C. J. Reynolds, 'Poststructuralism at Sydney', in Barbara Caine, Brian Fletcher, Meg Miller, Ros Pesman and Deryck Schreuder (eds.), *History at Sydney, 1891–1991: Centenary Reflections,* History Department, University of Sydney, Sydney, 1991

36 A relatively clear explanation of Saussure's theories is provided in Terence Hawkes, *Structuralism and Semiotics,* Methuen, London, 1977

37 Claude Levi-Strauss, *The Elementary Structures of Kinship,* Eyre and Spottiswoode, London, 1969, p 493

38 Jacques Derrida, *Of Grammatology,* trans. Gayatri C. Spivak, Johns Hopkins University Press, Baltimore, 1976; — *Writing and Difference,* trans. Alan Bass, University of Chicago Press, Chicago, 1978; — *Margins of Philosophy,* trans. Alan Bass, University of Chicago Press, Chicago, 1982

39 All references to Foucault's works are given in Chapter Five

40 Anthony Giddens, *The Consequences of Modernity,* Polity Press, Cambridge, 1990, pp 45-53

41 There are literally dozens of works written to explain what postmodernism is about but most leave the uninitiated reader more confused than when he or she started. For those with some familiarity with contemporary social theory, the most helpful general survey is Steven Best and Douglas Kellner, *Postmodern Theory: Critical Interrogations,* Macmillan, Basingstoke, 1991

42 Christopher Norris, *What's Wrong With Postmodernism: Critical Theory and the Ends of Philosophy,* Harvester Wheatsheaf, Hemel Hempstead, 1990; — *Uncritical Theory: Postmodernism, Intellectuals and the Gulf War,* Lawrence and Wishart, London, 1992

43 Jean François Lyotard, *The Postmodern Condition,* University of Minneapolis Press, Minneapolis, 1984

44 Hal Foster (ed.), *Postmodern Culture,* Pluto Press, London, 1983, especially essays by Kenneth Frampton on architecture, Rosalind Krauss on sculpture and Douglas Krimp on art

45 Fredric Jameson, *Postmodernism, or, The Cultural Logic of Late Capitalism,* Verso, London, 1991

46 John Frow, *What Was Postmodernism?,* Local Consumption Publications, Sydney, 1991

47 E. Ann Kaplan, 'Feminism/Oedipus/Postmodernism: The Case of MTV', in E. Ann Kaplan (ed.), *Postmodernism and its Discontents: Theories, Practices,* Verso, London, 1988; — *Rocking Around the Clock: Music Television, Postmodernism and Consumer Culture,* Methuen, New York, 1987

48 Steven Best and Douglas Kellner, *Postmodern Theory*

49 Perry Anderson, *In the Tracks of Historical Materialism,* Verso, London, 1983, pp 32-55; Terry Eagleton, 'Marxism, Structuralism and Post-Structuralism', *Diacritics,* 15, 4, Winter 1985, pp 2-12

50 Jürgen Habermas, 'Modernity versus Postmodernity', *New German Critique,* 22, pp 3-14; — *The Philosophical Discourse of Modernity: twelve lectures,* trans. Frederick Lawrence, Polity Press, Cambridge, 1987

51 Jürgen Habermas, *Theory of Communicative Action,* Vols 1 and 2, Beacon Press, Boston, 1984 and 1987

52 Bill Ashcroft, Gareth Griffiths and Helen Tiffin (eds), *The Empire Writes Back: Theory and Practice in Post-colonial Literature,* Routledge, London, 1989, p 2

53 Vijay Mishra and Bob Hodge, 'What is post(-)colonialism?', in John Frow and Meaghan Morris (eds) *Australian Cultural Studies: A Reader,* Allen and Unwin, Sydney, 1993, pp 30-46. Mishra and Hodge's essay is critical of this tendency in *The Empire Writes Back* and in the work of Stephen Slemon

54 Edward Said, *Orientalism,* (1st edn 1978), Penguin, Harmondsworth, 1985

55 Edward Said, *Culture and Imperialism,* Chatto and Windus, London, 1993

56 Mudrooroo Narogin, *Writing from the Fringe: A Study of Modern Aboriginal Literature,* Hyland House, Melbourne, 1990

57 Michel de Certeau, *The Practice of Everyday Life,* trans. S. Rendall, University of California Press, Berkeley, 1984; — *Heterologies: Discourse of the Other,* trans. B. Bassumi, Manchester University Press, Manchester, 1986; — *The Writing of History,* trans. Tom Conley, Columbia University Press, New York, 1988

58 Ian Buchanan, 'Writing the Wrongs of History: de Certeau and Post-colonialism', *Span,* (Brisbane), 33, May 1992, pp 39-46

59 *Representations,* Winter 1991

60 Michel de Certeau, 'Travel narratives of the French to Brazil: Sixteenth to Eighteenth Centuries'; and Luce Giard, 'Epilogue: Michel de Certeau's Heterology and the New World', both in Stephen Greenblatt (ed.), *New World Encounters*

61 Michel de Certeau, *The Writing of History,* pp xxv-xxvi, his italics

62 Michel de Certeau, *The Writing of History,* p 10

63 Michel de Certeau, *The Writing of History,* p 4, his italics

64 Michel de Certeau, *Heterologies,* p 191

65 Michel de Certeau, *The Practice of Everyday Life,* p 25

66 Michel de Certeau, *The Writing of History,* p 3

67 Michel de Certeau, *The Writing of History,* p 4

2

THE OMNIPOTENCE OF SIGNS

SEMIOTICS AND THE CONQUEST OF AMERICA

THE YEAR 1992 marked the five hundredth anniversary of the European discovery of the Americas by Christopher Columbus. Had the quincentenary occurred within the political and ethical environment that prevailed in 1952 or even 1962, the discovery would have been celebrated as a momentous event—the establishment of European civilisation in the New World and the beginning of a process of expansion that eventually encompassed the whole globe. Instead, the observance became the occasion for an extraordinary outpouring of moral outrage. What made this particularly remarkable was that the wrath came less from the indigenous peoples of the continents subjected to colonisation than from the ostensible beneficiaries, the descendants of the European conquerors themselves. In book after book written to observe the quincentenary, the whole process of European discovery and settlement was denounced by academics as one of the greatest calamities to have befallen not only the native Americans but the human species as a whole and, indeed, the planet itself.

In *American Holocaust: Columbus and the Conquest of the New World,* the American academic historian David Stannard accused Columbus of starting a process of unprecedented human destruction. 'The road to Auschwitz led straight through the heart of the Americas', he wrote.[1] In *The Conquest of Paradise: Columbus and the Columbian Legacy,* the American historian and environmentalist Kirkpatrick Sale accused Columbus of finding a land where human beings lived in harmony with nature and of transforming it into one where people not only exploited nature through an unprecedented pattern of rapaciousness, but exported this new variety of environmental abuse to the whole globe. All this has left us, Sale wrote, 'at risk of the imperilment— worse, the likely destruction—of the earth'.[2] Despite the passage of five centuries, 1492 appears still not remote enough to be studied in a detached way. In the 1990s, that era remains very much a moral issue that compels response.

The quincentenary also encouraged a number of American literary critics to take the plunge and write commentaries not only on the poetry and drama of the late fifteenth century but on its historical records as well. The journals of Columbus and of several other Spanish, English and French explorers, as well as the records of the Spanish conquistadors, became objects of attention for a number of America's well-known postmodernist, poststructuralist and 'new historicist' literary critics including Stephen Greenblatt, Louis Montrose and David Quint.[3] Greenblatt's book, *Marvellous Possessions,* is about the role of 'symbolic technology' and 'engaged representations'; that is, the role of writing, speaking and translating in the 'mimetic assumptions', 'shared metaphors' and 'imaginative operations' that he finds guided the European discovery and conquest of the New World.[4]

Someone who has done more than most to define both the political and literary dimensions of this critical environment is Tzvetan Todorov, a Bulgarian who, since the 1960s, has lived and worked in Paris as a theorist of literature and language. He built a successful international career by reviving the ideas of one of the earliest movements in literary theory, that of the Russian formalists of the 1920s and 1930s. He is a theorist of structuralism and semiotics whose books include *The Fantastic: A Structural Approach to a Literary Genre* (1970), *The Poetics of Prose* (1971) and *Theories of the Symbol* (1977). In 1982 he launched himself into history with the book *The Conquest of America,* which examined the roles of Christopher Columbus and the conquistador of Mexico, Hernando Cortés. Its initial publication in French was followed by an English translation in 1984. The book created a great deal of enthusiasm among literary critics, both for its example and for its methods. For here was one of their own not only breaking out of their discipline's confines into new territory but capturing the high ground with a new way of addressing historical issues. Todorov's moral stance, which identified European imperialism in the Americas as a scourge worse than the Nazi Holocaust, also won approval in the prevailing academic climate. 'The sixteenth century', he argued, 'perpetrated the greatest genocide in human history'.[5] He dedicated his book to an unknown Mayan woman whom the Spanish conquistadors had had torn apart by dogs.

Of all those now seen as the villains of post-Columbian America, Hernando Cortés is usually regarded as the worst. In November 1519, when Cortés and his band of Spanish soldiers crossed the eastern sierras and made their descent into the Valley of Mexico, they came upon the city of Tenochtitlan and the civilisation of the people who called themselves the Mexica. Cortés reported to Spanish Emperor Charles V that the city, with its population of two hundred thousand, contained more than twice as many people as the largest in Spain, which at the time was Seville, with around seventy thousand inhabitants. Tenochtitlan itself was a magnificent achievement. It was constructed on an island in Lake Texcoco (the site of modern Mexico City), bordered and crossed by canals, and linked to the mainland by three great causeways, each three leagues, or ten kilometres, long. The city was supplied with fresh running water from the surrounding hills by a stone aqueduct two metres wide and two metres deep. At its political and cultural centre, the buildings were all made of stone and the great pyramids of its religion towered sixty metres into the air, higher than the cathedral at Seville. Tenochtitlan's huge market square was bigger than any in Europe and attracted no less than sixty thousand people a day. Within less than two years, however, Cortés had wreaked such a trail of destruction that Tenochtitlan lay in ruins and most of its population were dead.

Tenochtitlan and its twin city Tlatelolco comprised a city-state and a military power that was the centre of a vast empire of tribute extending not only to the other cities of the valley but across most of what is now central Mexico. The Mexica were the most powerful of all the Nahuatl-speaking people of Mesoamerica.[6] The odds in favour of them withstanding any challenge from the Spaniards seemed immense. The numerical superiority of the Mexica over Cortés and his band of only about five hundred adventurers was overwhelming. The natives were fighting from their own home base and on their own territory. In contrast, their Spanish opponents initially lacked any lines of supply or reinforcement, were acting in defiance of their own authorities in Cuba, and had been ravaged by a series of bloody battles both with other natives and other Spanish forces. Yet by August 1521, Cortés was totally victorious. As Todorov and almost every other analyst of the issue has emphasised, the conquest of Tenochtitlan was the critical event in the invasion of the New World. The fall of the city left America subject to Europe.[7] The question that reverberates down the centuries is: how was so implausible but so portentous a victory possible?

The answers that have been offered, like so many in history, have reflected the concerns of their times. In the sixteenth century, the accounts written by the conquistadors themselves and the missionary friars who followed them emphasised the superiority of the courage, leadership and moral character of the Spaniards and the aid given them by Providence, whose designs they were said to be fulfilling. In the nineteenth century, an era of even more ambitious imperial expansion, W. H. Prescott's highly popular account, *History of the Conquest of Mexico and the History of the Conquest of Peru*,[8] saw the rational European intelligence and the superior military technology of Cortés triumphing over the irrational, superstitious, indecisive mentality of the Mexican leader Montezuma. And in the late twentieth century, Todorov offers us an answer drawn from semiotics and structuralism: 'by his mastery of signs Cortés ensures his control over the ancient Mexican empire.'[9]

Before explaining what he means, it is worth recounting the major events of the conquest upon which all historians so far agree. There were two major phases. The first phase began in April 1519 when the Spanish expedition landed on the Mexican coast. In defiance of the Governor of Cuba, Diego Velazquez de Cuellar, who was sponsor of the expedition, Cortés assumed independent command of the forces and advanced inland. He encountered the natives of the eastern provinces, defeated them in battle and then enlisted them as allies in his march on Tenochtitlan. The Spaniards were initially accepted into the imperial city as ambassadors of a foreign power. They were saluted with gifts and treated with great hospitality. However, they soon seized the Mexican ruler Montezuma as hostage and, through control of his person, held power in the city for the next six months. Meanwhile, Velazquez de Cuellar had despatched Panfilo Narváez to arrest Cortés and end the adventure. Cortés withdrew from Tenochtitlan to meet Narváez on the coast. Cortés forced Narváez and his troops to surrender and then incorporated them in his own ranks. In his absence, the Mexica reclaimed their authority through an uprising against those Spaniards whom Cortés had left behind guarding Montezuma. This was a bloody affair, sparked by a Spanish massacre of unarmed Mexican warriors and culminating in the death of Montezuma himself at Spanish hands. By the end of June 1520, the first phase of the encounter was concluded by the 'Nochte Triste' in which the Spaniards, suffering heavy losses, were routed and expelled completely from Tenochtitlan.

Like the first, the second phase lasted just over a year. The Spanish forces retreated to the province of Tlaxcala to recuperate. They nursed their wounds, restored their weapons and supplies, and planned their return. Part of their strategy involved the prefabrication of no less than thirteen brigantines. They then knocked down the vessels and employed eight thousand natives to transport them in parts over the mountains. The second Spanish advance was made via the smaller cities in the Valley of Mexico, which were first subjugated and then engaged as allies for the assault on Tenochtitlan. In May 1521, Cortés reconstructed his brigantines on the shores of Lake Texcoco, dug a canal to launch them and then laid siege by both land and water to the imperial city. By the middle of August the siege was raised and the Spanish and their native allies entered the city, destroying its buildings as they fought their way inside and killing most of the remnants of the now starving and disease-ridden inhabitants.

The generations of historians who have discussed the conquest, Todorov notes, have provided a wide range of explanations for the Spanish victory. These explanations fall into four categories. First are those that focus on the inadequacies of Montezuma's leadership. The Mexican leader has long been criticised for not recognising the threat posed by the Spaniards. They presented themselves as ambassadors and he accepted them as such. There were times before he was taken hostage, and even periods during his captivity, when he could have ordered that the Spaniards themselves be seized. However, he vacillated about taking action, tried to bribe the intruders with gifts, consulted his oracles and waited for them to give him guidance about how to handle the strangers. On this account, it was his indecision that proved fatal to himself and his subjects.

The second type of explanation has focused on the antagonistic political relations between the Mexica and other Aztec populations in the Valley of Mexico and beyond. Tenochtitlan had only recently risen to its position of dominance in Mesoamerica. The Mexica were resented by the other Aztecs as recent usurpers of power and as cruel overlords. The Mexican empire was one of tribute and the imperial city was dependent for food and other basic necessities on supplies that flowed from the surrounding subjugated regions. However, the Mexica had failed to develop a system for governing their territories that generated loyalty or allegiance. The entry of Cortés into the uneasy political truce of the valley shattered its foundations. He was quickly seen as a liberator by other Aztec cities who needed little persuasion to cut off the supplies they provided to Tenochtitlan and turn their arms against it.

The third explanation has centred on the superiority of Spanish military technology. Spanish weapons included cutlasses, lances, arrowheads and armour all forged from iron and steel, plus handguns, crossbows and cannon. Aztec weapons were wooden arrows, knives of flintstone and wooden clubs embedded with flakes of obsidian, a form of volcanic glass. On land, the Spaniards could make military movements and attacks on horseback. The Mexica kept no beasts of burden and went only on foot. They never knew horses existed until they saw the Spanish cavalry. On water, the Spaniards fought the final siege of Tenochtitlan largely from their heavily fortified brigantines while the Mexica defended their canals and waterways by canoe.

The fourth explanation concerns the epidemic of smallpox that ravaged the native populations in the second year of the invasion. It was carried ashore by one of the soldiers of Narváez and, unlike the Europeans, the natives had no inherited immunity to the disease. In 1521 smallpox was the biggest single cause of death in the Valley of Mexico and killed off many more Aztec warriors than did Spanish swords or guns.

Given the volume of scholarship that has been applied over the centuries to the conquest, one might have thought that a combination of these four accounts would go most of the way towards providing a satisfactory answer to the question. However, Todorov insists that neither individually nor collectively do they suffice. The impact of Spanish weaponry has been exaggerated, he claims—'the gunpowder was often wet'—and the numerical superiority of the Mexica was too great for an explanation in purely military terms to be adequate. Instead, Todorov puts forward an interpretation that he claims provides an underlying, common basis for all the previous versions as well as any others that might be advanced: the Mexica, he says, were defeated by a failure of communications.

I tend to take literally one reason for the conquest/defeat that we find in the native chronicles and which has hitherto been neglected in the west, doubtless being regarded as a purely poetic formula. The testimony of the Indian accounts, which is a description rather than an explanation, asserts that everything happened because the Mayas and the Aztecs lost control of communication. The language of the gods has become unintelligible, or else these gods fell silent.[10]

Todorov sees the communication problems of the Mexica through an orthodox version of structuralist theory: culture is a system of signs that orders experience, and the Aztecs were dominated by their culture in ways that proved fatal. Though 'masters of the art of ritual discourse', the dramatically altered circumstances created by the presence of the Spaniards left the natives incapable of adaptation and improvisation. They failed to produce 'appropriate and effective messages' either among their own people or in their dealings with the newcomers. Todorov analyses a number of the constituents of their culture to argue his case. The Mexica had a cyclic, repetitive view of time in which they saw events as 'frozen in an unalterable sequence, where everything is always predicted in advance, where a singular event is merely the realisation of omens always and already present'. In a world where time repeated itself, prophecy derived from an understanding of the past. Hence, when the foreigners arrived, Montezuma turned to a book to learn what they would do.[11] He was incapable of admitting that an entirely new event could occur. The belief that fate was already decided meant that there was no opportunity for Mexican individuals to effect change. The individual did not exist in the European sense but was merely the constitutive element of the collectivity.

The individual's future is ruled by the collective past; the individual does not construct his future, rather the future is revealed; whence the role of the calendar, of omens, of auguries. The characteristic interrogation of this world is not, as among the Spanish conquistadors (or the Russian revolutionaries), of a praxeological type: 'what is to be done?'; but epistemological: 'how are we to know?'[12]

In such a culture, ritual speech was the overwhelming form of cultural expression. Ritual speech was regular in its forms and functions and hence always quoted or recited. A vast range of social circumstances were covered by ritual speech: prayers, court ceremonies, rites of passage ceremonies, departures and encounters. 'Their function is that of all ritual speech in a society without writing: they materialise social memory, i.e. the body of laws, norms and values to be transmitted from one generation to the next in order to assure the very identity of the collectivity.'[13] Todorov regards the dominance of speech and the absence of writing as the most important elements in the encounter between Aztecs and Europeans. The stylised drawings, or cartoon-like pictograms, used by the Aztecs were not, he says, a lesser degree of writing but something different. They noted the experience but not the language. Societies that lack writing are locked into the past, Todorov maintains. When ritual speech becomes the principle vehicle of memory support, the society is dominated by its past rather than by its present. In the Nahuatl language, the word for ritual or memorised speech, *huehuetlatolli*, literally means 'speech of the ancients'. This is further support for his thesis that Mexican culture looked backwards to know how to act in the present.

Todorov says there was a direct relationship between the possession of writing and native attitudes towards Europeans on both continents of the Americas. The three great Amerindian civilisations encountered by the Spaniards—the Aztecs, Mayas and Incas—each had forms of writing at a different stage of development and each of these stages produced a different response to the Europeans, especially as reflected in their belief that the Spaniards were gods. The Incas were the least familiar with writing and, of the three, were the most convinced of the divinity of the conquistadors. The Aztecs, who had pictograms, initially succumbed to the 'paralysing belief' that the Spaniards were gods: Cortés himself was supposedly a reincarnation of the Mexican god, Quetzalcoatl. According to Todorov, the Mexica even believed that Spanish horses were divine creatures. Only later in their encounter did it dawn on the Aztecs that Cortés and his followers were men like themselves and that their horses were mortal. By then, says Todorov, it was too late. The Mayas of Yucatan, who had developed a rudimentary form of phonetic writing, were the only people of the three to reject the foreign gods thesis. The Mayas called the Spaniards 'strangers' and even 'powerful ones' but never gods.[14]

Ritual dominated the native mentality even in battle. Todorov says that the Mexica expected warfare with the Spaniards to be 'subject to ritualisation and to ceremonial'. In Aztec warfare, the place of combat was always agreed upon by rival cities. Battles were preferably conducted on the stretches of cleared land that were specially set aside on the periphery of most settlements. Aztec warriors had long accepted not only that each city had its appropriate place for battle but that these battles were always fought over predetermined and fixed periods of time. They could not imagine tactics of striking from a concealed distance with long-range weapons. Aztec warfare was governed by strict codes of honour in which the ideal contest was that between two evenly matched warriors. Their religion dictated that the aim of warfare was not to kill one's opponents immediately but to take them prisoner so they could later be sacrificed to the victors' gods.[15] The Mexica were no match for a culture that did not share their scruples.

By contrast, Cortés acted in ways that suited the moment. He could weigh up the balance of advantage and adapt his tactics to any situation. The secret of his success was that he was a great communicator.

What Cortés wants from the first is not to capture but to comprehend; it is signs which chiefly interest him, not their referents. His expedition begins with a search for information, not for gold. The first important action he initiates—and we cannot overemphasise the significance of this gesture—is to find an interpreter.[16]

The mastery Cortés displays in his innovation is not simply a distinctive talent peculiar to him as an individual but, says Todorov, an inherent feature of European culture. This derives partly from the European possession of writing, which permitted a more developed form of 'mental structure', thus giving the Spaniards both greater flexibility in the way they viewed their position and more sophisticated communication skills. It also derives from the Christian concept of time, 'which is not an incessant return but an infinite progression toward the final victory of the Christian spirit'.[17] Overall, Todorov's thesis is that it was European culture that triumphed in Mexico, thanks to its superiority in the art of semiotics.

Masters in the art of ritual discourse, the Indians are inadequate in a situation requiring improvisation, and this is precisely the situation of the conquest. Their verbal education favours paradigm over syntagm, code over context, conformity-to-order over efficacy-of-the-moment, the past over the present. Now the Spanish invasion creates a radically new, entirely unprecedented situation in which the art of improvisation matters more than that of ritual. It is quite remarkable, in this context, to see Cortés not only constantly practising the art of adaptation and improvisation, but also being aware of it and claiming it as the very principle of his conduct.[18]

IMPROVISATION AND AZTEC CULTURE

The concepts and terminology of Todorov's interpretation derive from semiotics and structuralist theory. Todorov was neither the only one nor the first working in this field to make claims about the power of signs. His claims about the Spanish experience in Mexico are, as the next chapter shows, very similar to those of the structuralist Marshall Sahlins about the British in Hawaii, particularly the notion that the natives viewed the Europeans as gods from their own pantheon. Yet, despite their novel idiom, the claims by these writers to be breaking new ground and to be seeing events through fresh perspectives, are questionable. Todorov, for instance, remains bound within the framework of some very traditional European views about the Spanish invasion. His most formidable critic, the Australian academic Inga Clendinnen, says that his main argument is actually little removed from the interpretation offered by W. H. Prescott in the 1840s: the Spanish triumph because of their cultural superiority, especially because of their mental and moral qualities. The 'general contours of the Prescottian fable', she says, are clearly discernible in Todorov's account. Clendinnen has published several journal articles on pre-conquest Mexico as well as books on the Mayas and the Aztecs. One of her articles, which deals specifically with the military history of the fall of Tenochtitlan, is a damaging critique of Todorov's thesis.[19] Quite contrary to his claims that the ritualistic discourse and mentality of the Mexica left them immobilised in the face of the Spanish challenge, Clendinnen has found considerable evidence of Aztec improvisation, adaptation and innovation when confronted by the new circumstances and technologies.

Clendinnen has emphasised that, of the two phases of the Spanish–Mexican confrontation, it was the second that was the most decisive. Although the first phase has attracted the most attention from historians, since it is largely composed of the intriguing cultural and political relationship between Cortés and Montezuma, its conclusion saw the Spaniards by far the weaker of the two parties. It was the second, largely military phase—the recruiting of native allies, the construction of the brigantines and the siege of Tenochtitlan—that defeated the Mexica and gave the Spaniards victory. So any explanation of the Spanish triumph has primarily to address the second phase, which, Clendinnen insists, was a close-run thing. Against Todorov's picture of Aztec warriors frozen in time and unable to change either strategy or tactics when confronted by situations new to their ritualised mind-set, Clendinnen finds evidence of a different kind. After their initial, fatal introduction to gunshot, cannon fire and crossbows, Mexican warriors quickly learned not to leap and shout and display themselves in battle, as they would against other Aztecs, but to weave and duck. Their canoeists learned to zigzag in the water to avoid the cannon shot from Spanish brigantines, so that in time the carnage was less.

Although siege warfare had been hitherto unknown in Mesoamerica, the Mexica responded with flexibility to its challenges.

They 'read' Spanish tactics reasonably accurately: a Spanish assault on the freshwater aqueduct at Chapultepec was foreseen, and furiously, if fruitlessly, resisted. The brigantines, irresistible for their first appearance on the lake, were later lured into a carefully conceived ambush in which two were trapped. The horses' vulnerability to uneven ground, to attack from below, their panic under a hail of missiles, were all exploited effectively. The Mexicans borrowed Spanish weapons: Spanish swords lashed to poles or Spanish lances to disable the horses; even Spanish crossbows, after captive crossbowmen had been forced to show them how the machines worked. It was their invention and tenacity that forced Cortés to the desperate remedy of levelling structures along the causeways and into the city to provide the Spaniards with the secure ground they needed to be effective.[20]

The Aztecs' alleged belief that Spanish men and horses were divine creatures gets short shrift from Clendinnen. At the initial encounter between the Spaniards and the warriors of Tlaxcala, on their first sight of horses the natives made a deliberate and successful attempt to kill two of them. They cut the bodies of the animals into pieces and distributed them throughout the towns of their province to show their mortal nature. The Aztecs admired the horses for their ferocity and courage in battle, but they were always well aware that they were simply animals. The notion that Cortés was regarded as the god Quetzalcoatl who had returned to his people from the east has a similar lack of credibility. Todorov claims that it was the Aztecs' lack of writing that led them to this belief. Clendinnen, however, says there is no evidence the idea existed during the years of the conquest. It was actually an invention of the Spanish monks who wrote their own histories of the conquest much later in the sixteenth century.[21] This is identical to the process through which the navigator James Cook came to be seen by the natives of the Hawaiian Islands as the god Lono. European missionaries to Hawaii, supported by compliant native converts, 'discovered' this native 'belief' decades after Cook's death when they too came to write their histories of the British arrival. As Gananath Obeyesekere has shown, the concept of Europeans as gods has no place in the theology of the natives of the Pacific. The idea of apotheosis is, rather, part of the euhemeristic traditions of Indo-European religion, including the Christian cult of sainthood and its ancient Roman predecessors.[22] In other words, it was European culture that was predisposed to the belief that the natives regarded the strangers as gods, not the other way around.

There are other aspects of Todorov's thesis that also strain credulity, even though the meagre sources available about pre-conquest beliefs do not provide us with a knock-down argument. He describes the Aztec world as one where time seemed frozen in an unalterable sequence. However, the sense of time in Tenochtitlan must have been felt quite differently. Until the four-teenth century of the European calendar, the Mexica lived a nomadic exist-ence far to the north of Lake Texcoco. In about 1325, when they settled on their island in the lake, they were an inferior, marginalised group, subject to the then-dominant cities of the valley. Their rise to imperial power took place only in the century before the Spanish landing. In 1520, much of the construction of Tenochtitlan, especially the magnificence of its temples and market square, had taken place in living memory. The Mexica's imperial splendour, as uncontested rulers of central Mexico, was less than fifty years old.[23] In other words, the Mexica lived within a dynamic society, familiar with social and political transformation, and well aware of their own dramatic changes in fortune. The enormity of empire building—the development of a workable political system, the raising of armies, the management of the me-tropolis, the external diplomatic manoeuvrings and alliances, the cultivation of a religious world view to sanctify the whole edifice—speaks of a people imbued far more than most with a sense of development over time and with the arts of adaptation and improvisation that Todorov claims were beyond them.

CULTURE AND WARFARE

Todorov's main critic, Inga Clendinnen, is Reader in History at La Trobe University, Melbourne, and is one of the most impressive practitioners of the discipline working today. She impresses both in the depth of her scholarship and through her sheer ability as a writer. She is a rare creature: an academic who can write stylish and striking prose. Her latest book, *Aztecs: An Interpretation* (1991), was written partly in Melbourne and partly at the Institute for Advanced Studies, Princeton. She is one of a group of Melburnians who have been welcomed to Princeton by the postmodernist anthropologist Clifford Geertz. She avoids, however, the theoreticist displays so characteristic of the work of the Princeton School and she is a severe critic of the structuralist, European visions of native peoples found in the work of writers like Todorov. *Aztecs* is a study of the culture, religion and daily life of the Mexica of pre-conquest Tenochtitlan as experienced by the city's inhabitants. Though the fragmentary and cloudy sources do not allow the portrayal of any historic individuals, Clendinnen has created a convincing account of the vivid drama of Aztec social existence, of the performance art that dominated their religion, and of the meaning the Aztecs derived from their constantly practised ritual of human sacrifice. It is a stunning piece of work which deserves the admiration it has received in the academic press in both the United States and Australia.

Nonetheless, in her own explanation of the Spanish military victory, Clendinnen remains a captive of the central positions of the cultural studies movement. In her account of the fall of Tenochtitlan, she acknowledges many of the points made by political and military historians but wants, ultimately, to subsume them all beneath a cultural explanation. It is ironic that while she criticises Todorov for simply repeating, under a new guise, the traditional Eurocentric vision of the conquest, her own account lies squarely within the same culturalist domain as that of Todorov himself.

Clendinnen's thesis is that warfare needs to be understood in cultural terms. Warfare is not a situation where the veils of culture are finally ripped away and natural man confronts himself. Combat is a phenomenon, she says, that exposes how ways of acting and meaning are understood and responded to in crisis conditions. Though it is not a contest that is as cultural as cricket, warfare is nonetheless rule-bound. Its high intensities expose 'what lessons about the other and about oneself can be learned in this intimate, involuntary, and most consequential communication'.[24] The reasons for the Mexican defeat, she argues, have to be understood in terms of the society's views about the nature and purpose of warfare and about how combat should be properly conducted.

All the Aztecs regarded warfare as a sacred duel between peoples. Their warriors had a religious view of how battle should be fought. They saw no virtue in defeating an inferior enemy. In their combat between each other, they would send food and weapons to the opposing side if they judged it too inferior to defeat as it was. Clendinnen agrees with Todorov's claim that the ideal form of battle was a hand-to-hand duel between matched warriors, a contest in which the taking of a fitting captive for presentation as sacrifice to one's own deity was the true measure of valour; or of one's fate if defeated. She says the Mexica were inhibited about killing on the battleground. The real aim of combat was capture; the meaning of warfare was the subjection of humans to the fate determined for them by the gods. Aztecs would fire arrows and darts at their enemies from a distance, but their aim was 'to weaken and draw blood, not to pierce fatally'. They had a fascination with the tactic of ambush, but only as a device by which to confront the enemy more dramatically, and so strike terror through surprise. But, Clendinnen insists, 'to strike from hiding was unthinkable'.[25]

The Spanish, on the other hand, preferred the ambush as part of their wider predilection for killing with least risk. They valued their crossbows and muskets for their ability to pick off selected warrior leaders well behind enemy lines before any formal challenges had been made and accepted. To the Mexica, these tactics were psychologically demoralising because men killed at a distance without proper engagement in battle died trivial deaths, unlike the warrior killed in direct confrontation who died nobly. The Aztecs thought that to kill from a distance without putting one's own life at risk was a shameful and cowardly action. The Spaniards also developed a new tactic for entrapping enemy warriors. In traditional battles between Aztecs themselves, the moment when one side prevailed and the opposition turned and fled was a compelling signal for the victors to pursue them to take captives. Cortés discovered how to exploit this by ordering his horsemen to pretend to flee and then, when the Mexican pursuit had begun, to turn on them suddenly and gain a sure crop of kills from among the boldest. Tactics like these earned loathing and derision from the native warriors, but also worked to baffle them and keep them off balance. During the siege of Tenochtitlan, the Mexican contempt for Spanish tactics intensified. 'Mexican warriors continued to seek face-to-face combat with these most unsatisfactory opponents, who skulked and refused battle, who clung together in tight bands behind their cannon, who fled without shame.'[26]

Clendinnen says Cortés himself owed his life to Aztec religious ideals about the appropriate conduct of war. His status as leader meant the natives thought it imperative he be taken alive to be offered as sacrifice to their gods. Many times on the battlefield, she says, Cortés was actually seized temporarily by native hands, but he became the subject of a 'disorderly tug of war' rather than a quick knifing. 'Mexican warriors could not kill the enemy leader so casually: were he to die, it would be in the temple of Huitzilopochtli, and before his shrine.'[27] Some Spanish soldiers who were captured were taken to the temple and sacrificed and their heads brought back and displayed before their compatriots. However, if the exigencies of the moment of battle meant that a Spaniard had to be killed, he was either turned around and his head beaten in—the form of death reserved for criminals—or else was stripped of clothing and weapons—thus reduced in status from warrior to slave—and then despatched.

Overall, Clendinnen argues, it was the Aztecs' religious definition of warfare that decided the whole issue. She acknowledges that on many combat-related issues the Mexica could be innovative. 'But on the basic measure of man's worth, the taking alive of prestigious captives, they could not compromise.' It was this commitment that bore most heavily on the outcome. 'Had Indians been as uninhibited as Spaniards in their killing, the small Spanish group, with no secured source of replenishment, would soon have been whittled away.'[28] It was Mexican culture and religion, moreover, that made it necessary for Cortés to destroy Tenochtitlan and kill most of its inhabitants. The Mexica had no concept of surrender and the transfer of power to the victor. During the final stages of the siege, Cortés made several attempts to negotiate with the remaining Mexican lords but was rebuffed. They refused any terms save a swift death. Even with all their warriors either dead or un-armed and the people starving, they responded to further mass killings from cannon and handgun not by surrendering but by pressing on to destruction. Exasperated, Cortés decided to raze the city, and unleashed his native allies who massacred the remnants of the defenceless men, women and children.

Since the Aztecs had no written literature, their attitudes towards warfare have to be inferred from other, less reliable, evidence. There are three principal sources: the reports of Cortés himself about the campaign; reminiscences made many years later by soldiers who served with him; and accounts from the native perspective also collected much later by Spanish monks trying to reconstruct the meaning of Aztec culture and religion. Some of the monks' native informants had been children and young men at the time the city fell and had direct experience of the final collapse. Clendinnen's interpretation of Aztec battlefield behaviour is drawn principally from the last kind of source. It is also heavily swayed by the culturalist agenda in history that prevails today. However, even within her own accounts of Aztec warfare and the battle for Tenochtitlan there is enough evidence to show that the older political, military and technological arguments, while they might be less fashionable and less exciting to the current generation of theorists, remain the more convincing. Some of her internal evidence itself also contradicts her thesis and, despite her best efforts, cannot be argued away. Let me make four different types of argument to bring out these points.

Aztec politics. The first and most important argument to make is a political one. As both Clendinnen and Todorov insist, the big question about the conquest of Mexico has always been how such a small band of Spaniards could have defeated such a powerful native force. The answer has never been difficult to comprehend. Cortés neutralised his numerical inferiority by recruiting large numbers of native allies. By the time of the final siege of Tenochtitlan, he had almost all the other Aztec cities and settlements in Mexico on his side. The reason for this has never been a mystery either. Tenochtitlan was seen as a murderously cruel and authoritarian imperial power whom the other Aztecs were pleased to see overthrown. In their swift rise to power, the Mexica had overlooked the diplomatic need to generate loyalty and self-interested support from their neighbours. They exacted tribute by threat of terror and retribution. In fact, each year, the agricultural harvest heralded the onset of a six-month 'season of war' in which warriors from Tenochtitlan would go out to other settlements to challenge them to battle, to bring back captives for sacrifice and to carry off women, children and slaves. One doesn't need much understanding of Mesoamerican religion to realise that such practices were bound to generate the desire for revenge.

Military technology. The second type of argument is the obvious one of military technology. By the fifteenth century, the Europeans had developed hard-edged weapons made of iron and steel but Aztec weaponry had not progressed beyond wooden and stone implements. Clendinnen says that, because of the Aztec predilection for taking captives rather than killing opponents, their arrows and darts were not meant to kill but to weaken and draw blood. But the fact remains that this was the most that their technology could hope to achieve anyway. The arrows and darts were made of wood and some were tipped with flintstone. Weapons of this kind were incapable in battle of piercing warriors to the heart. The same was true of the flint and obsidian knives carried by the Aztecs and of their wooden lances tipped with flint. The most powerful weapon in the Aztec armoury was the club embedded with obsidian. Like the rest, this was not a killing weapon. It was normally directed at an opponent's legs, to cripple or throw him so he could be grappled to the ground and subdued. In contrast, the Spanish steel cutlass was physically capable of decapitating a man with one blow. Spanish lances could kill with one strike, especially from the height and thrust given by horseback. Even if we disregard the overwhelming superiority provided by brigantines, horses, cannon and arquebuses (handguns), the Spaniards had weapons for hand-to-hand combat that killed easily, while their opponents had weapons that injured or, at best, disabled. Spanish soldiers, in fact, found Aztec weapons so inconsequential that they abandoned their own heavy metal armour in favour of quilted cotton.[29] Although their cultural beliefs about battle may well have meant that the Aztecs thought it dishonourable to strike from a distance, it was also true that they had no weapons that would have allowed them to do so. In fact, reading Clendinnen's account of their cultural strictures on battlefield behaviour, one cannot help but think that the Aztecs were making a virtue out of necessity. It looks very much like their technology had placed strict limits on the kind of warfare that was available to them and so their religion and codes of warrior honour had sanctified the only practices that were possible.

In accounting for the Spanish conquest, it is just as necessary to explain the Spanish military environment as that of their opponents. This is something that Clendinnen omits to do. The Spanish invasion of America took place in the midst of what was the greatest transformation in European warfare in a thousand years—the gunpowder revolution. By the early 1490s, French foundrymen had perfected a new bronze-cast cannon that fired wrought iron balls. In 1494, the possession of forty cannon allowed Charles VIII of France to cut a swathe through Italy, conquering Florence then marching south and overwhelming in eight hours the fortress at Naples, which had once with-stood a siege by traditional military means for seven years. 'The whole of Italy quaked at his passage', records the military historian, John Keegan. 'His guns had brought a true revolution in warmaking.'[30] By the turn of the sixteenth century, on the eve of Cortés's departure for the Americas, firearms in the form of arquebuses and muskets were added to cannon and the crossbow (itself invented in Europe only a century before) to complete the supremacy of missile weapons over cavalry and pike. Some of the older European aristocratic powers, especially in France and Germany, preferred to resist the new kind of warfare that firearms permitted. However, the military class of the then lesser powers, especially England, Italy and Spain, sensed the opportunities that the inventions created and embraced firearms more eagerly. Keegan records that the Spaniards, with the largest wars on their hands at the time, were the most enthusiastic advocates of the new weapons. In two notable battles, at Cerignola in 1503 and Bicocca in 1522, numerically superior French and Swiss infantry were destroyed by the firepower of Spanish handgunners.[31] In Mexico, Cortés had all this new technology at his disposal—cannon, firearms, crossbows—not to mention cavalry. He faced an enemy whose weapons were still in the stone age.

Military tactics. A third case that should be made is that of military tactics. The Mexica had never before experienced the kind of siege warfare practised by Cortés. Europeans, on the other hand, had been conducting sieges for more than two thousand years before the Spanish landfall in America. European cities had over this time adapted their construction, supplies and defences to the possibility of siege. Moreover, at the time the Spaniards were departing for America, European fortifications were going through a period of rapid redesign because of the challenge presented by the invention of cannon. In Tenochtitlan, however, Cortés found a people who had never even conceived of European-style siege warfare, let alone constructed defences against it. Once he saw this, both the possibility of conquering the city and the strategy needed to accomplish it were clear to him.

Culturalist explanations. A fourth problem that may be raised is Clendinnen's own argument against Todorov. Despite their culture and religion, the Mexica were not people frozen within a mentality that made it impossible for them to respond to the Spaniards. Given the degree of the shock they received confronting Europeans who had such different ways and means of fighting, the Mexica responded and adapted fairly quickly. In other words, Clendinnen's own case against Todorov neutralises the impact of her own attempt to provide a culturalist explanation. If the Aztecs were not as disadvantaged by their culture as Todorov claims, they could not be as disadvantaged as Clendinnen claims either.

Let me elaborate this last point using her own account of the conquest. Two things that are essential to Clendinnen's case are the Aztec insistence on capturing rather than killing enemies and their belief that anything less than hand-to-hand combat was shameful and cowardly. However, her description of the last days of Tenochtitlan provides enough evidence to the contrary to undermine her case. When Spanish soldiers made their forays into the city streets, they were pelted from the rooftops with large stones that had been stored for the purpose by Aztec warriors. There was little ritual in these efforts. The stones were intended to kill, injure and disable as many of the enemy as possible. When some Spanish crossbowmen were captured during the assault, the natives took their weapons, forced their captives to demonstrate how to use them and then fired upon the invading Spaniards. In other words, Clendinnen herself provides two examples of the Mexica adopting the 'unthinkable' Spanish tactic of hurling missiles from a distance with the intent to kill, despite her claim that this would have been a breach of their most sacred principles of battle. When two of the Spanish brigantines, patrolling the lake as part of the siege, ran aground, the Mexica who overran them did not capture their captains and crew for sacrifice nor invoke any other ritual. They killed them on the spot. The final massacre of the population, in which up to forty thousand people may have perished, was carried out not by Spaniards but by their native allies. These were from the province of Tlaxcala and, at the very outset of the campaign in 1521, long before the fighting began, they told the Spaniards their views about what to do when they encountered the enemy.

In fighting the Mexicans, they said, we should kill all we could, leaving no one alive: neither the young, lest they should bear arms again, nor the old, lest they give counsel.[32]

This statement poses some obvious difficulties for Clendinnen's views about the creed of Meosamerican warriors. It shows that some of the Nahuatl-speaking people, though sharing similar language and religious beliefs, had a radically different code of warrior honour to that which she says held sway in Tenochtitlan. Clendinnen herself acknowledges this quite openly, but attempts to explain it away by arguing that the Tlaxcaltecs were underdogs and outsiders within the Mexican empire. Their hatred of the Mexica was particularly intense and this gave them a unique set of attitudes.[33] However, these are essentially secular grounds for breaking with what Clendinnen has described as fundamental religious beliefs. If there were political reasons for one group of Aztecs to abandon a supposedly uncompromising religious principle, it is quite understandable that the Mexica would do the same. When faced with total defeat and subjugation, the warriors of Tenochtitlan abandoned their religious scruples and tried to kill as many of the enemy as they could. In other words, the central cultural point on which Clendinnen rests her case for the Mexican defeat is inherently implausible.

In making the case here, the last thing I want to do is deny that culture is a highly influential determinant of the kind of warfare that people practise. Nor am I arguing that Clendinnen's account of Mexican warrior culture is mistaken in some kind of fundamental way. These, however, are not the central issues at stake. The issue is why the Spaniards defeated the Mexica and, while Clendinnen's account certainly increases our understanding of the conflict, it shifts the cause of the defeat onto Aztec culture and away from the true and overpowering causes: the Spanish political and military superiority. The cultural aspects of Mexican life were by no means irrelevant but, clearly, they influenced the outcome far less than the principal causes. It is quite fair to say that, had Mexican culture been radically different but their political, military and technological situation the same, the outcome would still have been much as it was. Once Cortés had determined to capture the Mexican empire, his adroit exploitation of local politics, the supremacy of his weaponry and the nature of his military tactics combined to guarantee him victory.

THE QUESTION OF 'THE OTHER'

As well as being a thesis about the power of signs, Todorov's book on the conquest of America is about the discovery of 'the other'. The subtitle of his book is 'The question of the Other' and he describes his subject as 'the discovery self makes of the other'.[34] The concept of 'the other' has become a favourite one of structuralists, postmodernists and other radical academics. It holds that one group of people define the prevailing system of normality or convention in such a way that other values and people are placed outside the system. Feminists claim that in patriarchal society, woman is the 'other'; radical blacks argue that their own values and ideals are suppressed by the dominant white culture, which casts their people as 'other'. Followers of Jacques Lacan's neo-Freudian theories give the term a capital letter. For them, 'the unconscious is the discourse of the Other'. It is a term that is bandied about with varying degrees of consistency across the whole of the contemporary theoreticist spectrum.

  Todorov says that when Christopher Columbus came upon the natives of the Caribbean in 1492 he responded to them with two contrary attitudes, which he bequeathed to all subsequent generations of Europeans, down to the present. On the one hand, he saw them as human beings with no fundamental differences from himself. They were equals, save for minor differences of language, clothing and technology. Todorov says this view initially led Columbus to believe the natives could be assimilated into European society. He even had some dressed in European clothing and taken back to Spain so they might learn European customs and religion, which, when they returned, they would spread among their own people. On the other hand, Columbus also betrays a view that saw the Caribbeans as different, a perspective that was quickly translated into terms of inferiority. This second view of natives as a lower form of humanity justified an attitude that was indifferent to their death and suffering and that allowed them to be captured and turned into slaves. Todorov classifies the first view as that of the 'noble savage' and the second as that of the 'dirty dog'. Despite appearing as opposites, both rested on a common basis: 'the failure to recognise the Indians, and the refusal to admit them as a subject having the same rights as oneself, but different.'[35] In other words, he is saying that Columbus saw the natives either as equal and the same, or different and inferior, but never equal and different. Columbus was a captive, says Todorov, of the egocentric nature of European culture, which identified itself with the human condition as a whole and which could not accept radically different notions of humanity.

What is denied is the existence of a human substance truly other, something capable of being not merely an imperfect state of oneself. These two elementary figures in the experience of alterity are both grounded in egocentrism, in the identification of our own values with values in general, of our *I* with the universe—in the conviction that the world is one... Columbus has discovered America but not the Americans.[36]

The year 1492 was symbolic of the triumph of European egocentrism over the 'other' in more ways than one, Todorov reminds us. In this year not only did Columbus find the New World, but the Jews were expelled from Spain and Ferdinand and Isabella finally defeated the Moors in the Battle of Granada, thereby establishing a homogeneity of religion and race throughout the whole of the Iberian Peninsula. Columbus's voyage was thus the harbinger of the modern era, Todorov says, which has since imposed its universalist notion of humanity, written in its own image, across the entire globe. Shifting into a more visionary gear, Todorov then goes on to tell us that the apparent victory of Europe in the Americas was really a defeat for the greater cause of human diversity.

The silence of the gods weighs upon the camp of the Europeans as much as on that of the Indians. By winning on one side, the Europeans lost on the other; by imposing their superiority upon the entire country, they destroyed their own capacity to integrate themselves into the world. During the centuries that follow, they would dream of the noble savage; but the savage was dead or assimilated, and this dream was doomed to remain a sterile one.[37]

Todorov did not derive this idea from his scrutiny of the documents of the European discovery of America. Rather, he went to these documents for confirmation of a theory that had already become popular among radical academics. This is the critique of the Enlightenment concept of universal human nature and values. By the early 1980s, this critique had become accepted by a wide range of groups, especially postmodernists, feminists and black activists. The eighteenth century claim that human nature was one, and that all had the same rights to liberty and equality, was being widely denounced as nothing but the ideology of dead, white males. Michel Foucault summed up the critique in his attention-getting phrase, 'the death of man'. I look in more detail at what Foucault meant by this in Chapter Five. Here it is enough to note that the critique replaces a universalist view of human nature with a relativist one. Postmodernists believe that human nature equals human culture and, since cultures are diverse, natures must also be diverse. Cultural relativism sees other cultures as legitimate in themselves—equal but different—no matter what the content. The idea of underlying values, common to all humanity, is seen as nothing but a myth of European culture and an oppressive imposition on those with different ways of life. We cannot use the values of our own culture, we are told, to judge those of others.

It is this critique that is the basis for so much of the moral outrage expressed by leftist historians and literary critics on the anniversary of 1492. They are denouncing what they see as the egocentric universalism of Europe, which brought about the destruction of the 'other', and they are affirming the virtue of an alternative, relativist approach to human culture. As I write this in 1993, the United Nations Year of Indigenous Peoples, the critics appear to have swept all before them. Both academic and popular sympathies these days have taken the critique to their hearts and seem firmly on the side of the natives.

One of the problems for Todorov in all this is that he lets his moral outrage get the better of the logic of his case. In trying to show the Aztecs as innocent victims who are worthy of our sympathy he ends up contradicting his major thesis about them as 'other'. He is led to argue, in fact, that in one central aspect of their culture, they are not so other at all. Let me use the next section to explain this.

HUMAN SACRIFICE AND CULTURAL RELATIVISM

One of the problems for those who profess sympathy for the indigenous peoples of the Americas is the widespread practice of human sacrifice which prevailed at the time of the Spanish conquest. Human sacrifice was practised by the Aztecs of Mexico, the Mayas of Yucatan, the Incas of Peru, the Tupinambas and the Caytes of Brazil, the natives of Guyana and the Pawnee and Huron tribes of North America. In societies that had developed urban settlements, such as those of the Aztecs and Mayas, victims were usually taken to a central temple and lain across an altar where priests would cut out their hearts and then offer them to the gods. In the less technologically developed societies of Guyana and Brazil, victims would either be battered to death in the open and then dismembered, or tied up and burned to death over a fire. The early European explorers were shocked to find that sacrifice was often accompanied by cannibalism. In Tenochtitlan, the remains of sacrificed victims were taken from the temples and distributed among the populace, who would cook the flesh in a stew. In Guyana and Brazil, limbs of victims were skewered and roasted over a spit before being consumed. The Caytes of the Brazilian coast ate the crew of every wrecked Portuguese vessel they found. The American anthropologist Harry Turney-High writes: 'At one meal they ate the first Bishop of Bahia, two Canons, the Procurator of the Royal Portuguese Treasury, two pregnant women and several children.'[38]

Todorov acknowledges all this and even publishes in his book some early Spanish drawings of acts of both sacrifice and cannibalism. The existence of these practices is something that most people brought up in Western society find very hard to come to terms with. For most of us, they would appear to provide evidence for Todorov's thesis that the natives of the New World did, indeed, constitute some unfathomable 'other' who were culturally at variance with Europeans in radical ways. Yet this is not how Todorov uses this material at all. In fact, his major concern is to play down, or explain away, these practices. He tries to argue that they are not as monstrously bizarre as they first appear but are simply the other side of the coin of practices in which European societies had indulged for centuries. First, he cites a long argument from one of the sixteenth century Dominican bishops in Mexico, Bartolomé de Las Casas, that these native practices have the same religious significance as the Eucharist of the Christian church. This is the ritual deriving from the last supper of Jesus in which, in the Roman Catholic interpretation, the congregation symbolically consumes His flesh and blood in the form of wafers and wine. The Old Testament also has examples of God ordering some of His followers to sacrifice their own children. God, of course, sacrificed His only son so that mankind might be redeemed. In other words, the practice is not as alien to the Judeo-Christian tradition as European contemporaries might think.[39]

Second, Todorov attempts to characterise both Europe and America as societies that are guilty of mass murder, with the principal difference being the cultural means to the end. While the native Americans had produced what he calls 'sacrifice societies', the Spaniards were representative of the 'massacre societies' of European culture. Of the two, Todorov believes the sacrifice society to be the more civilised. Sacrifice is performed in the name of the official ideology; it is perpetrated in public places, in sight of all, and to everyone's knowledge. The victim's identity is determined by strict rules. The sacrifice testifies to the power of the social fabric and to its mastery over the individual. By contrast, Todorov says, massacres reveal the weakness of the social fabric. They are performed in some remote place where the law is only vaguely acknowledged. The more remote and alien the victims the better: they are exterminated without remorse, identified with animals, and their individual identity is irrelevant. Unlike sacrifices, Todorov points out, massacres are generally not acknowledged or proclaimed; their very existence is kept secret and denied. This is because their social function is not recognised.[40]

Unfortunately for Todorov, his belief that he can characterise the two cultures along these lines is hopelessly confused. He is forced to admit such major exceptions to his division that he robs it of any intellectual force. He says that the 'massacre societies' also practised sacrifice when, for example, he likens the executions for heresy carried out by the Spanish Inquisition to native religious sacrifice.[41] He is also well aware that some of the Mesoamericans prepared for and indulged in massacres, especially the final massacre by the Tlaxcaltecs of the Mexica at the siege of Tenochtitlan. And he invents a new, third category, the '*massacrifice* society' to classify the mass murders of the twentieth century: 'These states, certainly modern in that they cannot be identified either with sacrifice societies or massacre societies, nonetheless unite certain features of both, and deserve the creation of a portmanteau word.'[42]

Todorov's failure to make this distinction stick leaves his wider thesis in a cleft stick. He wants to impose a moral judgement on the Spanish conquest, and yet he also wishes to play down the issue of human sacrifice so that his readers will still see the Aztecs as victims who have the greater virtue and who deserve the greater sympathy. To do this he is forced to argue that all human societies are guilty of systematic mass murder; only some are more guilty than others. But once the distinction between sacrifice/massacre societies evaporates, he is left with nothing but a common human nature to explain the murderous proclivity of the species. And the idea of a common human nature is something that his whole book was designed to deny.

Where, then, does all this leave the question of 'the other'? Once one gains more than a nodding acquaintance with the culture that prevailed in Mesoamerica before the coming of the Spaniards, a simplistic view of the Aztecs as morally defensible casualties is very difficult to sustain. Certainly, for the historians of the American quincentenary to use the term 'holocaust' and to say that 'the road to Auschwitz' led through Mexico is to make comparisons that are not only wildly anachronistic but conceptually odious. The victims in Europe, the Jews, did not have a culture before the Second World War that was warlike and domineering, nor did they have a religion that practised incessant, ritualistic murder. The victims in America, the Aztecs, by contrast displayed all these characteristics.

Inga Clendinnen has said that most recent historians of Aztec America have either set aside the issue of human sacrifice while they concentrated on other things—political and economic matters—or else have discussed it at levels of considerable ideological and theological abstraction.[43] In her book, *Aztecs* she makes the explanation of human sacrifice one of the central objectives of her account of Mexican cultural, religious and social life. She thrusts the issue right into her readers' faces. The result is one of the most disturbing books that many will have ever read. It is impossible to do justice to her whole story in the space available here, but allow me to select some points that bear on the moral issues raised by the historians of 1492 with which this chapter started its discussion.

The Mexica practised human sacrifice on a regular, seasonal basis as well as on special occasions to celebrate great moments in their imperial rule. Killings were scheduled four times a year to mark the four seasonal festivals in the Aztec calendar. During the season of war, which continued for half the year, warriors from Tenochtitlan would attack surrounding settlements to capture warriors like themselves and to exact tribute in the form of goods and slaves. The most prestigious sacrifices were those of captured warriors, but slaves were frequently killed as well. The Aztec empire of warfare and tribute extended across modern central Mexico, from coast to coast, and the sacrificial victims were mainly from Nahuatl-speaking tribes. Aztec sources do not provide enough evidence for historians to calculate precisely how many were put to death each year, but the numbers involved were immense. When one of the conquistadors, Bernaz Diaz del Castillo, first entered Tenochtitlan he saw that: 'in the plaza where their oratories stood, there were piles of human skulls so regularly arranged that one could count them, and I estimated them at more than one hundred thousand.' Another conquistador, Andrés de Tapia, estimated the number of skulls hanging on racks in Tenochtitlan to be no less than 136 000. Though twentieth century scholars believe these and other contemporary observations exaggerate the picture, the most plausible estimates are that the numbers executed every year ran to several thousand.[44]

Those killed were not regarded as some lower form of life. The Mexica knew they were killing human beings like themselves: that was the whole point. Human bodies and blood were offered as sustenance to their gods, the powers of the earth and of the sun—especially to Tezcatlipoca, the omnipotent and omnipresent god of the interior of the earth, and to Huitzilopochtli, the tribal deity of the Mexica and the god of the sun and god of war. 'The killings', Clendinnen notes, 'were also explicitly about the dominance of the Mexica and of their tutelary deity: public displays to overawe the watcher, Mexica or stranger, in a state theatre of power, at which the rulers of other and lesser cities, allies and enemies alike, were routinely present'.[45]

The executions were performed before shrines of the gods, on the platform at the top of great pyramids that were constructed for the purpose of sacrifice.

The victim walked or was dragged up the temple steps to the platform, was spreadeagled alive across the large killing stone, and was held down by five priests. Four would hold the limbs and one the head. The angle of the plane of the stone meant that the victim's chest cavity was arched and elevated. The executioner priest then plunged a knife of flint under the exposed ribs and sawed through the arteries to the heart, which was pulled out and held high as an offering to the gods. The execution was a messy affair, with priests, stone, platform and steps all drenched by the spurting blood. The head of the victim was usually severed and spitted on a skull rack while the lifeless body was pushed and rolled down the pyramid steps. At the base of the pyramid, the body was butchered and, after being distributed to relatives and friends of the warrior who had offered the sacrifice, the parts were cooked and eaten.

After certain kinds of sacrifices, the skin of the victim's back was split open and the skin peeled from the body. A priest would then dress himself in the flayed skin, with the wet side out, dead hands and feet dangling from live wrists and ankles, and continue the ceremony. During Ochpaniztli, the festival of the eleventh month, the sacrificial victim was a woman who for four days was bedecked with flowers and teased by the women attending her about her impending doom. On the fifth night, the women accompanied her to the temple of the Maize Lord where she was stretched across the back of a priest and killed. Clendinnen continues:

Then, still in darkness, silence, and urgent haste, her body was flayed, and a naked priest, a 'very strong man, very powerful, very tall', struggled into the wet skin, with its slack breasts and pouched genitalia: a double nakedness of layered, ambiguous sexuality. The skin of one thigh was reserved to be fashioned into a face-mask for the man impersonating Centeotl, Young Lord Maize Cob, the son of Toci.[46]

Not all of those executed were outsiders; some were low-born citizens and slaves from within the community of Tenochtitlan itself, and some were children of families within the city. The children were those offered to Tlaloc, the god of agricultural fertility, over the first months of the ritual calendar. Priests chose children to be killed from among those who had been born on a particular daysign and whose hair was marked with a double cowlick. The children, aged between two and seven years, were taken by the priests from their homes and kept together in nurseries for some weeks before their deaths. As the appropriate festivals arrived, they were dressed in magnificent costumes and paraded in groups through the city. The pathos of the sight moved those watching to tears. The children, who knew their fate, also wept. The priests welcomed this because their tears were thought to augur rain. The children's throats were then slit and they were offered to Tlaloc as 'bloodied flowers of maize'.[47]

While human sacrifice was practised by all Nahuatl-speaking peoples, the killings that most distinguished the Mexica were those of their great ceremonies: the installation of a new ruler, and the dedication of a new temple or a great work of engineering. There is a contemporary description of the fate of the Huaxtec people who launched an unsuccessful revolt in 1487 at a time that coincided with one of these great ceremonies. The Mexican army herded their Huaxtec prisoners back to Tenochtitlan where the priests greeted them with the news that they were all to die for the inauguration of the newly completed Temple of Huitzilopochtli (the same pyramid recently excavated in the square of the Cathedral of Mexico). Clendinnen describes 'the men linked by cords through the warrior perforations in their septums, the maidens and the little boys still too young to have had their noses pierced, secured by yokes around their necks, all wailing a pitiful lament'. Though the conquistador, Bernaz Diaz, claimed that more than eighty thousand people were killed for this one inauguration, Clendinnen argues that a more realistic figure was closer to twenty thousand, all executed over four days: 'four patient lines stretching the full length of the processional ways and marshalled along the causeways, slowly moving towards the pyramid.'[48]

It is difficult for anyone brought up in Western culture to know how to respond to the dreadful details of these Mexican rituals. There are some Marxist commentators, ever ready with a theory to impute unspeakable motives to anyone in authority, and always seeing the lower orders as paragons of virtue, who have claimed the rituals were a form of state terrorism launched by the Aztec ruling class to preserve its power. Clendinnen, however, dismisses this kind of thing from the outset.

The killings were not remote top-of-the-pyramid affairs. If only high priests and rulers killed, they carried out most of their butchers' work *en plein air*, and not only in the main temple precinct, but in the neighbourhood temples and on the streets. The people were implicated in the care and preparation of the victims, their delivery to the place of death, and then in the elaborate processing of the bodies: the dismemberment and distribution of heads and limbs, flesh and blood and flayed skins. On high occasions warriors carrying gourds of human blood or wearing the dripping skins of their captives ran through the streets, to be ceremoniously welcomed into the dwellings; the flesh of their victims seethed in domestic cooking pots; human thighbones, scraped and dried, were set up in the courtyards of the households—and all this among a people notable for a precisely ordered polity, a grave formality of manner, and a developed regard for beauty.[49]

Five centuries later, those who read this might well feel their insides turn to learn that there has been a human society that could foster such practices. Mexican culture must seem to many readers to be so perverted and alien to all the natural springs of life that its people indeed justify the label of 'other'.

Todorov's comparison of Mexican sacrifice with the consumption of wine and wafers at a Christian Holy Communion is a Pythonesque grotesquerie.[50]

Those academics and multiculturalists who insist we should always take a relativist stand on culture—that we cannot condemn other cultures; they are equal but different—should, to be consistent, accord the Mexica the same status. This would seem to me to make as much sense as accepting the cultures of Nazi Germany and Stalinist Russia as equal but different. To say this is not simply to adopt the other side of the coin. The truth is that it would now be entirely beside the point to rail against the Mexica for the monstrous injustices perpetrated in the name of their religion. Their extermination of the Huaxtec people, their execution of tens of thousands of unarmed men, women and children, their whole bloodthirsty regime organised to gorge the appetites of their imaginary gods, seems at this distance more depressingly futile than worthy of outrage.

It makes just as little sense to adopt a moralistic attitude towards the sixteenth century Spaniards who destroyed the Aztec empire. If we took a strictly utilitarian view of the human blood that was deliberately shed between 1492 and 1521, the Mexican priests emerge with a much higher body count than the Spanish soldiers. Of course, once we start seeing both sides of this picture, such comparisons immediately become pointless. It is also worth recalling the facts about how most died. The accumulated deaths from warfare and atrocities that Todorov and other recent writers have painstakingly tallied all pale before the biggest single killer of native Americans at the time: smallpox. Even Todorov, who claims that Spanish actions in the New World amount to a genocide far worse than anything in the twentieth century, has to admit that the number of direct killings during the conquest was 'relatively small' and that the great majority of the native population were actually eliminated by disease.[51] Here again, moral outrage seems an inappropriate and indulgent response. It makes as much sense to blame Cortés for the deaths from smallpox as it does to blame Montezuma for all those who have subsequently died from the venereal diseases that originated in Mexico. Neither side had a germ theory of disease nor any knowledge of the workings of the human immune system. Neither were responsible.

If the historians of the quincentenary were genuinely interested in sympathising with the indigenous peoples of the past, they might have done more to resurrect the views of the Huaxtecs and the Tlaxcaltecs and to have told us how these neighbours regarded the Mexica and their culture. Except for genuine scholars like Clendinnen, the rest have completely avoided doing this. This is partly because it would make their moral outrage appear ludicrous: they would have been hard put to find words to express the understandable hatred these other Mesoamericans felt for the Mexica. The main reason for their reluctance, however, is because the interest of these writers in the events of 1492 derives only in small part from any real sympathy they might have for the natives and far more from their fervour to adopt a politically correct stance against their own society. They themselves, in other words, bear all the characteristics of the Eurocentrism they condemn in Columbus, Cortés and their other historical characters. In taking the high moral ground on behalf of the indigenous dead of five centuries ago they are making a transparently insincere political gesture.

The final ground upon which these linguists and critics might want to stand is to claim that we are still living with the egocentric, universalist assumptions of the European culture bequeathed by the European explorers and conquistadors. Hence, those who are the inheritors of this culture share the guilt of its founders. Hopefully, what this chapter has by now demonstrated is that this position, too, is untenable. All the arguments about culture put forward by Todorov and his cohorts have proven so empirically inaccurate and logically inconsistent—not to mention so demeaning in their assumptions about native mentalities—that they are worthless as guides to how we should respond.

1 David Stannard, *American Holocaust: Columbus and the Conquest of the New World*, Oxford University Press, New York, 1992

2 Kirkpatrick Sale, *The Conquest of Paradise: Columbus and the Columbian Legacy*, John Curtis, Hodder and Stoughton, London, 1991

3 The works of those named are collected in Stephen Greenblatt (ed.), *New World Encounters*, University of California Press, Berkeley, 1993

4 Stephen Greenblatt, *Marvellous Possessions: The Wonder of the New World*, Clarendon Press, Oxford, 1991

5 Tzvetan Todorov, *The Conquest of America: The Question of the Other*, Harper Collins, New York, 1985, p 5

6 In this chapter, the term Mexica refers to the inhabitants of the imperial city-state, Tenochtitlan, and the term Aztecs refers to the Nahuatl-speaking natives of the wider Valley of Mexico and surrounding provinces

7 Tzvetan Todorov, *The Conquest of America*, p 77

8 W. H. Prescott, *History of the Conquest of Mexico and the History of the Conquest of Peru*, (1843) The Modern Library, Random House, New York n.d.

9 Tzvetan Todorov, *The Conquest of America*, p 119

10 Tzvetan Todorov, *The Conquest of America*, p 61

11 Tzvetan Todorov, *The Conquest of America*, pp 85-7

12 Tzvetan Todorov, *The Conquest of America*, p 69

13 Tzvetan Todorov, *The Conquest of America*, p 80

14 Tzvetan Todorov, *The Conquest of America*, pp 80-81

15 Tzvetan Todorov, *The Conquest of America*, p 92

16 Tzvetan Todorov, *The Conquest of America*, p 99

17 Tzvetan Todorov, *The Conquest of America*, p 87

18 Tzvetan Todorov, *The Conquest of America*, p 87

19 Inga Clendinnen, 'Fierce and Unnatural Cruelty: Cortés and the Conquest of Mexico', in Stephen Greenblatt (ed.), *New World Encounters*

20 Inga Clendinnen, 'Fierce and Unnatural Cruelty', p 26

21 Inga Clendinnen, 'Fierce and Unnatural Cruelty', p 16

22 Gananath Obeyesekere, *The Apotheosis of Captain Cook: European Mythmaking in the Pacific,* Princeton University Press, Princeton, 1992, p 124

23 Inga Clendinnen, *Aztecs: An Interpretation,* Cambridge University Press, Cambridge, 1991, pp 21-44

24 Inga Clendinnen, 'Fierce and Unnatural Cruelty', p 24

25 Inga Clendinnen, 'Fierce and Unnatural Cruelty', p 26

26 Inga Clendinnen, 'Fierce and Unnatural Cruelty', p 31

27 Inga Clendinnen, 'Fierce and Unnatural Cruelty', p 27

28 Inga Clendinnen, 'Fierce and Unnatural Cruelty', p 27

29 Inga Clendinnen, *Aztecs,* p 116

30 John Keegan, *A History of Warfare,* Hutchinson, London, 1993, p 321

31 John Keegan, *A History of Warfare,* p 331

32 Inga Clendinnen, 'Fierce and Unnatural Cruelty', p 40

33 Inga Clendinnen, 'Fierce and Unnatural Cruelty', p 40

34 Tzvetan Todorov, *The Conquest of America,* p 3

35 Tzvetan Todorov, *The Conquest of America,* p 49

36 Tzvetan Todorov, *The Conquest of America,* pp 42-3, 49

37 Tzvetan Todorov, *The Conquest of America,* p 97

38 Harry Turney-High, *Primitive War: Its Practice and Concepts,* 2nd edn, Colombia, 1971, p 193

39 Tzvetan Todorov, *The Conquest of America,* pp 186-192

40 Tzvetan Todorov, *The Conquest of America,* p 144

41 Tzvetan Todorov, *The Conquest of America,* p 144

42 Tzvetan Todorov, *The Conquest of America,* p 253

43 Inga Clendinnen, *Aztecs,* p 3

44 A summary of the various estimates is in Hugh Thomas, *The Conquest of Mexico,* Hutchinson, London, 1993, n50, pp 646-7

45 Inga Clendinnen, *Aztecs,* p 92

46 Inga Clendinnen, *Aztecs,* p 201

47 Inga Clendinnen, *Aztecs,* pp 98-9

48 Inga Clendinnen, *Aztecs,* p 91

49 Inga Clendinnen, *Aztecs,* p 2

50 Greg Dening makes exactly the same comparison in *Mr Bligh's Bad Language: Passion, Power and Theatre on the Bounty,* Cambridge University Press, Cambridge, 1992, when he compares human sacrifice on Tahiti with his own offering of the Eucharist in his previous career as a priest. Dening's book is discussed in the next chapter

51 Tzvetan Todorov, *The Conquest of America,* p 133

3

BAD LANGUAGE AND
THEATRICAL GESTURES

STRUCTURALISM AND ETHNOHISTORY IN THE PACIFIC

O F ALL THE historical issues about which it is possible to write, one
small incident of British maritime history in the Pacific Ocean in the
eighteenth century has attracted probably more attention in proportion to its
importance than any other. The mutiny on the HMS *Bounty* in April 1789
has generated more than a thousand books and articles and its progeny includes
an epic poem by Byron, a nineteenth century English musical, a pantomime
and no less than five movies, two made in Australia and three in Hollywood.

One of the latest additions to this list of interpretations is Greg Dening's
book, *Mr Bligh's Bad Language: Passion, Power and Theatre on the Bounty,* which
was published by Cambridge University Press in 1992.[1] The book has received widespread and flattering acclaim from Dening's colleagues, who have
endowed it with nothing less than adulation.[2] Some of its Australian academic
reviewers nominated it as one of the two or three best books published any-
where on any subject in 1992. It won the 1993 Victorian Premier's Literary
Award for non-fiction. Dening is the recently retired Professor of History at
the University of Melbourne and one of a number of historians from his own
institution and nearby La Trobe University who in recent years have spent
some time at the Institute for Advanced Studies, Princeton, with Clifford
Geertz, one of the early postmodernist anthropologists. These historians, whom
Geertz has named 'the Melbourne group', include Inga Clendinnen, Rhys
Isaac and Dening's wife, Donna Merwick. In the late 1980s and 1990s, they
have produced books on Dutch New York, colonial Virginia and the Aztecs

of Mexico.[3] Dening finished writing his own book on the *Bounty* at the Princeton Institute, which he describes as an 'academic nirvana'.

Compared with other mutinies of the same period, that of the *Bounty* was a mild affair. On the HMS *Hermione* in 1797, for instance, the crew massacred all the officers, whereas the mutiny on the *Bounty* eight years earlier was a bloodless event in which the mutineers put William Bligh and his supporters into a launch, in range of land, and gave them arms and provisions. At Spithead and the Nore in 1797, the sailors combined a volatile mixture of revolutionary Jacobinism, Irish nationalism and complaints about bad food, with the result that the whole British fleet mutinied not once but twice. On the *Bounty*, the conflicts had more to do with personal relationships, and half the ship's company remained loyal to the captain. Most of the handful of books and articles published on the 1797 mutinies are now out of print and familiarity with most of them was, anyway, largely confined to professional historians. By contrast, the story of the *Bounty* is not only still taught in university courses but has entered the popular imagination in a way that is almost unprecedented. In the Hollywood movies, for example, the role of the chief mutineer, Fletcher Christian, has always been played by the current matinee idol—Clark Gable in the 1930s, Marlon Brando in the 1960s and Mel Gibson in the 1980s. Why so much attention to the one rather than to the others?

Part of Dening's aim is to throw light on this question. His book not only retells the story of the mutiny but examines its subsequent interpretations, especially those reflected in the theatre and the cinema. His conclusion is that different ages have used the story of the *Bounty* to reflect their own interests and prejudices. In the late eighteenth and early nineteenth centuries when Britain's naval power was in the ascendancy, the typical response was to treat Bligh as a national hero—a 'Gallant Chief' of 'Old England's welcome shore', according to even the radical poet Byron—and the mutineers as dark, guilt-ridden usurpers of legitimate authority whose search for paradise in the islands of the South Pacific ended appropriately in self-destruction. Later in the nineteenth century, a more democratic era saw Bligh as a representative of old Tory corruption and viewed Fletcher Christian as the victim of Bligh's despotic and unpredictable behaviour. This tale of class conflict, of tyranny versus just cause, remained the basis of the 1935 Hollywood clash between Charles Laughton's Bligh and Clark Gable's Christian. By 1962, the movie reflected a reassessment by historians that it was Christian who was both better bred and better mannered and that Bligh was an uncouth, opportunistic upstart from the lower orders. As befitted the period, the Trevor Howard–Marlon Brando movie was a defence of humane and liberal values against the dictates of profit—the mutiny was caused by Bligh's ruthlessly mercenary stance on fresh water, which he conserved for the breadfruit plants he had collected rather than provided to his thirst-maddened crew. The 1984 film was an even more predictable creature of its time. It was based on the 'gay thesis' developed in the book by Richard Hough.[4] The cause of the mutiny now lay in the homosexual attraction of Anthony Hopkins's Bligh to Mel Gibson's Christian. Bligh's rages were the product of his uncontrolled jealousy of Christian's petulant posturing.

Now, those who assert that historians are always dominated by the interests and dictates of their time are obliged to regard themselves in the same light. In this, Dening is consistent. In the postmodern 1990s, when the social sciences are pervaded by textual analysis and theories of language, he offers a thesis derived from the same stock. His argument is that Bligh's language so offended the decorum that governed the relationships between men during the trials of long sea voyages that it drove them to rebellion.

Bligh was not unduly cruel or violent, Dening argues. To scotch the 'common myth' of Bligh the sadist, Dening searched the records and counted the number of floggings given to seamen aboard the British ships that sailed the Pacific in this era to show that Bligh was far less inclined to use the lash than any other captain of the era, especially less so than James Cook and George Vancouver.[5]

In blaming the mutiny on Bligh's 'bad language', Dening wants this phrase to mean something different from and much more extensive than most people's usage. He does not mean that Bligh's language was obscene, though he does acknowledge that it was seen as 'abusive and intemperate'. Bligh used to call his officers 'scoundrels, damned rascals, hounds, hell-hounds, beasts and infamous wretches'. The day before the mutiny he berated the assembled crew about some stolen coconuts and told them he would make them 'eat grass like cows'.[6] Dening says that Bligh had problems in communicating with the crew, since he could not see things from their perspective nor express himself fully. He 'found it difficult to grasp the metaphors of being a captain, how it could mean something different to those being captained'. He 'tended not to hear the good intentions or catch the circumstances and context in the language of others but demanded that others hear them in his'.[7] Dening also shows that some of the mutineers had adopted their own in-group dialect during their five-month stay in Tahiti. They had lived ashore with Tahitian women and had added a number of Tahitian words and phrases to their own seamen's English to create their own patois, which both bound them together and set them apart.

Yet Dening insists that it was not merely language at the level of words or expressions that led to the rebellion. The cause of the mutiny ultimately lay in the style of Bligh's captaincy, in his misunderstanding and misuse of the rituals and theatrics of authority.

I make the thesis that Bligh's bad language was the ambiguous language of his command. It was bad, not so much because it was intemperate or abusive, but because it was ambiguous, because men could not read in it a right relationship to his authority.[8]

Dening describes a number of the ambiguities that Bligh perpetuated on the *Bounty*. Many of them stemmed from the fact that the purpose of the voyage was not to serve national goals such as exploration or defence. The *Bounty* was a public vessel on a commercial assignment to transport breadfruit plants from Tahiti to England's colonies in the West Indies, where they were to be cultivated to provide cheap food for plantation slaves. This entrepreneurial mission, Dening says, produced conflicts with the naval culture that had governed previous voyages to the Pacific. Bligh's loyalties were more civilian than military. He acted as his own purser, keeping expenses firmly within budget and generating a suspicion among the crew that, instead of receiving the traditional captain's generosity, they were short-changed in food and supplies so that Bligh could profit personally. He also adopted an unorthodox layout below deck. The social space on his 'privatised' ship was subordinated to its botanical function, with the normally lavish great cabin used by captain and officers transformed into a nursery for 750 pots of plants, and the crew's living space reduced and forced forward and down.[9]

Bligh's behaviour towards officers and crew oscillated between rage and reconciliation. At one moment, he could humiliate his officers publicly with a tirade of abuse, and the next would invite them to dine with him. Two nights before the mutiny, some of the coconuts collected from the nearby Tongan islands went missing. Bligh accused Christian of being a thief, then, the next day, sought rapprochement by asking him to dinner. Christian declined and, instead, armed himself and his followers in order to take the ship. Dening's claim is that this was the ultimate response to the ambiguities of Bligh's command.

Dening's book, though focused on the mutiny, is ambitious to explore a number of wider issues as well. The chief of these is the contact between Europeans and Polynesians in the Pacific in the late eighteenth century. Dening wants to write what he calls ethnographic history. This means seeing things not only through the eyes of the British but from the perspective of Polynesian culture as well. Dening provides a lengthy analysis of the first of these contacts, that between the islanders of Tahiti and Samuel Wallis of HMS *Dolphin* in 1767.[10] In a later section he provides another lengthy account of the death of James Cook in Hawaii in 1779.[11] In both these sections he argues that the Polynesians saw the English as gods who, as their religion predicted, had come to them from across the sea. On Tahiti, the islanders saw the arrival of Wallis and the *Dolphin* as a materialisation of their god 'Oro, the coloniser of islands. On Hawaii, the natives thought Cook was Lono, one of the four major gods in their pantheon. Dening's aim in these sections is to show how the beliefs and rituals of both these cultures responded to the arrival of Europeans, how Polynesian culture accommodated the appearance of the strangers, just as Europe's own sense of its place in the world was affected by the discoveries of the societies in the Pacific Ocean.

At the end of the book he says that his ultimate aim has not been simply to offer a new explanation of the mutiny on the *Bounty* but to use the event as a parable, that is, as a narrative that leads to larger meanings than the story itself.[12] He is really trying to write a work about what he calls the 'double helix' of past and present. Not only do those of us in the present see the past through our own cultural binoculars, but the past itself is not some static entity that is there in itself, waiting to be discovered. What we see of the past has already been shaped by others before us in ways we do not expect, and the versions of the past we inherit in turn act as the cultural binoculars through which we look back at the past. The historian can help unravel these strands to show us the position we are in. An historian can do this by acting as an ethnographer, that is, as an anthropologist who can deconstruct (or analyse and expose) both the signs and the structures of a culture. This kind of anthropologist is one who stands outside a culture to adopt a perspective that is not available to insiders, who are too immersed in their speech to recognise their language (or, in Saussurean terminology, who see their *parole* but not their *langue*).[13] So *Mr Bligh's Bad Language* is ultimately a treatise on historical method and theory, written in the form of a parable about the mutiny on the Bounty and a discussion of the European impact on the Pacific Islands in the eighteenth century.

Dening's work bears all the hallmarks of recent linguistic and cultural theory. He pays homage to the familiar pantheon of continental structuralists, post-structuralists and neo-Marxists—Roland Barthes, Claude Levi-Strauss, Michel Foucault, and Walter Benjamin. From Foucault he adopts the idea that there was a major shift underway in the 'episteme' of discipline at the time of the mutiny.[14] From structuralism and cultural studies he takes the concept that the historian is primarily involved in textual analysis: 'I retext the already texted past.'[15] From structuralism he also takes a position of cultural and moral relativism. Dening describes how Europeans arriving at Tahiti and Hawaii frequently observed Polynesians engaged in ritual human sacrifice and cannibalism. He explains to those readers who might be inclined to regard such practices as barbaric that the islanders had their British counterparts. For example, he wants us to understand that the execution in Britain of three of the mutineers who were tried and found guilty was the ritual equivalent of Tahitian sacrifices, such as those of the thirty low-born islanders whom the *Bounty* crew witnessed being executed as part of the celebrations to mark the inauguration of the new king Pomare.[16] Similarly, after the Hawaiians killed Cook, their chiefs separated his remains and stripped the bones bare of flesh. Dening wants us to see the action of Cook's officers in dividing up and auctioning his personal effects after his death as an understandably similar cultural response.[17]

Although Dening says he is offering a parable in the form of a narrative tale, the structure he gives the book is nothing so mundane and old-fashioned as a chronological sequence. He begins not with the outward voyage but with Bligh's return to England and the trial and execution of three of the mutineers. The sojourn at Tahiti that preceded the mutiny is described in the middle of the book after he has discussed the rebellion itself. The narrative is also broken up by sections devoted to the experiences of Cook, Wallis and other explorers before Bligh, as well as by lengthy reflections on the nature of such concepts as naval discipline, sacrifice, the possession of territory and the London stage in the early nineteenth century. To underline the theatrical claims of his enterprise, Dening divides the book not by chapters but by acts and scenes, as if he had written a play. There is a Prologue followed by Act One, Scene One; Act One, Scene Two and so on. This device, however, fails to come off because there is no dramatic sequence to the discussions he offers. The book is more a series of disparate essays on related topics than something that has a perceptible direction which carries the reader along with it. His structure is collage, not drama. It is ironic that Dening should choose such an inappropriate contrivance, since in the final one-third of the book he proffers himself as a critic of the various theatrical representations of the mutiny that others have produced on stage and in cinema over the last two hundred years.

Like the littérateurs in cultural studies, Dening endorses the view that history is fiction, though he adds the rider that this does not mean it is fantasy. He says that while teaching undergraduates at the University of Melbourne:

I have always put it to them that history is something we make rather than something we learn... I want to persuade them that any history they make will be fiction—not fantasy, fiction, something sculpted to its expressive purpose.[18]

In other words, history is not made up out of our dreams and wishes, but it is made up, or invented, none the less. In particular, history is not something to be learned from the past, not something to be *discovered*. The attempt to use history to show the events of the past 'as they really were' has always been, Dening says, an 'illusion'. He cites approvingly the German Marxist Walter Benjamin, who wrote that 'the history that showed things "as they really were" was the strongest narcotic of our century'.[19]

The purpose of writing and researching history, Dening argues, is not to gain knowledge about the past but to satisfy the cultural needs of the present.

In this, he says, history serves functions similar to those of religion and mythology. 'History, myth, sacrament, ritual ... all serve to colligate the past and make understandings that bring order to the present. They make sense of what has happened by economising the wealth of possible causes of events down to principal determinants that really matter.'[20] The social role that history performs is to generate what Dening calls 'cultural literacy'. What he means by this is the system of learning and the sum of information that go to make up the typically cultured or educated person. It also includes the range of moral judgements and attitudes that people accept as appropriate to adopt towards the well-known events of the past. Cultural literacy is 'that knowledge of the past that sustains the values of the present'.[21] Different ages, however, have different social values, so their interpretations of history change. Hence the mutiny on the *Bounty* has meant different things to different generations, and hence history itself is really about the present rather than the past. 'The past, as we know it, is indistinguishable from the ways in which it is realised in the present.'[22]

Dening appears to see his own role in this whole process as one of creating a new agenda for the present era drawn from the assumptions of structuralism, ethnography and postmodernism. Being culturally literate in the 1990s, he argues, means recognising the power of language and signs to create our sense of reality—'words do not mirror the world but make it'—and also involves understanding that the meanings of words change over time.[23] Given today's prevailing academic deference to linguistic studies, a new history of the mutiny, from Dening's perspective, simply had to be a study couched in terms of language and its shifting meanings.

THE ILLUSIONS OF HISTORY

To begin to reply to all of the above, allow me to make an uncomplicated point about the logic of claiming that we cannot really know what happened in the past. Dening's thesis that it is an 'illusion' to try to know the past 'as it really was' and that our views of the past are interlocked with our present value systems, is relativist in terms of historical knowledge. He says history is not 'something we learn' from the past but is a matter of interpretation, of reading off from the past whatever our present values, systems and preoccupations dictate. In other words, the past is a text or series of texts, which we interpret, the same as we would a work of literature. Different people and eras will make different interpretations. Hence history is not a process in which objective knowledge is discovered and accumulated. Unfortunately for Dening, it is not difficult to show that his own practice in *Mr Bligh's Bad Language* contradicts his theory. There are at least two important parts of his book where he relies upon knowledge of the past 'as it really was' in order to argue his own case.

The first of these is the one piece of real knowledge he has contributed himself. This is his conclusion about the level of floggings that Bligh ordered aboard the *Bounty*. Since Dening has published his statistics, no one in the future will be able to argue that Bligh was more violent than the other commanders of British ships in the Pacific at the time. Indeed, the conclusion appears inescapable that he was one of the captains least inclined to use the lash on his crew. To argue that Bligh was less violent, Dening does not put forward his statistics as merely an interpretation with which others might legitimately take issue. He uses his conclusion to demolish what he calls the 'common myth' of Bligh the sadist. He can only do this if he uses it as a truth in an objective or absolute sense. Moreover, he uses the two points he has now established—(1) the statistics show that Bligh was less violent; and (2) previous explanations of the mutiny based on Bligh's violence merely reflected the values of the time they were written—as the central premisses of his wider argument that different ages generate their own myths about history to suit their own needs and values. So his major thesis, that we never know history 'as it really was', is itself derived from an argument based on a point about what really happened in history. His case is self-contradictory.

Dening makes the same mistake in his critiques of the Hollywood movies about the mutiny. He delights in pointing out some of their grosser inaccuracies, such as in the 1935 film which made Bligh the captain of the *Pandora*, the ship that sailed from Britain to capture the mutineers and bring them to justice. Dening says when he shows these films to his students—who know that Bligh actually stayed at home while the *Pandora* was under the command of Captain Edward Edwards—they become 'angry and scornful' about how 'irresponsible' and 'negligent' Hollywood can be when it comes to representing the past. He also points out that the 1962 movie saw Marlon Brando's Christian dying on Pitcairn Island after he had heroically tried to stop the other mutineers from burning the *Bounty*. Dening tells us the real Christian was, like most of the remaining mutineers, murdered by their Tahitian slaves on Pitcairn four years after the ship had been burned and sunk.

However, someone with Dening's view of history cannot talk about what 'actually' happened, nor can he discuss the fate of 'real' characters. Since he believes that history is not something we 'learn' or discover, but is only a procession of shifting interpretations made by successive generations, he lacks any solid ground of fact upon which to stand and make the kind of criticisms that he does. To be able to write about who actually commanded the *Pandora*, or how Christian really died, or any of the numerous other facts that Dening uses to disparage other people's accounts of the mutiny, one has to accept that history is not merely something that successive generations invent for their own purposes. Rather, it must be a process that provides a record that contains some truths and that gives us knowledge about the past. Of course, it is possible for historians to be mistaken and misguided, and, of course, they often ask questions and find answers that reflect their own culture. But if we are to talk sensibly about the past, we have to accept that some of the historical record is true, that there are facts about the past which we know from history, and that the past is not merely an invention of the present but is something that happened quite independently of those of us who have inherited its consequences.

GESTURES OUT OF SEASON—STRUCTURALISM ON HAWAII

The discipline of anthropology has provided one of the principal routes through which concepts derived from structuralism have entered the mainstream of the humanities and social sciences. This is particularly true of the United States, where cultural anthropology has been the most prominent version of the field. When it was founded early in the twentieth century, American cultural anthropology focused on the language, art, rituals and religious practices of native peoples, especially those of North America itself and of the Pacific Islands. In Britain, by contrast, the discipline's main concerns were about social organisation, and so it came to be known as social anthropology. The descriptive activities of cultural anthropology, as distinct from its theory, have long been known as 'ethnography'. When ethnographers turn their attention to the past to write the history of non-literate peoples they usually describe their work as either 'historical anthropology' or 'ethnohistory'.

In 1949, the French anthropologist Claude Levi-Strauss published *The Elementary Structures of Kinship*, the first of his many influential texts in cultural anthropology. He argued that language and the modes of thought that corresponded to it constituted the culture of a society, which determined a wide variety of kinship behaviour and social institutions. The language thesis of Levi-Strauss was in harmony with the existing concerns of American cultural anthropology and, over the next twenty years, the assumptions of structuralism worked their way into the discipline.

As well as the story of the mutiny on the *Bounty*, one of the major concerns of Dening's book, *Mr Bligh's Bad Language*, is to provide an ethnographic account of the way that the Polynesian islanders of Tahiti and Hawaii responded to their discovery by European sailors in the eighteenth century. In this, Dening follows both the example and the arguments of the American ethnographer Marshall Sahlins. One of Dening's chapters—sorry, one of his entr'actes—is a largely verbatim reproduction of an article he originally wrote for the Melbourne journal *Meanjin* in 1982, which was an extended review of the 'radical brilliance' he found in Sahlins's book, *Historical Metaphors and Mythical Realities: Structure in the Early History of the Sandwich Islands Kingdom*. The central focus of Sahlins's work is the death of James Cook in Hawaii in 1779. Sahlins accepts the view, which dates back to early nineteenth century accounts of Hawaiian history written both by American missionaries and the first native historians, that the islanders regarded Cook as the god Lono.

In the late eighteenth century, the Hawaiians had a pantheistic religion dominated by four major gods—Ku, Kanaloa, Kane and Lono—and a powerful goddess of the volcano, called Pele. Lono was associated with peace, games and fertility. The Hawaiians believed that Lono arrived as an invisible presence during their Makahiki festival, which Sahlins argues was held each year around January of the European calendar. Lono was believed to arrive from across the sea in a sailing boat. Dening reproduces on page 164 of his book a sketch of a crosspiece and sail icon of Lono alongside a drawing of Cook's ship *Resolution* under sail to show the similarity of the two images. Sahlins argues that Cook arrived at the Hawaiian islands for his second visit in 1779 (he saw them first in 1778) during the Makahiki festival. After tacking around Hawaii and Maui for almost two months, Cook landed at Kealakekua Bay on the island of Hawaii on 17 January. The landing site he chose was the same point where the Hawaiians began and ended a Makahiki procession behind the icon of Lono. When Cook waded ashore, the estimated ten thousand natives who greeted his ship cleared the way and prostrated themselves before him chanting 'Lono, Lono, Lono'. Cook was taken by priests into their temples and swathed in red cloth.[24]

Cook departed Hawaii on 3 February, which Sahlins has calculated by computer was the day after the end of Makahiki that year. The period after Makahiki belonged to the warlike god Ku. After ten days at sea battling huge swells and springing the mast of the *Resolution*, Cook returned to Kealakekua Bay. This time, however, there were no greetings, no prostrations and no more red cloaks. Instead, the people were insolent and their chiefs sullen. After a native stole one of the ship's cutters, Cook went ashore to take the local chief Kalani'opu'u hostage for the boat's return. A crowd gathered to prevent the chief's abduction and, in the ensuing conflict, Cook and four marines were stabbed, and beaten to death with rocks. The body of Cook was then taken to the temple of the now-prevailing god, Ku, where it was dismembered, the flesh taken off the bones, and the bones ceremonially divided among the chiefs. One of the parcels of bones and flesh was taken out by canoe to the *Resolution* and offered to the English who were asked by the natives when Lono would return again. For many years afterwards, Cook's bones were taken up by the priests of Lono and carried around the island at the head of the annual Makahiki procession.

Dening, following Sahlins, explains the radically different response to Cook's arrival in mid-January and his return in mid-February, in terms of the symbolism of the Hawaiians' religious beliefs. Cook as Lono was unassailable during the festival of Makahiki. The islanders saw him as supreme and bowed to every wish he made clear to them through his gestures. However, in the following season of Ku, the chief Kalani'opu'u, their warrior leader who united them in battle against the peoples of the other Hawaiian islands, now eclipsed the authority of Lono and so could kill his embodiment. On the return visit, says Dening:

All Cook's gestures and threats, done in his eyes for the sake of property and discipline, were gestures out of season... Cook was not Native now, but Stranger, a shark that walked on the land. In those circumstances the killing was easy and the death made everything come true again. So they kept asking when Lono would come again.[25]

To explain why Dening is interested in retelling the Sahlins version of Cook's death in 1779 in a book ostensibly about the mutiny on the *Bounty* ten years later, we need to look again at the theory and method of structuralism and its relationship to the discipline of history. According to structuralist theory, the world of human beings is an interconnected semiotic system. It is an arbitrary system of signs, dominated by the structure of *langue*, the formal dimension of language, which rules over *parole*, or the actual words that people pronounce. *Langue* is a synchronic structure, that is, it is an abstract set of rules that has no history. *Parole*, the utterances made by people, is said to be diachronic, that is, it exists in real time. Structuralists and ethnographers are primarily interested in *langue*, the underlying structure. Levi-Strauss extended the idea of the structure of language to that of culture, which he described as a system of signs that orders experience. Culture thus sits inside people's brains, like a computer program, dictating the way they see the world and determining how they respond to it. Levi-Strauss distinguished between non-civilised and civilised societies. He argued that the invention of writing by the latter, which occurred as part of the formation of the modern state, altered the character of time as lived experience. Non-civilised, prewriting cultures are thus, in his view, prehistoric, lacking a sense of social change over time.[26] Prewriting cultures are 'cold cultures' which, unlike the 'hot' cultures of the West, are not caught up in the flux of change, and which lack the ability to adapt or modify their values and their institutions.

For ethnographers who want to write about the momentous impact that European culture had on prewriting, indigenous cultures, especially during the European expansion of the seventeenth and eighteenth centuries, the assumptions of structuralism pose a number of difficulties. In essence, the problem is how to discuss 'cold cultures', which cannot handle change, at a time when change was forced upon them. Traditional ethnography, as instituted by Levi-Strauss, only sought to deal with a non-civilised culture in its prehistoric mode. What do you do, then, when history manifestly intervenes as it did so brutally in the lives of the natives of the Americas, the Pacific Islands and Australasia? This was the issue that Marshall Sahlins set out to answer in his work on the death of Cook in Hawaii, and that Dening has addressed both in repeating Sahlins's interpretation and in making his own analysis of the impact of Wallis on Tahiti in the 1760s. Sahlins was trying to use Cook to introduce history and practical action in the world into structuralism, and to overcome the distinction between diachrony and synchrony, or between history and structure. In doing this, his aim was not to merge history and ethnography on an equal footing, but to subsume history within the domain of structuralism on terms dictated by the latter.

Since, according to structuralist theory, the 'cold culture' of the Hawaiians was incapable of adapting to change, the islanders could not respond to so remarkable an event as the appearance of white-skinned, strangely clothed Europeans in large sailing ships by rethinking their situation. The mind-set that their culture had supposedly programmed into their brains would not allow this. Instead, Sahlins says, they reacted according to prearranged scenarios. They interpreted the arrival of Cook and his men during Makahiki as the return of Lono. So the identification of Cook as Lono is not simply an isolated incident in early Hawaiian–European contact but a conclusion that lends powerful support to structuralist theory itself.

Similarly, the death of Cook four weeks later is also interpreted by Sahlins as an event that confirmed the structuralist view of the world. Cook returned at a ritualistically unscheduled time—the time of Ku, not Makahiki—and suffered a ritual death for his wrong move. Cook was killed not as the result of a simple skirmish over a theft, but as part of a ritualistic conflict between Lono and the Hawaiian chief Kalani'opu'u. Cook's reaction to the theft produced a 'structural crisis' in which all social relations changed their signs and left the god and the king to 'confront each other as cosmic adversaries'. The Hawaiians, says Sahlins, perceived the attempt to take Kalaniopu'u hostage as a version of the ritual of Kali'i in which, on important occasions, the king wards off the spears aimed at him by a party representing the god. On this occasion, it was the god who was forced to defend himself against the king's party—but the Hawaiians would have perceived this, Sahlins claims, as the ritual enactment 'played in reverse'.[27] Similarly, he believes the dismemberment of Cook's body and the use of his bones for years later as part of the annual Makahiki rites allowed all the events the Hawaiians perceived about the Cook visit—the arrival of Lono, the killing of the god and his resurrection—to be accommodated in their existing culture.

The irruption of Captain Cook from beyond the horizon was truly an
unprecedented event, never seen before. But by thus encompassing the
existentially unique in the conceptually familiar, the people embed their present in
the past.[28]

In other words, cultural categories, or structures of signs, are pregiven. Historic events, when they occur, are fitted into these pre-given categories. There are no 'facts' that can come from outside the culture to disrupt or contradict it. Humans always see things the only way the structuralists insist is possible: through their own pregiven categories. Sahlins feels the contribution he has made to structuralist theory is to show that, although structures dominate, particular events—especially when they are as momentous as Cook's visit—nonetheless do have an effect. An important event can actually synthesise with a structure, though always on the structure's terms. Such events are accommodated in the existing culture, but, in the process, they help produce a new, modified structure through which future events will be perceived. History is thus eternally subservient to structure.

THE POSSESSION OF TAHITI

Dening's own contribution is actually much more ambitious than that of Sahlins. He repeats Sahlins's interpretation of the events in Hawaii and then goes on to offer his own account of the arrival in Tahiti of Captain Samuel Wallis on HMS *Dolphin* in 1767. When Wallis sailed into Matavai Bay to trade for food and fresh water, he was surrounded by between four hundred and six hundred canoes containing about eight thousand Tahitians. Some canoes contained women who came close to the ship and, as they danced, lifted their clothing and made sexual gestures towards their naked bodies. One large, double canoe had an awning on which stood a man dressed in red cloth looking like a chief and apparently orchestrating the action. The sailors labelled him the 'king of the island'. Unlike the Hawaiians when they first met Cook, the Tahitians did not prostrate themselves before the strangers nor did they chant any of the names of their gods. On the chief's direction, they pulled stones from their canoes and hurled them at the sailors and their ship. The British replied with cannon and musket, which smashed the canoes, killed many of the islanders and drove off the rest.

The typical modern reader, on having these events recounted, would understand them in commonsense terms and read what we would think were obvious meanings into them. Most of us would interpret the scene as an ambush in which the islanders coaxed the sailors within range of their stones through a display of lascivious dancing by their women. Once they could attack, they did so with what we would regard as the fairly understandable motive of defending their territory from interloping outsiders. If you think this, says Dening, you would simply be betraying your own cultural mind-set. He argues that we need to see the scene through the 'cosmological familiarities' of Tahitian culture. The women were not performing 'wanton tricks', as the sailors thought, but were engaged in a sacramental dance to catch the eye of the divine. Instead of defending their territory, the islanders were actually engaged in a dramatic play that made sense of the occasion for them through the cosmology of one of their principal gods, 'Oro.

... the 'king of the island' was likely to have been an *arioi* master of a lodge or a priest of 'Oro. His double canoe was no battle ship. It was likely to have been 'Rainbow', his sacred transportation. The awning he stood on was likely to have covered the ark of 'Oro's accoutrements. What the Tahitians saw on the *Dolphin* was Tahitian gods, divine in the Tahitian way.[29]

Hence, the arrival of the English at Matavai Bay was interpreted by the Tahitians in terms of their existing culture, in particular their myths about the god 'Oro. Even the attack on the ship and the slaughter of their own people, says Dening, fitted their expectation that the god's arrival would be an occasion of human sacrifice. Let me quote a longish passage from his book to make it quite clear how he claims the Tahitians responded to the English and the killings they perpetrated.

If the tone and direction of myths of 'Oro collected later are any indication, the *Dolphin* came like one of the marvellous canoes of old from afar, and Tahitian expectancy would be that she would make a landing, be the centre of sacrifice, be the occasion for reinstatement and investiture of the *ari'i rahi,* be the circumstance for alliance and treaty, and the establishment in them of some hegemony. The arrival at Matavai was true to the myth of how 'Oro would arrive to colonise a new place. It had happened at Taiarapu long ago and more recently at Atehuru. The novelties did not matter, not even the contradictions. The Tahitians were entertained and wholly satisfied by its simple meaning.[30]

Now, even the most broad-minded cultural relativist would have to admit that this is a rather extraordinary claim: a mass killing by strangers can leave the relatives and friends of the victims 'entertained and wholly satisfied'. What a powerful set of cultural and religious beliefs the Tahitians must have had, which could not only obliterate their desire to mourn their dead but could leave them pleased with the outcome! I will return to discuss this dubious claim shortly, but let us first follow Dening's story about Tahiti to its conclusion.

Into his history of events in the South Pacific, Dening weaves an account of how those events were interpreted back in England. In fact, he spends almost as many pages in discussing the London response to the discoveries in Tahiti as he does in describing what happened on the islands. Central to his case is the notion of 'possession'. English naval officers took possession of the Tahitian islands; readers of London journals and pamphlets, and audiences at pantomime matinees, took possession of the Tahitian people and culture; but the Tahitians, in turn, took their own possession of the strangers.

Dening does not use the term 'possession' in its customary sense of acquiring ownership. Rather he uses it in the same way as Sahlins does to describe how existing cultures accommodate remarkable events without any undermining of their fundamental beliefs. When Dening says the Tahitians possessed the strangers through 'Oro, he means that they accommodated the arrival of the English in their culture by believing them to be the incarnation of the god 'Oro. Similarly, he argues that the British possessed the Tahitians, not so much by declaring the islands the property of the Crown but by seeing the Tahitians through the eyes of their own culture. One of the most remarkable features of Tahitian society for the English was its attitude towards sexuality. Among the ceremonies that the Tahitian chieftess Oberea staged for James Cook was a public copulation between a young man and a twelve-year-old girl. Oberea herself had sex with Joseph Banks in her canoe, and took his pistol and some clothes as recompense. All the sailors readily found Tahitian women who would have intercourse with them. When the sailors' journals and diaries recounting these events were published in the 1770s, English moral certitude was in no way shaken by evidence of a society that readily engaged in such apparently sinful practices but seemed to suffer no harmful consequences. Instead, the English ridiculed and joked about the Tahitians in verse, pamphlets and pantomime, deflating the status of 'Queen Oberea' for having a tattoo on her bottom, and sending up Banks for being caught without his pants. The Tahitians and their royalty were denounced for their sexual licence and given a public status below that of the lowest-class English. The Tahitians were not seen as a radically alternative version of humanity, writes Dening, rather 'they were the same, only worse'.[31] In other words, just as the Tahitians responded to the shock of the English arrival by incorporating them into their traditional culture, so did the English public come to terms with their discovery of the Tahitians' sexual mores. The English 'possessed the natives with a laugh', that is, they accommodated them in their existing mind-set by ridiculing their behaviour. Hence, Dening the ethnographer is arguing that culture responds the same way in both preliterate and literate societies. He is confirming Sahlins's view that it is possible to inject momentous historic events into structuralist anthropology while preserving the underlying principles of structuralist theory.

Not only this—and here we come to the reason that Dening is more ambitious than Sahlins—our own society in the 1990s operates in the same way. We can see the world, including the world of the past, only through the structures that are given to us by our culture. There are no objective facts to 'discover', no history to be 'learned'. All we can do is frame the past through the culture we are given, a culture that itself has been framed by the varying interpretations of the cultures of the past. This is why Dening says it is an illusion to think we can cut through the myths of history to get at the truth. We can no more do this than could the Polynesian islanders in the eighteenth century. One of the main reasons Dening has chosen to write about the mutiny on the *Bounty* is because there have been so many versions offered by diarists, historians, theatrical producers and film-makers. The shifts in the story reflect shifts in the structure of the culture. Hence the history of the changing interpretations of the mutiny, he thinks, both confirms the central tenet of structuralist theory and demonstrates how the theory applies to both non-civilised *and* civilised societies like our own. When they try to account for historic events, both 'cold' and 'hot' societies are in the same boat.

THE MYTHS OF ETHNOGRAPHY

Dening was both very lucky and very unlucky in the timing of the publication of his book. Within weeks of his own work coming onto the market, a new study of Cook in Hawaii was published that completely pulled the rug out from under his ethnographer's feet. The book, *The Apotheosis of Captain Cook: European Mythmaking in the Pacific,* written by the Sri Lankan-born Professor of Anthropology at Princeton University, Gananath Obeyesekere,[32] is a devastating critique of Marshall Sahlins's theories about Cook and of the view, endorsed so enthusiastically by Dening, that the Polynesian islanders regarded European sailors as gods. Dening's bad luck was that his own composition, so long in gestation and so freshly published, was so quickly reduced to ruins, albeit in the eyes of the small number of scholars who have read Obeyesekere's work. His good luck was that neither the Australian historians who lavished such generous praise on him in both the popular and academic press, nor the judges of the Victorian Premier's Literary Award, had absorbed Obeyesekere's work before they announced their opinions. Let me summarise Obeyesekere's case against Sahlins and show its implications for Dening's own interpretations. Obeyesekere's main point is that, rather than it being an Hawaiian belief that Cook was the god Lono, it is a European myth that the islanders thought this way.

It may be possible for Europeans to believe Cook was a Hawaiian god but hard to believe that Hawaiians thought this, given that Cook did not look Hawaiian, spoke no Hawaiian and said he came not from Kahiki (Lono's home) but from Brittanee.[33]

Instead of believing the English to be gods, Obeyesekere argues, the Hawaiians actually thought the half-starved sailors had come from a land where the food had run out, to fill their bellies. Instead of conforming to the mythical arrival of Lono, as Sahlins claimed he had done, Cook did something quite different. He was seen to circle the islands in his ships for nearly two months, mapping them and looking for an opportune time and place to land. The ritual of Lono, however, had the god circle the island of Hawaii on the land. Soon after he disembarked, Cook was taken by the Hawaiians to a temple where he was persuaded by the priests to prostrate himself before an image of the god Ku. In the Hawaiian belief system, this is something that a chief would do, but that a god such as Lono could not.

Obeyesekere argues, using the details of the rituals the islanders performed on Cook's arrival, that he was treated not as a god but as a chief. For instance, the Hawaiian chiefs did not prostrate themselves before Cook, only the common people did. Prostration in Christian or Muslim culture might mean religious worship, adoration or devotion, but it was an act that Hawaiian commoners performed habitually before their chiefs. Obeyesekere quotes Captain Charles Clerke of the *Discovery*:

The respect they pay the King and two or three chiefs here is, whenever they see one of them coming they fall flat upon their faces scarcely daring to look up, and in this position they continue till he is twenty or thirty yards past them; if in canoes, they leave off paddling and prostrate themselves along the boat.[34]

Hence natives who prostrated themselves before Cook were simply according him the ceremonial obeisance known as *kapu moe* by which their own important chiefs were honoured. This same obeisance was also extended to Captain Clerke, but never to ordinary seamen. Hawaiians inhabited a highly hierarchical society, Obeyesekere observes, and were sensitive to hierarchies other than their own.

As everyone who has written on the subject acknowledges, Cook was certainly called Lono by the Hawaiians. However, Obeyesekere points out that they merely gave him the name of the god, but did not regard him as the god himself. The islanders were making the same distinction that Christians would when they give a child a divine name, such as calling a girl Mary, or that Muslims would when naming a boy Mohammed. Obeyesekere reinterprets the temple ceremonies that Sahlins thought showed the worship of Cook as Lono, to argue that what the Hawaiians were doing was investing Cook as a chief, with a status similar to their own, and with the name of one of their gods. Moreover, they did this not to fulfil their myths, legends or culture but for the rather materialist and opportunist motive of enlisting the English, with their vastly superior ships and weapons, on their own side in their interminable wars with the chiefs of the other islands.

Despite Sahlins's computer calculations, it is actually unlikely that Cook landed on Hawaii during the Makahiki festival. Obeyesekere points out that not one of the many journal writers on Cook's ships mentions the word Makahiki, not even those who, with an eye to publishing their observations for an eager public in England, had made detailed recordings of the names of all the rituals, ceremonies and festivals they had so far encountered on their long voyage through the Pacific. Given the present state of scholarly research into the Hawaiian past, Obeyesekere writes, it is impossible to say for certain whether there was a Makahiki festival being conducted during either of Cook's visits in 1778 or 1779 but it is 'inherently improbable' that one occurred without the English being aware of it, as they apparently were not.[35]

Obeyesekere shows how, at some of the most critical points of Sahlins's account, he takes liberties with the evidence to make his story more credible. In trying to argue that, just before he was killed, Cook was re-enacting a 'mirror image' of the legendary role of Lono in the Hawaiian belief system, Sahlins writes: 'The god Lono (Cook) was wading ashore with his warriors to confront the King.' In fact, Cook and his marines had been on shore for some hours and had gone to the village to find the chief they wanted to take hostage. The English were not attacked by the Hawaiians while wading ashore but when they were running in the opposite direction, trying to get to their boats to save their lives.[36]

Similarly, we can add that Dening also plays fast and loose with the facts of Cook's arrival. Dening writes that, when Cook first landed, no Hawaiian chief met him—'There were no chiefs in all that welcoming crowd'[37]—and that the high chief, or king, did not appear for several days. His aim is to try to make it look as if the Hawaiian people spontaneously recognised Cook as a god and bowed before him chanting 'Lono, Lono' without being prompted by their superiors. However, Obeyesekere records that, although the high chief, Kalani'opu'u, an old man, was not presented for several days, two younger chiefs, Kamina and Palea, boarded the *Resolution* as soon as it anchored in Kealakekua Bay. At the time, it was overrun by hundreds of the islanders who clambered aboard, but who, at this stage, made no prostrations. The two chiefs then introduced Cook to the king's priest, Kao.[38] Obeyesekere argues that the commoners' chants of 'Lono, Lono' were probably not even meant for Cook but for Kao's son, Omiah, who was also known as Lono (multiple names for chiefs and priests being common) and who was one of the most sacred and powerful priests on the island. Lieutenant James King of the *Resolution* said Omiah was revered like the Dalai Lama. Before Cook was invested as Lono, he walked among the commoners accompanied by Omiah (Lono). Obeyesekere says that the prostrations and the chants of 'Lono, Lono' were at this time more likely to have been meant for Omiah than for Cook.[39]

In a wider sense, Obeyesekere demolishes not only the myth that Cook was regarded as a god but the whole attempt by Sahlins to read history through structuralist theory. The Hawaiians did not respond to the arrival of the English in the way that structuralism said they would. Not only did they not see Cook as Lono but their traditional culture, rather than accommodating the visitors, was devastated by the events of 1778–79 and by the visits of the small number of sailing ships that came to the islands in the following decade. In less than a generation, the Hawaiians had abandoned their traditional religion and the tabu system that had preserved their traditional class divisions. The position of women changed dramatically and Hawaiian chiefs quickly adopted English styles of authority. In fact, Obeyesekere points out that Cook's visit made a demonstrable impact on the vulnerable areas of Hawaiian society— chiefly authority, the status of women, economic relationships—all in a matter of weeks.[40]

Where, then, does this leave Dening's thesis that the islanders of Tahiti also responded in a structuralist manner by incorporating the coming of the strangers into their own mythology by regarding them as gods? We do not have to wait for someone to produce another book like Obeyesekere's to see that this view lacks any foundation. Dening's whole claim for this thesis rested on the credibility of Sahlins's much more detailed account of the events in Hawaii. Given that he had very limited local evidence to offer, Dening's account of the first contact on Tahiti was based on deductions he made from his understanding of Tahitian religion. His interpretation was not something the islanders actually reported or confirmed themselves. The most that Dening felt justified in claiming about Tahitian beliefs was that the Tahitians 'probably' and 'were likely' to have responded in the way he thought the Hawaiians had. It is plain that this interpretation now lacks any credibility whatsoever. Moreover, we certainly do not need any more research to see that Dening's claim that the Tahitians were 'entertained and satisfied' by the slaughter of their own people is both absurd and offensive. To put his view in its place, let me quote the diary of one of the naval officers on the *Dolphin*, George Robertson. Writing later on the day when he had taken part in killing the Tahitians, but lacking the benefit of structuralist theory to see the entertainment he provided them, Robertson recorded:

How terrible must they be shockd, to see their nearest and dearest of friends Dead, and toar to peces in such a manner as I am certain they neaver beheald before.[41]

An explanation far more credible than any of those derived from culture or religion about how the Polynesians and English reacted to each other on first contact can be gleaned by considering the military nature of the encounter. The policy that English naval officers adopted towards the natives of the Pacific was to prepare the acceptance of their landing by creating an initial sense of terror among the indigenous populations. Given any sense of resistance or conflict, real or imagined, the English responded by killing some natives with gun fire. Third Lieutenant Williamson was the first Englishman to kill an Hawaiian. The event occurred during the first attempt to land a boat on the island on 20 January 1778, when Williamson, unsure whether the islanders who surrounded his boat were trying to steal from him or simply trying to help his crew to land in the surf, shot a man through the head. To justify his action he cited a naval authority in his journal. 'These barbarians must be [initially] quelled by force, as they afterwards readily believe that whatever kindness is then shown to them proceeds from love, whereas otherwise they attribute it to weakness, or cowardice, and presents only increase their insolence.' Obeyesekere argues that this was but a minor variation of the views held by naval officers, Cook included, about the need to create a sense of shock and terror in the minds of the natives and to thereby induce them to accept without challenge the landing of the strangers.[42]

The actions of the islanders of Tahiti towards the English can be explained in ways that are perfectly understandable in human terms without recourse to any structuralist cultural theory. Initially they sought to defend their own territory from the strangers by luring them into an ambush and then driving them off with stones. Enough of them were killed by overwhelmingly superior weaponry to make them quickly abandon the attempted resistance and to accept the outsiders on the terms the latter imposed. On Hawaii, the English were more warmly received from the outset, but a killing at the point of first contact taught the islanders the power and menace of the strangers. In both cases, once it became clear to the natives that the English were only visitors and not conquerors, things improved to the point where something like normal diplomatic relations between people from such divergent backgrounds could be established. This is the commonsense view, so derided by Dening, to which all the evidence clearly points. Why have structuralists been so reluctant to accept it? The next section takes up this issue.

STRUCTURALIST METHODS AND 'IMMACULATE PERCEPTIONS'

Once we demolish the myths that European ethnographers have created about Polynesian cultural and religious beliefs, we can see the whole structuralist enterprise in a different light. Its major problem is the preference it gives to theory rather than facts. The chief structuralist theoretician, Levi-Strauss, postulated that native peoples had a mentality different from that of peoples from more modern cultures. In developing the distinction that I noted earlier between 'cold' and 'hot' societies, Levi-Strauss in *The Savage Mind* claimed that native peoples had 'pre-logical' or 'mystical' ways of thought, which left them more emotive, more adept at manual than intellectual tasks, and thus more childlike. This meant they always tried to annul the impact of historical factors, such as the arrival of strangers, on the equilibrium of their minds and the continuity of their cultures.[43] The theory, when stripped of its structuralist jargon, is patronising and latently racist, but this has not prevented ethnographers from continuing to apply it, right to the present day. Instead of taking the evidence they found in the historical records and then drawing their conclusions, the ethnohistorians of the Pacific have done the reverse. They have given primacy to their theory and have then tried to make the evidence fit into its all-encompassing mould.

One of the most impressive aspects of the book on Cook by Obeyesekere is the care and intelligence with which he marshals the evidence for each of the points he makes. For all of our understanding of the events in Hawaii in 1778 and 1779, including the details of the Hawaiians' rituals and ceremonies and the way their chiefs and priests responded to the strangers, we have to rely upon the journals and diaries of the English officers aboard the *Resolution* and the *Discovery*. Like most human observations, these accounts differ considerably in their descriptions of a number of the same events, especially some which are crucial to understanding how the Hawaiians (who had no written records) themselves responded to Cook and his men. Whenever Obeyesekere argues a point about which there are conflicting accounts, he is careful to ask which of the diarists was on the spot at the time, which one had only written down reports he had heard from others, how their unpublished notes written on the island itself compared to their books published years later (a number of these books were elaborated upon and garnished to suit the taste of the English reading public), and which of them, for various reasons, were the most accurate and reliable observers. Though his profession is ethnography, Obeyesekere acts like a traditional historian in the best sense of that term.

Sahlins and Dening, on the other hand, both come to these events with their theory in hand, looking for signs that will confirm what they already believe. Sahlins parodies the idea of historical facts as 'immaculate perceptions',[44] as the delusion that it is possible to see through the veils of our mentalities to find what really happened or what really existed. The empirical world that we imagine we can perceive, he claims, is always mediated by cultural values through a consciousness that is itself always culturally constituted. Instead of discovering facts, we can only regurgitate our culture. However, his theoretical self-assurance leads him into a cavalier abuse of his source material which Obeyesekere exposes time and again. 'There are virtually no instances in Sahlins's corpus where a source is critically examined, beyond two references to Ledyard labelled as unreliable without any reason given for this judgement', Obeyesekere writes. He found over a dozen cases in Sahlins's work of erroneous use of source material, misleading translations of Hawaiian terminology, manipulation of evidence and selective quotation that distorted the intended meaning of the writer. Despite the frequent claims made by structuralists about their great expertise in the analysis and deconstruction of texts, the charges Obeyesekere makes about the quality of Sahlins's methodology are pungent.

Information from any text is used as long as it fits the structuralist thesis, the assumption being that because it fits the theory it must be factually correct. A variety of early native histories and missionary texts are given the same prominence as are the ship's journals. Brief visits by seamen in the nineteenth century are mined for useful information. There is no real probing into the agenda underlying the writing of different kinds of texts.[45]

We should not regard Sahlins's work on Hawaii as the simple aberration of one ethnographer. Dening, with his proselyte's views on how the Tahitians regarded Wallis and his sailors as gods, is guilty of exactly the same errors. Their mistaken approach is inherent in the whole structuralist project. Anyone who adopts their basic methodology—that theory determines the facts—will always fall into the same mire. Anyone who adopts structuralist theory or methodology abrogates the claim to be working as an historian.

Overall, then, Dening's use of the mutiny on the *Bounty* story and his account of the British discovery of the Polynesian societies of the Pacific deserve to be rejected, not only because his major interpretations are demonstrably mistaken but because of the pernicious precedent his book sets. If we accept his version of 'cultural literacy' and disown a realist and empiricist account of history, anything goes. We would have no means of distinguishing between history and myth, between biography and hagiography, between eyewitness reports and fairy tales. Without facts, we would lack one of the most important grounds for debate, for contesting someone else's versions of history. One Hollywood version of the mutiny on the *Bounty* would be just as good as any other, and each would be just as valid as Dening's own account. Who could say any of the Hollywood versions was inferior? Certainly not Dening, who could only conclude that each was an appropriate product of the culture of its time.

---

1   Greg Dening, *Mr Bligh's Bad Language: Passion, Power and Theatre on the Bounty,* Cambridge University Press, Cambridge, 1992

2   See especially Professor Donald Denoon's review in *Australian Historical Studies*, 100, April 1993, p
    483

3   Alan Frost, review of *Mr Bligh's Bad Language*, *Weekend Australian*, 10–11 October 1992. Inga
    Clendinnen, *Aztecs: An Interpretation*, Cambridge University Press, Cambridge, 1991; Rhys Isaac, *The
    Transformation of Virginia, 1740–1790*, University of North Carolina Press, Chapel Hill, 1987; Donna
    Merwick, *Possessing Albany 1630–1710: The Dutch and English Experiences*, Cambridge University
    Press, Cambridge, 1990

4   Richard Hough, *Captain Bligh and Mr Christian*, E. P. Dutton, New York, 1973

5   Greg Dening, *Mr Bligh's Bad Language*, pp 63, 114

6   Greg Dening, *Mr Bligh's Bad Language*, p 58

7   Greg Dening, *Mr Bligh's Bad Language*, p 61

8   Greg Dening, *Mr Bligh's Bad Language*, p 61

9   Greg Dening, *Mr Bligh's Bad Language*, p 20

10 Greg Dening, *Mr Bligh's Bad Language*, pp 191–213

11 Greg Dening, *Mr Bligh's Bad Language*, pp 160–73

12 Greg Dening, *Mr Bligh's Bad Language*, p 338

13 Greg Dening, *Mr Bligh's Bad Language*, p 228

14 Greg Dening, *Mr Bligh's Bad Language*, p 138. Foucault's concept of the 'episteme' is discussed in
    Chapter Five

15 Greg Dening, *Mr Bligh's Bad Language*, p 5

16 Greg Dening, *Mr Bligh's Bad Language*, p 229

17 Greg Dening, *Mr Bligh's Bad Language*, pp 170–1

18 Greg Dening, *Mr Bligh's Bad Language*, p 366

19 Greg Dening, *Mr Bligh's Bad Language*, p 292

20 Greg Dening, *Mr Bligh's Bad Language*, p 196

21 Greg Dening, *Mr Bligh's Bad Language*, p 340

22 Greg Dening, *Mr Bligh's Bad Language*, p 338

23 Greg Dening, *Mr Bligh's Bad Language*, p 341

24 Greg Dening, *Mr Bligh's Bad Language*, pp 163–7

25 Greg Dening, *Mr Bligh's Bad Language*, pp 170–1

26 Claude Levi-Strauss, *Structural Anthropology*, Allen Lane, London, 1968, pp 365–6

27 Marshall Sahlins, 'Captain James Cook; or the Dying God', in his *Islands of History*, University of
    Chicago Press, Chicago, 1985

28 Marshall Sahlins, *Islands of History*, p 146

29 Greg Dening, *Mr Bligh's Bad Language*, p 195

30 Greg Dening, *Mr Bligh's Bad Language*, pp 197–8

31 Greg Dening, *Mr Bligh's Bad Language*, p 269

32 Gananath Obeyesekere, *The Apotheosis of Captain Cook: European Mythmaking in the Pacific*, Princeton
    University Press, Princeton, 1992

33 Gananath Obeyesekere, *The Apotheosis of Captain Cook*, p 61

34 Gananath Obeyesekere, *The Apotheosis of Captain Cook*, p 120

35 Gananath Obeyesekere, *The Apotheosis of Captain Cook*, p 58

36 Gananath Obeyesekere, *The Apotheosis of Captain Cook*, p 181

37 Greg Dening, *Mr Bligh's Bad Language*, p 165

38 Gananath Obeyesekere, *The Apotheosis of Captain Cook*, pp 46, 82

39 Gananath Obeyesekere, *The Apotheosis of Captain Cook*, p 94

40 Gananath Obeyesekere, *The Apotheosis of Captain Cook* p 56

41 George Robertson, *The Discovery of Tahiti*, The Hakluyt Society, London, 1948, p 156

42 Gananath Obeyesekere, *The Apotheosis of Captain Cook*, p 41

43 Claude Levi-Strauss, *The Savage Mind*, University of Chicago Press, Chicago, 1966

44 Marshall Sahlins, *Islands of History*, p 147

45 Gananath Obeyesekere, *The Apotheosis of Captain Cook*, p 67

4

THE DECONSTRUCTION OF IMPERIAL HISTORY

POSTSTRUCTURALISM AND THE FOUNDING OF AUSTRALIA

HISTORIANS have always written their work in narrative form. This is because their subject matter has been not just the past but the movement of past events through time. If anything has been central to history, it has been the dimension of time. Historians have believed that, in incorporating this dimension through narrative, they have been reflecting the nature of reality itself. So, if you wanted to challenge the very core of history writing, time and narrative would be the quarry to pursue.

This is the project Paul Carter has set for himself. To date, he has published three books, each of which, in varying degrees, contributes to his aim. The first, *The Road to Botany Bay,*[1] which appeared in 1987, was devoted entirely to Australian history. The second and third, *Living in a New Country*[2] and *The Sound in Between,*[3] both contain essays on Australian historical themes and were published in 1992. Carter is a poststructuralist who contests the writing of history on at least three grounds.

First, he rejects the notion that narrative writing can reflect reality. This kind of writing is linear, he says, whereas experience is multidimensional. Carter observes that, because of the limitations of the linear, the poststructuralist theorist Jacques Derrida has called for a different kind of writing, one that lets people 'reread past writing according to a differerent organisation of space'.[4] Carter calls his own attempt at this kind of rereading 'spatial history'.

Second, he claims that narrative history is neither value-free nor objective but is charged with ideology. In particular, it is a product of the imperial era and was initially designed by imperialists to record their own creation of order out of chaos. Carter says that all such narratives deserve the label 'imperial history'.

Third, the narrative historian's notion of time itself is mistaken and out of date. Temporal experience is always portrayed by historians in a linear fashion. In doing this, they are simply reflecting their discipline's origins in pre-twentieth century, mechanistic thought. 'Temporality has continued to be conceived of in Newtonian terms, as a pure intuition independent of space.'[5] Carter insists that historical events are spatial as well as temporal, and so, by implication, historians in the era of Einstein should be operating with the notion of space–time. Spatial history is his version of this concept.

THE ROAD TO BOTANY BAY

When Paul Carter's first book on Australian history, *The Road to Botany Bay*, was published in 1987, it attracted far more attention than might have been expected for a new author writing for a specialised, academic audience. It was discussed not only in the academic press but in all major Australian newspapers, attracting reviews from some of the senior figures of Australian historiography, including Manning Clark and Russel Ward. Unusually for such an esoterically Australian work, it was also reviewed in London in the *Times Literary Supplement*, the *Times Educational Supplement* and the *London Review of Books*.[6] Not all the reviews were favourable—some, in fact, were unremittingly hostile—but the book was widely regarded as something significant which, like it or not, could not be ignored.

On its first appearance, the book's dust jacket carried enthusiastic commendations from three of Australia's internationally best-known novelists, David Malouf, Peter Carey and Barry Hill. By the time a reprinted edition appeared, publisher Faber and Faber had organised even more heavy-weight endorsements from the New York literati for its cover blurb. Columbia University's postcolonialist literary critic, Edward Said, was full of praise:

Astonishingly original methods of cultural research ... This is a compelling work of great intellectual power.

The postmodern cultural essayist Susan Sontag concurred:

Paul Carter's bold, ingenious account of nation-founding is itself a kind of founding book—of the adventurous discipline of spatial history ... A brilliant book for many appetites.

Part of the explanation for the book's instant celebrity lay in Faber and Faber's coup in gaining such illustrious recommendations, but the main reason lay in the promise of the content itself. *The Road to Botany Bay* announced itself as a radical, new and iconoclastic approach to the early history of the British in Australia—the discovery of the east coast, British exploration and settlement, the convict system and contact with the Aborigines. Its author claimed not only to be offering a fresh version of all these old, familiar, school curriculum topics but to have invented a new kind of history altogether: spatial history. The book, moreover, was peppered throughout with quotations from fashionable Continental philosophers such as Jacques Derrida, Paul Ricoeur, Giles Deleuze and Edmund Husserl—plus some reverent citations of the works of Edward Said himself—a tactic guaranteed to intrigue local readers, who had regarded Australian history as an uneventful sideshow, hard to fit into the annals of the rest of the world.

The Road to Botany Bay combines a critique of traditional methods of writing history with the advocacy of a new approach to the subject. The critique is fundamental rather than piecemeal. Two of Australia's best-known historians, Manning Clark and Geoffrey Blainey, who would be regarded by most readers as having quite different perspectives on their subject matter, are lumped together by Carter as members of the one camp. Though Clark's work leans, politically, to the Left, and Blainey's to the Right, and though most would regard these two historians as being Australianist in their approach, Carter sees them both as representatives of the one thing: 'imperial history'. Henry Reynolds who, during the previous decade, had been widely revered in the profession for his pioneering work in uncovering evidence of how the Aborigines responded to the British occupation of their lands, is dismissed by Carter as someone whose book 'merely continues by other means two hundred years of white history'.[7]

These historians, and virtually every other who wrote on Australia before Carter appeared, are fundamentally flawed, he says, by their adoption of the traditional, empirical, narrative approach to their subject. When historians write what Carter calls 'linear, narrative history', they attempt to create a long chain of causes and effects about lives, events and facts. They are trying, through the sequential pattern they create, to show how one period in the past caused another, more recent period, to come into being. Ultimately, they want to show how the past created the present. Carter maintains that the cause and effect patterns they find are mere artifices. From the perspective of historical narrative, which is always written from hindsight, the past appears to move relentlessly towards the present. But Carter argues that from the perspective of the historical actors themselves, history is experienced differently—there is no sense of inevitability, and the world is full of possibilities. Traditional history, he writes, is an illusory vision of the world which locks us out of an understanding of how things were actually experienced by people in the past: 'it is precisely the particularity of historical experience, the material hereness and nowness which cannot be repeated, that such [narrative] history crowds out in favour of a transcendent classification in terms of multiplying causes and effects.'[8] Carter likens the methodology of the empirical historian to that of the botanist of the eighteenth century. Just as the aim of the botanist was to translate the living, breathing, natural world into the artificial classifications of Enlightenment science, the viewpoint of the narrative historian is contaminated by hindsight and the attempt to explain how things came to be as they are now.

Carter maintains that, despite their various political leanings, the narrative empiricism of traditional historians binds them all to the one ideological position. He regards their descriptions of the first European settlements, of the making of roads, buildings and laws, as defensive attempts to demonstrate the emergence of order from chaos and therefore as endorsements of the 'unlawful usurpation and constitutional illegitimacy' of the colonial founders. 'Empirical history of this kind has as its focus facts which, in a sense, come after the event. The primary object is not to understand or to interpret: it is to legitimate. This is why this history is associated with imperialism.'[9]

In working out his own alternative, 'spatial' version of history, Carter traverses the familiar topics and characters associated with the exploration, discovery and initial settlement of Australia by the British. His book is more a collection of essays on related themes than a sustained and integrated argument. He begins with a study of James Cook and Joseph Banks on the *Endeavour* and offers his own account of why Cook chose the names he did for the geographic features he recorded on his maps of the coastlines of eastern Australia and New Zealand. He then follows the First Fleet as it sails into Botany Bay in 1788 and as it subsequently abandons that site for the more congenial shores of Sydney Cove. Founding figures such as Watkin Tench brought with them, Carter writes, the rhetoric of an imperial vision that sought to expunge the explorer's logic of Cook. He next analyses the journals of some of the famous explorers of the inland, including Charles Sturt, Thomas Mitchell and Edward John Eyre, as well as that of his favourite character, the continent's first circumnavigator, Matthew Flinders. There are essays exposing the ideology of mid-century real estate developers' urban grid plans for Melbourne and Adelaide, plus other pieces on white settlement and domestication of the rainforest and bush of the Victorian countryside. He finishes with discussions of the existentialist and spatial perspectives held by the early convicts and by the Australian Aborigines.

The title of the book carries a least two meanings. In its wider sense, the road is the process of discovery and exploration of the east coast of Australia, via the eighteenth century intellectual baggage that Cook and Banks brought with them, leading to the eventual establishment of the British settlement in

New South Wales. In its other sense, it is also the title of one chapter in the book devoted to understanding the experience of the convicts. When the First Fleet, after having been anchored for some days on the shores of Botany Bay, moved camp a few kilometres north to Sydney Cove, the site of Botany Bay became 'the first *other* place in the colony' and the overland route to it came to be seen by the convicts as a way of escape, that is, escape to another place rather than simply escape into the wilderness. This 'road', which was at best a barely discernible Aboriginal track through bush and swamp, was more symbolic than real. The belief that it existed, and that at the end of it there were French ships that would take them aboard (the French explorer La Perouse had sailed into Botany Bay within days of the First Fleet's arrival), was an important convict fantasy. As long as this imaginary road existed, Carter writes, the convicts' dream of escape was kept alive and their independent, anti-establishment mentality and language could be sustained.

In opposition to the grand narratives of 'cause and effect empirical history' in which the end of the story is known before the writer starts, Carter presents 'a form of non-linear writing'. He traces 'the spatiality of historical experience' through his reinterpretations of some of the familiar texts used by other historians, 'letters home, explorers' journals, unfinished maps.' He argues that the historian's use of these texts should not be to plot the story of nation-building nor to write heroic biographies of historical individuals, as he sees Clark and Blainey both doing. To read them this way:

is to exclude precisely what distinguishes them: their active engagement with the road and the horizon. For the historical significance of the explorers' journals and the settlers' diaries does not reside in any stylistic illusion of picturesque completeness ... Quite the contrary, it is their open-endedness, their lack of finish, even their search for words, which is characteristic: for it is here, where forms and conventions break down, that we can discern the process of transforming space into place, the *intentional* world of the texts, wherein lies their unrepeatability and their enduring, if hitherto ignored, historical significance.[10]

The 'facts' of his spatial history, Carter writes, are 'not houses and clearings, but phenomena as they appear to the traveller, as his intentional gaze conjures them up. They are the directions and distances in which houses and clearings *may* be found or founded'.[11] To readers brought up on traditional history, none of this is easy to follow, so let me try to explain what he means. When he writes about 'the *intentional* world of the texts' and the 'intentional gaze' of the traveller, Carter is describing how explorers and travellers write about and give meanings to what they see. The language they use to generate their meaning has itself the power to make history. 'Such spatial history—history that discovers and explores the lacuna left by imperial history—begins and ends in language.'[12] The most important use of language that he finds in the making of history is that of naming. He says that we make a mistake in assuming that land is 'already there' before it is named. The act of naming brings land into being, in the historical sense. He does acknowledge that the land actually exists in the geological sense before it is named but says that this is not historically relevant.

For by the act of place-naming, space is transformed symbolically into a place, that is, a space with a history. And, by the same token, the namer inscribes his passage permanently on the world, making a metaphorical word-place which others may one day inhabit and by which, in the meantime, he asserts his own place in history.[13]

Other kinds of language-use that also made history were mapping, plotting directions and even the act of imagining, as in the case of the imaginary inland sea sought by Charles Sturt. Understanding the significance of these language forms, Carter says, allows us to dispense with the imperial historians' myth of a theatrical settlement followed by linear progress, and to substitute a demonstration of 'the dialectical nature of foundation'. We need to understand 'the sense in which the new country was a rhetorical construction, a product of language and the intentional gaze'.[14] The geological forms that early explorers of the inland such as Sturt, Mitchell and Eyre came across were not significant in themselves. They became so only because they were named as being different from their surroundings. A slight rise on a flat inland plain was named as a 'mount' or a 'hill' to distinguish it rhetorically from the 'succession of conceivable places' that the explorer could read from the landscape. 'Whether they existed or not was by the way: they were necessary differences without which a distinct idea of the landscape could not be formed.'[15] 'Historically speaking', Carter says, 'the country did not precede the traveller: it was the offspring of his intention ... he found there what he was looking for'.[16] In other words, the countryside was not a given entity, waiting to be settled. It was something that was brought into being for European comprehension by explorers and settlers in their acts of naming and describing the kinds of differences—differences between hills, plains, creeks, lakes and valleys—that they wanted to define. Hence, the historical object called Australia was not discovered; it was created by the application of language.

Carter rests most of his claim for offering a new perspective on Australian history on his analysis of the journals and diaries of explorers. In many cases, he argues, these journals are the opposite of the foundation documents that historians have assumed them to be. Instead, he interprets them in an original manner to reveal 'the logic of travelling'. The explorer who serves best to reveal this 'logic' is James Cook, and the practice through which he revealed it most clearly was the naming of places. There was a world view embodied in Cook's naming practice, Carter says, that stood at odds with the aims of imperialism. Cook's significance in Australian history was not that he founded a country. Instead, 'by establishing a tradition of travelling, Cook inaugurated Australia's spatial history'.[17] Let me try to explain what this means.

Carter says it is wrong to try to categorise or sum up in some taxonomic way the names that Cook gave to the places he found on his first voyage to the Pacific, in which he mapped the east coast of Australia and circumnavigated both islands of New Zealand. Any classification of this kind would fail to understand the historical circumstances in which the names were given—the fact that they unfolded in the time and space of the journey. Pigeon House Mountain was named because it looked like a pigeon house, but Ram Head was named after Ram Head in Plymouth Sound rather than because it resembled a male sheep; the Three Brothers were named because they bore some likeness to one another but Northumberland Isles and Cumberland Isles were given these names not because they resembled the English counties but to honour the two younger brothers of George III in whose reign the *Endeavour* sailed. Carter explains that such disparities do not signify a purely arbitrary or frivolous naming practice. Instead, the names bore a relation to one another in terms of the progress or logic of Cook's journey.

'Botany Bay', for instance, was chosen because of the epistemological differences that had emerged between Cook's travelling perspective and Joseph Banks's empiricism. The name was an example of Cook's ironic wit in satirising Banks's mania for collection and classification. Carter claims the name was chosen to underline the difference between Banks's science and Cook's 'nomadic discourse'. The reason it was called Botany Bay, and not Botanists' Bay, was because Cook wanted to make a linguistic analogy between the last place he named in New Zealand, Admiralty Bay, and the first he named in Australia, Botany Bay. To readers who might be bewildered by an analogy that apparently consists of nothing more than both names ending with the letter 'y', Carter says the link might not work empirically but it does rhetorically. 'It faithfully preserved the traveller's sense of facts, not as discrete objects, but as horizons increasingly inscribed with spatial meanings.'[18] Nowhere in his journals is there a discussion by Cook himself about why he gave Botany Bay this name. Nonetheless, Carter says he is justified in reading Cook this way and in drawing this conclusion from the patterns he interprets as lying within the explorer's maps and journal.

This kind of reading, which interprets rather than explains, which relocates the text in the context of its writing, can be applied more generally: taken as a whole, Cook's place names express the navigator's active engagement with the space of his journey. They are figures of speech characteristic of the explorer's discourse.[19]

To help explain his concept of the 'explorer's discourse', Carter contrasts it with what he describes as 'that other great eighteenth-century naming discipline, botany'. He does this through an analysis of the naming practice of Cook's major sponsor and passenger, Joseph Banks. The disparity between the two, in terms of both scientific method and epistemological aims, could hardly have been greater, Carter claims. Banks was a representative of the Enlightenment project of universal knowledge; Cook's travelling mind knew how vain was the hope that the accumulation of empirical detail would reveal the nature of the world. 'For where Banks was preoccupied with the typical, Cook was concerned with the singular; where Banks tended to generalise, Cook tended to specify.'[20] According to Carter, Banks's problem was that he was a follower of the Swedish botanist Carl Linnaeus and so was engaged in a 'beguilingly simple' project to classify the plants of the planet. By using a 'superficial comparison of a limited number of characteristics', gentlemen botanists such as Banks travelled the world naming and collecting plant specimens. In the pre-Darwinian era, this activity became very popular among the scientifically minded of the European upper classes. Carter is a scathing critic of their empiricism which he portrays as a mindless pastime of collecting and naming. Disregarding plant morphology, they attempted to fit the specimens they found into the pregiven, artificial classification system devised by Linnaeus. The methodology of this eighteenth century pseudo-science, Carter maintains, was not confined to botany. It also provided the model for the study of history. But whereas botany has had its Darwinian revolution, those who labour on today as historians are unwittingly replicating this hopelessly outmoded approach.

The pleasure of the plant collector, then, was a pleasure in naming uniquely and systematically. It was the pleasure of arrangement within a universal taxonomy, a taxonomy characterised by tree-like ramifications—in short, a pleasure analogous to that felt by the imperial historian, who assimilates occasions and anomalies to the logic of universal reason.[21]

Having established in his own mind that Cook's explorer's logic stands opposed to Banks's classification practice, and since he thinks that he has also successfully linked botany, via imperial history, to imperialism itself, Carter feels justified in claiming that Cook's naming practice 'stood at odds with the aims of imperialism'. Unfazed by the circuitousness of his reasoning, Carter declares that Cook, therefore, 'inaugurated Australia's spatial history'.[22] In the early nineteenth century, the explorers of the continent's vast interior continued the alternative, 'epistemological strategy', or the mode of knowing, that Cook had begun. One of the most common expressions of spatial history was the explorer writing his journal or diary. Explorers who wrote up their journeys, Carter says, aimed to bring the country before their readers' eyes. The primary function of these journals was 'to name the world of the journey'. Whether he found anything or not, the explorer's 'account of his route would serve to bring the country into historical being'. This state of 'historical being' was the text of the journal, which had a kind of logical primacy over the landscape itself.

The logic they used to discover the country did not derive primarily from the realm of contemporary geographical hypothesis or even from the economic incentives offered by governments or squatters: it originated in the logic of travelling itself, in the continuity of the journal, which, kept day after day, left no spaces unrelated and brought even the most distant objects into the uniform, continuous world of the text. If there was a principle of association at work, it was to be found in the orderly succession of diary entries, not in any logic of the landscape.[23]

According to Carter, the journal of Matthew Flinders, *A Voyage to Terra Australis*, published in 1814, was 'the first great Australian work of spatial history'. This was a journal that was not merely the account of a voyage but a model of how explorations should be written up. 'It had become the exploration of a literary genre as much as the record of a journey.' It began with a 204-page historical introduction; followed by 550 pages devoted to the two years in which Flinders explored the continent's entire coastline on his ship *Investigator*; followed by Book Three devoted to his detention and imprisonment by the French on the island of Mauritius for six years.

The aspect of Flinders' work that attracts most of Carter's attention was his practice of naming the islands of Spencer Gulf after villages in his home county of Lincolnshire. Carter insists that these names, far from reflecting a simple sentimentality for the familiar places of his childhood, were an expression of 'something about exploring as a mode of knowing'. Carter reproduces a map of the mouth of Spencer Gulf and a map of Lincolnshire to argue that the essential point about the islands' names is that 'they preserve the spatial and topographical relationship of the Lincolnshire villages'. The villages are grouped into three constellations, a pattern reflected in the islands and in some of the ports, capes and points of the gulf coast. Carter realises that anyone who peruses his maps will see that there are some marked differences between the two. Port Lincoln in South Australia, for instance, is in the centre of the map and its place names, whereas in England, the city of Lincoln is on the western perimeter of the same place names. In Spencer Gulf, Tumby Island is to the north of Louth Island which is to the north of Boston Island. In England, the village of Tumby is halfway between Louth in the north and Boston in the south. He acknowledges that Flinders' names do not reproduce the layout of English Lincolnshire exactly but, rather, they 'revise and clarify its spatial relationships' in a way that resembles the 'extended views and regions' of Flinders' homeland.[24]

Carter's aim in all this is to show something that has escaped Flinders' previous biographers. He claims the navigator was operating with a coherent theory of knowledge that bears remarkable similarities to Carter's own poststructuralist travelling theory: 'he wanted to show his method of exploring as a mode of knowing, and the means of doing this was to reveal the true nature of associative logic and, in particular, the validity of the argument from analogy.'[25] In using the term 'associative logic', Carter is referring to the doctrine of associationism, an eighteenth century theory of psychology subscribed to by British philosophers such as David Hume and David Hartley, which held that the mind joined together ideas to form associative chains of reasoning. Carter says that, although no one has previously recognised it, Flinders must have been an adherent of this theory, a claim based partly on the internal evidence of his writings—which refer to a poem written about the theory—and partly on the hypotheses Flinders drew about navigation and geography.

Carter offers two examples of Flinders using the theory. When, accompanied by George Bass, he circumnavigated Tasmania in 1798-99, Flinders was the first to prove that the island was separated from the mainland by the strait he named after his colleague. At the time he noted that unusually strong tides were associated with the presence of the strait. In 1802, when exploring the mainland's southern coastline, then called the 'Unknown Coast', Flinders encountered Spencer Gulf. The existence of strong tides emanating from the gulf led Flinders to believe that he was in the presence of another strait that, initially, he thought might lead all the way from the southern coast to the northern. Carter thinks that the analogy Flinders made from one example to the other (an analogy, of course, that quickly proved mistaken) was evidence of a new, anti-Enlightenment kind of mentality: 'by an internal operation of the mind, Flinders can argue from the past to the future, from what was before to what was possible again. In this way, he can advance logically beyond the horizon.'[26] The logic of this argument, Carter claims, is 'in complete contrast' to the thinking of the empiricist Joseph Banks. According to Carter, Banks had deduced that the interior of the continent was uninhabited, since he accepted as a universal truth that all savages depend on the sea. Since the sea shore did not dissect the continent in any major way, Banks said the inland must be uninhabited. Carter says this showed Banks's logic 'was only capable of denying difference ... Banks reduces the possible future to conformity and uniformity with the present'. Flinders, however 'by contrast, employs what might be called a logic of travelling'.[27]

This same logic was in evidence in what all writers on Flinders agree was his major scientific achievement: his recognition of the deviation from true north caused in the magnetic compass by the presence of iron in a ship and by the direction of the ship's head, which led to his invention of the compensating

device that still bears his name. Rather than this discovery being an achievement of the Enlightenment methods of observation and induction, Carter
wants to chalk it up to Flinders' travelling logic. It was a 'triumph for associative reasoning'.

It underlined the point that, for Flinders, motion and orientation, the twin
conditions of travelling, were instrumental aspects of knowledge. Travelling, if it
was properly understood, if it was subjected to the proper reasoning processes,
could yield a truth that eluded merely static deduction.[28]

Apart from explorers, the other group of early Australian colonists whom
Carter sees operating with a travelling logic were the first settlers of the bush.
This, of course, is a rather surprising claim since most of us would assume that
settling was a process that was the opposite of exploring. Not so, says Carter,
and he puts forward an argument to claim that settlers were travellers too.

By reading the diaries of some of the settlers of Victoria, Carter finds that
the process of settlement was radically different from that portrayed by the
imperial historians. 'Contrary to the imperial paradigm of colonisation, in
which settlement follows on smoothly from discovery and exploration, the
settlers inhabited the new country strategically. They were themselves dis-
coverers and explorers.' Hence the imperialists' 'great drama of colonisation'
is a myth. More often than not, Carter says, the explorer and the settler were
one and the same person. They did not stay long in one place: they were
restless souls that yearned to wander. The reason they cleared the land and
built their houses was not because they wanted to set down permanent roots
or to raise families. Their houses were simply depots or staging posts, which
they created in order to serve as points of departure for more exploration and
wandering. In other words, settlers and squatters preferred not to settle or
squat; they chose a wandering foot over a heart at rest. Carter claims that
'settling' and 'exploring' are not contrary terms but actually have a close relationship to each other: they 'simply refer to two aspects of a single epistemological mode, to do with the getting of spatial knowledge'. The main evidence he offers for this is 'the fact that both adopt the journal as their obvious
literary medium'.[29]

This textualist interpretation of the actions of Australian settlers who sailed
halfway around the world, and spent years of their lives clearing land, constructing houses on it, stocking it with animals and ploughing it with crops,
simply so they could have somewhere from which to travel on again—this
backpacker's theory of history—is the most obviously questionable of all Carter's theses. If those settlers who built the pastoral dynasties which have attracted the attention of so many historians were simply laying down depots
and staging posts, why did they do it using such imposing and costly structures, with their homesteads often outdoing in splendour the architecture of

the British gentry to which they had been born? Why was the principal political issue of the Australian colonies for the first half of the nineteenth century centred on the pastoralists' determination to add ever greater tracts of Crown land to their holdings? The history of Australian land settlement has been so well canvassed by historians and the evidence of the aims of the settlers have been so well recorded[30] that Carter's theoretical speculations do not deserve to be taken seriously. Nonetheless, it is worth pausing at this point to go back over some of his other arguments which I have outlined, to reveal how little they too have to recommend them.

NAMES, SPACE AND TRAVEL

Naming: We should start with the issue on which Carter hinges most of his arguments: the process of naming. When he says that we cannot assume that any piece of land is 'already there' before it is named, he is not taking the old philosophical idealist position that things do not exist unless they are perceived by someone. Rather, his claim is that land does not exist in a historical or cultural sense until it is named: 'by the act of place-naming, space is transformed symbolically into a place, that is, a space with a history.'[31] There are a number of difficulties posed by this thesis.

For a start, it is not difficult to show that the act of naming can be quite irrelevant to the occurrence of history. This is readily revealed by Carter's own discussion of the topic in his chapter on Matthew Flinders. Flinders sailed the 'Unknown Coast' of South Australia in 1802. However, he did not give the coast and its islands their names until he returned to England and wrote up the journal of his voyage in 1812. According to Carter's thesis, this must mean that during this ten-year interval the coastline did not exist in an historical sense. This, of course, is nonsense. The place had a 'history', that is, it figured as part of the history of European discovery and exploration of Australia, from the moment Flinders entered its waters. At one point during the voyage, at the entrance to Spencer Gulf, Flinders lost six of his crew through drowning. A few weeks later, to the east of Kangaroo Island, Flinders encountered the French navigator Nicholas Baudin and his ship *Le Géographe*. According to Carter's thesis, none of these historic events could have happened because, without names at the time, there was no historic space for them to happen in.

Further, the relationship between names and history very often occurs in the opposite sequence to that described by Carter. As the maps he reproduces testify, there are many spaces which the first explorers left nameless and gave only descriptive terminology: boggy creek, mud flat, dry lake, yellow hills, white cliffs, sandy bay. In Hobart one space on the map defined by the last of these descriptive terms has been transformed into the upmarket suburb of Sandy Bay, a name now synonymous with the city's best gardens and mansions, the Wrest Point Casino and the University of Tasmania. It was not the first cartographer but the experience of people living around this bay that made the term into a name with this significance. In other words, the history made the name, the name did not make the history. As Carter's own discussion of the use of Aboriginal place names in Australia shows, a great many of them are inaccurate translations or have no meaning at all in the local dialect. This makes it clear that, in terms of making history, names are purely arbitrary signs: almost any name will do, and even a description without a name will suffice. The meaning that a name will come to assume will be determined by its history.

Some of the evidence Carter himself provides for his thesis turns out, on closer inspection, to be completely unconvincing. This is especially true of his discussion of the way Flinders named the islands of Spencer Gulf after villages in Lincolnshire. As I noted above, Carter claims that these names expressed 'exploring as a mode of knowing' and that they 'preserve the spatial and topographical relationship of the Lincolnshire villages'. As I also noted, Carter acknowledges that the geographic relationship is not exact but he gives the impression that it remains fairly close. This is quite misleading. Anyone who takes the trouble to study his maps for some time will actually find more discrepancies than similarities in the comparisons he is trying to make. In the Sir Joseph Banks group of islands, for instance, the names, north to south, are: Winceby, Reevesby, Marum, Partney, Lusby, Kirkby, Dalby, Hareby, Langton, Sibsey, Spilsby and Stickney. However, in Lincolnshire, the north–south order is: Dalby, Langton, Winceby, Partney, Lusby, Mareham, Spilsby, Hareby, Kirkby, Revesby, Stickney and Sibsey. If you track both sets of names from east to west there is a similar degree of disparity. In the gulf, all these islands are to the east of Louth Island, but in England the same villages are all due south of Louth. In the gulf, all the islands are to the east of Point Bolinbroke but, in England, Bolinbroke is right in the middle. In short, Flinders certainly named these islands after some of the villages of north-east Lincolnshire but his selection appears to have been made largely at random. Any 'spatial' relationship or pattern between the two exists solely in Carter's mind.

For a thesis so concerned about names, Carter's book is strangely silent about one of the most common naming practices of all those used in Australia and the Pacific. This is the use of the prefix 'New' followed by a place name from Europe. Let me list just a few of the larger territories that were labelled this way at one some stage in their history: New Holland, New South Wales, New England, New Zealand, New Hebrides, New Britain, New Caledonia, New Ireland. Even though these names cover virtually the whole of the geographic area that he is discussing, Carter offers no comment on any of them. The reason for this is that this practice suggests a quite different explanation about why the early European explorers gave the names they did. There is no 'travelling logic' or linguistic rationale evident in any of these names, nor, with the possible exception of New South Wales, do the areas named bear the slightest resemblance to the physical characteristics of their European name-sakes. Rather, they were given these names for political and legal reasons. From the first expansion overseas by the Portuguese in the early fifteenth century, international diplomacy between the European powers accepted that the legal act of possession of a newly discovered territory customarily in-volved naming it. Lawyers for the crowns of Europe argued that 'no one could well lay claim to any nameless city, and that a province without a name was hardly a province at all'.[32] While a name given by one explorer did not preclude explorers from another country laying their own claims, the earlier publication of a map with names applied to the major topographical features was taken, in any territorial dispute, as prima facie evidence of discovery and initial possession. The prefix 'New' followed by a European place name was one form of declaration of the imperial interests claiming possession. This was, for example, one of the reasons why Cortés gave the name New Spain to the territory he conquered in Mexico, and why the changing names of colo-nial New Amsterdam/New York reflected the dominant imperial power of the era.

Scientific method: Carter's critique of the scientific method of the Enlightenment—especially as found in the work of Joseph Banks—and his attempt to identify it with the methods of traditional history, is another example of how he has got both the sequence of events and the logic of his categories the wrong way around. It is well known that Banks was a follower and friend of Linnaeus and a member of the Linnaean Society. While he was not committed to the Linnaean system of nomenclature in the mindless way Carter claims, and while there is no evidence to support Carter's claim that Banks was engaged in naming simply for pleasure or for its own sake, it is nonetheless true that Banks, Linnaeus and every other naturalist at the time was engaged in a great project to classify nature in all its variety. This classification meant ordering nature, putting all living things in their place and giving each its rank in a fixed hierarchy. From the mid–eighteenth century to the mid–nineteenth, naturalists vied with one another to produce a system of classification of flora and fauna that could satisfactorily explain them all. The system of Linnaeus was one of the most prominent, but was by no means regarded by Banks or anyone else as laying down a set of universal laws to which all discoveries must conform. In opposition to Linnaeus's tree like structure, competing naturalists (some of whom were influenced by the spirit of the Enlightenment;

but others of whom, contrary to Carter's belief, remained committed to the spirit of Christianity) put forward circular classification systems within which clusters of groups revolved; others developed mathematical formulae that they hoped would reveal the plan of creation devised by God.

There was one thing that all these classificatory systems had in common, however. They were all static and lacked the concept of change over time. This was the fundamental point that Charles Darwin grasped. To classify nature, Darwin said, the naturalist must devise a system that contains 'order in time of creation'. The Darwinian revolution occurred because Darwin injected the concept of time, the dimension of history, into the understanding of nature. In the study of human society, however, the concept of change over time had already been taken for granted by historians for centuries. The rise and fall of peoples, governments and empires had defined their discipline. In fact, as Darwin's most recent biographers show, some of the most important influences that allowed his conceptual breakthrough were the historical, time-series data on population produced by his compatriot, the political economist Thomas Malthus.[33] So, in drawing a parallel between the static, timeless classification systems of eighteenth century botany and what he calls 'imperial' history, Carter is guilty of a considerable misrepresentation. Indeed, one should point out that today's principal representative of the immobile, time-deprived study of human affairs is French structuralism, the basis of the very genre in which Carter himself is working. It is this, in fact, that seems to be his main problem. He so readily misrepresents history largely because he is so opposed to its central principle.

Carter's other attempt at delving into eighteenth century scientific method is his claim that Matthew Flinders was an adherent of Hume and Hartley's theory of associationism. It was this theory that supposedly allowed Flinders to develop the conceptual breakthroughs that Carter claims for him: a travelling logic, the process of argument from analogy, and his identification of compass drift. As I noted above, apart from Flinders' solution of the compass problem, the achievements and the philosophical turn of mind ascribed to him by Carter have not been recognised by anyone else who has written about him. Let us look a little more closely at how Carter arrives at his findings.

There is only one piece of evidence that Carter offers to show that Flinders supported associationism. This is a phrase from a letter Flinders wrote to his wife from his prison in Mauritius in 1804. He tells her he has dedicated the first day of the year to ' "the pleasures of memory" '. Carter emphasises that Flinders put the phrase within inverted commas. Before showing the alleged philosophical import of this, let me add some biographical details that Carter omits. In April 1801, aged twenty seven, and domiciled briefly in England,

Flinders married Ann Chappell of Lincolnshire. Three months later, denied permission to take his bride with him, he sailed on the *Investigator* for the 'Unknown Coast' of South Australia. He did not see his wife again until his release by the French in 1810. Carter claims this one phrase, 'the pleasures of memory', represents much more than the kind of understandable sentiment we might expect from young lovers separated so abruptly. Flinders does not say it, but Carter recognises that the phrase is really a reference to the poem written by Samuel Rogers in 1792, titled *The Pleasures of Memory*, which was a poetic exposition of the philosopher Hartley's doctrine of associationism. Carter follows this with a page of exposition about how Rogers' poem explains Hartley's ideas. He then goes on to 'interpret' Flinders as if he had thereby established him as a committed associationist, but there is nothing else in the chapter to connect Flinders in any way at all with this philosophical system. Carter's whole case is built on what must surely rank as the flimsiest piece of evidence ever used in a book on Australian history. Hence, the claims that Flinders was operating with some kind of 'travelling logic' and that he founded Australia's 'spatial history' have nothing to recommend them but Carter's own textual interpretations. In terms of evidence from Flinders himself, they remain completely unsubstantiated.

Travelling logic versus imperial history: When *The Road to Botany Bay* first appeared, some of the author's less sympathetic reviewers wrote that, after reading almost four hundred pages, they were none the wiser about what 'spatial history' actually was. This is a little unfair because, though difficult to follow and never given a summary definition, the concept recurs often enough in the book for the dedicated reader to glean what Carter means. Spatial history is the expression of the travelling logic that Carter finds in the writings of Cook, Flinders and some other explorers. The real problem with the concept is not that it remains undefined but that Carter's deployment of the term is inconsistent and, in some places, quite illogical.

We need to remember that his aim is to establish spatial history as a kind of knowledge different from that provided by the contaminated hindsight of traditional historians, who write their works knowing how the events concluded and how their characters eventually fared. Time and again, Carter gives the impression that the value of spatial history and travelling logic is that they are records of a kind of immanent presence of the events they discuss: 'where we stand and how we go ... the intentional world of historical individuals, the world of active, spatial choices'.[34] But in his discussion of the writings of some of the explorers, Carter is forced to admit that they often did not record events in their journals on a day-to-day basis. Cook, for instance, did not name Botany Bay in Botany Bay itself. He wrote most of the journals about his first exploration of the Pacific after the voyage was largely complete, when he was sojourning with Dutch colonists in their East Indies capital of Batavia. Some of Cook's passages of writing were not even his own but were modified copies of observations Banks had made in his own journal. In Batavia, moreover, Cook took the time to revise, correct and add new names to the maps that he had drawn as he went along. In other words, Cook wrote up his journals with the benefit of the dreaded hindsight, just like the historians that Carter condemns. And some of the journals' contents were not Cook's own intentional meanings about where he stood and how he went but were poorly disguised transcripts from the journal of that hopeless empiricist and imperialist, Joseph Banks. The worst offender in this regard is Carter's favourite hero, Flinders. As I noted before, Flinders was not able to complete his maps and diaries, nor to give his names to the 'Unknown Coast', until he had returned to England ten years after his voyage, when his mind must have been virtually saturated with hindsight.

In other places in his book, Carter recognises that it is inappropriate to discuss spatial history as a direct record of the experience of events. Spatial history sometimes becomes an analysis of the *experience of writing* about the experience of events: it 'relocates the text in the context of its writing'.[35] Now, this is something quite different. Instead of directly plugging into the minds of the travelling explorers, we have to make do with Carter's reflections about the writing habits they adopt and the texts they produce once they become stationary—in other words, nothing more immanent than the second-hand observations of a literary critic.

Carter displays a similar confusion and lack of consistency when he tries to characterise the writings of traditional historians. In his introduction, he provides a textual and theoretical analysis of a passage in Volume One of Manning Clark's *A History of Australia,* in which Clark describes how Governor Phillip and the First Fleet landed and pitched camp at Sydney Cove in 1788. As part of his attempt to reveal the imperial intent in Clark's account, Carter writes: 'Clark's description does not simply reproduce the events: it narrates them, clarifies them and orders them.' Yet in the very next paragraph, a mere twenty-five lines later, Carter has apparently forgotten what he has just written and chastises Clark for using the words of a contemporary observer to describe the scene. But now, Carter advises us, 'the historian does not order the facts, he conforms to them'.[36] Poor Manning Clark—in a single passage he stands exposed as an imperialist because, on the one hand, he has ordered his facts but also because, on the other hand, he has not ordered them. Since this appears on only the second and third pages of Carter's book, it is plain that publishers Faber and Faber would have served their author better if they had found him a good copy editor instead of the ridiculously flattering cover blurb puffs from Sontag and Said.

There is a similar but perhaps even more embarrassing inconsistency involved in another of Carter's comparisons between spatial history and imperial history. In several places he criticises the latter as 'cause-and-effect, linear history'. The most incisive abuse he seems able to heap on traditional history is to call it 'linear' and the warmest praise he can find for those he favours is to describe their approach as 'spatial'. However, like some other poststructuralists who pose as linguistic experts and lecture their readers about the nature and theory of metaphorical language, Carter has neglected to ponder the meaning of the metaphors he himself employs. He has borrowed the term 'linear history' from French theorists without considering the implications of using it as a contrast to his own concept of 'spatial history'. He should have realised that a line is itself a figure in *space* and, though it is only in one dimension, is nonetheless a spatial concept. To label history as 'linear' is to therefore apply a spatial metaphor. Hence, those who accept that imperial history is linear thereby commit themselves to conceiving it as a form of spatial history. To have avoided such a miscarriage of terminology, Carter might have distinguished between traditional history and spatial history on the grounds that the former was one dimensional and the latter was of two or more dimensions. But this, of course, would have exposed the incongruity of his comparisons. It is his own work, engrossed so narrowly in travelling, naming and interpreting, that obviously contains the fewer dimensions.

In any event, the French use of the term 'linear' to describe traditional history is itself a pejorative misnomer. There is no history book that is accurately described by the term. Not even the most dedicated narrative historian writes in a strict linear sequence, with each event plotted in single file, one after the other. This is so obvious and so well known that, were it not for the straw man constructed by Carter, the issue would hardly be worth debating. Every narrative writer makes provision for events that happen not in sequence but simultaneously. Every time historians use that common term 'meanwhile' they are writing of events that have occurred at the same time as those they have just discussed, that is, events that obviously take place in a non-linear progression.

Not only this, but it has always been clear to historians that some phenomena operate on quite different time scales from others. Some events, such as the fate of individuals in politics, unfold very quickly, in days or weeks; while others, especially national issues such as economic status or military power, fluctuate in the medium term over years, while others still, for example supranational phenomena such as demographic patterns or religious beliefs, change at paces that are perceptible only over decades or the course of centuries. Historians, operating as far back as Edward Gibbon or even Tacitus, have always based their work on such non-linear assumptions.

CONVICTS AND EVIDENCE

One of Carter's principal aims in deploying his spatial history is to recover voices and experiences that have been lost to us through the selection processes of imperial history. Carter tells us that when historians compose their work they draw primarily on the writings of contemporary observers of the events under consideration. These writings are treated as primary sources, but because they themselves are, of necessity, partial, selective and value-impregnated, Carter says they should properly be regarded as secondary sources. Rather than constructing their case from first-hand evidence, he says, historians practise what is 'essentially a legitimation of selected earlier documents'.

As my own quotations from the First Fleet writers illustrate, even the primary sources consist largely of the narration of quotations and are themselves, in this sense, secondary. Quotations are the historian's raw facts. By arranging and narrating them, he not only constitutes certain documents of the past as 'authorities', but also earns his own writing the authority and legitimacy of history.[37]

He is particularly concerned to rescue the mentalities and dreams of the convicts who were transported to Australia from the British Isles and who constituted the colony's underclass for the first fifty years of settlement. Carter views the convicts as the main anti-establishment force in the new settlement. As such, they were not only anti-authoritarian and hard to discipline; their rebelliousness ran deeper, he claims, and derived from a rejection of Enlightenment empiricism and the imperialism that came in its train. Were it not so anachronistic, he might have claimed the convicts as the first Australian postmodernists: he says they invented fantastic stories, including one about an escape route to China; they not only subverted Enlightenment reason but held up an ironic mirror to it; they could 'parody the language of reason' and 'send up the pretensions of power'. Their intransigence 'was a rebuff to the Enlightenment boast that it could vindicate its world view empirically. It was a rebuff to the view that saw history occurring in a world already fully furnished with barracks, court-houses, prisons and roads'.[38]

Carter draws these conclusions despite his insistence that, in the conventional historical records, the immediate perspectives of the convicts have been lost. There are no narratives or journals written by convicts themselves recording their experience, he says. We can only view them through the 'distorting mirror' of the chronicles written by those in authority, the governors and officers who were drawn from and who shared the ideologies of the upper classes. From the perspective of authority, the convicts were barely human: 'these writers tend to treat the convicts as irrational beings little superior in either intellect or morals to the Aborigines'. Carter says that, because of this, we cannot have confidence in the descriptions of convicts provided by these traditional sources.

Is it likely then we can recover their history? The 'convict' who comes down to us in the pages of his oppressors is a social and political construction: he exists as a reflection of a body of rules, as a personification of transgression, a figure of speech necessary to the ruling class's self-justification and the perpetuation of its power. To let the convicts speak for themselves would have been to entertain the unthinkable: mutiny, another history.

There is another possibility, however, that Carter says can be grasped through the application of spatial history. By 'returning to Botany Bay reflectively' and by interpreting the accounts of the ruling-class chroniclers spatially:

we can recover from the Enlightenment logic of cause and effect something of what that logic suppressed. In particular, we may be able to recover that dimension of the convict's existence which imprisonment and transportation were specifically designed to exclude: his occupation of historical space. Recovering this lost space may not change the official history but, proposing another place, another Botany Bay, it does represent a timely mutiny against imperial history's methodological assumptions.[39]

In other words, the hitherto silenced voice of the convicts can at last find its tongue. By reading between the lines in a spatial way, the poststructuralist interpreter can open for us minds that would otherwise have remained locked forever.

It is little wonder that those who have heaped such lavish praise on Carter have all been novelists and literary theorists and that some historians who reviewed his book were full of scorn. The arrogance of Carter's claim to rescue the convicts from oblivion is equalled only by his total ignorance of what Australian historians have been writing for the last forty years. If ever there was a topic that has attracted those interested in history from below it is that of the Australian convicts. Unlike other anti-establishment nineteenth century characters such as England's Luddite machine breakers, whose total documentary legacy was a few threatening letters, the Australian convicts produced more documents recording, in their own words, their observations and activities, their dreams, hates and loves, than almost any other underclass in history. Moreover, there have been more history PhDs, lectureships and chairs in Australia earned from this source material than from almost any other single topic. The convicts have provided Australian academics with one of their major industries.

Carter's claim that the sources of the historians of the convict era all come from the officer classes, and are nothing better than secondary source narrations of quotations and partial observations, betrays that he knows next to nothing of the 'imperial' history he wants to overthrow. Russel Ward began collecting works written by the convicts themselves—their letters, poems and songs—in the 1940s and 50s. His landmark work, *The Australian Legend,* has been in print since 1958. Carter assumes, falsely, that all convicts were illiterate, but even for those of whom this was true there is still a wealth of material available that records their own voices. Historical archives hold so many volumes of transcripts of verbatim evidence given by convicts in court cases in both Britain and Australia that historians will probably never wade through them all. These transcripts record not only evidence from the trials from which the convicts were transported but even more fruitful and socially revealing material from civil matters in the colonies such as conflicts over property, divorce, licence applications and suits for injury and defamation. This evidence records the words of both the literate and the illiterate.

While it is true that those in authority responded to any sign of convict dissent with summary violence, Carter's claim that convicts were regarded as barely human is pure invention. The shortage of skills in the colonies meant convicts, while still under sentence, were appointed to a wide range of trade and professional positions—clerks, architects, builders, surgeons, musicians and artists—positions that demanded both literacy and responsibility. Historians have found enough evidence in existence to write studies of convict religious beliefs and of their differing attitudes to the Protestant and Catholic churches.

There is so much material available in the convicts' own words that lexicographers have been able to produce dictionaries devoted to convict or 'flash' slang. Convicts and ex-convicts alike wrote letters, journals, poems, songs and plays. At least eight convicts, mainly trade unionists and Irish nationalists who had been transported for political offences, wrote and published critical analyses of the convict system itself. Two convicts wrote novels that reached publication. One of these, *Quintus Servinton* (1830) by the convict Henry Savery, was the first novel published in book form in Australia. There is no form of literary output in which convicts are not represented.[40]

Against this great volume of sources, to which Carter appears completely oblivious, the best that his alternative history can offer is third-hand interpretations of the yarns, gossip and 'spatial fantasies' of convicts that he finds recorded in the published journals of colonial officers. If this is all that poststructuralism has to put in place of all the years of research accumulated by empirical historians, it is clear how much we stand to lose if Carter and the other exponents of cultural studies succeed in strangling the discipline with their theoretical ligatures.

ABORIGINES AND NARRATIVE

Another aspect of Australian history about which Carter says he has something dramatically new to offer is the study of Aboriginal society. As usual, he is confident that everyone before him who has approached this topic has got it all completely wrong. He thinks it is worse than mistaken to discuss Aborigines as if they were a dispossessed and subsequently disadvantaged underclass. Aborigines, he says, inhabit a different realm, which cannot be fathomed by the kind of history written by Europeans. The writers he most sharply rebukes are those whom many had regarded as the most sympathetic academic rescuers of the Aboriginal perspective: Henry Reynolds, who tracked down and compiled the evidence of Aboriginal resistance to the British occupation of their lands in the nineteenth century; and Stephen Muecke, the editor of an anthology of visual, oral and written works, who had attempted what Carter calls the 'editorial illusion' of presenting Aboriginal voices with no white intervention. Both emerge as imperial historians like all the rest.

To treat the Aborigines as an oppressed group within white society or for that matter to write of their history beyond the frontier, as if they were spirited opponents of white colonisation, is only to achieve by different means what Tench [one of the chroniclers of the First Fleet] and his colleagues had already done before: their appropriation to a white discourse, history. It is to suppose that the Aborigines moved in the same historical space as the Europeans—a space constituted culturally, according to social, economic and, above all, intellectual criteria. And, while this assumption may be made for the convicts, it is not valid for the Aborigines: we have no grounds for presuming that aboriginal history can be treated as a subset of white history, as a history within history.[41]

Works of this kind, says Carter, act to suppress the difference of Aboriginal history, 'a difference not simply of content but of form'. The critical issue that conceals this difference is, predictably, historians' linguistic blindness. 'The constitutional inability of imperial history to engage the Aborigines, to recognise the possibility of a different history, emerges in a variety of ways. But underlying them all, is the question of language.'[42] Carter, though he is white, English-educated and speaks no Aboriginal languages, nonetheless presents himself as the one who has the key to crack the code that has eluded everyone else. Thanks to poststructuralist linguistics, he has been permitted a vision denied to ordinary mortals. The Aborigines, he reveals, inhabit a 'genuinely oral and spatial culture', while Europeans are locked within a 'book-like, museum-like discourse of a culture that claims universal validity'.[43] Perhaps not so surprisingly, Carter decides that the Aboriginal cosmos fits very neatly into the same travelling logic he found inhabiting the other, non-Aboriginal characters of his book.

For theirs was a world of travelling, where succession, rather than stasis, was the natural order of things: succession as a spatial, rather than temporal, phenomenon. It was space which was problematic, the field of history and tactical address, not the metaphysical past and future. ... the Aborigine did not travel for the sake of seeing new countries, but in order to inhabit his own. If the white historian feels the need to validate his present by reliving the past, the Aborigine travelled in order to stay where he was.[44]

From this point, Carter goes on to argue that, despite the conceptual gulf, it remains possible for a white historian to write Aboriginal history. This could not, of course, be another version of imperial or empirical history: it would have to be spatial history.

An aboriginal history of space would, then, be a symbolic history. It would not be an anthropologist's account of the Aborigines' beliefs. Nor would it be a history of frontiers and massacres. Rather than seek by a newly ingenious means to translate the otherness of their experience into empirical terms, it might take the form of a meditation on the absent other of our own history.[45]

This Aboriginal history, he says, would begin 'in the recognition of the suppressed spatiality of our own historical consciousness'. But he emphasises that this kind of history would not actually discuss any of the *content* of our spatial experience. It would simply recognise the 'historically constitutive role' of our spatial experience. In other words, it would not describe the look and feel of spatial experience, but would confine itself to telling us how spatial experience is a very important factor in determining what history is. Carter says that a spatial history of the Aborigines would stand in a 'metaphorical relationship' to the history the Aborigines tell themselves. It would not be a book *about* the language of recollection, rather it would have to *enact* the language of recollection. For those who find this distinction rather enigmatic, Carter unfortunately does not offer any explanation. Instead, he goes on to conclude with a flourish: 'Such a history, giving back to metaphor its onto-logical role and recovering its historical space, would inevitably and properly be a poetic history.' Now, for the uninitiated, this is the kind of in-talk that any self-respecting treatise on cultural studies or postmodernism will regurgi-tate on cue. In saying that metaphor has 'an ontological role', Carter is mak-ing the stock claim that figures of speech have the ability to make what there is, to create reality, that the world is made of language.

But how does all this help us understand how to write Aboriginal history? Carter is nothing if not inventive. He tells us in the end that the 'Aboriginal history of space' he is elucidating would probably not even mention Aborigi-nes. Yes, he is serious.

A history of space which revealed the everyday world in which we live as the continuous intentional re-enactment of our spatial history might not say a word about 'The Aborigines'. But by recovering the intentional nature of our grasp on the world, it might evoke their historical experience without appropriating it to white ends.[46]

Those readers who follow Carter's thesis all the way and who come across this statement near the end of the book, might well reflect upon it and come to a conclusion that the author is too modest to suggest outright himself, but which he leaves lying there, none too carefully concealed, waiting to be discovered. If the faithful reader thinks long enough about which author could write a work to reveal the everyday world as the 'intentional re-enactment of our spatial history', or who could 'recover the intentional nature of our grasp on the world', he or she may well jump to the obvious conclusion: why, Paul Carter himself! And those who do this may then go one step further and realise that *the very book they have just read* fulfils all the criteria that the author has laid down. Just like the hypothetical book he recommends, his own is a 'meditation on the absent other'. It contains no facts about Aborigines, no attempt to describe their experiences. It is all theory about, rather than examples of, history writing. In other words, from very thin cover, Carter is advancing *The Road to Botany Bay* not only as a deconstruction of imperial history, but as the model for the first genuine work of Aboriginal history to be written by a white man.

Like most who inhabit the genre of poststructuralism, Carter advances his critiques of others from the high table of theory. Nowhere does he give the 'imperial' historians he denounces the sort of consideration I have afforded him here, with a lengthy exposition of their ideas backed by generous selections of verbatim quotations. He appears very reluctant to climb down among the rank and file and read closely, or indeed read very much of, what they have had to say. Had he done so—had he taken the trouble to study the nitty-gritty of the historiography of Aboriginal people in Australia over the last twenty-five years—he might have displayed less of his own illustrious ego on this topic.

The study of Aboriginal history has been largely a phenomenon of the period since 1970. At the end of the 1960s, most Australian history, despite its ostensibly nationalist concerns, had been defined by English historiography. Conservatives celebrated the British influence, tracing the development of parliamentary democracy, English law and British industriousness in this new environment. The Left was equally celebratory of British influences, but its champions were trade unions, the labour parties and English socialist and anti-imperialist writers. Only a minority broke from this pattern, notably Russel Ward in his study of the myths and culture of the lower orders and Manning Clark in his antipodean saga of Enlightenment secularism versus the Protestant and Catholic versions of Christianity.[47] At the time, hapless postgraduate students like myself, blown by the prevailing winds from the Left, tacked fruitlessly in search of local examples of working class heroes who could emulate those found in Britain by Edward Thomspon and Eric Hobsbawm. If ever there was an academic scene that deserved the postcolonial term Eurocentrism—or, more accurately, Anglocentrism—this was it. Into this manifestly evaporating pond in 1970 lobbed the book by Charles Rowley, *The Destruction of Aboriginal Society*.[48] Before Rowley, historians had confined Aborigines to the first few pages of their general surveys of Australia and, once 1788 was reached, allowed them to disappear. The great dramas of nineteenth century Australian history were all assumed to have taken place within the realm of the new arrivals: convicts versus jailers, gold diggers versus troopers, selectors versus squatters, labour versus capital. Without commenting at all on the pertinence of the existing picture, Rowley cut it down to size overnight. He showed what most people had assumed to have been small, isolated outbreaks of violence against blacks, coupled with some sporadic, pathetic gestures at welfare, actually formed a great unbroken arch of systematic brutality, dispossession and incarceration stretching from the late eighteenth century to the twentieth. Rowley redefined the great drama of Australian history as the conflict between Europeans and Aborigines. Since 1970, many other writers have come into the field and either added to or reshaped some of Rowley's themes. Rowley had drawn his sources primarily from government records and his work was essentially a European view. It was not until the early 1980s, especially with Henry Reynolds's breakthrough in discovering and deploying previously untouched evidence, that historians found it was possible to use Aboriginal voices to tell the story. Nonetheless, since Rowley's book was published, no one has seriously challenged his underlying revelation of an unbroken chain of self-perpetuating attitudes, policies and responses that whites have imposed upon blacks.

Before Rowley, Aboriginal people themselves knew of their treatment and their condition, including the massacre of many of their forebears, only as temporally isolated, unconnected events confined to local areas. The central methodological tool that enabled people to break free of these limited visions was narrative history. It was only when all these events were linked through the method of narrative that people could see what had been done across the whole of the continent and across the whole of the period since 1788. Once the basic narrative structure had been established, it created room for an explosion of interest and a booming academic publishing industry, which quickly grew impatient with the limitations of the predominantly European perspective that prevailed and which demanded a greater role for Aborigines themselves both in providing evidence and in writing the story.[49] It remains nonetheless true that all of these demands have been made within the paradigm established by Rowley. Without the kind of overarching narrative he provided, both Aborigines and Europeans alike would have lacked the means to see the portentous nature of their relationship. Today's political movement by Aboriginal people for restitution of their position would have lacked its most compelling argument.

Where, we might well ask, would Aboriginal understanding be if all they had ever found in the writings of historians was the Paul Carter brand of non-empirical, anti-narrative, spatial discourse? What would Aborigines say about white academics who wrote so-called 'Aboriginal history' that was more intent on exploring the arcane linguistics of French theory than condescending to describe the real experiences of real people?

I HAVE NOT devoted so much space in this book to discussing *The Road to Botany Bay* because I think it is intellectually formidable in any way. On the contrary, it is replete with so many self-contradictions, factual inaccuracies and trite interpretations, and is so continuously and odiously pretentious, that it is hard to take seriously. However, to be taken seriously is what it deserves, for it displays all the characteristics of the methodological approaches that have now surged to the front in history, not to mention in the other humanities and social sciences. These methodologies are based on the discovery that contemporary literary analysis provides an attractive, new, fast track to academic prominence. Tackling the major issues of human experience no longer requires the hard work of steeping yourself in the writings of all those practitioners of your discipline who have gone before you, and then putting in the even harder slog of doing your own original research. Instead, all you need do is take a small selection of the more prominent and familiar authors, label them in terms used by the currently fashionable theoretical guru, add some linguistic speculations about the textuality of everything, and then wait for the self-same guru or his acolytes to recognise your genius and lavish you with hyperbole. With this kind of inside running, and with the empirical method still plodding along its own slow and arduous turf, it is no surprise the smart money is on the new favourite.

It should also be clear from Carter's book how trenchant is the opposition these littérateurs have to those who still practise empirical methods. The work of the latter is automatically dismissed as being of utterly no consequence. One of the characteristics of history teaching until the past decade was that most academic departments felt an obligation to provide a reasonable spread of political opinion for students. Even at the height of the Cold War, when most new lecturers who joined Australian arts faculties fitted the then-dominant conservative mould, there were enough leftists appointed to inject some alternative views into the most reactionary subject stream. The postmodern ascendancy has no such scruples. As his book so pointedly demonstrates, Carter and those like him regard members of the traditional discipline not as peers whose different politics and perspectives may be tolerated, but as people operating with such a deeply flawed set of assumptions that they would be better off in institutions for the feeble minded.

In this environment, the prospects of a new, younger generation being attracted to empirical history dwindle all the time. The shrinking rewards on offer today to academics in the humanities are going elsewhere. Empirical work is a visibly deteriorating path to research grants, publication, conferences and academic employment. Unless all this changes dramatically, the retirement dinners given to the current generation of traditional historians, now mostly middle-aged and older, will represent the funeral of their discipline.

1 Paul Carter, *The Road to Botany Bay: An Essay in Spatial History*, Faber and Faber, London, 1987

2 Paul Carter, *Living in a New Country: History, Travelling and Language*, Faber and Faber, London, 1992

3 Paul Carter, *The Sound in Between: Voice, Space, Performance*, NSW University Press and New Endeavour Press, Sydney, 1992

4 Paul Carter, *The Road to Botany Bay*, p 158

5 Paul Carter, *Living in a New Country*, p 26

6 Reviewers included: Manning Clark, *Sydney Morning Herald*, 12 December 1987; Russel Ward, *The Australian*, 5 December 1987; Barry Hill, *Times on Sunday*, 13 December 1987; Peter Porter, *Times Literary Supplement*, 27 November 1987; Jennifer Breen, *Times Educational Supplement*, 4 December 1987; Clive James, *London Review of Books*, 18 February 1988; David Malouf (ABC Radio interview), *Thesis Eleven*, No. 22, 1989

7 Paul Carter, *The Road to Botany Bay*, p 160

8 Paul Carter, *The Road to Botany Bay*, p 22

9 Paul Carter, *The Road to Botany Bay*, p xvi

10 Paul Carter, *The Road to Botany Bay*, pp xxii–xxiii

11 Paul Carter, *The Road to Botany Bay*, p xxiv

12 Paul Carter, *The Road to Botany Bay*, p xxiii

13 Paul Carter, *The Road to Botany Bay*, p xxiv

14 Paul Carter, *The Road to Botany Bay*, p 36

15 Paul Carter, *The Road to Botany Bay*, p 50

16 Paul Carter, *The Road to Botany Bay*, p 349

17 Paul Carter, *The Road to Botany Bay*, p 33

18 Paul Carter, *The Road to Botany Bay*, p 16

19 Paul Carter, *The Road to Botany Bay*, pp 16–18

20 Paul Carter, *The Road to Botany Bay*, p 18

21 Paul Carter, *The Road to Botany Bay*, p 20

22 Paul Carter, *The Road to Botany Bay*, p 32

23 Paul Carter, *The Road to Botany Bay*, p 69

24 Paul Carter, *The Road to Botany Bay*, pp 184–6

25 Paul Carter, *The Road to Botany Bay*, p 187

26 Paul Carter, *The Road to Botany Bay*, p 189

27 Paul Carter, *The Road to Botany Bay*, p 189

28 Paul Carter, *The Road to Botany Bay*, p 190

29 Paul Carter, *The Road to Botany Bay*, p 140

30 The most recent and accessible bibliography is B. H. Fletcher and J. M. Powell, 'Land Settlement', in D. H. Borchardt (ed.), *Australians: A Guide to Sources*, in the series *Australians: A Historical Library*, Fairfax, Syme and Weldon, Sydney, 1987, Chapter 25

31 Paul Carter, *The Road to Botany Bay*, p xxiv

32 George R. Stewart, *Names on the Land: A Historical Account of Place-Naming in the United States*, Houghton Mifflin, Boston, 1958, p 12

33 Adrian Desmond and James Moore, *Darwin*, Michael Joseph, London, 1991

34 Paul Carter, *The Road to Botany Bay*, pp xiv, xvi

35 Paul Carter, *The Road to Botany Bay*, p 18

36 Paul Carter, *The Road to Botany Bay*, pp xiv–xv

37 Paul Carter, *The Road to Botany Bay*, p 325

38 Paul Carter, *The Road to Botany Bay*, p 317

39 Paul Carter, *The Road to Botany Bay*, p 295

40 The most recent survey of convict writings and of literature about the convict system is A. G. L. Shaw, 'Transportation of Convicts', in D. H. Borchardt (ed.), *Australians: A Guide to Sources,* Chapter 23; for an analysis and dictionary of convict slang see Robert Langker, *Flash in New South Wales 1788–1850*, Australian Language Research Centre, University of Sydney, Occasional Paper No. 18, September 1980

41 Paul Carter, *The Road to Botany Bay*, p 325

42 Paul Carter, *The Road to Botany Bay*, p 332

43 Paul Carter, *The Road to Botany Bay*, p 333

44 Paul Carter, *The Road to Botany Bay*, p 336

45 Paul Carter, *The Road to Botany Bay*, p 350

46 Paul Carter, *The Road to Botany Bay*, p 350

47 Russel Ward, *The Australian Legend,* Oxford University Press, Oxford, 1958; C. M. H. Clark, *A History of Australia*, Vol. 1, Melbourne University Press, Melbourne, 1962

48 C. D. Rowley, *The Destruction of Aboriginal Society*, Australian National University Press, Canberra, 1970

49 For a survey and bibliography of this literature, see Ann McGrath and Andrew Markus, 'European Views of Aborigines', in D. H. Borchardt (ed.), *Australians: A Guide to Sources,* Chapter 15

5

THE DISCOURSES OF MICHEL FOUCAULT

POSTSTRUCTURALISM AND ANTI-HUMANISM

MICHEL FOUCAULT deserves an extensive treatment in this book because he is the French theorist who has contributed most to the directions history is now taking. While almost all of his underlying ideas derive from those of the nineteenth century German philosopher Friedrich Nietzsche and his successor, Martin Heidegger, Foucault himself has been very influential, first, in reviving these ideas in France in the 1960s and, second, in transmitting them to the English-speaking academic scene in the 1970s and 1980s. Many of the radical claims about history discussed in earlier chapters have come to be widely countenanced because of the intellectual climate created by Foucault. As a professor of history, Foucault contributed to two distinct fields. One was the history of ideas, the other the history of institutions such as asylums, prisons and hospitals. It was through history that he rendered many of the concepts of his two German mentors palatable, by translating their philosophical abstractions into a more worldly realm.

Foucault's influence on history in English-speaking countries can be seen clearly today in the sort of topics that now attract researchers. Pick up the current edition of an academic history journal in the United States, United Kingdom or Australia and you are likely to find articles that derive from the agenda he established. This includes the study of insanity, psychiatry, medicine, criminology, penology, the rise of the professions, sexuality, 'the body' and, especially, criminals, sexual deviants and other individuals living on the margins of society. Foucault and his followers all take the view that, far from being marginal, society's outcasts hold the key to understanding the mainstream.

Although he has had an influence on most of the disciplines within the humanities and social sciences, history was Foucault's defined area of expertise. From 1970 until his death from AIDS in 1984, he was Professor of History and Systems of Thought at the *Collège de France,* one of France's most prestigious educational institutions. However, anyone who comes to his work with expectations derived from their reading of traditional histories will find his work anything but familiar. As one of his interpreters has written:

Foucault offers a new way of thinking about history, writing history and deploying history in current political struggles... Foucault is an anti-historical historian, one who in writing history, threatens every canon of the craft.[1]

Foucault's writings include *Madness and Civilisation* (1961),[2] which is a history of responses to insanity and the growth of the psychiatric profession; *The Birth of the Clinic* (1963),[3] a study of the history of medicine in the eighteenth and nineteenth centuries; *The Order of Things* (1966),[4] and *The Archaeology of Knowledge* (1969),[5] which are both books on the methodology of the history of ideas; *Discipline and Punish* (1975),[6] a history of the origins of prisons in the nineteenth century; a three-volume work entitled *The History of Sexuality* (1976–79); and two books on individuals, one about a nineteenth century triple murderer, the other about a nineteenth century hermaphrodite.[7] He also wrote a number of articles on the methodology of studying human affairs and, once he had attained celebrity status, he published his views in the form of interviews. The best-known English-language versions of the latter are *Language, Counter-Memory, Practice* (1977),[8] *Power/Knowledge* (1980)[9] and *Foucault Live* (1989).[10]

THE MAKING OF A RADICAL CELEBRITY

The English translation of *Discipline and Punish* appeared in 1975 and turned Foucault from a French identity into an international celebrity. He was particularly welcomed by a number of the radical groups that had emerged in the late 1960s and early 1970s, which found his ideas were just what they needed to give their causes some intellectual substance.

Foucault's appeal derived from his stance as a radical but a non-Marxist. Although the movements of students and anti-Vietnam War activists in the 1960s promoted a great revival of Marxist ideas within the universities, some of the other radicals who emerged found the central tenets of Marxism difficult to follow. In particular, movements of radical feminists, homosexuals, prisoner activists, ex-psychiatric patients and other marginalised minorities were not impressed by the Marxist concept that the leading role in history was to be played by the industrial working class. Radical feminists saw the working class as a phenomenon defined by male theorists and dominated by men. They found in Foucault a more androgynous theory. Gay liberationists found that not only was Foucault one of their own but that he had a theoretical approach that rejected universal norms, including those that defined heterosexuality as the social ideal. To political activists inside prisons and other institutions who could see little point in joining political parties or trade unions, Foucault said that local struggles, not universal programs such as socialist revolution, were the real stuff of resistance.

To those members of the academic Left of the Vietnam War era who regarded Marxism as contaminated by its connection with the USSR, Foucault offered an attractive alternative. He saw the main struggle against modern society being carried out by those groups with whom many former student radicals still identified: the deviants and the outcasts. As it became increasingly difficult in the 1980s for even the most devoted Sixties radical to believe that Marxism could offer either a plausible critique of or a political alternative to bourgeois society, Foucault's popularity grew. For those who were prepared to overlook some of his bizarre political judgements—including his public defence of the Ayatollah Khomeini's bloody purges in post-revolutionary Iran, even while the regime executed homosexuals—Foucault provided an alternative system of thought and a convenient package of esoteric slogans through which the radicals' loathing for the bourgeoisie could be sustained.

Foucault's approach, moreover, was peculiarly suited to the university environment. He held that the main revolutionary struggle was not against political or economic institutions; rather the true radicals were those who challenged the major Western philosophies or 'systems of thought'. This was a radicalism perfectly suited to practice in the academic realm of tutorials, conferences, cafes and bars. There was no longer any need to do anything as concrete or practical as working for political parties or trade unions, going on strike or demonstrating in the streets. Instead, followers of Foucault could spend their time reading, debating and writing their criticisms of the academic disciplines of philosophy, history, sociology, criminology and psychiatry. None of this, Foucault argued, was a less practical or inferior variety of politics. 'Theory', Foucault declared , 'does not express, translate, or serve to apply practice: it is practice'.[11]

ANTI-HUMANISM AND THE PRIMACY OF LANGUAGE

Much of the notice Foucault initially attracted derived from his ability to coin the striking phrase. The most notorious was his declaration, at the end of his 1966 book, *The Order of Things,* of 'the death of man'. His obvious allusion to

Nietzsche's proclamation of 'the death of God' drew a considerable degree of attention both to himself and to the then-burgeoning school of anti-humanist philosophy.

Foucault meant by 'the death of man' that humanist philosophy had now been overthrown. Although, as we shall see, Foucault's attempts to define humanism leave a great deal to be desired, there is a clear enough core to the concept. Humanists have long shared a commitment to the idea that man himself, the human subject—understood as man's consciousness and will—is the originator of human actions and understanding. The notions of individual freedom and individual responsibility, and the philosophies that support them, have long been based upon it. However, according to Foucault, this movement had now run its course. His proclamation was based not only on his own rejection of this 'philosophy of man' but on its demise from its position at the centre of contemporary thought and culture. The humanism of the modern era had been toppled by the anti-humanism of the postmodern.

One of anti-humanism's central philosophical claims is that humanism's belief in the autonomy of the subject is an illusion. The two characteristics of 'the subject' that come under strongest attack are those of *free will* and *consciousness*. From a humanist perspective, the individual is a free agent who normally weighs up the issues confronting him and makes his own, rational decision about what to do. The anti-humanist rejects this as naive, for it omits the dimension of the unconscious. The concept of the unconscious, which originated in mid-nineteenth century German philosophy, has allowed anti-humanists to proclaim that the entire humanist tradition has been wrong to assign to the conscious mind the central role in the functioning of a human being. They believe that the unconscious is the dominant influence on behaviour and thought, and that we must abandon the assumption that purposive action is consciously directed. Hence, we must reject our belief in the autonomy of the individual subject.

Foucault also insists that we have to abandon the common sense assumption that there is a real world outside ourselves and that we can have knowledge about it. This is another illusion of humanism, he claims. Our minds are confined to the realm of our language. Though he shares this assumption with structuralist theory, Foucault denied he was a structuralist. He took the 'primacy of language' thesis straight from Nietzsche. Through language, Nietzsche contended, human beings imposed their own arbitrary constructions of meaning on what would otherwise be nothing but chaos. If we could think of the world beyond our minds, Nietzschean philosophy holds, there would be none of our categories, causes, or hierarchies, and none of the boundaries that we think separate one realm of existence from another. We create these things and fashion these forms of order through language. Moreover, we should not think that our language reflects reality in any way, or that the words we use correspond in some direct sense to objects in the world outside. We have no way of knowing about any such reality. All we have access to are the words and meanings we create ourselves which are, of necessity, distortions of whatever reality might be. From this perspective, those who are influential enough to define the concepts of an era consequently define the sense of reality held by their fellow human beings. If we accept this, theory can indeed be practice.

DISCOURSE, GENEALOGY AND POSTMODERNISM

Two of Foucault's major projects in the 1960s were devoted to the history of ideas, or what he called the history of 'systems of thought'. They were examinations of how theory, especially as expressed in philosophy and the social sciences, had defined and influenced the major epochs of the recent past. As a follower of Nietzsche, Foucault accepts the concept of historical categories and the idea that thought is intrinsically linked to the dimension of time. However, he rejects the idea that history revealed any continuum or pattern of development. The concepts used by other historians of ideas to express the notion of people learning from others or building upon the ideas of those before them—described by terms such as 'tradition', 'influence', 'development', 'evolution'—are all dismissed by Foucault. In laying down another axiom of poststructuralism, Foucault says there is no sense of forward movement or progress in the history of ideas, only discontinuities: the ideas of one era are not an improvement on those of the past, only different.

The books, *The Order of Things* and *The Archaeology of Knowledge,* put forward Foucault's notions about how we are to understand the history of ideas. Like many continental philosophers, Foucault makes it difficult for the reader to understand what is going on, and what is going wrong, in these books by insisting on using his own 'private' version of words in ways that are often at variance with their 'public' uses. So, I will try to provide an exegesis of both books via an explanation of his terminology.

Archaeology: Foucault has used this word in the names of three of his books. *The Birth of the Clinic* is subtitled 'An archaeology of medical perception'. The subtitle of *The Order of Things* is 'An archaeology of the human sciences'. Foucault's term 'archaeology' bears little relationship to the excavation of ancient tombs and buried cities. It is a metaphor for 'digging deep' into the underlying rules and assumptions of the human sciences. It is also a metaphor designed to suggest that other theorists who have written about the history of ideas have so far been more superficial. Foucault is trying to analyse what he sees as the unconscious rules of formation that regulate the emergence of the human sciences. 'It is these rules of formation, which were never formulated in their own right, but are to be found only in widely differing theories, concepts and objects of study that I have tried to reveal, by isolating, as their specific locus, a level that I have called ... archaeological.'[12]

Despite his adoption of this metaphor, one of Foucault's main conclusions in *The Archaeology of Knowledge* is that there are no deep truths to be found. Scientific theories and concepts of history have not produced any process that might count as a pattern underlying thought. Nor is there anything like an evolutionary process at work within human reason, as grand theorists such as Hegel argued. Each historical era simply has its own way of thinking. The thought of each era is 'discontinuous'. Each new era is defined by a 'transformation' in thought that owes nothing to the preceding era. There is no underlying law, model or unity to be discovered that might unite historical eras. All that exists is a 'multiplicity of discourses'.

Episteme: In *The Order of Things* Foucault employs the term 'episteme' to refer to an era that is defined by a structure of thought. He is not referring to any specific content of this thought, only to 'the totality of relations that can be discovered for a given period, between the sciences' when they are examined to see what methods they have in common. Foucault describes three epistemes in the recent past: the Renaissance; the classical age or Enlightenment; and the modern age. He also writes of a fourth, future age which can only be seen now as 'a light on the horizon'. The Renaissance could be defined by its assumption of the resemblance between words and things. The classical age was an era in which all the sciences were dominated by systems of classification, but in which there was no science of man himself. The modern episteme is the age of humanist philosophy and of the invention of the human sciences.

In *The Order of Things*, Foucault lays down two principles about epistemes. First, each era can have only one of them: 'in any given culture and at any given moment, there is always only one episteme that defines the conditions of possibility of all knowledge.' Second, each episteme is 'discontinuous' with the next, so that from one era to another 'things are no longer perceived, described, expressed, characterised, classified, and known in the same way'.[13] The task of the historian of ideas, or rather the historian of the episteme, is to examine the writings of the period, not for the knowledge they tried to establish but for what their work reveals of the episteme itself. In other words, the historian should read the works of nineteenth century intellectuals, even those as different as Charles Darwin, Cardinal Newman and Karl Marx, not for what they said in their different fields, but for what their common assumptions and methods reveal about their era. In this way, the historian can uncover 'a sort of great, uniform text, which has never before been articulated, and which reveals for the first time what men "really meant" '.[14] However, the idea of one great text lying underneath and directing everything later struck Foucault as 'totalitarian' and 'mortifying'. His next book abandoned the term 'episteme', and substituted the concept of the 'discursive formation'.

Discourse and discursive formations: In *The Archaeology of Knowledge*, Foucault retracts some of his previous work and says he had not been trying to show that 'from a certain moment and for a certain time' everyone thought in the same way or that 'everyone accepted a number of fundamental theses'. He now uses the term 'discursive formation' to describe the historic eras he had previously called epistemes. He also abandons the metaphor of depth in his text (though he retains it for the title). He says he is no longer studying 'underlying' ideas or 'foundations' of thought, nor looking for 'a secret discourse, animating the manifest discourse from within'.[15] Everything is now on the surface.

A discursive formation is composed of the statements that may be made in the 'discourses' of an era. 'Discourse' is one of the most recurrent terms in the works of Foucault and, especially, of his followers. Sometimes he indicates it corresponds to what we would know as an academic discipline: 'thus I... speak of clinical discourse, economic discourse, the discourse of natural history, psychiatric discourse.'[16] But part of his aim is to reject the conventional nomenclature that defines academic disciplines into separate categories such as 'science', 'literature', 'philosophy' or 'history'. He wants to show that these apparently disparate fields share common assumptions once they are analysed from his archaeological perspective. The discourses that go to make up a discursive formation are statements made in various fields of study within an era. A discursive formation can be identified by the fact that the statements made within it all belong to a single system. An archaeological analysis is now one that is undertaken not to reveal any underlying meaning but simply to describe the existing discourses of an era and to identify what they have in common.

Despite all this change of nomenclature, however, there is very little change in content. There is as much discontinuity between discursive formations as there was between epistemes. From one era to the next, the conventions of each field of study undergo a major shift. The 'discursive formation' of the modern era remains for Foucault the one that is dominated by the assumptions of humanist philosophy and the human sciences.

As a postscript to this section, two related and recurring terms used by Foucault and his followers may be noted: 'discursive practices' and 'non-discursive practices'. For the uninitiated these mean nothing more than, respectively, 'statements, speech and writings made by people' and 'actions taken by groups or institutions'. A discursive formation is composed of discursive practices. Foucault is forced to admit that non-discursive practices—those of institutions such as the Church, the military and the university—do have lives that extend across several ages and thus straddle more than one discursive formation. The implication of this implausible position is that institutions and institutional practices can be continuous from one era to another but the statements and ideas related to them are strictly discontinuous.

Genealogy: In the 1970s, Foucault shelved 'archaeology' as a description of his work and adopted that of 'genealogy'. This marked his emergence as a militant critic not only of modern philosophy but of modern society itself. 'Genealogy' is a concept derived from Nietzsche's work, *On the Genealogy of Morals*, where the idea of the objectivity of science is dismissed: there is '*only a perspective seeing, only a perspective knowing*'.[17] Foucault combined this idea with those in another of Nietzsche's books, *The Will to Power*, to argue that not only was all so-called scientific knowledge subjective but that it was a 'tool of power' in the hands of those who formulated it. In 'archaeology', the task was to analyse the content of a discourse; in 'genealogy' the task is to analyse who uses discourse and for what ends. In his new, militant phase, moreover, Foucault declares that the genealogical method is 'anti-science' and that it is waging a struggle 'against the effects of the power of discourse that is considered to be scientific'.

In a theme similar to Marxism's support for the working class, Foucault's genealogy claims to serve a different but still oppressed group, the deviants and the afflicted. Again, in parallel with Marxism, Foucault argues that theories which call themselves scientific are not disinterested but are linked to relations of authority. However, unlike Marx who believed that some knowledge could be objective (notably, that of his own writings), Foucault goes on to insist that knowledge and power are always and necessarily interdependent. A site where power is enforced is also a site where knowledge is produced; and conversely, a site from which knowledge is derived is a place where power is exercised. In *Discipline and Punish* he wants to show the prison as an example of just such a site of power, and as a place where knowledge essential to the modern social sciences was formed. Reciprocally, the ideas from which the social sciences were formulated were also the ones that gave birth to the prison. The belief that a scientist can arrive at an objective conclusion, Foucault argues, is one of the great fallacies of the modern, humanist era.

Modern humanism is therefore mistaken in drawing this line between knowledge and power. Knowledge and power are integrated with one another, and there is no point of dreaming of a time when knowledge will cease to depend on power; this is just a way of reviving humanism in a utopian guise. It is not possible for power to be exercised without knowledge. It is impossible for knowledge not to engender power.[18]

So, instead of referring to 'power' and 'knowledge' separately, he prefers the compound term 'power/knowledge'.

Foucault defines the principal methodology of the genealogist as that of history. In fact, he calls the genealogist 'the new historian'.[19] The role he prescribes for this new historian is essentially political: to foster the 'insurrection of subjugated knowledges', which are opposed to 'the centralising powers which are linked to the institution and functioning of an organised scientific discourse within a society such as ours'.[20] In the early 1970s, he said this 'insurrection' was being led by those outcast groups who were then engaged in struggles against authority, especially psychiatric patients and prisoners. At the time he proclaimed these ideas, Foucault himself became engaged in the radical prison activist movement, attending meetings and offering advice. He argued that the 'local knowledges' of groups such as prisoners were crude responses to their immediate situation. These groups lacked an historical understanding of others who had responded similarly. So their demands needed to be supplemented by the interpretations of a sympathetic academic such as himself, to unite what he called his 'erudite, historical knowledges' with the 'disqualified knowledges' of the outcasts. This union would produce what he called 'subjugated knowledge' or a 'historical knowledge of struggles', that is, a genealogy formidable enough to challenge the power of those sciences that had sided with authority.[21]

Postmodern politics: Foucault never used the term 'postmodern' to describe his work, but some of his interpreters have argued that he was one of the first radicals to break with the revolutionary socialist tradition and to introduce a postmodern approach to politics.[22] In place of the Marxist claim that modern history represents one big struggle between the working class and the middle class, Foucault argues for a multiplicity of independent struggles. Rather than conflict taking place at the heart of the economy, between labour and capital, Foucault sees conflicts diffused throughout the microlevels of society, in prisons, asylums, hospitals and schools. In place of macropolitical forces battling for control of the source of central power in society—the state—Foucault substitutes a postmodern concept of micropolitics where local groups contest decentralised forms of power.

Hence there is no single locus of great Refusal, no soul of revolt, source of all rebellions, or pure law of the revolutionary. Instead there is a plurality of resistances, each of them a special case.[23]

In taking this position, Foucault rejects most of the central concepts of Western radical politics. He rejects the idea of liberation or emancipation because it implies there is some inherent human essence waiting to be freed. He thinks the idea that there is a 'human essence' is one of the illusions of humanism. He rejects the concept of ideology and its assumption that false consciousness, which enshrouds the minds of the populace, can be replaced by a true consciousness. There are no truths to discover, Foucault believes, only different perspectives to take. He also rejects the notion of political revolution based on the large-scale transformation of society following the overthrow of the central state. The bases of power come not from the centre, he argues, but from the 'capillary' levels of the political body. From these outer levels, power flows to the larger, centralised structures, just as the blood flows from the capillaries to the central organs. Hence, without changes to the outer, local sources of power, changes made at the centre will be ineffectual. Postmodern politics holds that because power is decentralised and pluralised, so too must be the forms of political struggle. And since all forms of power are based on who defines the 'knowledge' that prevails at the outer levels, political struggle is largely a matter of the redefinition of local knowledge by those who are subjugated, assisted by sympathetic academics such as Foucault. Hence postmodern politics can be conducted more effectively through debate than through action.

There is one area, however, where Foucault demonstrably fails to break with the Western revolutionary tradition. Every grand scheme to transform society that has ever been dreamed up by an intellectual or academic has always given a major role to intellectuals and academics themselves. Foucault rejects the idea of the 'universal intellectual' who claims to represent or speak on behalf of the oppressed masses in order to institute a new world order. Instead, he substitutes the idea of the 'specific intellectual' who advises the locals to help them with their immediate struggle. However, the essential role for the intellectual is different in nominal terms only. In Marxist theory, the proletarian masses need the universal intellectual to inform them of their historic mission and to help them realise it; in Foucault's version of politics, more specific groups, such as prisoners, identify their own immediate issues but still cannot define their historic significance nor conduct an effective resistance without the intervention of the intellectual. Despite his support for a less centralised politics, Foucault's postmodern intellectual still wants to be the centre of attention, just like all the radical intellectuals who have gone before him.

TRUTHS AND KNOWLEDGES

Before making a critique of Foucault's writings on the history of ideas, there is one issue about his overall approach that deserves to be raised. This is the relativism of his concepts of truth and knowledge. Foucault insists, whether he is talking about epistemes, discursive formations, or genealogies, that throughout history there is no accumulation of knowledge. There are only discontinuities. The thought of one era is not better, not *more knowledgeable*, than another, only different. Foucault is led to this position by Nietzsche who always insisted that progress was an illusion. If he were to admit that one era learns from, and builds upon, the work of its predecessors, then he would let the idea of progress into history, which is the last thing an adherent of Nietzsche would want to do. However, the consequence of rejecting the idea of the growth of knowledge is to be forced to claim that knowledge is relative to particular historic eras. Each era, Nietzsche and Foucault both assert, devises its own truths and its own knowledges.

Foucault also argues that knowledge is relative not only to historic eras but to social groups as well. Within each discursive formation, or each historic era, different social groups can have their own versions of knowledge, even if they are mutually inconsistent. Those who have power generate the kind of knowledge that they need to maintain their power; those who are subject to this power need their own, alternative kinds of knowledge in order to resist. Foucault is also committed to a relative concept of truth. Truth for him is not something absolute that everyone must acknowledge but merely what counts as true within a particular discourse.

Each society has its regime of truth, its 'general politics' of truth: that is, the types of discourse which it accepts and makes function as true; the mechanisms and instances which enable one to distinguish true and false statements, the means by which each is sanctioned; the techniques and procedures accorded value in the acquisition of truth; the status of those who are charged with saying what counts as true.[24]

However, it is not difficult to show that a relativist concept of truth of this kind is untenable. If what is true is always relative to a particular society, there are no propositions that can be true across all societies. However, this means that Foucault's own claim cannot be true for all societies. So he contradicts himself. What he says cannot be true at all.

The relativist fallacy also applies to the concept of knowledge. One cannot hold that there are alternative, indeed competing, forms of knowledge, as Foucault maintains. Inherent in the concept of knowledge is that of truth. One can only know something if it is true. If something is not true, or even if its truth status is uncertain, one cannot know it. To talk, as Foucault does, of opposing knowledges is to hold that there is one set of truths that runs counter to another set of truths. It is certainly possible to talk about *beliefs* or *values* that may be held in opposition by the authorities and by their subjects, since neither beliefs nor values necessarily entail truth. But Foucault's idea that there are knowledges held by the centralising powers that are opposed to the subjugated knowledges of the oppressed is an abuse of both logic and language.

Despite its logical untenability, the genealogical method holds a great attraction for Foucault and his followers. In debates with their opponents, especially if the opponent is a 'positivist' or a 'piecemeal empiricist', they hold what they believe is an unassailable position by focusing on *who* is speaking rather than on *what* is being said. They use the genealogical method to absolve themselves from the need to examine the content of any statement. All they see the need to do is examine the conditions of its production—not 'is it true?' but 'who made the statement and for what reasons?'. This is a tactic that is well known in Marxist circles where, to refute a speaker, one simply identifies his class position and ignores what he actually says. If someone can be labelled 'bourgeois' everything this person says will simply reflect the ideology of that class.

The Foucauldian version is little different. In debate, any question about the facts of a statement is ignored and the focus is directed to the way what is said reflects the prevailing 'discursive formation' or how it is a form of knowledge that serves the power of the authorities concerned. One of the reasons for Foucault's popularity in the university environment is that he offers such tactics to his followers—tactics which should be regarded as the negation of the traditional aims of the university: the gaining of knowledge and the practise of scholarship. Foucault's influence on the type of academic debate so frequently found today should be a matter of great concern. Instead of talk about real issues, all we get is talk about talk. Instead of debates based on evidence and reason, all we get is a retreat to a level of abstraction where enough is assumed to have been said when one has identified the epistemological position of one's opponent.

HUMANISM AND THE DEATH OF MAN

Apart from the example provided by his methodology, Foucault's main claim to influencing the history of ideas, or, as he prefers to call it, the history of systems of thought, has been his identification of the three major epistemes, or discursive formations, of recent history, plus his critique of humanism. As recorded at the start of this chapter, the three discursive formations correspond to the Renaissance, the classical age or Enlightenment, and the modern era. The critique of humanism, celebrated by Foucault as 'the death of man', marks the end of the modern age. Humanism, as noted earlier, is the philosophy that holds that the human subject is fully self-conscious and acts in an autonomous way, according to reason. Anti-humanism emphasises the influence of the unconscious on behaviour and claims that the human mind is not free but is locked within the structures of language.

As an account of the major systems of thought of the periods he defines,

Foucault's thesis contains a number of problems which he never resolves. In a 1967 interview on *The Order of Things,* Foucault acknowledges an observation made by his questioner about 'the absence of detailed notes and bibliographies, accumulated and acknowledged references, customary for this kind of work'. By abandoning the normal scholarly apparatus of footnotes, references and bibliographies, Foucault can talk about the terminology and concepts of other writers without detailing the texts and pages to which he is referring. By not tying himself to the customary conventions, he can make his work wide ranging, but at the same time he runs the risk of becoming so imprecise that it is difficult to know exactly to whom or what he refers when he cites certain philosophical tendencies and assumptions. This not only becomes a problem for the reader trying to follow all his allusions, but it becomes a problem for Foucault himself because it leads him to use several key terms and concepts in different and contrary ways.

In *The Order of Things,* and in the interpretations offered by his followers, the normal, careful reader can interpret Foucault as saying that there is a correlation between the modern age and humanist philosophy. The modern age, Foucault says, 'begins around 1790–1810 and goes to around 1950'.[25] Humanist philosophy, he indicates at one point in *The Order of Things,*[26] began with Immanuel Kant and the publication in 1781 of *Critique of Pure Reason* in which Kant argued that the objects of the external world only become real when the human mind focuses on them, and that human understanding is, in Kant's words, 'the lawgiver of nature'. However, in interviews that discuss the same book, Foucault talks about humanism beginning some one hundred years later, at the end of the nineteenth century.

The humanist movement dates from the end of the nineteenth century... When one looks rather closely at the culture of the sixteenth, seventeenth and eighteenth centuries, one can see that man literally had no place in it. Culture at the time was busy with God, the world, the resemblance of things, the laws of space, and also of course the body, the passions, the imagination. But man himself was entirely absent.[27]

This statement conflicts not only with the views he has expressed about Kant, but with the normal public uses of the concept of 'man'. The culture of the eighteenth century, when Foucault claims 'man' was 'entirely absent', produced several momentous testimonies to the presence of just this concept, including Tom Paine's *The Rights of Man,* the French Declaration of the Rights of Man, and the Constitution of the Republic of the United States of America. It also conflicts with the works of some of Foucault's mentors, notably Heidegger, who saw the philosophical emergence of the concept of self-conscious man in the writings of René Descartes in the mid-seventeenth century. Two of Foucault's most incisive French critics, Luc Ferry and Alain

Renaut, argue that Foucault is not unaware of objections like these. Thus all he can be allowed to mean by the claim that humanism dates from the end of the nineteenth century is that the human sciences that have man as an object of study, such as sociology, anthropology and psychology, date from this period. 'But in that case', they ask, 'why not say that in the seventeenth century the sciences of man did not yet exist? That might have been less striking than saying that man was entirely absent at the time, but the formulation would have been more accurate'.[28]

There are more problems about the definition of humanism itself. Foucault says at one stage that 'those most responsible for contemporary humanism are obviously Hegel and Marx'. It is difficult to understand what he means by labelling these two as humanists. Hegel's philosophy was an idealism that believed the ultimate reality was spiritual and that history was the unfolding of mind or spirit. Marx's philosophy was materialist, which held that there was an objective world beyond the human mind and that history was a real-life struggle between social classes. These opposing, religious-versus-materialist world views shared two things: the use of a dialectical method that, in itself, hardly rates as a 'humanism'; and the fact that they are both grand, teleological theories that purported to explain all of history. But the latter does not make them 'humanist', since they share the same characteristic with a number of traditional religious doctrines, including that of Christianity.

There is also a problem with Foucault's concept of 'the death of man'. He actually puts forward two mutually inconsistent versions of what this 'death' means. On the one hand, he talks about the critique of humanism made by anti-humanist philosophers, most notably Nietzsche and Heidegger. By arguing that the human subject was fragmented, that is, it had both a conscious and a (more dominant) unconscious dimension, they showed that the subject's self-understanding was largely incomplete. They thus brought about the death of the humanist understanding of man. On the other hand, in *The Order of Things*, Foucault argues that the human sciences turn man into an *object* of study. In doing this, they fail to grasp the authentic selfhood of man. This also represents a 'death of man', according to Foucault, since it is a failure to establish a form of understanding appropriate to both the conscious and unconscious dimensions of the human subject. However, if this second version is correct, the first cannot have done what Foucault claims. That is, if the human sciences fail in their attempt to comprehend man, their major critics, Nietzsche and Heidegger, must surely have succeeded in producing a better comprehension, or else their critique could not be effective. But because Nietzsche and Heidegger are also responsible for another version of 'the death of man', their alternative must have a meaning that is quite incompatible with its opponent.

This last confusion, which has been exposed most transparently by Ferry and Renaut, led Foucault through a labyrinth of themes, mostly borrowed from Heidegger's analyses of Kant's metaphysics, to eventually claim that the real meaning of 'the death of man' was that 'man does not exist and never did'.[29] One does not need to wade through the maze of judicious philosophical equivocation that leads Foucault to this point to see that his conclusion is not merely inconsistent but is yet another wilful abuse of the normal principles of debate. As Ferry and Renaut have put it: 'The strategic potential of such discourse is very great; it seems to defy beforehand any attempt to determine its content.'[30]

We can also raise questions about Foucault's use of the concept of anti-humanism, the rejection of the autonomous, self-conscious subject, especially as he applies it to history. One group of anti-humanist historians he admires for their creation of 'a very important mutation in historical knowledge' is the *Annales* School of French historiography.[31] The *Annales* School, especially the work of Fernand Braudel and Emmanuel Le Roy Ladurie, regards history as the unfolding of processes that have an inevitability that surpasses the efforts of individuals. They see long-term influences, such as geography and climate, as far more powerful than political and military events and personalities. History for them is a process without a subject. The problem for Foucault is that this approach is in direct conflict with the role we saw him prescribing earlier for the 'new historian' as someone who should foster an 'insurrection of the subjugated knowledges' of local, outcast groups in their struggle against authority. By calling for the emergence of this new historian, the 'specific intellectual', to advise these groups, Foucault is appealing to a conscious subject who can act upon his or her own free will. When he says that power breeds resistance, he offers no analysis of the internal structure of oppressed groups that will lead them to resist. The reason he fails to do this is clear: people will not automatically resist unless their conscious mind gives them some reason to believe there might be some point in it; and they simply cannot resist unless they have the will to do so. Foucault's politics are a contradiction of his philosophy. He cannot even begin to express a political program without letting into his discourse the very concepts of autonomy and consciousness whose existence he is committed to denying.

With all these problems, it is little wonder that in the last years of his life, Foucault finally recognised the untenability of much of his earlier work. In the second and third volumes of his *History of Sexuality* he brings the vocabulary and concepts of the previously maligned doctrine of humanism into his own writings. Both 'the subject' and the 'freedom' of the individual to act ethically form part of his attempt to revive the ethics of classical Greece. The individual, according to this new Foucault, needs to shape himself as an 'ethi-

cal subject'. He defines the basic practice of ethics as self-mastery that is derived from 'the thoughtful practice of freedom'.[32] Unfortunately, neither he
nor his supporters like to admit that he has thereby jettisoned key passages of
his earlier work. Instead of simply admitting he was mistaken or wrong, again
we find equivocations such as 'shifts of emphasis', 'discontinuities' and a similar range of euphemisms. Foucault himself says that his last two books 'formulated the framework of the thought in a slightly different way' and that he was
really returning to an issue that he had once left aside. One supporter has
written:

Reading Foucault's work it is apparent that there are particular continuities, of
theme and interest. It is also evident that there are shifts of emphasis, changes of
direction, developments and reformulations which have licensed commentators to
talk of breaks, differences and discontinuities within the work.[33]

However much dissembling of this kind is produced, one thing remains
clear. In terms of the history of ideas, the grand thesis put forward in *The
Order of Things* and *The Archaeology of Knowledge* is riddled with inconsistencies and incoherence. Foucault has not even come close to giving a satisfactory account of the various systems of thought that have prevailed since the
Renaissance. His critique of humanist philosophy and of the human sciences
can best be described as a shambles. He cannot even give consistent definitions of either of his key terms, humanism and anti-humanism, let alone deploy these expressions in a convincing historical analysis. And his most famous aphorism, 'the death of man', turns out to be even more inconsistent
than the other concepts he uses.

HISTORY AS FICTION

According to Foucault, the historian cannot avoid taking on the role of a
political activist. All knowledge exudes power, he insists, so the knowledge
produced by the historian must serve political ends, of one kind or another.
The role that Foucault himself decided to take, as I noted above, was to join
the side of the outcasts and deviants and help foster an 'insurrection of subjugated
knowledges' in opposition to mainstream historians whose work, he said,
supported the existing authorities and power arrangements. The pursuit of
this aim partly involved him in writing the perspective of the outcasts into the
historic record. But it also involved making an effort to undermine the received
interpretations of existing history.

In 1971, Foucault spelled out in some detail his views on the writing of
history. In the article, 'Nietzsche, Genealogy and History', he declares the
need to distinguish between 'effective history' (a term of Nietzsche's) and
traditional history.[34] He says that the aim of traditional history to discover in

the past a pattern, or a rational sequence of events, is impossible because there is nothing constant or universal in either human nature or human consciousness. Different historic eras cannot relate to one another, and a new era is not born within and nurtured by its predecessor. A new era, or 'episteme', simply appears in a way that cannot be explained. History does not display any pattern of evolution, he says, because the past is nothing more than a series of discontinuities or unconnected developments.

'Effective history' differs from traditional history in being without constants. Nothing in man—not even his body—is sufficiently stable to serve as the basis for self-recognition or for understanding other men. The traditional devices for constructing a comprehensive view of history and retracing the past as a patient and continuous development must be systematically dismantled.[35]

The discipline of history, Foucault claims, cannot aspire to produce objective knowledge. Rather, it should aim at purging us of the pretence that historians are detached, objective observers of the past. This can only be accomplished by the 'affirmation of knowledge as perspective'.

Historians take unusual pains to erase the elements in their work which reveal their grounding in a particular time and place, their preferences in a controversy—the unavoidable obstacles of their passion. Nietzsche's version of historical sense is explicit in its perspective and acknowledges its system of injustice. Its perception is slanted, being a deliberate appraisal, affirmation, or negation; it reaches the lingering and poisonous traces in order to prescribe the best antidote.[36]

In other words, objectivity is impossible, so historians should be deliberately biased in their interpretations. However, if one takes this view, where does this leave the pursuit of the truth about what happened in the past? Foucault is quite explicit—everything that happened in history has to be seen from a perspective. Even what most people would regard as fairly basic historic facts should not be seen as standing on their own. The details of events such as the storming of the Bastille, or the Battle of Waterloo, can never be seen in objective terms but only through a political interpretation.

An event, consequently, is not a decision, a treaty, a reign, or a battle, but the reversal of a relationship of forces, the usurpation of power, the appropriation of a vocabulary turned against those who had once used it.[37]

Where, then, does this leave Foucault's own claims to be an historian? On his own admission, he cannot be attempting to write objectively. In this, at least, he is consistent. He acknowledges at more than point that his own histories deserve to be called fictions. In 1967, discussing his history of ideas, *The Order of Things,* he said: 'My book is a pure and simple "fiction": it's a novel.'[38] He added that it was not he who invented this fictional status; it was an inevitable consequence of the epistemology of the era in which he wrote.

That is, no historian of ideas at the time could help but write anything other than fiction. By 1977, however, while still acknowledging his histories were fictional, he was at the same time attempting to insert into them the concept of truth.

I am well aware that I have never written anything but fictions. I do not mean to say, however, that truth is therefore absent. It seems to me that the possibility exists for fiction to function in truth, for a fictional discourse to induce effects of truth, and for bringing it about that a true discourse engenders or 'manufactures' something that does not as yet exist, that is, 'fictions' it. One 'fictions' history on the basis of a political reality that makes it true, one 'fictions' a politics not yet in existence on the basis of a historical truth.[39]

Now, one could agree that the notion of truth in fiction is credible. It does make sense to say that some works of literature, such as a novel or a play, may capture a certain truth about people, or that they are 'true to life'. This is a familiar and acceptable notion. It is also well known how difficult it is for historians to be objective because they start their work within the assumptions and concepts of their own position in time, space and culture. Is Foucault right, then, to replace traditional history, and its claims to objectivity, with 'effective history', a form of study of the past that is openly partisan?

One way to test the credentials of Foucault's case is to climb down from the level of abstraction adopted here so far and look at some actual written history. In particular, we might examine the texts of the 'effective history' that Foucault has written himself, and then compare them to the work of more conventional historians who have contributed to the same fields. This is the approach adopted in this rest of this chapter, which provides an analysis of Foucault's major historical works plus a test of their credibility in light of the work of some of his traditionalist critics.

THE ORIGIN OF MODERN INSTITUTIONS

Foucault's first major work, *Madness and Civilisation,* was not conceived as a history of a condition that concerns only the relatively small number of people who have made up the ranks of the insane and the institutional staff who have treated them. Rather, it is a topic that he regards as central to understanding the nature of the history of the West over the last three hundred years: 'the Reason–Madness nexus constitutes for Western culture one of the dimensions of its originality.'[40] In particular, he wants to overturn the traditional stories told about the treatment of insanity and about the wider growth of medicine as a science. Instead of a history of progress and increasing knowledge over the last two hundred years, Foucault tells quite a different story. The period covered by his book, the 1650s to the 1790s, was a time, he argues, in which the human sciences founded a new regime of widespread repression. Most historians have regarded this period as the Age of Reason or Enlightenment when rational, scientific method replaced religious faith and superstition as the basis of knowledge. For Foucault, this elevation of reason meant the denial of madness as part of the human condition. This had dire consequences, he asserts, not only for the insane but for the ethical values that came to dominate Western society.

Foucault claims that in the Middle Ages and the Renaissance the insane were familiar figures within society, and the concept of madness was accepted as falling within the common parameters of the human experience. The mad roamed free in villages and throughout the countryside. In some cases, the insane were used in public displays and were made to perform in spectacles and entertainments. Foucault says the essence of the medieval response was captured by the Ship of Fools, which he asserts was a real vessel that ferried the mad up and down the Rhine on a pilgrimage in search of their reason. The ship, 'conveying its insane cargo from town to town', was a floating symbol, which provided witnesses with a haunting image of the immanence of insanity within the human predicament. Some medieval doctrines held that the insane enjoyed insight into sacred forms of knowledge; but, more often, they were tolerated within local communities as defectives and unfortunates. 'In the Renaissance', Foucault writes, 'madness was present everywhere and mingled with every experience by its images or its dangers.'[41]

However, from 1650 onwards, European society began what Foucault calls 'the great confinement'. Suddenly, a large number of people—up to one per cent of the population of Paris, he says—were incarcerated in hospitals, charitable institutions and workhouses that were quickly established in France, England, Holland, Germany, Spain and Italy. Some people were held in newly constructed institutions, others in buildings that, centuries before, had been lazar houses or leprosariums—this new population, however, was 'excluded more severely than the lepers'.[42] Initially, the incarcerated included several groups from the lower orders: the unemployed, the poor, the criminal and the insane. This was because institutions originated in times of economic recession and were targeted at 'a population without resources, without social moorings, a class rejected or rendered mobile by new economic developments'. As such, the great confinement 'constituted one of the answers the seventeenth century gave to an economic crisis that affected the entire Western world: reduction of wages, unemployment, scarcity of coin'.[43] However, Foucault insists that the authorities at the time did not themselves recognise these economic imperatives. Rather, they saw the growth in poverty and idleness as stemming from the failings of the poor themselves: 'the weakening of discipline and the relaxation of morals.'[44] Their remedy was to incarcerate people in institutions in which they would be forced to labour all day. The work ethic, in other words, became a universal prescription for all members of society.

Foucault ties this development to the rise of the European middle class: it was the trading and new industrial cities that gave the lead in establishing institutions of confinement to enforce the work ethic. He argues that this reveals the essentially authoritarian underside of the moral values that accompanied the rise of the middle class and the attempt by this class to make its own values universal. This is an interpretation that might have been offered by an orthodox Marxist historian. However, the main thesis of Foucault's book derives not from Marx but from Nietzsche. The latter held that the central feature of Western philosophy was its definition of man as a rational being, a creature who reasons. Nietzsche believed that this was the major failing of the traditional view, for it denied other aspects of humanity such as its unconscious, voluntaristic, orgiastic and self-destructive sides. Foucault's book argues that the history of insanity is really the story of the way the concept of reason has suppressed that of madness.

In the Middle Ages, Foucault contends, madness was a concept that had its own autonomy and was recognised as a part of the human condition. But with the arrival of the Age of Reason, madness became defined as 'unreason', the opposite of reason. 'It was in relation to unreason and to it alone that madness could be understood.'[45] Hence, because 'reason' had now become the definitive characteristic of humankind, the person who was not rational lost the status of a human being and became nothing more than an animal.

During the classical period, madness was shown, but on the other side of bars; if present, it was at a distance, under the eyes of a reason that no longer felt any relation to it and that would not compromise itself by too close a resemblance. Madness had become a thing to look at: no longer a monster inside oneself, but an animal with strange mechanisms, a bestiality from which man had long been suppressed.[46]

Foucault writes that, at the close of the classical period of the Enlightenment, when the French Revolution marked the arrival of the modern era, a new form of repression took over. In the eighteenth century institutions, the insane had marked themselves off from other inmates by their unwillingness and incapacity to work. The authorities of the modern period responded in three ways: first, by establishing asylums for the exclusive use of the insane; second, by freeing the insane from chains and other forms of physical restraint that had been common in institutions; third, by defining the concept of insanity as a medical problem.

The change in the mad person's status from that of a beast to someone who was ill might be seen as the acknowledgement both of the humanity of the mad person and of the temporary nature of the person's condition. Foucault insists, however, that such a view is mistaken. Medical practitioners were given new power to legally incarcerate a person whom they defined as being insane. Moreover, the purpose of this incarceration was to allow the person to become the subject of medical treatment. Hence, medical definitions abrogated legal protections and the rights of the person to live with the rest of the community—they created a non-person. The only way the mad person could regain legal and communal status, that is, the status of a fully human person, was to respond positively to the medical treatment. The appropriate response that psychiatrists and other doctors sought, Foucault emphasises, was acceptance of the norms of the community. Overall, he presents psychiatric laws and treatment of the insane as pernicious weapons that modern societies wielded in order to enforce their own definitions of normality and to punish those who transgressed them.

Madness and Civilisation made Foucault's academic reputation in France and, in 1964, earned him his first chair as Professor of Philosophy at the University of Clermont-Ferrand. His next book, *The Birth of the Clinic,* published in France in 1963, attracted less attention but it nonetheless develops the key themes of his book on madness. Medicine's claim that its history is one of progress is false, he argues. The scientific approach of the nineteenth century did not represent a gradual unfolding of objective knowledge about the causes and cures of disease. Instead, he argues, it merely substituted a different form of medical science. The book is not, he insists in the preface, a critique that takes sides 'for or against' any particular kind of medicine. Nor is it a study of the origins or history of ideas about scientific medicine and disease. Rather it is a study of the way in which the ill person came to be 'constituted as a possible object of knowledge'. What does this mean?

In *The Birth of the Clinic,* Foucault claims to have discovered 'the great break' in the history of Western medicine, which occurred at the end of the eighteenth century. This represented a 'mutation in medical knowledge' that transformed the things medicine studied and the ways of practising medicine.[47] Up to the end of the eighteenth century, doctors were more interested in diseases themselves than in individual patients. Early medical science was primarily an attempt to classify and categorise various diseases, according to their similarities and differences, and to then try to make sense of their patterns of occurrence. An individual who was ill represented only a space occupied by the disease. The medical scientist was primarily interested in the wider issue of the disease itself rather than its single manifestation in one person. In the nineteenth century, the 'scientific appetite' of doctors moved to the pathological anatomy of the individual. This shifted the emphasis of medicine to the study of the individual body and to the way that the symptoms of disease were present in bodily tissues. Once this shift had taken place, dissection of corpses and autopsies became a central part of medical training and analysis. The institution where these events were located became the clinic (which was initially confined to the hospital) and the practice became known as clinical medicine. Foucault says that the new structure was indicated by a change in the way doctors questioned their patients. In the eighteenth century, the central question was: 'What is the matter with you?' In the nineteenth century, doctors asked: 'Where does it hurt?'[48]

Foucault's aim in writing this book is not merely to provide a revision of the history of medicine. He also wants to show the way in which medical science affected all the human sciences. He believes the conceptual break he identified in medicine provided a model that the others followed. The shift from the classification of diseases to the study of illness in the individual was 'the first scientific discourse concerning the individual'. Henceforth, 'Western man could constitute himself in his own eyes as an object of science'.[49] From this, the study of human behaviour and of groups and societies derived three central principles: first, the human sciences proclaimed their methods were empirical and objective; second, the study of corpses led to the integration of the concept of individual death and finitude into Western culture and its social sciences; third, the study of groups and societies became rooted in a distinction, derived from medicine, between the normal and the pathological.[50]

Foucault's ultimate objective in both *Madness and Civilisation* and *The Birth of the Clinic* is to demonstrate that there is a dimension of power involved in all of the human sciences that are derived from the medical model of knowledge. By their power to separate individuals into the healthy and the sick, the sane and the insane, the normal and the pathological, the professions based on these sciences have assumed an authority that amounts to repression. Those who do not fit into the prescribed moulds are institutionalised and made to undergo treatment until they conform. According to Foucault, this system derives, not from the state or the middle class as in Marxist theory, but from our modes of thought, especially the way in which the human sciences are conceptualised.

In his third book on institutions, *Discipline and Punish*, Foucault extended his theses to encompass not only the main object of this study, prisons, but several other types of institutions. This is the book and the subject matter that made his name in English-speaking countries. He argues that the birth of the modern era in the eighteenth century created the disciplinary institution that made the power to punish a more essential function of the social body than it had ever been before. For whatever purpose it was established, the institution was always based on certain standard concepts: strict timetables; standardised architecture; institutional uniforms; and ranks, classes and grades of inmates. Its aims were nearly always the same: to control the individual's use of time and space; to change the personality and values of the inmate; to segregate members from their former culture; to provide members with an identity that derived only from the institution; and to instil a disciplinary ethos in all those within the institution. These methods and objectives, which originated in the Middle Ages in the monastic practice of religious orders, became widely adopted in the modern era, and not only in prisons, he argues. They came to form the underlying organisational structure of all our institutions: hospitals, schools, military barracks and factories. A gradual process, which saw different institutions repeat or imitate the practices of others, eventually converged in the blueprint of a general method.

They were at work in secondary education at a very early date, later in primary schools; they slowly invested the space of the hospital; and, in a few decades, they restructured the military organisation. They sometimes circulated very rapidly from one point to another (between the army and the technical schools or secondary schools), sometimes slowly and discreetly (the insidious militarisation of the large workshops).[51]

The thesis is striking, though not necessarily original. The American sociologist Erving Goffman had made a similar critique (not acknowledged by Foucault) of what he called 'total institutions' in his 1961 book *Asylums*. Foucault's study, however, is more ambitious because it claims to identify not only the common nature of institutions, but the very basis of the discipline and power relations to which all of us are still subject today. What has emerged from the modern system of penology, he claims, is a 'capillary' system of power which has no centre but which reaches everywhere, affecting us all.

Foucault begins *Discipline and Punish* with an account of the public dismemberment in Paris in 1757 of 'Damiens the regicide'. It is the story of a prolonged and partly botched process in which the executioner is forced to partially sever the limbs of the prisoner, while he is still alive, before the horses employed to pull the arms and legs from his torso can do the job. Foucault then provides a contrasting account of penal practice some eighty years later in the House of Young Prisoners in Paris. The contrast is indicated by a timetable that prescribes the precise times and activities that must occupy each day of the inmate's incarceration.[52] The reader is led to see a transition from a penal regime based on terror to one based on order and punctuality. Foucault, however, does not see this as an improvement or an indication of a growing human concern. The decline in pain and cruelty over these eighty years is more than matched, he claims, by a 'displacement in the very object of the punitive operation'.

The expiation that once rained down upon the body must be replaced by a punishment that acts in depth on the heart, the thoughts, the will, the inclinations. Mably formulated the principle once and for all: 'Punishment, if I may so put it, should strike the soul rather than the body'.[53]

The switching of attention to 'the soul' was accompanied by an increase in the power and authoritarianism of those involved in penal practice, Foucault says. Those who pretended to be more liberal were really the opposite. As well as dispensing justice, they now wanted to 'cure' the criminal. They were not only interested in punishing the prison inmate, he says, but they also wanted to become involved in the criminal's treatment and rehabilitation. The result was the expansion rather than the contraction of society's penal regimen and the emergence of a new system of values and new theories and disciplines within the social sciences. The most direct result was the growth of a new class of people and interests to be satisfied—psychologists, psychiatrists, social workers and penal reformers—to add to the traditional personnel, such as judges, lawyers and police, who made their livings out of the existence of criminal behaviour. The apparent 'reforms' instituted by these new professional classes had the effect, Foucault claims, not of humanising the penal system but of extending it further into social life: 'to make of the punishment and repression of illegalities a regular function, coextensive with society... to punish with more universality and necessity; to insert the power to punish more deeply into the social body.'[54]

The combined effect of these new values and personnel was to create what Foucault calls a 'technology of power over the body'. The concept of a 'technology of power', of a 'political technology'; is one that Foucault borrowed directly (though he did not acknowledge it in this book) from the philosophy of Martin Heidegger, who claimed that modern society had produced a technological system which amounted to general enslavement. Foucault adapted this idea to make his own distinction between the 'body' and the 'soul'. He did not use the idea of the 'soul' in any religious sense; rather the soul represented the form of internalised subjugation produced by modern society.

It would be wrong to say that the soul is an illusion, or an ideological effect. On the contrary, it exists, it has a reality, it is produced permanently around, on, within the body by the functioning of a power that is exercised on those punished—and, in a more general way, on those one supervises, trains and corrects, over madmen, children at home and at school, the colonised, over those who are stuck at a machine and supervised for the rest of their lives. This is the historical reality of this soul, which, unlike the soul represented by Christian theology, is not born in sin and subject to punishment, but is born rather out of methods of punishment, supervision and constraint... the soul is the prison of the body.[55]

Overall, Foucault's aim is to show that the histories of the institutions he has studied—the mental asylum, the hospital and the prison—provide models for the general form of power held by the authorities who dominate modern society. The sciences that control these institutions—psychiatry, clinical medicine and criminology—have established an objectifying 'gaze', an all-seeing eye that turns people into objects of study. This has permitted a shift in authority from the practice of laying down laws towards an increasing reliance on the mobilisation of norms, or the enforcement of morality. Foucault's aim is to indicate that most aspects of modern life are, similarly, subject to the tyranny of the social sciences and the professional practices that derive from them. Inside schools, within families, in factories and in the colonies of the Third World, people are not free, as they imagine. Their lives are ordered by concepts that originated in the birth of the modern era more than two hundred years ago.

MADNESS AND THE ENLIGHTENMENT

Foucault's interest in the history of madness was inspired by the claim of both Nietzsche and Heidegger that one of the defining characteristics of the modern concept of reason lies in its rejection of difference, or otherness. Foucault's study of madness argues that in the Middle Ages there was a place in society for the mad. However, once the Enlightenment of the eighteenth century had defined man in what was then a new way, as an essentially *rational* creature, the insane became figures of fear and loathing because they were such conspicuous representatives of *the other*, or the different aspect of humanity. This was why, according to Foucault, the period from around 1650 to 1789 went to such lengths to construct asylums to quarantine the mad from the rest of society. In his history of madness, Foucault is attempting to provide support for Heidegger's claim that the humanist concept of rational man was a stifling, backward step in its rejection of difference and in its imposition of a single concept of identity. When other historians have examined the details of Foucault's account, however, they have concluded that the historical record provides very little support for this or any other of the philosophical points he wants to make.

In France, a recent account of the origins of asylums by the French historians Gauchet and Swain[56] has shown that Foucault's claim that the 'great confinement' coincided with the Enlightenment is quite inaccurate. The great confinement did occur, it is true, but not between 1650 and 1789. In this period, the total number incarcerated in France grew at little more than the rate for the population as a whole, from two thousand to about five thousand. Incarceration on a large scale, however, was essentially a product of the *nine-*

teenth century, in particular, from 1815 to 1914. In this latter period, the number of asylum inmates rose from five thousand to one hundred thousand. Gauchet and Swain argue, therefore, the great confinement was a product not of the era of the Enlightenment *philosophes* but rather of the democratic era that followed the French Revolution and the fall of Napoleon.

In Britain, the story was similar. Andrew Scull's history of the treatment of the insane between 1700 and 1900 shows that there was no substantial state-led move to confine the mad during either the seventeenth or the eighteenth century.

Indeed, the management of the mad on this side of the Channel remained ad hoc and unsystematic, with most madmen kept at home or left to roam the countryside, while that small fraction who were confined could generally be found in the small madhouses, which made up the newly emerging 'trade in lunacy'.[57]

Scull adds that in England during Foucault's so-called classical age of the great confinement, 'there was no English "exorcism" of madness; no serious attempt to police pauper madmen ... and so far from attempting to inculcate bourgeois work habits, ...what truly characterised life in the handful of eighteenth century asylums was idleness'.

Historians have pointed to similar illusions in Foucault's account of medieval attitudes. The insane who roamed free in the Middle Ages did so not because the period was more generous towards difference, nor because it was more ready to accept a multidimensional concept of man. This was a time, in fact, when Church and state were one, and where religious doctrine and political ideology coincided. Because medieval societies were hierarchical and inegalitarian, they found it much easier than modern democracies to define some people as less than fully human, or as beyond the human. Hence the toleration accorded the mad was based on the definition of their status as either subhuman or superhuman (and semi-divine). Whichever view prevailed—and subhuman was the most common throughout Europe—the mad were regarded as outside humanity and beyond communication. In this environment, those who were not accepted as fully human could nonetheless live in a community and, as long as they caused no trouble, did not need to be locked away. Since it was accepted that they lacked the understanding and the capacity to suffer of the fully human, the insane could be ridiculed, chased by children and put on display. The status of the village idiot was not much higher than that of domestic animals and he was accepted, like domestic animals, as a familiar feature of village life. 'Where the mad proved troublesome', Scull observes, 'they could be expect to be beaten or locked up; otherwise they might roam or rot. Either way, the facile contrast between psychiatric oppression and an earlier, almost anarchic toleration is surely illusory'.[58] As for the Ship of Fools, the historian Erik Midelfort has searched in vain for any evidence that it ever existed. He concludes it is an invention, a figment of Foucault's overactive imagination. 'Occasionally the mad were indeed sent away on boats. But nowhere can one find reference to real boats or ships loaded with mad pilgrims in search of their reason.'[59]

Foucault is just as unreliable in his account of the response of modern society to the insane. Madness became an issue of public policy with the rise of democratic, egalitarian societies, primarily because these societies accepted the madman not as *the other,* or as someone outside humanity, but as *another human being,* as an individual with the same basic status as everyone else. Democratic societies do not make a display of their insane because they do not regard them as less than human. And if the insane are ill-treated, those responsible are usually held up to public criticism and correction. Insanity is no longer a cause of amusement or curiosity. For most of the modern period, the majority of people were happy to see the insane kept at a distance, but this was not because they were regarded as sub-human but because the insane were seen as people whose behaviour was disturbing or threatening. However, governments in the late twentieth century in Australia, the United States and a number of other Western countries, faced with the considerable cost of institutional care, have adopted decarceration policies and closed down most asylums. Today, the distance that was formerly maintained between society in general and the insane has shrunk dramatically.

If the modern era conferred similarity of rights, why then did democratic societies in the nineteenth century nonetheless produce the great confinement that quarantined the insane in asylums rather than integrate them into society? The initial enthusiasm for institutional confinement was based on the idea that it could insulate the inmate from the influences of the outside world whose environment was held responsible for the condition that needed treatment. In the first half of the nineteenth century, the moral corruption of this environment was largely blamed for insanity, criminality, alcoholism and poverty. Later in the century, this moral explanation was dropped in favour of a medical model of illness, which largely prevails today, as Foucault himself has argued. However, contrary to Foucault's assertion, the asylum represented a social will to integration, not exclusion. By transforming the social environment, the founders of asylums believed, you could create a new person, cured of old problems and habits, who could eventually be released into the outside world.

Now, of course, it is clear to anyone who has read the history of institutionalised care[60] that the social experiment represented by asylums largely failed in its aims. It was impossible to exclude the external environment, and the actual process of insulation produced unforeseen problems, including inmate dependency and conformity, and authoritarian internal management. Psychiatry itself failed to properly diagnose or heal the majority of patients in asylums. By the late nineteenth century, citizen campaigns in some Western countries had begun to demand that large institutions be closed down. By the 1950s, the great confinement had entered its last days. But despite these problems and failures, the representation of madness provided by the asylum does not accord with Foucault's claim that it was fundamentally repressive. Across its several aspects, the asylum always treated madness as a contingent and temporary condition of a person whose basic humanity was still legally asserted. Even when the insane were deprived of normal human rights because of their condition, they were still subject as citizens to due process of the law, and their rights were always conditionally, not permanently, deprived. The insane were never defined by democratic society as a lower form of humanity, as they had been in the Middle Ages. Foucault's central claim—that the history of insanity supports Nietzsche's and Heidegger's thesis that the modern era has imposed a stultified concept of humanity by rejecting 'the other', or the irrational side of man—cannot be sustained.

PENAL THEORY AND PENAL EVIDENCE

Foucault's treatise on prisons, *Discipline and Punish,* may be subjected to just as damaging an empirical critique as his thesis on madness. Again he attempts to make what happened in history fit into his theoretical schema and, again, he can be found making a number of chronological errors. Changes that he claims happened in one era actually happened at another, much later stage. Given the grandeur of Foucault's scope, any corrections to his work on the question of timing might appear triflingly pedantic, but, when exposed, they actually suggest alternative explanations for the origins of the changes he is discussing. Although he is frequently vague about chronology in his writings, in the case of penal reform Foucault is quite specific. He claims that the late eighteenth century marked 'a new age for penal justice'.

It saw a new theory of law and crime, a new moral or political justification of the right to punish; old laws were abolished, old customs died out. 'Modern' codes were planned or drawn up: Russia, 1769; Prussia, 1780; Pennsylvania and Tuscany, 1786; Austria, 1788; France, 1791, Year IV, 1808 and 1810.[61]

Although he is reluctant to discuss the details of all the above reforms, Foucault says their common principle was that of eliminating punishments directed at the body of the criminal. 'Among so many changes', he says, 'I shall consider one: the disappearance of torture as a public spectacle'. He then gives a broadly correct, and uncontroversial, account of the decline of the torture that once accompanied execution in some European countries, and records how executions themselves eventually became more efficient, through the trap-door gallows and the guillotine, as well as less public. Unfortunately for Foucault's argument, however, there is some equally uncontroversial evidence, which he ignores, that shows that legislation directed at 'the body' rather than 'the soul' increased dramatically in the very period in which he claims it declined. For, rather than the institutional timetable, the major contribution the late eighteenth century made to European penal practice was the extension of the death sentence.

The English evidence for this was well established at the time that Foucault wrote. The number of crimes in England bearing the punishment of death increased from about 50 in 1688 to about 160 by 1765, and reached approximately 225 (no one is certain of the number) by 1815.[62] Contemporary jurists and modern historians of both conservative and leftist persuasions agree that there were two main reasons for this: first, the commercialisation of agriculture, which turned what had been either customary rights or minor infringements (taking underwood from forests and fish from ponds, or stealing hedges and fruit from trees) into capital offences; and second, the growing needs of commerce, which led to the death penalty for forgery and counterfeiting to protect the new system of paper credit and exchange. Two-thirds of those convicted of forgery in the eighteenth century were actually executed. 'With the exception of murder', Michael Ignatieff notes, 'no offence was more relentlessly punished'.[63]

Up to the 1780s, most major crimes such as murder, robbery, forgery and machine breaking were punished by whipping, branding, the pillory, banishment and execution. One hundred years later, such punishments had been largely replaced in most of western and northern Europe by imprisonment. However, Foucault is as inaccurate about the timing of this shift in penal practice as he is about the confinement of the insane. In England, the range of capital offences was greatly reduced only after the democratic reforms of 1832. Both executions and commuted sentences of death decreased in the years that followed.[64] The British legal system developed a distaste for corporal punishment at the same time, but did not remove it from the statutes until the Whipping Act of 1861 was passed; even then flogging was retained as punishment for robbery with violence. The English continued public ceremonies of execution until 1868, the same year in which they finally ended transportation to Australia, again following a new surge of liberal and democratic reforms. It was the 1880s—not the 1780s as intimated by Foucault—when the 'old customs died out', when judicial execution and corporal punishment became rare events and when the prison became the 'ordinary mechanical punishment for every new offence created by the Legislature'.[65] In other words, it was not a 'new theory of law and crime' devised by the Enlightenment that reformed the prevailing systems of punishment, but, once again, the rise of the values of democracy, liberalism and egalitarianism.

In *Discipline and Punish,* Foucault's objective is not merely to trace the history of penology. His ultimate aim is to show the development of the disciplinary power that he believes dominates modern society. Under the *ancien régime,* the king imposed social order by empowering his officers to inflict immediate punishment on the body of offenders. The modern era, Foucault claims, introduced a regime of 'generalised surveillance' which replaced the 'relations of sovereignty' with those of 'the relations of discipline'. Moreover, he says, while punishment by the sovereign was directed at the *act of crime,* the discipline of modern society is directed at the *nature of the criminal* and aims not so much to punish as to transform, not to dole out summary justice but to change the offender so that he conforms to the behaviour that society wants.

Foucault claims these developments amounted to an historic transformation: 'the gradual extension of the mechanisms of discipline throughout the seventeenth and eighteenth centuries, their spread throughout the whole social body, the formation of what might be called in general the disciplinary society.'[66] He acknowledges that some forms of modern discipline had histories that stretched back to the Middle Ages and beyond. The institution of the prison, and its division into cells, derived from the model provided by Christian monasteries; the ordering of schools came from another model provided by religious orders; public hospitals derived from examples of naval and military hospitals; workshop disciplines were centuries old. In the late eighteenth century, however, a point was reached where a multiplication of the effects of power was gained through the formation and accumulation of new forms of knowledge within institutions.

At this point the disciplines crossed the 'technological' threshold. First the hospital, then the school, then, later, the workshop were not simply 'reordered' by the disciplines; they became, thanks to them, apparatuses such that any mechanism of objectification could be used in them as an instrument of subjection, and any growth of power could give rise in them to possible branches of knowledge; it was this link, proper to the technological systems, that made possible within the disciplinary element the formation of clinical medicine, psychiatry, child psychology, educational psychology, the rationalisation of labour.[67]

Foucault argues that there was one version of the design of prisons that emerged to provide the general model for the 'disciplinary society'. This was the Panopticon invented by the English Enlightenment thinker Jeremy Bentham. The Panopticon consisted of a central observation tower surrounded by a circular building comprising several stories of cells, each of which had an open, barred wall which faced the observation tower. Bentham proposed that the prison warden, from the 'all-seeing' observation tower, could know at a glance what was going on in each of the several hundred cells that faced him. According to Foucault, 'panopticism' is the model of how the social sciences monitor the activities of the members of the modern society. It is discipline by surveillance: 'an interrogation without end, an investigation that would be extended without limit to a meticulous and ever more analytical observation, a judgement that would at the same time be the constitution of a file that never closed.'[68]

Foucault insists that the change that occurred was essentially a philosophical one. There was a moment in time when a new idea was invented. Such was the power of this idea that, eventually, it caused dramatic political changes including the overthrow of the king and the court in France and the reorganisation of the political system in England.

Interviewer: You determine one moment as being central in the history of repression: the transition from the inflicting of penalties to the imposition of surveillance.

Foucault: That's correct—the moment where it became understood that it was more efficient and profitable in terms of the economy of power to place people under surveillance than to subject them to some exemplary penalty... The eighteenth century invented, so to speak, a synaptic regime of power, a regime of its exercise *within* the social body, rather than *from above* it. The change in official forms of political power was linked to this process, but only via intervening shifts and displacements. It was the instituting of this new local, capillary form of power which impelled society to eliminate certain elements such as the court and the king. The mythology of the sovereign was no longer possible once a certain kind of power was being exercised within the social body. The sovereign then became a fantastic personage, at once archaic and monstrous.[69]

One can see from passages such as this why Foucault became so popular within universities. The fall of political dynasties is but a consequence of one momentous idea. Unlike Marx, who made philosophers dependent upon the revolution of the blue collar proletariat for their power, Foucault elevates social thinkers to the most powerful members of society, all by themselves.

This may be very heady stuff in undergraduate tutorials but there are a number of problems with it. For a start, when one examines the writings of the philosophers of the Enlightenment to whom Foucault credits these developments, they do not fit very well into his thesis. For instance, the eighteenth century thinker who originally argued for prison sentences to replace capital and corporal punishment, Cesare Beccaria, was a rationalist who believed that criminal acts were the result of individual choice. Beccaria eschewed the idea that the nature of the criminal's character and background should be a factor in his punishment and insisted that criminals should be treated equally before the law, and that punishment should fit the crime. This philosopher, in other words, was operating firmly within the old 'relations of sovereignty'. Despite Foucault's claims, Beccaria specifically rejected the proposal that his system of imprisonment should aim at the reform or the transformation of the criminal. 'Reformation is not to be thrust even on the criminal', Beccaria wrote, 'and while for the very fact of its being enforced, it loses its usefulness and efficiency, such enforcement is also contrary to the rights of the criminal, who can never be compelled to anything save suffering the legal punishment'.[70]

Jeremy Bentham, upon whose shoulders Foucault places so much of the responsibility for the present system, was even more of a classic liberal. Bentham's utilitarian psychology held that every individual was a free and calculating agent engaged in the pursuit of pleasure and the avoidance of pain. From a utilitarian perspective, the point of punishment was to show the criminal that he had calculated wrongly when he chose crime instead of obeying the law. Again, punishment should fit the nature of the crime rather than the nature of the criminal. Bentham's plans for the Panopticon made no attempt at reform apart from providing a site where the criminal could contemplate his loss of liberty, compared with the liberty he might have had if he had not offended. Any work the criminal did in jail was designed not to make him a better citizen when released but to help make a profit for the contractor who constructed the prison, for Bentham was one of the earliest advocates of what are now called 'privatised' prisons.[71]

The human sciences about which Foucault is so concerned—psychiatry, criminology, child psychology et al—did not emerge in the late eighteenth century as part of Enlightenment philosophy. They only arose, in fact, some one hundred years later, and came as a *critique* of the view of human nature expressed by Beccaria, Bentham, James Mill and other liberals who wrote on penology. The Scottish historian David Garland has recently published a study of the late-Victorian penal system in England, which clearly identifies its theoretical inspirations. Up to the 1880s, this system insisted on treating each individual 'exactly alike' with no reference being made to his or her criminal type or individual character. The criminal's nature was simply that of the legal subject. Only children and the insane were accorded a status that varied in any way from that of the legal subject. It was not until the 1890s, however, that the philosophies and practices that characterise the penal system of today came into being. These philosophies and practices rejected the classic liberal system in three ways. First, they denied the formal equality of legal subjects and began to take account of the peculiarities of specific individuals, especially the degree to which some could be held responsible for their actions. Second, they recognised fields of study outside the law itself and accepted some of the conclusions of these human sciences as factors that could mitigate criminality, such as the psychological problems of adolescence, the medical nature of alcoholism and the economic difficulties of some offenders. As a result, they began to classify inmates into various social and psychological categories that required different institutional programs, including distinct institutions for juveniles, inebriates and those defined as mentally defective. Third, they developed a range of alternatives to prison to include reform schools for adolescents, training and work experience programs, parole and supervision without detention.[72]

This new jurisdiction, which was introduced in England between 1895 and 1914, and in several other Western countries at about the same time, is the one that comes closest to Foucault's characterisation of the disciplinary regime. It allowed the state to treat the offenders not as equal, free and rational legal subjects but as individuals of varying character and responsibility. The relation between state and offender was no longer presented as a contractual obligation to punish, but as a positive attempt to produce reform and normalisation. This new state regarded itself as a benefactor, intervening to relieve conditions that detracted from formal equality and attempting to rescue its subjects from vice and crime.[73]

This new, interventionist state represents a dramatic change from the liberalism of the late-eighteenth century Enlightenment. It reflects the reorientation of the role of government in the early twentieth century as part of the movement towards what later came to be known as the 'welfare state'. It is the early twentieth century, not the late eighteenth, that corresponds most to Foucault's thesis. For instance, among the first historians of prison reform in Britain were the early twentieth century welfare state advocates, Beatrice and Sidney Webb, who were also pioneers of a number of the techniques of social investigation that Foucault identifies as part of the modern apparatus of surveillance.[74]

Now, at this point, even though we can acknowledge that there may be some correspondence between what Foucault calls the 'disciplinary society' and the institutional policies and practices of the welfare state, he is still not left with much of an argument. The complete lack of any correlation between the penal reform of the Enlightenment and that of the twentieth century destroys his central claim about the power of philosophy. There was no single idea, born at one moment in the eighteenth century, from which all the history of the disciplinary society has unravelled. Moreover, this is not even true for the period where there is some connection between Foucault's account and the findings of other historians. As David Garland has shown in some detail, the normalisation and categorisation that took place after 1895 was neither natural nor inevitable, nor the simple unfolding of 'penality's true essence'. It was the outcome of a definite struggle between contesting forces, between administrators seeking the efficient conduct of institutions, between professionals from the new social and medical sciences seeking to encompass new territories within their ambit, and between politicians responding to incompatible demands from their constituents to impose punishments according to principles of justice, to reduce rates of crime and recidivism, and at the same time to economise on the costs of conducting the prison system. In other words, theories of penology were never more than one ingredient in a real and often messy political contest, and the outcome was never inevitable.

It is clear, then, that Foucault's attempt to portray the present period as dominated by a system of thought that could be read off from the philosophy of the Enlightenment is a failure in every way. Where, then, does this leave his fictionalised, perspective-based, effective history? Whatever view one takes about the ability of historians to free themselves from the perspective of their own times, it remains nonetheless true that Foucault's own work and that of his critics is constructed through the use of empirical data and information: the numbers of inmates in asylums, the dates of penal reforms, the words of the texts of reformers of medical and disciplinary regimes. When Foucault's own data are held up against those of others there are two conclusions that may be drawn. The first is that in the cases discussed above, the critics clearly have the best of the debate and effectively demolish Foucault's conclusions. The second, and methodologically more important, conclusion is that what decides these issues is actually the empirical data that is being deployed, and appealed to, by both sides. Even though Foucault has an obviously careless and cavalier attitude towards the use of evidence, he does not admit to inventing or distorting it. He uses evidence as though it is given by the historic record; given, that is, in an objective way.

Foucault's histories of institutions, therefore, are demonstrations of the falsity of his own theories. History is not fiction, nor is it merely 'perspective'. The core of history—the basis for the conclusions that individual historians reach and the basis of the debates that historians conduct between each other—is factual information. Despite the speculations of Foucault and his followers, history remains a search for truth and the construction of knowledge about the past.

---

1   Mark Poster, *Foucault, Marxism and History: Mode of Production versus Mode of Information*, Polity Press, Cambridge, 1984, p 73

2   Michel Foucault, *Madness and Civilisation: A History of Insanity in the Age of Reason*, (French edn 1961), Vintage Books, New York, 1988

3   Michel Foucault, *The Birth of the Clinic: An Archeology of Medical Perception*, (French edn 1963), Vintage Books, New York, 1975

4   Michel Foucault, *The Order of Things: An Archaeology of the Human Sciences*, (French edn 1966), Pantheon Books, Random House, New York, 1973

5   Michel Foucault, *The Archaeology of Knowledge*, trans. A. M. Sheridan Smith, Pantheon Books, New York, 1982

6   Michel Foucault, *Discipline and Punish: The Birth of the Prison*, (French edn 1975), Allen Lane, London, 1977

7   Michel Foucault (ed.), *I, Pierre Riviere, having slaughtered my mother, my sister, and my brother... A case of Parricide in the Nineteenth Century*, (French edn 1973), Pantheon Books, New York, 1975, and *Herculine Barbin, Being the Recently Discovered Memoirs of a Nineteenth Century French Hermaphrodite*, (French edn 1980), Pantheon Books, New York, 1980

8   Michel Foucault, *Language, Counter-Memory, Practice: Selected Essays and Interviews*, ed. and trans. by D. F. Bouchard, Cornell University Press, Ithaca, New York, 1977

9   Michel Foucault, *Power/Knowledge: Selected Interviews and Other Writings 1972–1977*, ed. Colin Gordon, Pantheon Books, New York, 1980

10 Michel Foucault, *Foucault Live: Interviews 1966–1984*, ed. Sylvere Lotringer, Semiotext(e), Columbia University, New York, 1989

11 'Intellectuals and Power: a conversation between Michel Foucault and Giles Deleuze', in Michel Foucault, *Language, Counter-Memory, Practice*, p 206

12 Michel Foucault, *The Order of Things*, p xi

13 Michel Foucault, *The Order of Things*, pp 168, 217

14 Michel Foucault, *The Archaeology of Knowledge*, p 118

15 Michel Foucault, *The Archaeology of Knowledge*, pp 28-9

16 Michel Foucault, *The Archaeology of Knowledge*, p 108

17 Friedrich Nietzsche, *On the Genealogy of Morals*, ed. William Kaufman, Vintage Books, New York, 1969, p 119, his italics

18 Michel Foucault, *Power/Knowledge*, p 52

19 Michel Foucault, *Language, Counter-memory, Practice*, p 160

20 Michel Foucault, *Power/Knowledge*, pp 81, 84

21 Michel Foucault, *Power/Knowledge*, pp 81-3

22 Steven Best and Douglas Kellner, *Postmodern Theory: Critical Interrogations*, Macmillan, London, 1991, pp 48-59

23 Michel Foucault, *The History of Sexuality, Volume 1: An Introduction*, Allen Lane, London, 1979, pp 95-6

24 Michel Foucault, *Power/Knowledge*, p 131

25 Michel Foucault, *Foucault Live*, p 30

26 Michel Foucault, *The Order of Things*, pp 315-18, 335-7

27 Michel Foucault in *Arts*, 15 June 1966

28 Luc Ferry and Alain Renaut, *French Philosophy of the Sixties: An Essay on Antihumanism*, (French edn 1985), trans. Mary S. Cattani, University of Massachusetts Press, Amherst, 1990, p 100

29 Michel Foucault, *The Order of Things*, p 322

30 Ferry and Renaut, *French Philosophy of the Sixties*, p 105

31 Michel Foucault, *Foucault Live*, pp 11-12

32 Michel Foucault, *The Use of Pleasure: The History of Sexuality*, Vol. 2, Vintage Books, New York, 1986, pp 4-13

33 Barry Smart, *Michel Foucault*, Routledge, London, 1985, p 41

34 Michel Foucault, 'Nietzsche, Genealogy and History', in Paul Rabinow (ed.), *The Foucault Reader*, Pantheon Books, New York, 1984, pp 76-100. Also published in *Language, Counter-Memory, Practice*

35 Michel Foucault, 'Nietzsche, Genealogy and History', in Paul Rabinow (ed.), *The Foucault Reader*, p 87-8

36 Michel Foucault, 'Nietzsche, Genealogy and History'; in Paul Rabinow (ed.), *The Foucault Reader*, p 90

37 Michel Foucault, 'Nietzsche, Genealogy and History', in Paul Rabinow (ed.), *The Foucault Reader*, p 88

38 Michel Foucault, *Foucault Live*, p 20

39 Michel Foucault, *Power/Knowledge*, p 193

40 Michel Foucault, *Madness and Civilisation*, p xi

41 Michel Foucault, *Madness and Civilisation*, p 70

42 Michel Foucault, *Madness and Civilisation*, p 45

43 Michel Foucault, *Madness and Civilisation*, pp 48, 49

44 Michel Foucault, *Madness and Civilisation*, p 59

45 Michel Foucault, *Madness and Civilisation*, p 83

46 Michel Foucault, *Madness and Civilisation*, p 70

47 Michel Foucault, *The Birth of the Clinic,* p xviii

48 Michel Foucault, *The Birth of the Clinic,* p xviii

49 Michel Foucault, *The Birth of the Clinic,* p 197

50 Michel Foucault, *The Birth of the Clinic,* pp 34-6

51 Michel Foucault, *Discipline and Punish,* p 138

52 Michel Foucault, *Discipline and Punish,* pp 3-7

53 Michel Foucault, *Discipline and Punish,* p 16

54 Michel Foucault, *Discipline and Punish,* p 82

55 Michel Foucault, *Discipline and Punish,* pp 29-30

56 M. Gauchet and G. Swain, *La Pratique de l'esprit humain: L'institution asilaire et la révolution démocratique,* Gallimard, Paris, 1980, cited by Luc Ferry and Alain Renaut, *French Philosophy of the Sixties,* pp 90-6

57 Andrew Scull, *The Most Solitary of Afflictions: Madness and Society in Britain 1700–1900,* Yale University Press, New Haven, 1993, pp 7-8

58 Andrew Scull, *The Most Solitary of Afflictions,* p 7. See also: 'Andrew Scull, 'A Failure to Communicate? On the Reception of Foucault's *Histoire de la Folie* by Anglo-American Historians', in Arthur Still and Irving Volody (eds), *Rewriting the History of Madness,* London, Routledge, 1992

59 Erik Midelfort, 'Madness and Civilisation in Early Modern Europe', in B. C. Malament (ed.), *After the Reformation: Essays in Honor of J. H. Hexter,* University of Pennsylvania Press, Philadelphia, 1980, p 254

60 Andrew Scull's work still provides the best overall approach to the English history of the subject. *The Most Solitary of Afflictions* is a rewritten version of his earlier *Museums of Madness: Social Organisation of Insanity in Nineteenth Century England,* Penguin, Harmondsworth, 1979. See also his *Decarceration, Community Treatment and the Deviant: A Radical View,* Englewood Cliffs, New Jersey, 1977

61 Michel Foucault, *Discipline and Punish,* p 7

62 Leon Radzinowicz, *A History of English Criminal Law and its Administration from 1750,* 4 vols, Stevens and Sons, London, 1948-1968, Vol. 1, chapter 1

63 Michael Ignatieff, *A Just Measure of Pain: The Penitentiary in the Industrial Revolution 1750–1850,* Macmillan, London, 1978. See also Douglas Hay, 'Property, Authority and the Criminal Law', in Douglas Hay, Peter Linebaugh and E. P. Thompson (eds), *Albion's Fatal Tree: Crime and Society in*

Eighteenth Century England, Allen Lane, London, 1975; E. P. Thompson, *Whigs and Hunters: The Origin of the Black Act,* Allen Lane, London, 1975

64 Leon Radzinowicz, *A History of English Criminal Law,* Vol. 4, pp 303-53

65 David Garland, *Punishment and Welfare: A History of Penal Strategies,* Gower, Aldershot, 1985, p 7, quoting from the Report of the Prison Commissioners, 1898

66 Michel Foucault, *Discipline and Punish,* p 209

67 Michel Foucault, *Discipline and Punish,* p 224

68 Michel Foucault, *Discipline and Punish,* p 227

69 Michel Foucault, *Power/Knowledge,* pp 38-9

70 Cited by Leon Radzinowicz, *A History of English Criminal Law,* Vol. 1, pp 277-83

71 Jeremy Bentham, *Panopticon,* in *The Works of Jeremy Bentham,* Vol. 4, New York, 1962; Gertrude Himmelfarb, 'The Haunted House of Jeremy Bentham', in her *Victorian Minds,* New York, 1968

72 David Garland, *Punishment and Welfare,* pp 12-15

73 David Garland, *Punishment and Welfare,* p 31

74 Sidney and Beatrice Webb, *English Prisons under Local Government,* (1922), London, 1963

6

THE FALL OF COMMUNISM AND THE END OF HISTORY

FROM POSTHISTORY TO POSTMODERNISM

WHEN THE Cold War ended in 1989, and while Russians, East Germans and other inhabitants of eastern Europe were pulling down the statues of the various dictators of their recently overthrown Communist regimes, Francis Fukuyama, an analyst with the American State Department, published an article that interpreted these events as having far more than European or even Western significance.[1] Fukuyama said the overthrow of communism had implications for the whole of humankind because it represented the 'end of history'. It confirmed, he said, that Western liberal democracy and technologically driven capitalism were end points of humanity's political and social evolution and the final forms of government and economic organisation. By 1992 Fukuyama had expanded his ideas from a fifteen-page article to a four hundred-page book entitled *The End of History and the Last Man*. The book is an exercise in what has been known variously as the philosophy of history, speculative history or universal history. In all its forms, this approach to history postulates that there is an overall logic or pattern to human affairs, from which a grand theory can be constructed not only to explain the entire past of the human species but to project the pattern forward to see into the future. In Fukuyama's version, he argues that, although human life will continue, history has come to an end. Behind this apparently contradictory idea lies a particular view of the meaning of history.

Fukuyama is arguing that what has come to an end is not the occurrence of events, even large and grave events, but History; that is, history understood as a single, coherent, evolutionary process. This understanding of history was most closely associated with the German philosopher of the late eighteenth and early nineteenth centuries Georg Wilhelm Friedrich Hegel. It became part of the intellectual atmosphere of both the nineteenth and twentieth centuries through the work of Karl Marx, who borrowed the concept from Hegel. The underlying principles of the thesis come from Judeo–Christian religion. The Bible saw the path of history as the realisation of God's plan for the salvation of humanity, and saw the end of history as the Last Judgement. Hegel secularised this process and saw history as the evolution of human rationality and freedom. History would end when humankind had achieved a form of society that satisfied its deepest and most fundamental longings. Marx offered a materialist version of Hegel. Marx saw the dynamic of history not as the evolution of reason but as the struggle between classes. Under Marxism, history would end with the achievement of a universal, communist society that would finally abolish the class distinctions that had themselves driven the historical process.

Fukuyama's version of universal history is a revival of Hegel's thought. Hegel believed he had himself witnessed the end of history when he saw Napoleon on horseback on a reconnoitre through the German university town of Jena in 1806. Napoleon's victory in the Battle of Jena, Hegel thought, had broken the power of the *ancien régime* in Germany and had thus cleared the way for the universal diffusion of the French Revolution's principles of liberty and equality. Fukuyama argues that Hegel's conviction was, in principle, correct. Although massive upheavals and revolutions over the next two hundred years were still in store, the big questions had all been settled. The basic liberties that Hegel had taken as constituting the ultimate form of social organisation had not changed since the fall of the *ancien régime*. Fukuyama's contribution is to revive the version of Hegel offered by his 1930s interpreter, the Russian–French philosopher and former Marxist Alexandre Kojève.

In raising the issue of a universal history, Fukuyama is resuming a discussion that had been largely abandoned, he says, because of the enormity of the events of, and the intellectual pessimism engendered by, the Second World War and the Cold War. He argues, however, that the final quarter of the twentieth century, the period since 1975, can be seen to confirm the 'end of history' thesis. This period has revealed the weaknesses at the core of the world's seemingly strong dictatorships. It has seen not only the collapse of communism in Europe but the corresponding demise of dictatorships of the military–authoritarian Right, with new, democratic regimes established in a number of countries including Greece, Spain, Portugal, Turkey, South Korea, the Philippines, Brazil, Argentina, Peru, Paraguay, Uruguay and Chile. Fukuyama says the implementation of democracy in South Africa should also be added to the list. 'Liberal democracy remains the only coherent aspiration that spans different regions and cultures around the globe.'[2] At the end of the twentieth century, he says, it makes sense once again to speak of a coherent and directional history that will eventually lead the greater part of humanity towards liberal democracy. Fukuyama argues his case from two separate directions: one from economics and the development of technology; the other from what he calls 'the struggle for recognition'.

His first argument, that modern natural science gives directionality and coherence to history, derives not from Hegel but from his own interpretation of the military imperatives of technology. The progressive conquest of nature through the scientific method developed in the seventeenth and eighteenth centuries has proceeded according to rules laid down not by man but by 'nature and nature's laws'. Technology confers decisive military advantages on those countries that possess it. Given the continuing possibility of war between countries, no state can ignore the need to defend itself through adopting technological modernisation. Moreover, all countries undergoing modernisation must increasingly resemble one another. They must unify nationally with a centralised state. They must urbanise and replace traditional forms of social organisation such as tribe, sect and family with economically rational ones based on function and efficiency. They must provide for the universal education of their citizens. These processes guarantee an increasing homogenisation of all human societies, regardless of their historical origins or cultural inheritances. Since modernisation means that societies become increasingly linked with one another through global markets, the process produces a universal consumer culture. While highly centralised, socialist economies such as those of the former USSR and China succeeded in replicating the level of heavy industrialisation of Europe of the 1950s, they proved woefully inadequate in transforming themselves into post-industrial economies in which information and technological innovation predominate. So the logic of modern natural science, Fukuyama says, leads not to socialism but produces a universal evolution in the direction of capitalism.[3]

However, there is no economically necessary reason that advanced industrialisation should produce political liberty. There are many examples of technologically advanced capitalism coexisting with political authoritarianism, Fukuyama points out, from Meiji Japan and Bismarckian Germany to present-day Singapore and Thailand. In fact, some authoritarian states can outperform the economic growth rates of democratic societies. Hence economic interpretations of history are incomplete, Fukuyama argues, because they cannot explain why evolution has produced democracy, the principle of popular sovereignty and the guarantee of basic rights under a rule of law. 'Man is not simply an economic animal.' To 'recover the whole of man', Fukuyama turns to Hegel and his account of history based on the 'struggle for recognition'.[4]

This second argument derives from Hegel's point that human beings differ fundamentally from animals because, as well as having needs and desires for food, shelter and the like common to all animals, they desire to be 'recognised'. In particular, they desire to be recognised by others as human beings, that is, as beings with a certain worth or dignity. Hegel says only man rises above his animal instincts, especially the instinct for self-preservation, for the sake of higher or abstract principles and goals. In the earliest periods of history, the desire for recognition led combatants to stake their lives to make their opponents 'recognise' their humanness. This produced a bloody battle to the death for the sake of prestige, a battle which ended when the natural fear of death led one combatant to submit. The outcome of this battle was a division of human society into a class of masters, who were willing to risk their lives, and a class of slaves, who gave in to the fear of death. This, Hegel says, was the relationship that produced the aristocratic societies that characterised the greater part of human history. The master–slave relationship, however, ultimately failed to satisfy either side. The slave lacked any recognition of his humanity; the master enjoyed the recognition merely of slaves who were less than human. The dissatisfaction arising from this relationship constituted a 'contradiction' that engendered the next stage of history. This was led by the democratic revolution in France, which abolished the distinction between master and slave by making the slaves their own masters. The former, inherently unequal relationship was then replaced by universal and reciprocal recognition whereby every citizen recognised the dignity and humanity of every other citizen, and whereby that dignity was recognised in turn by the state through the granting of rights.[5]

Hegel's psychological concept of the desire for recognition may, Fukuyama admits, appear to be an unfamiliar concept, but he argues that it is as old as the tradition of Western political philosophy. It was first described by Plato in *The Republic* as one of the three parts of the soul. As well as desire and reason, the soul contained a part that Plato called *thymos* or spiritedness. Today, Fukuyama says, we would call the propensity to invest the self with a certain value 'self-esteem'. The propensity to feel self-esteem, he says, arises out of the part of the soul called *thymos*.

It is like an innate human sense of justice. People believe they have a certain worth, and when other people treat them as though they are worth less than that, they experience the emotion of *anger*. Conversely, when people fail to live up to their own sense of worth, they feel *shame*, and when they are evaluated correctly in proportion to their worth, they feel *pride*. The desire for recognition, and the accompanying emotions of anger, shame and pride, are parts of the human personality critical to political life. According to Hegel, they are what drives the whole historical process.[6]

Fukuyama points out that the Hegelian concept of liberalism differs significantly from the tradition of liberalism in English-speaking countries. For Thomas Hobbes, John Locke and the American founding fathers, liberalism and human rights existed largely to define a private sphere in which individuals could enrich themselves, free from the interference of the state. Hegel, however, saw rights as ends in themselves because the primary satisfaction of human beings lay in the recognition of their status and dignity. In other words, the English and American liberals saw that the main purpose of government was to allow individuals to pursue material gain, whereas Hegel saw that it was to satisfy the desire for recognition.[7]

Overall, then, Fukuyama argues that Hegel's universal history has its basis in Plato's three-part division of the human soul. Desire and reason together explain the process of industrialisation, economic growth and the triumph of capitalism. *Thymos* leads people to demand liberal democratic governments. Fukuyama notes that the simple three-way connection he has drawn is much more complicated in real life. For example, the work ethic that imbued the Protestant entrepreneurs who created European capitalism and the elite who modernised Japan after the Meiji Restoration, was generated by the desire for recognition. In many Asian countries today, the work ethic is sustained not so much by material incentives as by the recognition it receives from the family or the nation. This suggests, Fukuyama says, that successful capitalism derives not only from liberal principles but from the drive generated by *thymos* as well.[8]

Fukuyama is also convinced that, as well as accounting for the internal development of economies and governments, his universal history can also explain international relations. At first sight, the original bloody battle for prestige that created masters and slaves would seem to lead logically to international competition, imperialism and the pursuit of world domination. Fukuyama agrees that, in a universal history, the relationship of lordship and bondage is naturally replicated on the world stage where nations seek their own recognition and engage in bloody battles for supremacy. However, he is critical of the 'realists' of power politics such as Henry Kissinger, who believe that such an environment is bound to be a permanent one. Fukuyama says that the ultimate logic of the process is that the liberal revolution that abolished the relationship of lordship and bondage by making former slaves their own masters should have a similar effect on the relationship between states. Both internally and internationally, liberal democracy replaces the irrational desire to be recognised as greater than others with the rational desire to be recognised as equal. Hence, a world made up of liberal democracies should have much less incentive for war, since all nations would reciprocally recognise one another's legitimacy. Fukuyama says there is substantial empirical evidence available to support his case. Over the past two hundred years, he says, liberal democracies have been quite prepared to go to war with undemocratic countries that do not share their fundamental values, but these liberal democracies have not behaved imperialistically towards one another. Even though there might be a rise of violent nationalism in eastern Europe and parts of the former Soviet empire, where people have long been denied their national identities, within the oldest and most secure countries nationalism is giving way to a kind of international cosmopolitanism. So, the sooner the world adopts liberal democratic capitalist values, the sooner we will put an end to warfare.[9]

Since it represents the end of history, does this mean that Western capitalism is the perfect human society? Far from it, Fukuyama replies. He acknowledges that contemporary democracies face a number of serious problems, from drugs, crime, homelessness and pollution to what he calls 'the frivolity of consumerism'. While these problems may be difficult to solve within liberal principles, he sees them as essentially technical issues and not serious enough to precipitate the collapse of the system as a whole, as communism collapsed in the 1980s. Fukuyama also admits that there is widespread inequality within capitalist societies deriving from economic inequality and the division of labour. Therefore, capitalist economies recognise equal people unequally.

Fukuyama regards this last critique from the Left, however, as minor compared with a much more powerful criticism from the Right that has been more concerned with the levelling effects of liberalism's commitment to human equality. The most prominent exponent of this view was Friedrich Nietzsche, who argued that modern democracy represented not the self-mastery of former slaves but the unconditional victory of the slave and of slavish values. Nietzsche coined the term 'the last man', which Fukuyama uses in his title to describe the type of personality that dominates the end of history. The last man, according to Nietzsche, was the typical citizen of liberal democracy who, whether male or female, gave up prideful belief in his or her own superior worth in favour of comfortable self-preservation. Nietzsche characterised such people as 'men without chests' who were composed of desire and reason but lacked *thymos*. They spent their lives calculating their long-term interest for the satisfaction of no more than petty wants. Nietzsche believed that no human excellence, greatness or nobility was possible except in aristocratic societies. Creativity and greatness could only arise out of *megalothymia,* that is, the desire to be recognised as greater than others. The last man did not desire to be recognised as greater than others, and without such a desire no excellence or great achievement was possible. Nietzsche argued that this self-satis-fied person felt no shame in being unable to rise above others and, hence, ceased to be human.[10]

Fukuyama believes that under liberal capitalism some entrepreneurs, such as Henry Ford, Andrew Carnegie and Ted Turner, still exhibit some of the characteristics of *megalothymia* by striving to make their businesses bigger and better than others. However, in essence, he agrees with Nietzsche's scenario. The end of history, he says, 'will be a very sad time'. The willingness to risk life for abstract goals and the struggle for recognition that demands audacity, nerve and imagination, will be replaced by calculation and the solving of merely technical problems. Politics will be replaced by economic manage-ment. The end of history will have neither a need nor a place for art or philosophy. Citing Kojève's conclusions from Hegel, Fukuyama describes the end of history:

It would no longer be possible to create the great art that was meant to capture the highest aspirations of the era, like Homer's *Iliad,* the Madonnas of da Vinci or Michelangelo, or the giant Buddha of Kamakura, for there would be no new eras and no particular distinction of the human spirit for artists to portray... Philosophy too would become impossible, since with Hegel's system it had achieved the status of truth. "Philosophers" of the future, if they were to say something different from Hegel, could not say anything new, only repeat earlier forms of ignorance.

Although war and poverty will not be totally eliminated. Fukuyama con-tinues, most of the human species will enjoy peace and abundance in a world where human culture reverts to a merely animal level.

Agreeing on ends, men would have no large causes for which to fight. They would satisfy their needs through economic activity, but they would no longer have to risk their lives in battle. They would, in other words, become animals again, as they were before the bloody battle that began history. A dog is content to sleep in the sun all day provided he is fed, because he is not dissatisfied with what he is. He does not worry that other dogs are doing better than him, or that his career as a dog has stagnated, or that other dogs are being oppressed in a distant part of the world. Human life, then, involves a curious paradox: it seems to require injustice, for the struggle against injustice is what calls forth what is highest in man.[11]

When, in the 1990s, he looks at the current generation of American uni-versity undergraduates, 'those earnest young people trooping off to law and business school', Fukuyama sees tangible corroboration of all his ideas. As they fill out their resumés and study for careers to maintain their lifestyle, they 'seem to be much more in danger of becoming last men, rather than reviving the passions of the first man'. The pursuit of material acquisitions and safe, sanctioned ambitions, he says, appears to have worked all too well. 'It is hard to detect great, unfulfilled longings or irrational passions lurking just beneath the surface of the average first-year law associate.'[12]

THE END OF COMMUNISM AND THE LAST MARXIST

The Fukuyama thesis attracted a great deal of attention both in 1989, when it was sketched in an article, and in 1992, when the book-length exposition and defence was published. The most passionate responses were made by the Cold War warriors of both the Right and the Left. There were some on the Right who quite gleefully declared that Fukuyama had finally proven that socialism was impossible and had thereby rendered all leftist intellectuals redundant.[13] Although there was at least one prominent Marxist intellectual who, as I discuss below, declared himself highly impressed, the majority of responses from the Left were either hostile or incredulous. By 1989, there were very few Western leftists who still supported the kind of regime established by Stalin and his successors in the USSR. Theoretically, the collapse of communism should have left their own versions of socialism intact. Instead, it forced the awful recognition that not only had communism been consigned to the dustbin of history but with it had gone the prospect of replacing capitalism with any kind of revolutionary regime based on socialism. Fukuyama aroused their hostility not simply because he articulated this realisation within a matter of weeks but also because he was operating with the very same philosophical system that Marx had derived from Hegel to teach the Left that history was on their side and would eventually produce a socialist utopia.

The most common response to Fukuyama from the Left was to repeat its traditional critique that modern, capitalist society does not satisfy the needs and aspirations of its members. Instead, it produces widespread social injustice, poverty, inequality, unemployment, crime, violence, drug abuse, family breakdown and urban decay, and produces these in such volume that there is a large, visible and growing underclass in almost every contemporary capitalist society. In other words, there are so many unresolved problems that liberal democracy could hardly be regarded as stable or secure. To this critique, Fukuyama's book responded in two ways.

The first response is to acknowledge that, while poverty and inequality certainly exist, they derive not from social class nor from the inherent economic nature of the system, but from cultural hangovers from a previous era. American blacks, he says, have high levels of unemployment, crime and family breakdown because of their culture. This is still influenced by the experience of blacks under slavery and by a premodern legacy of racism among whites. But neither of these hangovers are related to the logic of liberal democratic capitalism, which is sustained not by racism but by egalitarian values.

The logic of the capitalist system is that, in the long run, market forces will eliminate these and other kinds of cultural lags. Secondly, Fukuyama says that even if these kind of problems prove intractable, they still do not affect his argument. His thesis can still live with a social system that is imperfect and full of inadequacies, tensions and conflicts. None of these problems denies his central point that there is no other regime that could replace liberal democracy and do better. The communist experiment showed, indeed, that in terms of liberty, equality and community well-being, any other system, no matter how well- or ill-intentioned, would do far worse. To mount an effective response to Fukuyama in historical terms involves being able to show not merely that liberal capitalism produces problems but that there are powerful, systemic alternatives to it. At least four types of response of this kind have been made.

Nationalism. The first of these hinges on the question of nationalism. Given that the breakup of the Soviet empire almost immediately produced a veritable firestorm of nationalist warfare in the Balkans and in Central Asia, surely, it could be argued, national rivalry and ethnic hatred are underpinned by passion so great that they must constitute a force for the continuation of history as we have known it. Not only this, but in the 1980s and 1990s we have witnessed the emergence to Great Power status of two countries, Japan and China, who display many of the history-making characteristics of the European imperial powers of the pre-1914 era. None of these examples bothers Fukuyama. Nationalist and ethnic conflicts are in the same category as racism and black cultural disadvantage—symptoms of an earlier era of history that runs counter to the logic of the system. The passions that fan hatreds or produce demands for independence in small regions of the Second or Third World are largely irrelevant to the global economic and power system dominated by large states. In the Cold War, these conflicts could be regarded as, and often became the site of, fields of contest between the two Super Powers, but now the Cold War is over they affect only the small groups directly involved. Even if one or more of them used nuclear weapons against their neighbours, this would no longer lead to a nuclear conflict between any of the Great Powers. Imperial competition between the larger states, Fukuyama notes, is of far more consequence for his thesis. Were one or more of the current Great Powers to develop a form of nationalism that had global or international territorial ambitions, this would indeed destabilise much of the present system. But he argues that the Second World War was largely fought against this kind of nationalism and the outcome destroyed any potential for it to re-emerge. Recognising the forces lined up against such ambitions, not even a newly powerful China would run the risk of developing a nationalist creed of this nature.

Religious fundamentalism. The second kind of potential systemic alternative is religious fundamentalism. The Islamic revolution in Iran, the demand for Islamic states in Egypt, Algeria and other parts of North Africa, the growing political influence of Christian fundamentalism—especially in the United States—plus movements that appear to be capitalising on political and economic uncertainty in India, Japan and elsewhere in Asia, all offer radical competition to the principles of liberal democracy. Moreover, unlike nationalism, fundamentalism is inherently universal in its claims. Whatever its creed, the principles it proclaims are held to be true for all people, not merely for one ethnic, cultural or geographically defined community. Fundamentalism has ambitions beyond that of any nationalism that exists today. However, Fukuyama argues that these developments are more apparent than real. Islamic fundamentalism is confined to Arab ethnic identity and does not act as a movement trying to win converts or conquer nations around the world. In fact, it acts far more as a successor to failed Arab nationalism than as a movement with global pretensions. Other religious fundamentalist movements that have emerged in the last two decades have had even narrower limits. They have all been confined within national boundaries where they have been often highly visible, but nonetheless minority, expressions of essentially nationalist fervour. Moreover, Fukuyama's argument from technology—that the imperatives of military competition force industrialisation and Western scientific method upon all countries—means that fundamentalism or religious belief of any kind will find it increasingly difficult to survive in the secular culture that inevitably accompanies these developments. Every nation that introduces a modern education system sets in train a process that undermines the kind of thinking that produces faith in supernatural authority.

State corporatism. A third and different tack is to argue that Fukuyama is wrong about liberal capitalism being the end of history because it is already being challenged by an authoritarian form of state corporatism. This is an alternative that Fukuyama himself takes seriously. He recognises the growth of the 'bureaucratic–authoritarian state', or what could be called 'market-oriented authoritarianism', in Japan and some newly industrialising Asian states, and acknowledges that they achieve better overall economic results when they are more coercive and less democratic. South Korea, for example, enjoyed its highest economic growth in the 1960s by suppressing wages, banning strikes and forbidding talk of greater worker consumption and welfare. The transition to democracy in 1987, however, saw South Korea undergo a series of strikes and wage demands, which the government was forced to meet, thereby increasing production costs and decreasing the country's international competitiveness. Taiwanese planners were able in the late 1970s and early 1980s to shift investment resources from light industries such as textiles to high-technology electronic industries, despite the considerable pain caused by unemployment in the former sector, because they were shielded by an authoritarian regime from democratic political pressures.[14] However, rather than seeing these as examples of the success of a managerial society model over the democratic model, Fukuyama regards them as proof of his overall thesis. While the logic of modern science and the industrialisation process points in a single direction towards capitalism, the other component of his universal history, the thymotic struggle for recognition, points towards democracy. The South Korean example, in fact, confirms this. Once the logic of industrialisation had unfolded and the country had modernised, the demand for recognition through democracy had to follow, which it did. Those states that are capitalist but remain bureaucratic–authoritarian, like Taiwan, are still in a stage of political underdevelopment that will continue to generate pressure for democratic reforms until these too are realised.

Creeping socialism. The fourth response is to argue that, far from being the end of history, liberal capitalism is itself a myth, which is accepted only by those naive enough to take the free market propaganda of the 1980s seriously. Far from there being any kind of reversion to genuine capitalist values under the regimes of Ronald Reagan, Margaret Thatcher and right-wing economic gurus such as Milton Friedman, the 1980s were a continuation of the gradual undermining of these same values. Reagan and Thatcher may have talked about liberal values, but their periods in office saw massive increases in state debt and welfare payments. This was a critique offered by commentators from both the Right and the Left, who agreed with each other that the end of communism did not mean the end of socialism. Some on the Right were just as convinced as their opponents that the thesis was deeply flawed, since socialism, far from being rendered irrelevant, was alive and well in the form of the creeping statism that infected all capitalist societies.[15] On the Left, while some writers acknowledged that there were versions of socialism that had collapsed just as surely as the Soviet regime, they argued that the path was still wide open for reformist rather than revolutionary strategies.[16]

The most favoured of these strategies remains the concept of hegemony, borrowed in the 1960s from the pre-war Italian Communist theorist Antonio Gramsci. This involved leftist participation in the upper reaches of government, education, the law and the media, as well as in lobby groups concerned with environmental, feminist, homosexual, ethnic and welfare issues. The ultimate aim was, through gradual encroachment, to promote the evolution of capitalism into a system of democratic socialism. It is difficult, however, to regard such a strategy today as representing a serious contender to the hegemony of capitalism itself. It may well mean, as the German theorist Jürgen Habermas has put it, that the Left can continue to provide 'the radically reformist self-criticism of a capitalist society', but none of the recent contribu-tors to this debate has been willing to argue that there is a coherent goal for the process. With state enterprise and central economic planning now so discredited, no one is willing any more to describe even the outline of a socialism that could provide a feasible socio-economic system to compete with and eventually replace capitalism. The most likely outcome for Gramscian strategists, which is clearly observable in the outlook of one's former leftist colleagues who have engaged since the 1960s in 'the long march through the institutions', is that they become absorbed by and, indeed, supportive of, the values they initially set out to subvert.

Perhaps the most painful recognition for those on the Left was that Fukuyama was flaunting their own most cherished concept. Until Fukuyama, universal history, or the philosophy of history, had been virtually the exclusive prop-erty of the Left because of their adherence to Marxism. Hegel had not been regarded by leftists as a philosopher who should be accepted in his own right. Instead, he was taught primarily because he was the one who had developed the secularised philosophy of history that Marx had taken and inverted to produce historical materialism. Though the Left claimed Hegel as one of their own, they regarded his liberal politics not as something of great weight in itself but simply as one of the ideological stages through which universal history had to pass before it manifested itself in Marx's grand scheme. Hence, Fukuyama was doubly provocative. He not only declared socialism the dead end of a blind alley but he used the very methodology that had produced socialism to do it. By vaulting backwards over the head of Marx to land on the shoulders of Hegel, Fukuyama performed a feat of dazzling intellectual gymnastics. Most of the Left looked on, stunned, like supporters of a team just thrashed in the grand final.

One of the very few Marxists who appreciated the performance was Perry Anderson, the former editor of the London journal *New Left Review*, and now pastured, like a number of his old English stable mates, in a university in California. Though he disagrees with the end, Anderson applauds the means the author used to reach it.

Here for the first time, the philosophical discourse of the end of history has found a commanding political expression. In a remarkable feat of composition, Fukuyama moves with graceful fluency back and forth between metaphysical exposition and sociological observation, the structure of human history and the detail of current events, doctrines of the soul and visions of the city. It is safe to say that no one has ever attempted a comparable synthesis—at once so deep in ontological premise and so close to the surface of global politics.[17]

At first glance, this might seem a strange response for him to make. During the soul-searching of 1989, Anderson was the most prominent Marxist intellectual to refuse to admit either that Leninism and the Russian Revolution had all been a horrendous mistake or that the traditional concept of socialism was finished. Marx and Lenin had certainly made errors, Anderson admitted in 1992 in his eulogy for the death of communism, but up to the mid-1930s socialism had made greater achievements than any other political movement of the time. There were crimes and massive bloodshed, to be sure, he says: 'But no other body of theory in this period—the first third of the century—came near to the twofold successes, of anticipation and accomplishment, of the socialist tradition.' He argues that, at one time, liberalism appeared to be in just as much trouble as socialism seems to be in today. After the mass killings of the First World War, followed by the Great Depression and the rise of Hitler, liberal civilisation seemed to many to be a bankrupt and barbarous creed. 'By the end of the first third of the century, it looked to many observers as if liberalism might be destroying itself from within as a major historical force.' However, thanks to the trauma of the Second World War and the postwar recovery, liberalism restored its fortunes. Although he makes all the expected disclaimers about the use of historical analogies, Anderson wants us to believe that there is similar kind of crisis in the offing—fuelled by 'the tremendous pressures of poverty and exploitation in the South'—which will create 'a new international agenda for social reconstruction', similar to that which revived liberalism in the 1940s. He sees a need for 'an Environmental Revolution comparable in significance only to the Industrial and Agricultural Revolutions before it'. He claims only socialism has the internationalist potential to stage the Environmental Revolution. The main political tactic to be used to pursue this goal is the takeover of supranational bodies such as the European Parliament. The tensions generated will give socialism its big chance for a comeback and another shot at the title. 'Were it able to respond effectively to them, socialism would not so much be succeeded by another movement, as redeemed in its own right as a program for a more equal and livable world.'[18]

Although he admires Fukuyama's style and method, and although he thinks all the other Left critics have failed to dent his thesis, Anderson nonetheless rejects the idea that we have reached the end of history. Like Marxists of old, Anderson still thinks that a great conflagration is fermenting just beneath the ostensibly stable surface of contemporary capitalism. This brew is a combination of environmentalism, North–South conflict over resources, and the residue of the nuclear arms race. The central case against capitalism today, he says, is the combination of ecological crisis and the social polarisation it is breeding. He claims that it is impossible to emulate the standard of living of the West in the Third World, especially given the environmental problems produced by the population explosions that would accompany the industrialisation of the world's peasant economies. Therefore, immigration flows from the Third World to the First will continue and probably accelerate. This will generate conflict since the countries of the 'North' will be forced to establish 'border patrols' both to keep out immigrants and to guarantee oil supplies. But because some of those countries now holding 'South' status have nuclear weapons, no permanent peace will be possible. Hence, since there exists the potential for such monumental conflict, it does not make sense to talk of the end of history.[19] Anderson has another argument to go with this one. It is tossed in at the last minute to show his politically correct credentials, but it looks rather like a scraping from the bottom of the political barrel. Couched in the terminology of early 1970s feminism, Anderson claims the condition of women in Western society still 'remains massively far away from real sexual equality'. This being so, he says, we cannot regard either liberty or equality as being fulfilled within contemporary society. Hence, as well as North–South external conflicts, there is a great deal of internal history still left to unfold within liberal capitalism.[20]

Both these scenarios are rather strange coming from Anderson in this context. They both fall into the category of arguments that he himself rejected when they were used by other leftists in reply to Fukuyama. It is not good enough, he says earlier in this same essay, to simply point out problems that remain within the world Fukuyama predicts. Yet this is exactly what he does himself. Moreover, if we accept, as Anderson does, the Hegelian project of universal history, there is a range of defences Fukuyama can deploy. He can simply dismiss difficulties of this kind as merely technical and/or potentially solvable, or can go on to say we simply have to live with serious problems since the end of history is not the arrival of a perfect system, but the elimination of any better alternatives to this one. On an empirical level, Anderson's case is also unconvincing to anyone not already encased within the doomsday mentality of contemporary environmentalism. For instance, the Malthusian population projections of his futuristic environmental catastrophe are wildly astray, being based on the birth rate of peasant agricultural societies rather than the two-child family that quickly becomes the norm once a population becomes urbanised, industrialised and educated. If Fukuyama ever bothered to reply at this level, he would make a meal of him.

The one appropriate argument that Anderson does offer is based on the recognition that an effective critique should put a 'powerful systemic alternative' to the world Fukuyama predicts. 'It must be possible to indicate a credible alternative to it', Anderson argues, 'without resort to mere gestures at the unpredictable or changes that are no more than terminological'. While he might be correct in logic, the systemic alternative that Anderson finally advances—socialism resurrected via ecological catastrophe—is anything but powerful: it is no more than wishful thinking, his own gesture at the unpredictable, which he all but admits himself.

Anderson, then, comes out of this debate an unimpressive figure. He had set out to show that he, above all others on the Left, had the power to silence the cheers of triumph by the victors of the Cold War. He turned out to have nothing to offer but a regurgitation of old, unconvincing slogans and old, ineffective designs—a dismal effort. Domiciled under the California sun, Perry Anderson looks disconcertingly like the very thing he set out to deny, a 'last man' at the end of the history of Marxism.

EMPIRICAL EVIDENCE AND THE PHILOSOPHY OF HISTORY

The principal reason that intellectuals on the Left find such difficulty in refuting Fukuyama is that they, too, derive their underlying ideas from the philosophy of history. However, once we recognise that the philosophy of history is itself an illegitimate method for understanding the course of human affairs—in either its Hegelian liberal or Marxist socialist versions—the 'end of history' thesis collapses. The most direct way to demonstrate this is by examining the central idea on which Fukuyama's case depends: that there is one key that can unlock history. The notion that there is one concept that explains all has always held a powerful attraction. The Christian salvationist view of history was based on it. So too was Marx's materialist thesis that the class struggle could, on its own, explain 'the history of all hitherto existing society'. Marx thought that he had discovered the one thesis that could explain all human history in the same way that Charles Darwin's concept of natural selection could explain all biological evolution. Hegelian theory holds that the 'struggle for recognition' is the central dynamic of human history. Let us examine this thesis.

One of the persistent claims of twentieth century social scientists has been that none of us can shake ourselves free from theory or ideology. We each grow up within a particular framework or paradigm of theory that dominates our thinking, so this line asserts. Those who think they are free from ideology and can make judgements objectively—historians, for example, who think they are dealing with 'the facts'—are therefore merely deluding themselves. 'Facts' only make sense within an ideological framework and so theory is held always to be prior to empirical observation. 'Observation statements', one radical philosopher of science assures us, 'must be made in the language of some theory, however vague'.[21] The most that is possible, we are told, is to bring our assumptions to the surface and to declare our theories and values—whether they be liberal, Marxist or whatever—to others and to ourselves. The big problem for this claim has always hinged on the question of where the major thinkers of each paradigm themselves get their ideas. If everyone was really locked within a theory or an ideology, no one, not even the great theorists, could free themselves. The usual answer to this problem is to allow for a handful of exceptional intellectuals such as Hegel and Marx, and more recently Michel Foucault and Jacques Derrida, to break free from the shackles that still bind the rest of us lesser beings. This response, however, has two problems. The first is that it is inconsistent and simply avoids explaining what it is that allows Foucault to be able to think for himself but not your average history professor. The second is that when we look at the origins of the theories of these so-called exceptional thinkers, we find the sources on which some of them have founded their ideas are not theoretical at all but are decidedly observational. The best example of this is the work of Hegel himself.

At the time Hegel wrote his major works in the early nineteenth century, history was a long way from its current academic practice. Nonetheless, it is clear from the most 'historical' of his works, the lectures on *The Philosophy of History*,[22] that his ideas are derived from the available conventional narrative histories of the eras he discusses. His work spans the ancient history of China, India, Persia, Egypt, Syria, Judea, Greece and Rome as well as the history of Europe from Charlemagne to the Reformation, with a final very brief section on what was to him the 'modern time'—the fifteenth to the eighteenth century. He discusses and characterises the historians on whose work he has most relied. They include Herodotus, Thucydides, Xenophon, Guicciardini, Caesar, Livy, Diodorus Siculus, Cardinal Retz, Frederick the Great, and Johannes von Muller, as well as the monks of the Middle Ages, whom he characterises as 'naive chroniclers'.[23] So although the structure of Hegel's theory has a teleology in the same mode as the Christian version of the human story— history has both a purpose and a fulfilment—his account of the motivations of historical actors derives not from any theology or philosophy but from interpretations he draws from the accounts by historians of what happened in history. In the construction of the philosophy of Hegel, observation was prior to theory. It is legitimate, therefore, to test his philosophy by appealing to the empirical evidence of historians. If the 'struggle for recognition' really is the key to understanding both the pattern of history (its purpose) and the end of history (its fulfilment), it should be confirmed in every case by the historical evidence, just as every biological case can be supported by the principle of natural selection.

Unfortunately for both Hegel and Fukuyama, if one thing is clear from the historical evidence it is that the 'struggle for recognition' never comes even close to explaining it all. The idea that the aristocrats of ancient and feudal society risked everything they had, including their own lives, in mortal combat to subjugate other men into slavery, might once have been a plausible postulate, given the state of historical knowledge in the age of Hegel, but it is inexcusable in Fukuyama's time. As the English historian John Keegan demonstrates in his sweeping survey of the history of warfare since the Stone Age, nobles have seldom led their troops from the front and the incidence of princes killed in battle is notable for its rarity. Keegan notes that, until the Industrial Revolution, the history of Europe and Asia was dominated by a permanent and fundamental tension between the haves of the ploughed lands and the have-nots of soils too thin, cold or dry to be broken for cultivation. While it is true that the cultivators often fought one another to gain the fruits of territory and to capture and subjugate peoples, the have-nots from the waste lands beyond the fertile zone usually had other motives. The Huns, Mongols and Tartars from the Asian steppes, who periodically ravaged the cultivated lands of Europe, China and India between the fifth and the fifteenth centuries, sought neither land, nor slaves, nor recognition. Keegan explains the motives of these 'horse peoples':

They did not seek, as the Goths did, to inherit or adapt to the half-understood civilisations they invaded. Nor—despite a suggestion that Attila contemplated marriage with the daughter of the western Roman emperor — did they seek to supplant others' political authority with their own. They wanted the spoils of war without strings. They were warriors for war's sake, for the loot it brought, the risks, the thrills, the animal satisfactions of triumph... [Their warfare] was not a means to material or social advance; indeed, precisely the contrary, it was the process by which they won the wealth to sustain an unchanging way of life, to remain exactly as they had been since their ancestors first loosed an arrow from the saddle.[24]

If we take another of the periods that Hegel himself discussed, the Middle Ages in Europe, twentieth century historians have found the motivations and consequences of the great expansion of the Western feudal system had little to do with Hegel's account. One of the principal causes of the expansion lay in changes within aristocratic families rather than in any quest for recognition. Recent work by German and French historians has suggested that in the tenth and eleventh centuries, loosely linked kin structures among the nobility were replaced by clearly defined lineages and primogeniture. The eldest son came to be the sole heir of the family title and estates. Younger siblings and cousins were excluded, thereby providing them with a powerful impetus to emigration. Tracing these developments, the English historian Robert Bartlett has shown that the expansion was in many cases the opposite of a process of warfare and enslavement. In the more closely settled parts of Europe, the new immigrants were few in number and found it impossible to pursue a process of expropriation and expulsion. In southern Italy, for instance, 'the picture that emerges is of a small group of Normans and other northern French knights in a population overwhelmingly Lombard, Greek and Muslim'. In some parts of Ireland, the migrating aristocrats married and interbred with the local population; in other parts, they survived as a sealed elite, surrounded by antagonistic natives. The level of hostility between the newcomers and the locals varied greatly, Bartlett shows, and depended on the circumstances of the intrusion and the cultural and religious differences between the two groups. Summarising the process, he writes:

The intrusive aristocracies of the High Middle Ages had differing relationships with and attitudes to indigenous peoples and cultures and could turn out to be an alien and conquering elite, an elite monopolising power but receptive to native culture or a group mingling with native aristocrats.[25]

Hegel's theory does not even fit what we now know about the early history of the German people, to whom he devoted one-quarter of his work *The Philosophy of History*. Bartlett's study shows that when western German aristocrats migrated into the lands east of the River Elbe in the eleventh, twelfth and thirteenth centuries, in what is now eastern Germany and Poland, they took over territory that was formerly inhabited by Slav peoples. They did this not because they were seeking recognition from the Slavs but because they wanted their land. The Germans did not make slaves of the Slavs but rather expelled them from the region altogether and replaced them with German settlers who were neither slaves, nor serfs, but free immigrants. Throughout this German expansion, the subjects of the lords were not people they had vanquished in battle but their willing followers who wanted to participate in the process. These subjects were, to be sure, economically and socially inferior to their feudal lords, but they were a long way from the less-than-human slaves portrayed by Hegel's thesis. Instead of being a coercive direction of labour, Bartlett demonstrates that the process was one by which migrating aristocrats attempted to lure people by creating favourable and attractive economic and legal conditions.

The vast movement of new settlement, migration and colonisation that took place in the High Middle Ages was based on this model of labour recruitment, not on enserfment or capture. The free village, consciously designed to draw new settlers, could be found everywhere, most notably in the parts of Europe, such as the Iberian peninsula and the lands east of the Elbe, which were opened up to large-scale immigration in this period... The peasants change their birth status and become hereditary leaseholders. The lord grants them this new and favourable status in return for the peasants' activity as farmers and settlers. The lord augments his income, the peasants their income and status.[26]

The 'struggle for recognition', then, is a very poor contender for the title of the key to history. This conclusion, of course, will come as no surprise to anyone who has read widely in the discipline. There are so many variables and contingencies in the story of human affairs that it is inherently implausible that there ever could be one explanation for it all. Both the historians I have drawn upon above, John Keegan and Robert Bartlett, emphasise that in the aspects of the story with which they are dealing, the issues at every stage are 'exceedingly complex' and difficult. Unlike the evolution of species, the thing that distinguishes history is that it is made by human beings who intervene in the process with their will and their reason. Human emotions, luck, stupidity, good judgement and fatal errors all play their part, not to mention the unpredictable scientific discoveries that people make. Even Hegel had to admit that the invention of gunpowder altered the course of history in the fifteenth century by directing major shifts in power towards those peoples who took most advantage of the use of firearms in warfare. Principally, though, it is the intervention of human beings and the decisions they take as historical subjects that make it impossible that there could ever be anything that qualified as the one central or fundamental explanation for history. This is one of the reasons that so many of the recent 'grand theorists', from Althusser to Foucault, have been at such pains to deny the ability of human subjects—that is, individuals and groups with minds and wills of their own—to intervene and make history themselves.

One of the important consequences of an empirical approach, therefore, is that history cannot be determined. The historical process is not moving inexorably in one direction or towards any goal or end; it has no hidden pattern or itinerary waiting to be discovered. The job of the historian is not to search for some theory that will reveal all, nor some teleology that will explain the purpose of things. Rather, it is to reconstruct the events of the past in their own terms. The reason that narrative is the most appropriate method through which to do this is because the historian is dealing in unique events, in the realm of the contingent. Such events never repeat themselves, but they are nonetheless dependent upon, contingent upon, every other event that came before. What happens in history, therefore, is never random, but neither does it conform to any deep-seated design. Hence, as long as the human species survives, it can make no sense to speak of an end to history.

One of the most common findings in intellectual history is that new ideas that might seem to have universal application very often reflect more about the time and place in which they were produced than anything else. Fukuyama's thesis is an obvious example. It is a celebration by an American of the American triumph in the Cold War, a response that the author thinks all humanity should share. In other parts of the world, however, there are many who have a much darker view of their prospects in the new world order. The collapse of the Soviet ruling class and its empire obviously appears quite different if one is looking out from Sarajevo, Warsaw or Odessa rather than Washington.

Many of the Moscow correspondents of the Western media have made the observation that there are some uncanny parallels between Russia in the early 1990s and the German Weimar Republic of the early 1920s: a lost war that humiliated the armed forces; hyperinflation; the rise of a chauvinist nationalism; attempts at anti-democratic putsches; and nationals of the old regime who find themselves stranded as minorities in upstart new states. From the perspective of eastern Europe, the end of the Cold War, rather than settling all the big questions, has reproduced a number of the ingredients that once combined to generate the greatest conflagration of the century.

NAZISM, POSTHISTORY AND POSTMODERNISM

One of the most embarrassing series of revelations for the radical intellectuals discussed in this book has been the number of connections made between their theories and the philosophies of the Nazi regime in Germany. The disclosures began in 1987 when the Chilean-born author, Victor Farías, published in France an examination of the German philosopher Martin Heidegger, regarded by his supporters as the most important theorist and interpreter of language in the twentieth century. Farías revealed previously suppressed documents that showed Heidegger had been a financial member of the Nazi Party from 1933 to 1945, a Nazi informer against academic colleagues in the 1930s, an anti-Semite and someone who lamented the defeat of the Nazi regime right until his death in 1976. Farías's book caused a great stir within France because three of the most famous French radical intellectuals, Michel Foucault, Jacques Derrida and Jacques Lacan, had all been influenced by and were partly dependent upon Heidegger's philosophy for their own theories. Supporters of this trio replied that Heidegger's political career was something quite distinct from his philosophy, but this response always had a ring of implausibility about it. A substantial component of Heidegger's philosophy had been a critique of modern social existence and, as such, was overtly political. Heidegger himself had continued to affirm as late as 1962 that the founding principles of National Socialism—its 'inner truth and greatness'—provided the one successful answer to the central problems of 'modern man' and to the 'dreary technological frenzy' that had left modern society in a state of destitution.[27] Although, as his apologists emphasise, it is true that Heidegger did express some concerns about the direction the Nazi movement took during the late 1930s (the main one being that he believed it was he, Heidegger, who deserved to be the German messiah rather than Adolf Hitler[28]) his academic career flourished under its patronage. Despite the French protests, the point that stuck was that Heidegger's philosophy was perfectly compatible with a successful career as one of Germany's leading academics during the Nazi regime.

The Heidegger revelations did most damage to the reputation of the poststructuralist theorist Jacques Derrida. Before Farías's book was published, an iconoclastic analysis of French intellectuals of the post-1968 period by the philosophers Luc Ferry and Alain Renaut had identified Derrida's thought as the most dependent on Heidegger of all the French Heideggerians. Ferry and Renaut irreverently characterised the radical trio according to the following formulae:

Foucault = Heidegger + Nietzsche
Lacan = Heidegger + Freud
Derrida = Heidegger + Derrida's style.[29]

At the same time as Farías was doing his detective work, a Belgian scholar, Ortwin de Graef, was engaged in a similar investigation of the case of Paul de Man who, until his death in 1983, had been one of America's most celebrated and influential literary theorists. It had been de Man who, as a member of the Yale School of criticism in the 1970s, had done more to institutionalise Derrida's poststructuralist methods within American literary circles and university English departments than anyone else. Ortwin de Graef revealed that, as a young man in occupied Belgium during the Second World War, de Man had been a Nazi collaborator and had written a series of articles in Belgian newspapers supporting the Nazi cause. In 1941, in response to what he saw as Jewish 'pollution' of European literature and to 'Semitic meddling into all aspects of European life', de Man had published his own final solution to the Jewish problem: 'the creation of a Jewish colony isolated from Europe' to which all Jews would be deported.[30] Following de Man's subsequent migration to the United States and during the career that saw him rise to the position of Professor of Humanities at Yale University, he not only failed to acknowledge these pro-Nazi activities but lied about his wartime role, claiming he had been a member of the Belgian resistance to the Germans.

Derrida himself joined the chorus of literary academics who wrote articles attempting to restore de Man's reputation, affirming that although he, Derrida, was Jewish he thought it wrong 'to judge, to condemn the work of a man on the basis of what was a brief episode'.[31] Despite the rejoinders and denials, however, the simultaneous revelations about Heidegger and de Man left the reputation of Derrida and poststructuralism decidedly murky. The revelations raised the awkward question of just how firm was the connection between pro-Nazi attitudes of the 1930s and 1940s and the French radical theory that had become so influential in our own time. In 1989, a German historian, Lutz Niethammer, provided much of the answer.

At the same time as Fukuyama wrote his first end of history essay, Niethammer published a book on the same topic, *Posthistoire: Has History Come to an End?*[32] Niethammer's treatment, however, is radically different in both method and conclusions. It is a study of the evolution of the idea of the end of history—sometimes called *posthistoire* or posthistory—from the mid-nineteenth century to the mid-twentieth. The main focus of the book is on eight European writers of the 1930s, 1940s and 1950s who had all expressed variants of the notion. Rather than an endorsement of the concept, Niethammer's work is a dramatic exposé of it. Of the eight writers, two had been Communists when they endorsed the thesis (Alexander Kojève and Walter Benjamin) while the other six had been either German fascists (Martin Heidegger, Ernst Jünger, Arnold Gehlen, Carl Schmitt) or Nazi collaborators during the Second World War (Bertrand de Jouvenal and Hendrik de Man, uncle of Paul). Niethammer says the thesis of posthistory is not about the literal annihilation of the world through, say, nuclear warfare or environmental catastrophe. Rather, it is about the end of meaning or purpose in history. Posthistory is a 'culturally pessimistic inversion of the optimism of progress'. It holds that the teleology of history has reached an end, but has concluded in a form of social life that is lived without any seriousness, struggle or objective: an anti-utopia.

As it was expressed in the 1930s, 1940s and 1950s, there were two major components of the posthistory thesis. The first was a philosophy of history; the second a critique of modern society. The philosophy of history was expressed most clearly by Arnold Gehlen, who had been a prominent social psychologist under the Third Reich and who became influential as a conservative anthropologist and cultural critic in West Germany during the 1950s and early 1960s. Gehlen argued that, just as the history of religion had come to an end, with a finite number of major faiths to which no more could be added, so the history of ideology had unravelled all its possibilities. No more general philosophies of the kind developed by Hegel, Marx or Nietzsche were conceivable. All that remained to humankind was to accept one or other of the various positions worked out within these major ideological fields. Moreover, this meant that no further development of either art or politics was possible. The range of *avant gardes* in literature, painting and music had exhausted their potentialities; the different types of political and administrative structures that were possible were limited to the few that existed in the 1950s and were, moreover, destined to be reduced even further.

I will therefore stick my neck out and say that the history of ideas has been suspended, and that we have now arrived at posthistory... In the very epoch when it is becoming possible to see and report on the earth as a whole, when nothing of any import can pass unnoticed, the earth is in this respect devoid of surprises. The alternatives are known, as in the field of religion, and are in every case final.[33]

The reason for this, Gehlen argued, was that history lacked a heroic subject.

Europe once possessed an epoch-making spirit. This baton had been most recently carried by the German people but, with their defeat in 1945, all that was now over. Postwar Germany, Gehlen argued, had become Americanised which, as Goebbels had warned, had destroyed the heroic German spirit and left its people no better than other races—a mass reduced to an impersonal 'they' or 'id'. Without a heroic subject, history had come to an end.

The posthistorical critique of modern society resurrected a number of ideas of Nietzsche, especially his condemnation of popular sovereignty in politics and culture. Modern society, Gehlen argued, was a world of technological rationality controlled by bureaucrats, planners and social engineers. Materialism was the dominant ethos and the culture of the bourgeois (which in the past had produced both some great art and great leaders) had been replaced by the mediocre masses. Culture became dominated by mass taste and mass media. Gehlen was disgusted by the masses who were driven by their collective unconscious into a pursuit of security above all else: 'They no longer bother about the old magic word freedom; they think in terms of plans...to make the world futureless and at that price to buy security.' There was no longer the possibility of society throwing up some great individuals like those who in the past had acted as heralds or helmsmen of their era. In particular, mass society had permanently aborted the production of that outstanding individual, the great artist. Gehlen complained in 1961:

Now there is no longer any internal development within art! It is all up with art history based upon the logic of meaning, and even with any consistency of absurdities. The process of development has been completed, and what comes now is already in existence: the confused syncretism of all styles and possibilities—posthistory.[34]

Posthistory, then, is an expression of a particularly unpleasant form of intellectual elitism that exhibits both a complete disdain for ordinary people and an unwillingness to regard them as individuals. It adherents contend that the age of great ideas and of heroic causes such as Nazism is over, replaced by a boring, featureless and, in Heidegger's oft-repeated word, 'destitute' world peopled by mediocrities.

Niethammer argues that the fascist version of posthistory was both a precursor of, and remains a major constituent of, French radical thought of the 1970s and 1980s. He also finds that key intellectuals of the German New Left of the 1960s, especially those with connections to its terrorist wing, returned to the posthistory thesis in the early 1980s in response to the failure of their plans for social revolution. Overall, his argument is that intellectuals on both the Left (Marxist) and Right (fascist) turned to the concept of posthistory when it became clear to them that their revolutionary aspirations either had been defeated outright or else appeared doomed to little chance of success. Posthistory is a pessimistic reaction to the end of utopian politics.

In France, Niethammer argues, similar causes produced similar responses, only with a delay of more than two decades. In the wake of the events of 1968—the failure of the student-led revolts and the desertion by French intellectuals from the Communist Party with whom they had largely sympathised in the postwar period—the philosophy of history deriving from Hegel and Marx was also subject to a new kind of critique from the Left. It was denounced for its pretensions as an authoritarian language game. What began as a critique of leftist thought eventually turned into the cultural movement called postmodernism. One of its leading exponents, Jean François Lyotard, a former Marxist, said the postmodernist outlook was based on 'an incredulity toward metanarratives', that is, it renounced the philosophy of history.[35] Lyotard was reviving a term used by Nietzsche who claimed 'metanarratives' were all products of Enlightenment or modernist belief in rational progress.

Another French postmodernist, Jean Baudrillard, a former Communist Party intellectual, developed an approach to criticism of the mass media that had a similar thesis, again with some components borrowed from Nietzsche. Baudrillard writes in a form of associative language of outpouring of images or analogies to claim that social reality and its 'simulation' in the media can no longer be distinguished. Indeed, Baudrillard claims the 'hyperreality' conveyed by the media actually dominates people's primary consciousness. They experience life through terms defined for them by the media. They lose the possibility of recognising or differentiating a future period of time, and so lose the sense of history. The masses, passive and bored, reach a state of entropy where history implodes into a state of inertia and stagnation.[36] This 'exit from history' is not an end but an eternal sameness. Niethammer points out that the Baudrillard thesis, unlike that of its German predecessors, is not pessimistic nor an occasion for despair but is presented with that cheerfulness that Nietzsche had already praised as the road to redemption. Baudrillard's response to the end of metanarratives thus goes one step further than the German version because, in rejecting pessimism, it abandons the lament for a lost goal. Baudrillard's 'cheerful' account of posthistory is presented as an analogy to the acoustic disappearance of music in the ultraperfection of a quadrophonic system. History reaches a 'vanishing point' in the surfeit of information about events that are both too numerous and too close, and through the dissolution of social interrelations in microanalytic research. Each event sinks 'with musical accompaniment' into the timeless store of too many events, into a proliferation of memories without experience.[37]

Beneath the provocatively outrageous analogies and attention-seeking metaphors of Baudrillard's postmodernism, however, lies yet another example of the posthistory thesis. As such, it is not detached from, but simply one more conclusion derived from, the philosophy of history which both he and Lyotard purport to reject. Instead of abandoning the philosophy of history altogether, Baudrillard has formulated a reaction to it, that is, a reaction that remains dependent on the existence of that to which it is opposed. For history to reach a 'vanishing point' there has to have been some history at some stage to do the vanishing. In Baudrillard's scheme of things, this 'history' could not be that poor, artless variety found in the work of empirical historians, for that is neither the kind that can vanish nor the sort of methodology that Baudrillard's approach would ever countenance. The only history that can perform his trick is the teleological kind, which can end either by arriving at some version of utopia or by culminating in the anti-utopia of the post-fascists and other end-of-history theorists. French postmodernism, then, is another version of posthistory, this time reduced to an intellectual absurdity since it is trapped within the very concept from which it imagines it is emancipated. Thus, rather than abandoning metanarratives, as it claims, French postmodernism should be seen instead as merely substituting one metanarrative for another. Its leading lights have deserted the grand theory of Hegel and Marx but, in its place, have taken on board an alternative philosophy of history acquired from Nietzsche and Heidegger.

In this light, we can see those English-speaking academics who are investing their time, energy and personal endorsement in the concept of postmodernism as sorry figures indeed. They thought they were participating in an exciting and new theoretical movement. Instead, all they are producing, albeit unwittingly, is an English-language version of a French theory from the 1980s, which itself derives from a German thesis from the 1940s and 1950s that was originally developed by a group of ex-Nazis to lament the defeat of the Third Reich.

---

1 Francis Fukuyama, 'The End of History?' *The National Interest*, 16, Summer 1989, pp 3-18

2 Francis Fukuyama, *The End of History and the Last Man*, Hamish Hamilton, London, 1992, pp xiii, 13-15

3 Francis Fukuyama, *The End of History and the Last Man*, pp xiv-xv, summary of Part II, chapters 5-12

4 Francis Fukuyama, *The End of History and the Last Man*, pp xv-xvi

5 Francis Fukuyama, *The End of History and the Last Man*, pp xvi-xviii, summary of Part III, chapters 13-19

6 Francis Fukuyama, *The End of History and the Last Man*, p xvii, his italics

7 Francis Fukuyama, *The End of History and the Last Man*, p xviii

8 Francis Fukuyama, *The End of History and the Last Man*, Chapter 21

9 Francis Fukuyama, *The End of History and the Last Man*, Chapter 23

10 Francis Fukuyama, *The End of History and the Last Man*, Chapter 28

11 Francis Fukuyama, *The End of History and the Last Man*, p 311. His analogy reveals how little the author knows about dogs. In any household containing two or more male canines, there is a persistent and occasionally violent political campaign to decide the dominant dog. Our family terriers, Duff and George, refute this part of Fukuyama's thesis every day

12 Francis Fukuyama, *The End of History and the Last Man*, p 336

13 Norman Wintrop, 'Fukuyama's Challenge to Leftism', *Quadrant*, June 1993, pp 9-19

14 Francis Fukuyama, *The End of History and the Last Man*, pp 124-5

15 David Stove, 'The end of history? the Fukuyama thesis', *Quadrant*, 33, 10, October 1989, pp 32-3

16 Robin Blackburn (ed.), *After the Fall: The Failure of Communism and the Future of Socialism*, Verso, London, 1992

17 Perry Anderson, 'The Ends of History', in his *A Zone of Engagement*, Verso, London, 1992, p 341

18 Perry Anderson, 'The Ends of History', pp 372-5

19 Perry Anderson, 'The Ends of History' pp 352-5

20 Perry Anderson, 'The Ends of History', pp 356-7

21 Alan Chalmers, *What Is This Thing Called Science?* University of Queensland Press, Brisbane, 1982, p 28

22 Georg Wilhelm Friedrich Hegel, *The Philosophy of History*, trans. J. Sibree, Dover, New York, 1956

23 G. W. F. Hegel, *The Philosophy of History*, pp 2-6

24 John Keegan, *A History of Warfare*, Hutchinson, London, 1993, pp 74-5, 188-9

25 Robert Bartlett, *The Making of Europe: Conquest, Colonisation and Cultural Change 950–1350*, Allen Lane, The Penguin Press, London, 1993, pp 49-51, 56

26 Robert Bartlett, *The Making of Europe*, p 120

27 Victor Farías, *Heidegger and Nazism*, (French edn 1987), English edn trans. Paul Burrell, eds Joseph Margolis and Tom Rockmore, Temple University Press, Philadelphia, 1989, p 298. In 1960 Heidegger dedicated one of his books to the director of the Institute of Racial Hygiene in Berlin during the Nazi era.

28 Tom Rockmore, *On Heidegger's Nazism and Philosophy*, University of California Press, Berkeley and Los Angeles, 1992, pp 200-1

29 Luc Ferry and Alain Renaut, *French Philosophy of the Sixties: An Essay on Antihumanism,*(French edn 1985) trans. Mary S. Cattani, University of Massachusetts Press, Amherst, 1991, p 123

30 For an appropriately critical analysis of de Man's journalism and career, and the attempts of the American literary establishment to defend him, see Roger Kimball, 'The Case of Paul de Man', in his *Tenured Radicals: How Politics Has Corrupted Our Higher Education*, Harper and Row, New York, 1990, Chapter Four.

31 Jacques Derrida, 'Like the Sound of the Sea Deep Within a Shell: Paul de Man's War', *Critical Inquiry*, 14, Spring 1988, p 590

32 Lutz Niethammer, *Posthistoire: Has History Come to an End?* (German edn 1989), English edn trans. Patrick Camiller, Verso, London 1992

33 Arnold Gehlen, cited by Lutz Niethammer, *Posthistoire*, p 11

34 Arnold Gehlen, cited by Lutz Niethammer, *Posthistoire*, p 12

35 Jean François Lyotard, *The Postmodern Condition*, University of Minneapolis Press, Minneapolis, 1984

36 Jean Baudrillard, 'The Year 2000 Has Already Happened', in Arthur and Marilouise Kroker (eds), *Body Invaders: Panic Sex in America*, New World Perspectives, Montreal, 1988, pp 35-44

37 Lutz Niethammer, *Posthistoire*, p 29

7

HISTORY AS A SOCIAL SCIENCE
RELATIVISM, HERMENEUTICS AND INDUCTION

HISTORY is a discipline that straddles both the humanities and the social sciences. History's credentials as a science derive from three of its objectives: first, it aims to record the truth about what happened in the past; second, it aims to build a body of knowledge about the past; third, it aims to study the past through a disciplined methodology, using techniques and sources that are accessible to others in the field. The claim that history is a science is a highly contested issue, which calls for justification rather than mere assertion, and so later sections of this chapter discuss the scientific status of the methodologies employed by historians. To start, however, let us focus on the issues of truth and knowledge. The study of history is essentially a search for the truth. Without a claim to be pursuing truth, writing history would be indistinguishable in principle from writing a novel about the past. A work that does not aim at truth may be many things but not a work of history. Historical knowledge can either be discovered, by finding evidence that provides new revelations, or can be synthesised, by ordering what is already known in a way that provides a new perspective on events of the past. Either way, historians long believed they were engaged in an enterprise that had some claim to be adding to the knowledge produced by others, by making new discoveries, and by seeing things from different angles, even in the act of criticising and overturning other claims. No historian ever started on a topic completely from scratch. Until recently, all acknowledged they relied to some extent on those who had gone before them and all assumed they were, in turn, contributing to an accumulating body of knowledge that would be drawn upon by others.

In the academic environment of today, however, the pursuit of truth and the accumulation of knowledge have become highly questionable endeavours. One of the reasons that the nihilism of French radical theory has been able to gain such a grip on the study of human affairs is because there is now widespread scepticism about the concepts of truth and knowledge. Many academics believe that neither the social sciences nor even the natural sciences can provide us with any kind of certitude. The fashionable and some say the now-dominant view, is that knowledge can never be absolute and there can be no universal truths. Let me quote a random, but representative, selection of recent statements from academics in both the humanities and the social sciences about the concepts of science, knowledge and truth. Anthony Giddens, Professor of Sociology at the University of Cambridge, and one of Britain's most influential social theorists has written:

In science, *nothing* is certain, and nothing can be proved, even if scientific endeavour provides us with the most dependable information about the world to which we can aspire. In the heart of the world of hard science, modernity floats free.[1]

The feminist historian Professor Ann Curthoys, of the University of Technology, Sydney, has claimed:

Most academics in the humanities and social sciences, and as far as I know in the physical and natural sciences as well, now reject positivist concepts of knowledge, the notion that one can objectively know the facts. The processes of knowing, and the production of an object that is known, are seen as intertwined. Many take this even further, and argue that knowledge is entirely an effect of power, that we can no longer have any concept of truth at all.[2]

The literary critic Dr Harry Oldmeadow, of La Trobe University, Victoria, while making a trenchant criticism of postmodernist theory's rejection of traditional values, nonetheless accepts its critique of truth.

The epistemological objections to the liberal ideal of a disinterested pursuit of truth are more difficult to counter. The positivist rubric of 'objectivity' is now quite rightly in tatters: Kuhn, Rorty and others have shown how the apparently objective basis of the scientific disciplines themselves is illusory (never mind the more absurd pretensions of a positivist sociology or a behaviourist psychology.)[3]

As the last two quotations underline, the most pejorative insult to hurl in today's academic climate is the label 'positivist'. This term refers to a movement in philosophy that began in the nineteenth century and that, under the name adopted by its pre-war Viennese adherents, 'logical positivism', reached its greatest influence in the English-speaking world in the 1950s and early

1960s. During the Vietnam War, positivism became identified with the political Right because some of the leading positivists at the time were outspoken supporters of American intervention (even though others, such as Bertrand Russell, were equally well-known opponents of both the war and the nuclear arms race). Positivism is but one of a number of philosophical analyses that have supported and justified the scientific method that rose to prominence in Europe in the seventeenth and eighteenth centuries in the period now known as the Enlightenment. This scientific method, based on drawing conclusions from empirical observation and experiment, provided the apparatus for all our subsequent knowledge of the physical and biological worlds and has been the engine of the industrial and technological societies that have emerged in the train of this knowledge. When postmodernists and their fellow travellers write dismissively of 'positivist illusions' their real target is the claim of the empirical methods of science to provide the path to knowledge. Scientific method, in their view, has no universal validity; it is just another transitory product of an era that is now rapidly fading.

Those readers who have not followed the debates inside academia over recent years about the status of knowledge and science may find all this odd, to say the least. After all, most of the educated population today attribute the enormous explosion of knowledge of the last three hundred years to the methods of empirical science. It has freed our culture from the shackles of superstition, mysticism and quackery, and it appears, indeed, still to be taken for granted by most intelligent people in the world at large. Unfortunately, within many schools of humanities and social sciences today such views are few and far between. As a result, this chapter needs to make a longish diversion from the book's principal focus to examine the current status of scientific knowledge. For if the fashionable view is correct, and truth and knowledge are really beyond our reach, then we might as well give history away altogether. The debate on this issue has taken place in no less than three separate forums: the sociology of science, the philosophy of scientific method and the field of hermeneutics.

THE SOCIOLOGY OF SCIENCE

One of the major figures responsible for the current levels of doubt about scientific knowledge is the American author Thomas Kuhn, whose very influential book, *The Structure of Scientific Revolutions*,[4] has been in print continuously since it was first published in 1962. Kuhn is responsible for introducing the concept of the scientific 'paradigm' to provide a sociological explanation of how changes in scientific opinion and methods come about. Kuhn uses this term in his account of how a widely accepted scientific framework is overthrown and replaced by another. He distinguishes three phases in the life of any body of science. The first is the pre-science phase in which a range of unstructured and uncoordinated activities take place. If these activities are taken up and organised by what he calls a 'scientific community', that community adheres to a 'paradigm'. A paradigm is made up of the range of techniques, assumptions and theories that the members of the community work with in pursuit of their science. While they are working within the framework of the paradigm, they practise what Kuhn calls normal science, which is the second of the phases he identifies. Kuhn says that normal science is characterised by periods of calm and steady development dominated by one accepted set of concepts. The third phase is composed of a crisis within the science, which produces a period of radical change when the ruling paradigm is overthrown by another. This constitutes a paradigm shift or a scientific revolution. The most well-known examples are the overthrow of Ptolemaic astronomy by that of Copernicus, or the replacement of Newton's mechanics by Einstein's theory of relativity. Crises recur because any existing paradigm is almost always subject to anomalies, that is, observations that are difficult to explain or reconcile with the central doctrine. At first these might appear marginal, but they gradually accumulate to the point where the scientific community eventually loses faith in the existing paradigm. The door is then opened for a scientific revolution to occur which will establish a new paradigm that explains both the former body of data and the inconsistencies that the old paradigm could not handle. A new period of normal science then continues until it, again, is subject to its own crisis and revolution.

The Kuhn thesis is a radical challenge to familiar notions of science, especially the idea that our knowledge of nature has gradually built up over time. Kuhn replaces the picture of a cumulative and progressive model of growth with a discontinuous and revolutionary process of change. For example, Einstein's theory of relativity did not add a new increment of knowledge to the secure truth of Newton's theory of gravitation but overthrew it completely. However, because Einstein's theories are themselves destined ultimately for the same fate, as would be the paradigm of any successor of Einstein, the Kuhn thesis is committed to denying the possibility of any scientific knowledge at all, in the normal sense of 'knowledge' implying truth and certitude. Kuhn eschews talk of 'truth' and 'falsity' in science and insists that the beliefs of scientists are all 'paradigm-relative', that is, they make sense within their own intellectual environment but not in others.

Kuhn also argues for what he calls the *incommensurability* of scientific theories. New paradigms may borrow some of the vocabulary and apparatus of the old, but they seldom use these borrowed elements in the same way. Different paradigms operate with different concepts, sometimes changing the meaning of old terms, and they have different standards of acceptable evidence, as well as different means of theorising about their subject matter.

Consider ... the men who called Copernicus mad because he proclaimed that the earth moved. They were not either just wrong or quite wrong. Part of what they meant by 'earth' was fixed position. Their earth, at least, could not be moved.[5]

Overall, Kuhn's thesis on incommensurability argues, there is no common measure for the merits of competing theories, nor any common agreement about what constitutes either a scientific problem or a satisfactory scientific explanation. Hence, there is no way of ranking scientific theories and thus there are no grounds for arguing that science is progressive. Einstein is not superior to Newton, just different.

Kuhn insists that, although a paradigm has to be supported by compelling evidence and arguments in its favour, it is never accepted for purely objective reasons; rather, it gains acceptance because a consensus of opinion within a scientific community agrees to use it. He says the issue is not decided by purely logical argument but is more like sudden conversion or a 'gestalt switch'.[6] The factors that lead scientists to change their allegiance to paradigms, he argues, need to be explained in terms of the scientists' values and the personal relations within a scientific community. 'Paradigm choice can never be un-equivocally settled by logic and experiment alone.'[7] Following Kuhn, a bevy of sociologists have entered the field to take up what they see as one of the most enticing consequences of his position: the idea that what is believed in science is determined by the customs and power relations prevailing within a particular scientific community.

One of these sociologists, David Bloor, has gone so far as to suggest that the content and nature of science can be explained through the methods of the sociology of knowledge, and that scientists accept scientific laws primarily for reasons of justification, legitimation and control.[8] Another, H. M. Collins, has made a radical critique of the concept of scientific experiment. All experiments, Collins claims, are subject to 'experimenter's regress'. This argument contends that experiments cannot perform the function that scientists claim for them, that is, to independently assess the success or otherwise of competing scientific theories. This is because the theories themselves determine what counts as an effective experiment. Hence, there are no objective criteria that can be derived from experiments to separate the outcome of the experiment from the theory it has been designed to test. After interviewing scientists about the reasons why they accept or reject experimental results published by other scientists, Collins concluded that they were strongly influenced by such things as the size and prestige of the university where the experiment was done; the personality, nationality and reputation of the scientist; whether the experiment was performed within a university or within industry; and the way the results were presented. 'It is not the regularity of the world that imposes itself on our senses', Collins writes, 'but the regularity of our institutionalised belief that imposes itself on the world'.[9]

Many of the conclusions of Kuhn and his followers have parallels in French radical theory. In particular, Michel Foucault's version of the history of ideas follows the concepts of Kuhn very closely. Kuhn's notion of the 'paradigm' is the model for Foucault's more encompassing but still very similar 'episteme'. Kuhn's argument that consensual custom and power determine what is accepted as scientific truth is almost identical to Foucault's claim that truth is established by intellectual power groups. In fact, it is highly likely that, just as Foucault constructed his thesis on institutions by borrowing without acknowledgement the ideas of the American sociologist Erving Goffman (as shown in Chapter Five), Foucault did much the same with Kuhn's book to produce his history of ideas. Whatever is the case, though, it is clear that the work of Kuhn, and its subsequent popularity among sociologists and their students, helped pave the way for the acceptance of French radicalism and for the prevailing derision about the claims of historians or anyone else to be pursuing the truth and producing knowledge.

THE PHILOSOPHY OF SCIENTIFIC METHOD

At the same time as Kuhn's essentially sociological analysis was made, the philosophy of scientific method had arrived, by another route, at a similar set of conclusions. By the early 1960s, the Viennese-born, English-based philosopher Karl Popper was widely regarded as having solved one of the most vexatious problems in philosophy: the justification of empirical scientific method. Popper devised, and from the 1930s to the 1980s was the leading advocate of, the principle of 'falsifiability'. He argued against the view accepted by most scientists that evidence was used to verify scientific theories. The traditional scientific method of induction has held, since the writings of Francis Bacon in the early seventeenth century, that we gain scientific knowledge by generalising from our observations. Popper claimed, however, that the proper role of evidence is to falsify scientific conjectures. Thus, instead of the traditional view that a scientific theory is *verifiable* by observation, Popper contended that a scientific theory is one that is *falsifiable*. Theories, Popper said, are not the kind of things that can be established as being conclusively true in light of observation or experiment. Rather, theories are speculations, guesses or conjectures about some aspect of the world or the cosmos. The role of observation and experiment is to rigorously test these theoretical conjectures and to eliminate those that fail to stand up to the tests that are applied. Science advances by trial and error, with observation and experiment progressively eliminating unsound theories so that only the fittest survive. As the title of one of Popper's best-known books describes it, scientific method is a process of 'conjectures and refutations'[10] in which we learn not by our experience but by our mistakes.

Falsifiability appeared to solve a number of the philosophical problems surrounding the scientific method of induction in which evidence comes first and theory later. Following a critique made by the eighteenth century Scottish philosopher David Hume, it appeared that the method of induction is fatally flawed. Inductive arguments, Hume argued, are logically invalid. Against traditional, inductive scientific method, which held that, after repeated observations of A being B, and no observations of the opposite, one is justified in claiming that all As are B, Hume argued that such inductive arguments are invalid because it is always open to possibility that the next A we find will not be a B. Given the remarkable successes that science and technology enjoyed in the eighteenth and nineteenth centuries, Hume's argument was quietly ignored by most philosophers. In the twentieth century, however, when some of the old certainties, especially those of Newton's physics, were overthrown, a new generation headed by Popper argued that Hume had been right all along. Popper accepted that universal arguments such as all As are B are *un*provable. However, he added that they remain in principle *dis*provable. If we find just one A that is not a B then we can be certain that the theory that all As are B is false. The very mark of a scientific theory is that it can be disproved by experience, he said, and the more disprovable it is compared with its rivals, then the better than them it is.

Falsifiability also appeared to avoid another critique that has been made of induction: the theory-dependence of observation. Scientific induction assumes that the observations of the world that go towards constructing a scientific theory are themselves objective and theoretically neutral. However, critics have countered that theory of some kind must precede all observation statements. One of Popper's former students, the Sydney philosopher, Alan Chalmers, has claimed: 'Observation statements must be made in the language of some theory, however vague.' As well as some scientific examples, Chalmers gives the commonsense instance: 'Look out, the wind is blowing the baby's pram over the cliff edge!' and says that much low-level theory is presupposed even here. 'It is implied that there is such a thing as wind, which has the property of being able to cause the motion of objects such as prams, which stand in its path.'[11] Falsifiability avoids such a critique because it freely admits that observation is guided by and presupposes theory. The aim of falsification is to start not with observations but with theories themselves.

Popper's approach, then, appeared to have much to recommend it. He abandoned the logically problematic claim that evidence counted *towards* the acceptance of a theory and, instead, argued that evidence only counted *against* a theory. For example, the argument 'A black swan was observed in Australia; therefore, not all swans are white' is a logically valid deduction. The falsity of a universal statement can be demonstrated by an appropriate singular statement. Moreover, the falsifiability criterion had the added advantage of readily identifying certain kinds of statements as non-scientific. For example, a logically necessary statement such as 'A father is a male parent' is not a scientific statement because it is true by virtue of the meaning of the term used and is thus unfalsifiable. Similarly, many statements deriving from religion, mysticism or metaphysics could be labelled unscientific because there is no evidence that could be brought to bear to falsify them. Hence, Popper had an argument that seemed to have three advantages: it solved the problem of induction, it was an empirical not a metaphysical approach and it defended science. For these reasons, falsificationism won widespread support in the 1960s from both philosophers and scientists themselves.

Falsificationism gained this acceptance despite the fact that it introduced a large element of uncertainty into the notion of science. It said that a scientific theory holds until it is disproved and that science advances by a process of elimination. However, Popper agreed that no matter how many searches fail to find a negative instance to falsify a theory, this can never provide grounds for thinking the theory has been conclusively established. Hence, on the falsifiability principle, no scientific theory can ever be conclusive. It remains forever a conjecture or a hypothesis. So we can never have sufficient grounds for gaining from science anything as concrete as 'knowledge' in the usual sense of that word. We get good theories (those that are falsifiable but not yet falsified) and bad theories (those that have been falsified or that are unfalsifiable) but nothing more definite than this. In the 1990s, social scientists such as Anthony Giddens still cite Popper's early work as the basis for their belief that nothing can be proved and that nothing is certain.[12]

Despite its wide acceptance, Popper's theory was subject to some searching criticisms from the outset. Thomas Kuhn argued that Popper's approach was little different from the verification theory that it was designed to replace. All scientific theories are accompanied by anomalies that they find difficult to explain, Kuhn pointed out. These are rarely regarded as falsifications, but, rather, are seen as 'the incompleteness and imperfection of the existing data-theory fit that, at any time, define many of the puzzles that characterise normal science'. If these anomalous observations are regarded as so powerful as to overturn an existing theory, they act as something that 'might equally well be called verification' for the newly emerging paradigm in the field. Kuhn said he doubted if outright falsifications ever existed.[13] Other critics pointed out that Popper had not removed the major difficulties inherent in the observation process. Observations that refute theories had no higher a level of reliability than observations that confirmed them. Scientists, moreover, will often reject an apparently falsifying observation in order to retain a theory. For example, supporters of Copernicus's theory that the planets orbited the Sun found it difficult to account for naked-eye observations that the apparent size of Venus did not change throughout the year, as the theory said it should, yet they stuck to the theory anyway.[14] If they had followed Popper, they would have been forced to agree that this observation amounted to a falsification of the theory that the planets orbit the Sun. It took another seventy years before better observation technology was developed that showed that the apparent size of Venus did change and that Copernicus was right.

Popper's most influential supporter was the Hungarian-born philosopher Imre Lakatos, who succeeded him as Professor of Logic and Scientific Method at the University of London. Although a critic of a number of aspects of the way in which Popper had formulated his falsification thesis, Lakatos tried to improve upon, and overcome objections to, the doctrine. Lakatos was also a critic of Kuhn, but nonetheless adopted some elements of the sociological approach into his work. Lakatos argued that any description of science cannot be confined to statements of laws or singular observations. He added that simple falsifications are rarely fatal to a scientific theory. Scientific endeavour has to be regarded as a 'research program'. This is a structure or framework that provides guidance for future research in a way similar to Kuhn's 'paradigm'. A research program has a hard core of general theoretical hypotheses from which the future research of the program can develop. For example, the hard core hypotheses of Copernican astronomy are that the Sun is the centre of the solar system, that the Sun remains stationary while Earth and the other planets orbit it, and that Earth spins on its axis once every day. In the early stages of a research program, Lakatos said, there might be many observations that appear to falsify its core, but the program should not be rejected because of these alone. It needs time both to develop its potential and to see if it can answer or overcome what initially look like major stumbling blocks. In the case of the Copernican research program, it had to await technological developments—such as the invention of the telescope—and theoretical developments in related fields—such as Newton's theories of gravitation and motion—before it could be properly assessed. A good research program, according to Lakatos, is one that has a high degree of coherence, that has the potential to inspire a great deal of future research, and that makes novel predictions that are eventually confirmed. Instead of falsification by observation, Lakatos substituted the contrast between a research program that is progressing and one that is degenerating. A degenerating (rather than falsified) research program is one which no longer makes novel predictions compared to a more progressive rival. This is why the old Ptolemaic astronomy, which held that the Earth was stationary at the centre of the universe while the stars and planets circled it, was displaced by Copernican theory.[15]

Although it played down the concept of falsification and gave more weight to confirmation, the Lakatos reformulation left science with the same degree of epistemological uncertainty as Popper's account. How can one tell when a research program has deteriorated enough for its hard core assumptions to actually be disproved? How can one tell that a research program has really run out of novel predictions? How can one be sure that a rival new research program has long-term potential and is not just a flash in the pan? Lakatos had to concede that these were questions that can only be answered in hindsight and that, meanwhile, a high degree of uncertainty prevails. It always remains possible that a waning research program can be revived, as had happened many times in science when the assumptions of old and unfashionable theories were suddenly found to hold the answers to new questions. If this is true, no research program can ever be said, in principle, to be dead and buried and no rival can ever truly claim the field. Following Lakatos, science still stood on shifting sands.

FROM RELATIVISM TO ABSURDITY

According to Thomas Kuhn, the criteria used to assess whether a scientific theory is superior to its rivals are those upon which scientists themselves place most value: how it fits the facts better; how it makes the better predictions; how it has the ability to solve more problems; as well as its aesthetic appeal, that is, its simplicity and neatness. Kuhn argues that 'the importance of aesthetic considerations can often be decisive'.

Though they often attract only a few scientists to a new theory, it is upon those few that its ultimate triumph may depend. If they had not quickly taken it up for highly individual reasons, the new candidate for paradigm might never have been sufficiently developed to attract the allegiance of the scientific community as a whole.[16]

In other words, the value system and tastes of the scientific community are decisive factors. Kuhn is quite specific about this. 'As in political revolutions, so in paradigm choice—there is no standard higher than the assent of the relevant community.' Individual scientists embrace a new paradigm for more than one reason, and usually for several at once. 'Even the nationality and prior reputation of the innovator and his teachers can sometimes play a significant role.'[17]

Since Kuhn acknowledges that the values and standards that prevail within a scientific community vary considerably, depending on the cultural and historical background of the time, this means that in Kuhn's account there can be no universal standard by which to assess a scientific theory. In other words, Kuhn's position is a relativist one—a successful scientific theory is one that is judged so by its peers, relative to their own values, culture and taste. This is a point that Lakatos used to make a trenchant critique of Kuhn. Lakatos said that the relativist position, in which there is no standard higher than that of the relevant community, leaves no room for any way of judging that standard. If what counts is the number, faith and persuasive energy of its supporters, then 'truth lies in power', acceptance of scientific change is no better than 'mob psychology' and scientific progress is merely a 'bandwagon effect'.[18] Without an independent or rational guide to assessing theories, the acceptance of new theories was no better than religious conversion.

Though Kuhn himself has attempted to deny the charge of relativism, there is little doubt in the minds of later commentators on his thesis not only that the charge is correct but that Lakatos himself, through the sociological elements used in his thesis on research programs, is in the same position. One of those who makes this point is Paul Feyerabend, a Viennese-born former student of Popper and Lakatos who spent most of his academic career as a professor of philosophy at the University of California at Berkeley. Feyerabend has pushed the argument from the sociology of science to its furthest conclusion. He argues that the history of scientific research is in itself testimony against the universal validity of any rules to judge the correctness of a scientific theory. Since there are not, nor ever have been, any such universal rules, Feyerabend says Kuhn's theses about paradigms and Lakatos's theses about research programs both share the same, relativist status.[19]

Feyerabend has taken Kuhn's notion of the incommensurability of scientific theories and used it to argue some extraordinary conclusions. Rival scientific theories can be so different from one another, Feyerabend contends, that the basic concepts of one cannot be expressed in terms of the other and that what counts as an observation in one does not count as an observation in the other. He gives the example of classical mechanics and relativity theory. In classical mechanics, physical objects have shape, mass and volume. In relativity, properties of shape, mass and volume no longer exist. This means, Feyerabend says, that any observation about physical objects within classical mechanics has a meaning different from an observation within relativity theory. 'The new conceptual system that arises (within relativity theory) does not just *deny* the existence of classical states of affairs, it does not even permit us to formulate *statements* expressing such states of affairs. It does not and cannot share a single statement with its predecessor...'[20] Given the degree of incommensurability that Feyerabend sees between these two theories and a number of others he compares, he concludes that that there are no 'rational' or 'objective' grounds on which to choose between rival theories. Theory choice is essentially subjective. It is strongly influenced by propaganda and is made on the basis of 'aesthetic judgements, judgements of taste, metaphysical preju- dices, religious desires ... *our subjective wishes*'. Hence, he asserts, a fairer way to decide the merits of scientific theories would be to put them to the vote.[21]

Feyerabend applies the incommensurability principle not only to rival sci- entific theories but to the whole of science itself as compared with other fields that claim to understand the world. Because they, too, are incommensurable, he asserts there can be no argument in favour of science over other forms of understanding. He compares science with astrology and voodoo and claims that there is no general criterion that gives scientific knowledge priority over the latter. Hence, he argues, it is wrong to teach science to school children as if it had a monopoly on wisdom. Non-scientific ways of viewing the world deserve the same kind of attention. The grip that the ideology of science has on government policy deserves to be broken, he says, in the same way that secular educationalists last century broke the nexus between Church and state. This would clear the way for other approaches, such as magic, to be taught instead of science. 'Thus, while an American can now choose the religion he likes, he is still not permitted to demand that his children learn magic rather than science at school. There is a separation between state and Church, there is no separation between state and science.'[22] In Feyerabend's view, science should be studied not as some holy writ but as an historical phenomenon 'together with other fairy tales such as the myths of "primitive" societies'.[23] Consistent with this line, Feyerabend has defended Christian fundamentalists who want to have the biblical version of creation taught in American schools alongside Darwin's theory of evolution.[24]

Feyerabend's deliberately outrageous and attention-seeking epigrams might seem to many readers to put him in a different category from the other three authors discussed here. Certainly, in terms of reputation, his openly irration- alist and 'anarchist' position is seen by most scientists and philosophers as markedly different from that of Kuhn, Popper and Lakatos. For the past thirty years, the latter trio have been widely regarded as having provided the most plausible account of scientific activity available. Yet it should be apparent from the account given above that Feyerabend's views start from the central points made by Kuhn's thesis. Feyerabend himself argues persuasively that the philosophy of science of Lakatos is different from his own in words only, and not in substance.[25] Kuhn has done a similar job to show the great affinity between his own ideas and those of Popper.[26] Later writers about this debate, such as the Sydney philosopher Alan Chalmers, whose book *What Is This Thing Called Science?* has become a best-selling commentary, agree that

Feyerabend's views are a logical conclusion of the premises established by the other three. Let us consider some of the implications of this.

What we are looking at is a school of thought—a paradigm, if you like, in its own right—that contains a number of implicit conclusions that are absurd and that no rational person should accept. Since it believes that knowledge is not accumulative, this school is committed to denying that there has been a growth in knowledge since the sixteenth century. The idea that the Earth is flat and that the stars and planets circle the skies above it should not be regarded as wrong or false but, rather, as a set of statements from an older paradigm which is incommensurable with the later one established by Copernicus, Kepler and Galileo. Moreover, these three scientists did not actually prove that the Earth and the other planets orbit the Sun, since nothing can ever be proved conclusively. They simply persuaded many people for the next three hundred years, for largely aesthetic and subjective reasons, that their own paradigm was worth accepting. And, of course, Einstein's theory of relativity was no advance on their earlier position either, it was just different. In the same vein, the story that the world was made by God in seven days, that it is only about 4500 years old, and that the fossils of long extinct sea creatures found embedded in mountain peaks are nothing more than remnants of the great biblical forty-day flood, is not mistaken but is simply a set of statements that is incommensurable with later paradigms. Some of us might believe the earth is billions rather than thousands of years old but our grounds for this belief are not superior to those of religious fundamentalists. Similarly, astrologists, fortune tellers and faith healers are not misguided or dishonest, only different. Indeed, Paul Feyerabend will defend the rights of those who want to teach these beliefs to your children at school.

But surely, one might object, the theories of Karl Popper have been so widely accepted by such an eminent group of scientists—Popper records in his autobiography that he met both Albert Einstein and Niels Bohr at Princeton in the 1950s and, he says, they generally agreed with his views[27]—that he could not possibly be in the same camp as that anarchist Feyerabend? Surely Popper, who has repeatedly denied any connection with subjectivism and relativism, is not committed to a form of scepticism so deep that it cannot provide us with rational grounds for elevating science above magic and voodoo? To respond to these objections, let me bring the material in this chapter full circle with a discussion of Popper's views on the status of observation and knowledge in the field of history.

In *Conjectures and Refutations*, just after he has made a critique of Francis Bacon's methodology of induction, Popper turns to the issue of how we learn about what happened in society. He claims that if we try to establish the veracity of an observation of an event in society we are forced to ask questions that themselves inevitably lead on to others, in a sequence that can never end. Popper calls this sequence an 'infinite regress'. He gives the example of an apparently innocuous statement by a newspaper: 'The Prime Minister has decided to return to London several days ahead of schedule.' How do you know that the statement is true? he asks. You answer that you read it in *The Times*. Popper says two questions follow from this. First, how can you be sure it was *The Times* and not something disguised as *The Times*? Second, how can you be sure that the newspaper got the information right? If you ignore the first bit of scepticism and follow the second trail, you might approach the editor of *The Times*. He would confirm that the paper had a telephone call from the Prime Minister's office. You can speak to the reporter who took the call, and you can ask him how he was sure that the call was genuine and that the voice really came from the Prime Minister's office. Popper claims that for every answer you get you can always ask another question.

There is a simple reason why this tedious sequence of questions never comes to a satisfactory conclusion. It is this. Every witness must always make ample use, in his report, of his knowledge of persons, places, things, linguistic usages, social conventions, and so on. He cannot rely merely upon his eyes or ears, especially if his report is to be of use in justifying any assertion worth justifying. But this fact must of course always raise new questions as to the sources of those elements of his knowledge which are not immediately observational. This is why the program of tracing back all knowledge to its ultimate source in observation is logically impossible to carry through: it leads to an infinite regress.[28]

In the study of the past, this whole process is even more difficult, Popper continues, because we usually lack any eyewitnesses to the events we think occurred. Historians rely on documents and have learned that they can never accept them uncritically. 'There are problems of genuineness, there are problems of bias, and there are also problems such as the reconstruction of earlier sources.' Even those documents that purport to be the reports of eyewitnesses themselves nonetheless always provide grounds for doubt. As most lawyers know, he says, eyewitnesses often err. Even those most anxious to be accurate are prone to 'scores of mistakes', especially if the witness was excited at the time or became influenced just after the event by some 'tempting interpretation'. Even in the case of what most people would regard as an extremely familiar historical event—he uses the example of the assassination of Julius Caesar in the Roman Senate—the available observations such as the statements of eyewitnesses and spectators of the event, and the unanimous testimony of earlier historians are insufficient to avoid the 'infinite regress'. Hence, Popper concludes, those who believe that historical sources can be used to provide knowledge are entirely mistaken. What he calls 'the empiricist's ques-

tions', for example, 'How do you know? What is the source of your assertion?' are *'entirely misconceived'*.[29]

Now, this is an argument that is just as bizarre as anything to come out of
Feyerabend. It not only rejects, in principle, the idea that historians can ever
produce knowledge, but it is committed to being profoundly sceptical about
our ability to know *anything* about what happens in society at any time. Let us
take, for instance, Popper's case about the murder of Julius Caesar and update
it from the Ides of March 44 BC to 22 November 1963 and apply his very
same logic to the assassination of John F. Kennedy. According to Popper, any
eyewitnesses to that shooting must be regarded as unreliable because, as lawyers know, witnesses sometimes get things wrong. All the film footage of the
event must be just as subject to the 'infinite regress' as his example of *The
Times'* report about the Prime Minister's return to London. We could never
ultimately establish that any of the film was authentic. Nor could we trust any
of the journalists who wrote that they themselves saw Kennedy killed. They
might have been overexcited at the time or tempted into rash interpretations
by later events, such as the subsequent assumption of office by Lyndon Johnson
or the emotionally charged funeral of the allegedly dead President. This doubt
must extend even to the testimonies of Mrs Jackie Kennedy who cradled her
dying husband in her arms, of Governor John Connally who was shot at the
same time, and of the doctors who examined the President's body and pronounced him dead. According to Popper's theory, all these are mere 'observations' and, as such, are insufficient grounds for providing knowledge that
the assassination took place. Let us be clear about this. Popper's position commits him to doubting not simply whether Kennedy was killed by Lee Harvey
Oswald, or was shot by one gunman or several, but whether he was killed at
all!

This is the same man, and the same book, that leading social scientists of the
1990s have relied upon to claim that nothing in our understanding of the
social or natural worlds can be certain. Yet if his conclusion is as absurd as
this, there are two questions that arise. First, since the argument has obviously
gone wrong somewhere along the line, where has this actually occurred?
Second, how could such nonsense have been taken seriously for so long, that
is, what is there about it that has made it plausible? The next section examines
these issues.

THE LOGIC OF SCIENTIFIC SCEPTICISM

The most incisive critic of the Popper–Kuhn–Lakatos–Feyerabend position is
the Sydney philosopher David Stove. In his 1982 book, *Popper and After: Four
Modern Irrationalists*, Stove provides a devastating analysis both of why their

case is wrong and why many people have found this difficult to recognise. As I noted above, the starting point for Popper, Lakatos and Feyerabend is the philosophy of science whereas for Kuhn it is the sociology or the history of science. As the field of the philosophy of science was traditionally conceived, it was concerned with the logical relations between scientific statements, that is, what could and what could not be legitimately transmitted from one statement to another. The sociology of science, on the other hand, is about scientific practice, what scientists do and what they think. The two fields are distinct areas of inquiry. The philosophy of science is *prescriptive* in that it aims to establish what relations *must* hold between statements. The sociology of science is *descriptive* in that it is simply an account of scientific activity, irrespective of the degree of logic that prevails within it.

David Stove has shown that one of the central problems in the recent debate is the conflation of the two fields. The philosophers Popper, Lakatos and Feyerabend all derive the evidence for their claims from the history of science. This would be acceptable if they used this evidence simply to provide examples of statements whose logic they were examining. Time and again, however, Stove shows them *appearing* to be making logical statements about the relations between scientific propositions, while *actually* making statements about what scientists believe or accept, that is, using the latter as if they were examples of the former. There is a constant, subtle elision from one kind of statement to the other. Their radical scepticism derives from their attempt to resolve questions of logical value by appealing to matters of historical fact.

One of the problems for Popper's philosophy of science that has long been recognised is the central issue on which it rests, the notion of falsification. It is often very difficult to tell if a theory has really been falsified by an observation. In the case of the proposition 'All swans are white', the observation of one black swan fairly readily counts as a falsification. But in the example of Copernicus's theory of planetary motion, the naked-eye observation that Venus appeared not to change size was, for seventy years, until the invention of the telescope, held to be a demonstration that the theory could not be true. The question of who is to judge whether a scientific theory has been falsified is one that, in practice, is naturally left to scientists. This is what Popper supports. In *The Logic of Scientific Discovery*, he writes that 'a physicist is usually quite well able to decide' when to consider a hypothesis as 'practically falsified'; and 'the physicist knows well enough when to regard a probability assumption as falsified'; and 'we shall no doubt abandon our estimate [of probability] in practice and regard it as falsified'.[30] Now, in the theory that all swans are white, the discovery of one non-white swan falsifies the theory, that is, refutes it, as a matter of logic. It does not matter how many or how few scientists recognise this logic, the logical inconsistency remains. But in the examples from Popper above, falsification is a matter of judgement by scientists, not logic. Physicists 'decide' when an assumption has been falsified; they 'regard' estimates as falsified. Stove uses these examples to argue that Popper is involved in a process of 'epistemic embedding', by which he means changing the logical status of a word or of statements by embedding them in a sociological context.

They use a logical expression, one implying inconsistency, but they do not imply the inconsistency of any propositions at all. They are simply contingent truths about scientists. Yet at the same time there is a suggestion that not only *is* a logical statement, implying inconsistency, being made, but that one is being made with which no rational person would disagree.[31]

All of those who support this radical sceptical position, Stove argues, are guilty of using logical words but depriving them of their logical meaning by embedding them in epistemic context about scientists. Kuhn talks of arguments that appear to be decisive rather than being logically decisive: 'Ordinarily, it is only much later, after the new paradigm has been developed, accepted and exploited, that apparently decisive arguments [against the old paradigm] are developed.' And Lakatos often uses quotation marks to neutralise the logical force of a term: 'The anomalous behaviour of Mercury's perihelion was known for decades as one of the many as yet unsolved difficulties in Newton's program; but only the fact that Einstein's theory explained it better transformed a dull anomaly into a brilliant 'refutation' of Newton's research program.'[32] Another tactic is the use of terms that confuse logical with causal relations. Lakatos, in particular, is prone to applying to scientific theories expressions such as 'is defeated', 'is eliminated', 'is removed' and 'is abandoned' as though these *causal* expressions were logical expressions like 'is falsified'. All he can really imply by these terms is that scientists have *abandoned* the theories concerned, not that they have been *refuted* in the logical sense of having been proven to be false.[33]

The conflation of statements from the philosophy and the sociology of science has been responsible for two of the great myths perpetrated by Popper and his followers: first, that all scientific findings of the past have been rendered irrelevant by the findings of later theories; and second, that scientific knowledge is never cumulative. By applying Stove's distinctions to the most common example used by the radical sceptics, we can put these myths in their place. Even though the Copernicus–Galileo–Kepler theory that the Earth and the planets orbit the Sun has now been *replaced* (a sociological concept) by far more sophisticated and adventurous Einsteinian theories of cosmology, the central findings of the seventeenth century thesis have not been *refuted* (a logical concept) by the newer theories. The planets still orbit the Sun, just as the scientists of the Renaissance discovered 350 years ago, and nothing can alter the fundamentals of that piece of knowledge that those scientists discovered. Moreover, the history of science over the last four hundred years has been, overall, a story of the accumulation of knowledge. Even if we concede to Feyerabend that Einstein's theory does not share a single statement with its predecessor, this is not an argument against the accumulation of knowledge. Einstein, as a matter of historical fact, wrote his theory of relativity in response to Newton's mechanics. One might argue, indeed, that it would not have been *possible* for Einstein to have written his theory before Newton wrote his, nor, for that matter, before the development in the nineteenth century of new kinds of non-Euclidean geometry. But because we are arguing a sociological-cum-historical point, the case for accumulation does not require us to go even this far. It is simply enough to record that Einstein was working on similar subject matter to Newton, that he knew Newton's work in detail and that his own theory provided a better account of the subject matter. All of these sociological details are true and so we have a clear example of the accumulation of knowledge in the principal field where Kuhn and Feyerabend deny such a thing is possible.

What is also ironic is that, once their case is identified as being sociological, its logic becomes an interesting issue. Popper et al are arguing from a number of examples in science, almost all of which are confined to physics and chemistry, to the whole of science. Their logic is that some examples of science are of a certain kind (some A are B), therefore all of science is of the same kind (all A are B). But this, of course, is the logic of induction, the very thing that they are united in rejecting from the outset. None of them dissect the nature of other sciences, such as medical science or geological science (Feyerabend does not even give us a decent account of the principles of voodoo), so their notions of rival paradigms and deteriorating or progressive research programs can only be applied to all of science by drawing the kind of inductive conclusions that they deny have any validity.

Another furphy in this debate is the claim that all observation statements are already preladen with theory. Now, if all observations were laden with theory, we could ask of any observation which particular theory it is supposedly laden with. Once we do this, it becomes apparent that the claim cannot be sustained. Consider the case of Galileo's observation through a telescope of the planet Jupiter and its moons in 1609. At the time, Galileo was a convert to the theory of Copernicus that the planets orbited the Sun and that moons orbited planets. This might have influenced the fact that, when he saw Jupiter's moons for the first time, they appeared to him to be orbiting the planet. However, would anyone imagine that if a supporter of the old Ptolemaic theory of astronomy had looked through a telescope at the same time he would have seen anything different? Would we expect the Ptolemaic theorist to see the moons not in orbit but roaming the skies *above* Jupiter as his own theory might have expected them to be doing? If you look at Jupiter today, no matter whether you accept the theories of Edwin Hubble or Athena Starwoman, you still see the moons orbiting the planet, exactly as Galileo saw them. What you observe through the telescope is independent of any theory. How you *theorise* about your observation is, naturally, highly influenced by your theories, but the observation itself is never tied to them in any necessary way. Nor are we engaging in theory when we give names to the things we see in space such as 'moon' or 'planet' or when we describe a visible process as an 'orbit'. All we are undertaking is the common procedure of applying names to observable objects. A theory is always committed in some way to a statement about the unobserved, and the mere act of naming what we observe is nothing more than what it is. The 'low level' example cited by Alan Chalmers above (the warning about the wind blowing the baby's pram over the cliff) does not show that every observation statement must be laden with some scientific theory. Nothing in the statement he cites, which could have been made by a child, deserves the status of scientific theory. The example presupposes nothing more than the use of language and the attribution of meanings to words to describe common experiences.

All this is not to claim, it should be emphasised, that the observations of natural scientists or social scientists are never influenced by theories. Indeed, the opposite is often the case. People frequently go hunting for observations and evidence to prove a theory upon which they have already settled. However, to restate a previous point: this is a sociological fact not a point of logic. There is no theory *inherent* in every observation; observations are not, as a matter of necessity, dependent on any theory of any kind.

There is one more question of logic that should be discussed at this point. In making his case that we can never have any certainty about the death of Julius Caesar because observations by historical characters are always subject to an 'infinite regress' of questions, Popper raises another issue. Because historians are describing the past, they are dealing with a finite world, something that existed at one stage but is now completely behind us. Now, we cannot ask an 'infinite' number of questions about a finite world. We might be able to ask a great many questions, but an infinite number is a logical impossibility. When historians accept observations about the past as evidence that an event really happened, they are always reluctant to take one report as proof of this. They prefer the *corroboration* of observations from many observers. This is what they have with the death of Julius Caesar. Every report they have ever seen about the Roman Empire around 44 BC, no matter how close or how removed the source, corroborates the assassination, and not one has yet turned up to falsify or even raise doubts about whether the event occurred. We could, if we chose, calculate the probability that this event, out of all the possible things that might have been observed about Caesar and those around him at the time, did occur. For every corroboration, the odds in favour of the hypothesis that he was killed grow geometrically. There comes a point with historical corroboration about such a well-recorded event where any other scenario besides the one we have accepted becomes impossible. Because we are dealing with a finite world—the planet Earth in 44 BC—we can rule out the prospect that somewhere within an infinite number of scenarios lies one in which Caesar was not killed. Logical possibilities based on infinity do not count in this or any other historical case. There is, in fact, so much corroboration about this particular assassination that it is literally impossible for there to be a non-assassination scenario that fits everything else we know about what was happening in Rome at the time. We know that Julius Caesar was killed in Rome in 44 BC just as surely as we know that John F. Kennedy was killed in Dallas in 1963.

As I noted earlier, if we seriously entertained Popper's notion about the impossibility of observations providing us with historical knowledge, we would also have to agree that we can never know anything about society at all, including the most familiar of the everyday events that all of us experience. How could anyone have ever entertained such a ridiculous notion? Before answering this, let me turn to another set of ideas that makes the same assertion but has a different origin.

THE DOUBLE HERMENEUTIC AND REFLEXIVITY

There has long been a distinction in the humanities and social sciences between studying the *actions* of human beings and the *meanings* of human conduct. There have been times when one side of this division has been favoured at the expense of the other; and at other times the balance has tipped the opposite way. In the period between the Second World War and the late 1960s, action-based perspectives were very much in vogue. This was the heyday of behaviourism in psychology and sociology. Behaviourists argued that the meanings that people gave to what they did could be vague, contradictory and often difficult to either interpret or articulate. They thought it impossible to build a rigorous social science on such soggy foundations. Human actions, however, could be counted, measured and tested with precision and so appeared to provide the primary data from which a proper science of society could emerge. These days, the behaviourists' strictures to throw out meaning, interpretation and understanding and to focus only on measurement and overt actions looks both mistaken and fruitless. It is now a commonplace that the meanings people bring to what they do cannot be eliminated from any account of human activity. It is clearly impossible to portray the richness of society and the reality of life once meaning is set aside.

Until recently, most historians were happy to include both action and meaning perspectives in their works. Most assumed that they could study actions (about which they could produce knowledge) as well as meanings (where they were probably limited to producing interpretations). This meant that many historians accepted that history had a dual nature as, on the one hand, a social science and, on the other, a member of the humanities. In recent years, however, the balance has not only swung away from the side of action but has gone right over the edge in the opposite direction. For we now have cultural and literary theorists insisting that it is *only* meaning that matters. Just like the behaviourists of the 1950s and 1960s, they have produced an orthodoxy with its own badges of identity and in-crowd terminology. One of the banners under which they are marching is called hermeneutics.

Hermeneutics is the theory of interpretation. It began as the field of interpreting religious texts such as the Bible but was later extended to history and sociology. It holds that the proper way to study human affairs is not to examine the causes or to measure the incidence of behaviour but rather to interpret the meanings of social actions from the point of view of the agents performing them. Nineteenth century hermeneuticists who wrote history said their goal was to reproduce the mind, or the mental perspective, of the people who lived in the past. This objective became enshrined as one of the basic and enduring principles of historical practice, especially in some of the great nineteenth century studies of European culture, such as Jacob Burckhardt's *The Civilisation of the Renaissance in Italy*. Twentieth century hermeneuticists, however, have gone much further to claim that their approach is the *only* proper way to contemplate human affairs. The study of human conduct, they claim, is fundamentally different from the methods of the natural sciences because its aim is the 'understanding' of human meanings, not the gaining of objective information. Because it is based upon meanings, human activity can be understood 'from the inside', unlike the natural world to which we relate only as outsiders.[34] The leading contemporary exponent of hermeneutics, the German philosopher Hans-Georg Gadamer, a colleague and ally of Martin Heidegger, says the appropriate model in seeking to understand the meaning of human conduct is that of interpreting a text.[35] The field is strongly influenced by the ideas of Nietzsche, especially his assertion that 'there are no facts, only interpretations'. Hermeneuticists such as Gadamer insist that interpretation itself is never a simple exercise. This is because the interpreter always brings his own meanings, prejudices and preconceptions to the task. He is attempting to understand the meanings of others but can do this, not in any objective sense, but only through the web of his own meanings and culture.

The British sociologist Anthony Giddens has argued that there is an additional dimension involved when social scientists study their world. Social science, he says, is not insulated from its subject matter in the way that natural science is. For example. no matter what evidence a physicist finds or what theory he supports, his published work does not have any affect on the laws of physics. However, Giddens argues, the publications of social scientists often have a considerable impact on what happens in human affairs. The social sciences operate within what he calls a 'double hermeneutic' involving two-way relations between actions and those who study them. 'Sociological observers depend upon lay concepts to generate accurate descriptions of social processes; and agents regularly appropriate theories and concepts of social science within their behaviour, thus potentially changing its character.'[36]

The clearest example of this is the study of economics, which describes the motivations and institutions of economic life in terms defined by its participants. In turn, the theory of economics and the inferences that can be drawn from it have a considerable effect on the economic process itself, influencing activities ranging from market-driven phenomena such as the price of shares on the stock market or the value of the dollar, to more deliberated activities such as the formulation of national economic policy. Even those sociological activities that appear to be 'objective', such as the compilation of statistics on the distribution of population, birth and death rates, marriage and the family, all 'regularly enter our lives and help redefine them', Giddens says. One of the clearest examples of this, he says, is the self-fulfilling prophecy that social and economic analyses regularly provide. 'Theorising in social science is not about an environment which is indifferent to it, but one whose character is open to change in respect of that theorising.'[37] Giddens has used the concept of the double hermeneutic to develop what he calls his 'theory of reflexivity'.

The reflexivity of modern social life consists in the fact that social practices are constantly examined and reformed in the light of incoming information about those very practices, thus constitutively altering their character... In all cultures social practices are routinely altered in the light of ongoing discoveries which feed into them. But only in the era of modernity is the revision of convention radicalised to apply (in principle) to all aspects of human life, including technological intervention into the material world. It is often said that modernity is marked by an appetite for the new, but this is not perhaps completely accurate. What is characteristic of modernity is not an embracing of the new for its own sake, but the presumption of wholesale reflexivity—which of course includes reflection upon the nature of reflection itself.[38]

Giddens uses his explanation of this phenomenon to argue that not only is what passes for knowledge of the social world inherently uncertain but this knowledge itself contributes to the 'unstable or mutable character' of the social world. The conclusion he draws from this is that we cannot have any knowledge about society, in what he calls 'the old sense' of knowledge meaning certainty. The 'circulating of knowledge in the double hermeneutic ... intrinsically alters the circumstances to which it originally referred'.[39] Hence:

... the equation of knowledge with certitude has turned out to be misconceived. We are abroad in a world which is thoroughly constituted through reflexively applied knowledge, but where at the same time we can never be sure that any given element of that knowledge will not be revised.[40]

Knowledge, then, according to Giddens can no longer mean truth or certainty. When we use the term, he says, we should understand it as referring to nothing better than 'claims to knowledge'. Hence, 'action' perspectives that try to provide knowledge are misguided. Social science is essentially a hermeneutic exercise, which attempts to deal with a 'necessarily unstable' subject, the 'careering juggernaut' of the modern world.[41]

It should be pointed out that, within Giddens's work over the past decade, there has been a subtle and unacknowledged shift in his account of reflexivity and the double hermeneutic. In his early writings about this process from 1984 to 1986, reflexivity was something that 'could' happen, not something that 'must' happen. For instance: 'The "findings" of the social sciences *very often* enter constitutively into the world they describe.'[42] However, by the 1990s, Giddens was confident he had grasped one of the *inherent* features of contemporary society. He now writes that the modern world is 'thoroughly constituted' by 'wholesale reflexivity', and that 'knowledge reflexively applied to the conditions of system reproduction *intrinsically* alters the circumstances to which it originally referred'.[43] His later work thus argues, first, that reflexivity is a *necessary* component of contemporary society and, second, that it *must* change the world to which it refers.

In his writings in the 1990s, Giddens has so persuaded himself of the strength of his thesis that when he now discusses reflexivity he feels he can dispense with the need to justify it by referring to any evidence. However, if we go back and look at the early examples he provides himself, it is apparent that he is grossly overstating his case. For instance, it is likely that the publication of sociological statistics about divorce has some impact on the divorce rate. It is always easier for individuals to take difficult decisions if they know there are others doing the same. But this is not something that is inevitable or necessary. Divorce statistics might influence some individual decisions but they are just as likely to be irrelevant in many cases where the nature of the relationship between spouses is by far the overriding factor, no matter what the statistics might be. Similarly, if economic analysis indicates that the stock market is due to fall, the price of shares may well decline, but not necessarily so. If other factors are present, such as portfolio managers with large funds to invest, this economic analysis may not produce any self-fulfilling prophecy at all. In other words, material conditions can often render beliefs about society irrelevant. When beliefs about society really do alter the circumstances to which they refer, this is a contingent matter, not something necessary.

Giddens's argument, moreover, overlooks two things. First, most people carry out their lives completely oblivious to sociological statistics and economic analysis, especially the former. If the undergraduate students I have taught over the last twenty years are at all representative, most people who gain a higher education degree in the humanities, let alone the majority of the population, cannot read a statistical table properly nor draw any conclusions from a time series graph. Second, there is the issue of the poor quality and sullied reputation of most sociological analysis and economic prediction. One of the conditions of modernity that Giddens should have considered is that people today are so bombarded with contradictory opinions from academic 'experts' in the media that most take them all with a grain of salt. Most business people today know that all economic predictions are bound to be wrong in varying degrees. When television viewers these days see the typical sociologist on their screen, adopting a predictably provocative position on some controversial issue, their most common response is not belief but wonder at how someone with views so divergent from ordinary intelligence ever got a job at a university in the first place.

The 'double hermeneutic' thesis, then, commits the same fallacy as the theses of Popper and his fellow philosophers of science, that of shifting from a sociological statement to a logical statement. From the premise that there are some examples of reflexive understanding in society, Giddens slides into the claim that reflexivity is therefore a logically necessary component of modern society. From this he goes on to draw the same conclusion as the philosophers of science, that 'knowledge' cannot mean certainty. But since the argument is invalid, it provides no support whatsoever for this conclusion.

Even in those cases where we recognise reflexivity is at work (say, couples being more inclined to divorce in an era with a high divorce rate) they do not provide grounds for a total lack of certainty. Just because an aspect of society is constantly shifting ground does not mean you cannot have knowledge about it. You can have knowledge about its movement. You can construct a narrative of the pattern of its shifting ground. This, indeed, is the very point on which historians have insisted all along. There is no aspect of society that stands still long enough to be subject to a sociological analysis. The only accurate way to understand society is historically; that is, as a moving phenomenon, as something with a time dimension. There is nothing in Giddens's hermeneutics or theory of reflexivity that undermines history's claims to provide knowledge nor its status as the proper study of humankind.

THE LANGUAGE OF RELATIVISM

The scepticism about knowledge considered in this chapter has become so well entrenched that it deserves some discussion, not only about its logical fallacies, but about why scepticism itself exists. One could answer this with a long diversion into the politics of post-1960s intellectual fashions among all the familiar radical groups. However, let us confine the discussion to science and the philosophy about it. David Stove attributes scepticism largely to the impact on intellectuals made by Einstein's revolution in physics. For the two hundred years prior to Einstein's revolution, scientists had believed that Newton's laws of mechanics and gravitation provided them with certainty. Einstein's demonstration that this was not so, came as a great shock and, in the subsequent process of disillusionment, the notion of certainty itself was one of the major victims. Many philosophers concluded that, since Newtonian physics were not certain, nothing was. The subsequent intellectual environment was dominated by an anxiety that the vainglory that had existed before the fall of Newtonian physics should never recur. 'To philosophers like Popper', Stove writes, 'the moral was obvious: such excessive confidence in scientific theory must never be allowed to build up again'. Since the most irrefutable of all such theories had been shown to be not irrefutable, Stove argues that the mood was ripe for a response that denounced irrefutability and substituted its opposite: total suspension of belief.[44]

Now, radical scepticism is nothing new in philosophy. The ancient Greek philosopher Pyrrho, had defended the notion and in the eighteenth century the Scottish philosopher David Hume had argued for a general scepticism about the unobserved. The problem for philosophers in the early twentieth century who wanted to assert such a position was that science still seemed to be remarkably successful. In the era of such extraordinary phenomena as air transport, radio, and antibiotic medicines, the public at large ignored the implications of Einstein's revolution and continued to believe that scientific discoveries were not only certainties but that they were increasing at a geometric progression. To be taken seriously in such an environment, a philosophical sceptic could not express himself outright and deny that science made discoveries or assert that scientific knowledge was not growing. According to Stove, Popper solved this dilemma by continuing to use words such as 'discover' and 'knowledge' but changing their meaning.

Stove points out that words like 'discover' and 'knowledge' are *success*-words. He gives a number of examples and counter-examples such as 'prove', which is a success-word because you can only prove what is true, and 'believe', which is not a success-word because you can believe what is not true. Similarly, the verb 'refuted' is a success-word since it means 'proved the falsity of', but 'denied' is not since it only means 'asserted the falsity of'. 'Knowledge' is a success-word because you can only know what is true, 'discovery' is a success-word because you can only discover what exists, 'explanation' is a success-word because you cannot explain anything except what is the case. So, when Popper the radical sceptic writes books with the titles *The Logic of Scientific Discovery* and *The Growth of Scientific Knowledge,* and when Lakatos entitles a collection of his essays *Proofs and Refutations*, they are engaging in what Stove describes as 'neutralising success-words'.[45]

When writing about the history and sociology of science, Stove observes, it is very difficult to avoid success-words. The most common tactic adopted by Lakatos when he finds himself in this position is to put quotation marks around words such as 'proof', 'facts' and 'known' as in: 'One typical sign of the degeneration of a program which is not discussed in this paper is the proliferation of contradictory 'facts' ... His 1887 experiment 'showed' that there was no ether wind on the earth's surface.'[46] There are also examples of Kuhn writing that when one paradigm replaces another, 'new knowledge' replaces 'knowledge of another and incompatible sort'. Citing this, Stove points out that knowledge implies truth and truths cannot be incompatible with one another. He says that the worst example of the neutralisation of a success-word is a phrase that is central to Popper's whole account: 'conjectural knowledge'. To say that something is known implies that it is known to be true. To say that something is conjectural implies that it is not known to be true. [47] Hence, what these examples demonstrate is not simply the coining of neologisms nor the bending of the rules of language (in Lakatos's term 'language-breaking') but the direct contradiction of the accepted meaning of the terms used. To maintain its plausibility, radical scepticism in the philosophy of science has had to *reverse* the common meaning of its central terms.

Precisely the same thing is evident in the words of those social scientists who argue that today nothing is certain. When Anthony Giddens writes 'Let us first of all dismiss as unworthy of serious intellectual consideration the idea that no systematic knowledge of human action or trends of social development is possible', we need to read this in light of what he says he means by 'knowledge'. In the same chapter he tells us that 'the equation of knowledge with certitude has turned out to be misconceived'.[48] Now, if we are certain of something it must be true and we must know it to be true. Yet the same is true of knowledge. So Giddens's claim that we can have knowledge yet not be certain of it is, like the claims of Popper and Co., the assertion of a self-contradiction.

For the sake of argument, let us try a rescue operation on Giddens's ideas and accept that, if knowledge can never be certain, whenever he uses the success-word 'knowledge' we should interpret him as meaning the non-success-word 'belief'. In this light, his first sentence quoted above could be rewritten as: 'Let us dismiss the idea that no systematic belief about human action or social development is possible.' Put this way, we have a statement with which almost everyone would agree. That, of course, is the trouble with it. For it becomes immediately clear that, since beliefs do not have to be true, one systematic belief is as good as any other. The systematic beliefs about society held by religious fundamentalists or astrologists (all of whom will insist they have very good reasons for their beliefs) have the same status as that of the systematic beliefs of a sociologist or an historian. We are left with a relativist theory where what is counted as 'true' (though never 'certain') is determined by personality, aesthetics, money or, more likely, what Lakatos himself denounced as mob rule.

While this has implications for Giddens's own reputation as a scholar, the more serious issue is the extent to which he and the others discussed in this chapter—all of them highly placed academics in influential positions—are prepared to abuse the language in the way they have done. By trying to eliminate the truth content of words such as 'know', 'fact', 'proof' and 'discover', they are all involved in an arrogant but tawdry attempt to change the meaning of the language for no better reason than to shore up their own misconceived and otherwise self-contradictory theories.

IN DEFENCE OF INDUCTION

In 1628 the English physician William Harvey published his findings about the circulation of blood and the function of the heart in animals. In doing so, he overthrew the prevailing theory of the ancient Greek physician Galen, who believed that the heart functioned primarily as a source of heat. Over the 350 years since Harvey's findings were published, the details of his discovery have been refined, but no one has seriously questioned its central claim. Today, there are more than four billion human beings on the planet and many times that number of other mammals. No one has ever found a human or any other kind of mammal whose blood did not circulate through the body (unless of course it was dead). Throughout the world, every day of the year, there are millions of medicines administered orally and intravenously, each of which counts as a little experiment that confirms that blood does indeed circulate. Yet despite these millions and billions of observations that confirm that Harvey was right, and despite the absence of even *one* counter-observation, Karl Popper and his followers maintain that this is still not enough evidence for us to be able to say that we can be certain that the blood circulates. Not only this, but they are committed to the position that this enormous accumulation of data does not allow us to be certain that even *one* of the vast number of mammals that will be born at any time in the future will have a body through which the blood circulates.

The reason that they hold what is, when put like this, such an obviously ridiculous position is because all the observations and experiments described above amount to nothing more than an *inductive* argument. You make an inductive argument when, after a number of observations of a certain phenomenon occurring, there comes a point when you say you have good reasons for drawing a more general conclusion. The example used in philosophy textbooks is usually 'All the ravens observed so far are black. Therefore, all ravens, now and in the future, are black'. An inductive argument, then, is an argument from premises about what has been observed to a conclusion about what has not been, or in some cases could not be, observed. These days, however, anyone who advances a case based on induction, whatever the form it takes, runs the risk of being accused of engaging in what recent generations of humanities students have been taught is a hopelessly flawed exercise.

The reason inductive arguments are now held in low repute, and the reason why so many students of social theory and scientific method today would rather reject Harvey's theory as a piece of knowledge than accept the principle of induction, is that they have been taught by Popper that they should accept the views of the Scottish philosopher David Hume. In two of his major works, *A Treatise of Human Nature* (1739) and *An Enquiry Concerning Human Understanding* (1748), Hume argued, first, that the premise of an inductive argument was no reason to believe the conclusion and, second, that there was no reason whatsoever (neither from experience nor anything else) to believe any contingent proposition about the unobserved. Popper acknowledges Hume's argument as the basis of his own rejection of induction.

I approached the problem of induction through Hume. Hume, I felt, was perfectly right in pointing out that induction cannot be logically justified. He held that there can be no valid logical arguments allowing us to establish 'that those instances, of which we have had no experience, resemble those, of which we have had experience.' Consequently 'even after the observation of the frequent or constant conjunction of objects, *we have no reason to draw any inference concerning any object beyond those of which we have had experience*' [Hume, *Treatise*, Book I, Part III, sections vi and xii] ... As a result we can say that theories can never be inferred from observation statements, or rationally justified by them. I found Hume's refutation of inductive inference clear and concise.[49]

David Stove has argued that Popper, writing a generation before Kuhn, Lakatos and Feyerabend, felt the need to justify his own philosophy by citing Hume's argument as one of its foundations. While the latter trio do not identify Hume in the same way, they are nonetheless just as committed because, in this area, their own writings are extremely derivative of Popper. Hence, Stove concludes, Hume's argument about induction is the basis of the radical scepticism of all four authors.[50]

Hume's conclusion, cited in italics above, is that we have no reason to believe any contingent proposition about the unobserved. In a detailed analysis of all the premises and subarguments Hume needed to reach this conclusion, Stove shows the starting premise is the invalidity of inductive arguments. This, Stove agrees, is indisputable. 'Some observed ravens are black, therefore all ravens are black' *is* an invalid argument. The 'fallibility of induction' premise is linked in Hume's argument with a general proposition about deductive arguments that Stove calls 'deductivism'. Deductivism holds that the only good arguments are deductive ones, that is, for P to be a reason to believe Q, the argument from P to Q must be valid. Together, the invalidity of inductive arguments and the premise of deductivism produce the subconclusion that Stove calls 'inductive scepticism'. This holds that no proposition about the observed is a reason to believe a contingent proposition about the unobserved. This subconclusion is itself then linked to the general proposition of empiricism which holds that any reason to believe a contingent proposition about the unobserved is a proposition about the observed. Together, inductive scepticism and empiricism produce Hume's conclusion. Stove's summary diagram of the overall argument is:

Fallibility of Induction
+ Deductivism   →   Inductive Scepticism
                       + Empiricism   →   Scepticism about
                                                 the unobserved

Stove argues that the key premise to the whole case is the assumption of deductivism. The fallibility of induction, on its own, does not produce inductive scepticism. For from the fact that inductive arguments are invalid it does not follow that something we observe gives us no reason to believe something we have not yet observed. For instance, if all our experience of flames is that they are hot and they burn, this does give us a reason for assuming that we will get burned if we put our hand into some as yet unobserved flame. This might not be a logically deducible reason, but it is still a good reason. But once the fallibility of induction is joined with the deductivist assumption that the only acceptable reasons are deductive ones, that is, those from logically valid arguments, then inductive scepticism does follow. (The general proposition about empiricism in the second stage of the argument needs to be joined with inductive scepticism to produce the final conclusion because some people believe that you can know the unobserved by non-empirical means, such as faith or revelation. As an empiricist, Hume, as does Popper, rules these means out as proper grounds for belief.)

Stove argues that to embrace deductivism as the only criterion for accepting an empirical argument is not, as it might appear, to impose the highest standards possible on debate. It is, in fact, to accept a point that carries no weight at all in this kind of argument. To assert the deductivist position is to assert a necessary truth, that is, something that is true not because of any way the world is organised but because of nothing more than the meanings of the terms used in it. Necessary truths are void of empirical meaning. So when any sceptic claims that a flame found tomorrow *might* not be hot like those of the past, or that the next baby born *might* not have circulating blood, he has no genuine reason for this doubt, only an empty necessary truth. Stove comments:

If I have, as Popper says I should not have, a positive degree of belief in some scientific theory, what can Popper urge against me? Why, nothing at all, in the end, except this: that despite all the actual or possible empirical evidence in its favour, the theory *might* be false. But this is nothing but a harmless necessary truth; and to take *it* as a reason for not believing scientific theories is simply a frivolous species of irrationality.[51]

Outside the world of philosophers and sociologists of science and their students, there are very few people who believe that deductivism is true. Most people accept that observations often provide perfectly good reasons for believing a conclusion even though that conclusion might not be entailed by, or deducible from, these observations. Similarly, they accept that some observations provide good reasons for disagreeing with a conclusion, even though we might not have a knock-down, deductive case. In these cases, the logical relations involved are less than absolute but nonetheless persuasive. The terms we use to describe these relations are similarly less than absolute. We say that the observation P confirms the conclusion Q (rather than proves it), or that L disconfirms M (rather than refutes it), or that A is inconsistent with B (rather than contradicts it). The study of these kinds of logical relations has been called, variously, confirmation theory, non-deductive logic or inductive logic. The most important body of scholarship to come out of the study of these relations is probability theory. The development of probability theory began in the seventeenth century but its supporters agree that its major landmarks were made in the mid-twentieth century, especially in the writings of Rudolf Carnap and Carl Hempel.[52] These two were members of the pre-war Vienna Circle of logical positivists. Probability theory, in other words, is the product of those hopelessly unfashionable positivists who are so peremptorily dismissed today by social scientists and literary critics. Yet, in the study of human affairs, probability theory and its derivatives and affiliates, such as statistical method, provide a far more relevant logical foundation than the empty deductivism of radical scepticism. Non-deductive logic, for instance, allows us to have good reasons to believe well-known facts such as the assassinations of Julius Caesar and John F. Kennedy, unlike the radical scepticism that commits us to permanent doubt on both scores. Most importantly for the debate covered in this chapter, it shows that there is a rational alternative to the foundations of belief that are urged upon us by the radical sceptics and so willingly accepted by hermeneuticists, postmodernists and their kind. Neither the natural sciences nor the social sciences are doomed by logic to profound and perpetual uncertainty.

One who would not disagree with this last statement is no less a figure than David Hume himself. Despite being the progenitor of the radical sceptics' position, Hume later dismissed the thesis as 'a juvenile work'. It first appeared in the *Treatise on Human Nature,* published in 1739 when he was 28 years old, and was repeated nine years later in his *An Enquiry Concerning Human Understanding.* However, forty years on, in the work of his maturity, *Dialogues Concerning Natural Religion* (1779), one of the earliest positions that Hume summarily rejected was the inductive scepticism of his youth.[53] For the next 150 years, a period of unprecedented growth in scientific and technological marvels, the thesis was largely ignored by scientists and philosophers alike. It was revived in the twentieth century not because of its persuasive power but for psychological and political reasons flowing, as we have seen, from Einstein's theoretical revolution as well as from the general sense of instability that prevailed in Europe after the First World War. Its attraction in the 1980s and 1990s, similarly, owes far more to politics and psychology than to anything more compelling. And in this, at least, Thomas Kuhn was right. People often accept a theory for reasons of custom, fashion and peer pressure. As a sociological statement this is no doubt correct, but as a guide to the true worth of a theory it carries no weight at all.

THE STATUS OF HISTORICAL EXPLANATIONS

In the 1940s and 1950s there was a wide-ranging debate among philosophers in America and Britain about the scientific status of history. Some, including the logical positivist Carl Hempel, argued that the same kind of general laws that applied in the natural sciences also applied in history. He reasoned that since everything that happens has a scientific explanation and since all scientific explanations presuppose general laws, so everything that happens, including historical events, can be subsumed under general laws. The overall aim of the case was to demonstrate what Hempel called 'the methodological unity of empirical science'. His argument attracted a variety of replies, which ranged from complete rejections of his concepts of 'laws' and 'explanations' to agreement that, while it might be possible *a priori* for historical explanations to be subsumed under general laws, given the current state of play there was so little chance of this happening that the prospect remained 'purely visionary'.[54] Without going into the finer details of this debate, one can nonetheless record that, since the 1950s, Hempel's opposition has by and large prevailed and majority opinion has been against the idea that history is a science.

There are a number of very obvious differences between the way that most scientists study nature and the way that historians study human activity. On the one hand, a chief aim of natural science is to find generalisations or laws that are invariant in space and time. To pursue this, many adopt the method of experiment where the aim is to study their subject in a laboratory, isolated from all the variables that occur in the real world. Most scientists are dealing with phenomena that repeat themselves and their aim is to be able to generalise about these repetitions. On the other hand, the variance of time is one of the defining characteristics of the study of history. Historians deal in change over time of events that, by their nature, cannot be repeated. They study specific circumstances, not undifferentiated phenomena. They can never isolate their subject matter from outside variables; indeed, the variables of the real world are essential components of their explanations. Instead of finding general laws, historians aim to produce narratives of unique events.

While it is indisputable that these differences exist between history and many of the natural sciences, the same is not true of all the natural sciences. In recent years, the American evolutionary biologist Stephen Jay Gould has given us a powerful reminder of how closely his own field of study relates to the methods and assumptions of human history. In his reflections on the Cambrian fossils of the Burgess Shale of British Columbia, Gould argues that the study of many large domains of nature, including human society, evolutionary biology and geology, must be undertaken with the tools of history. Moreover, if the theory of the big bang and the expanding universe is correct, cosmology, too, is an essentially historical study.[55] In each of these cases, the research data used in the field come from the traces of the past that can be found in the present. In each case, the ultimate method of exposition is narrative explanation. In an historical explanation in any of these sciences, Gould says, an event, E, is explained in terms of narrative. E occurred because D came before it, preceded by C, B and A. If any of these stages had not taken place , or had emerged in a different way, E would not exist. Thus event E is intelligible and can be explained rigorously as the outcome of A through D.[56]

A narrative is an explanation of the causes and effects of events, incorporating the dimension of time. Although it had long been the defining technique of history, by the end of the Second World War narrative had earned itself a bad name by its association with the then discredited view that the story of humanity was one of progress. However, the historian does not have to believe that history has any purpose at all, let alone see its movement in progressive terms, to still remain dependent upon the technique of narrative. This is due to the ineluctable reality of time. Although there have been some philosophers who have held that the passage of time is an illusion, time and its arrow, pointing from past to future, is something to which not only human life but all the animate and inanimate matter of the world is bound.[57] Narrative is a representation of reality.

One thing that narrative cannot do is engage in prediction. An historical explanation does not involve a direct deduction from any laws of nature or of human society that may then be projected into the future. An outcome in history is not even predictable from any general property of a larger system. For example, while the victory of the Northern states in the American Civil War may seem with hindsight to have been determined by their superiority in population and industry, we cannot speak of any predictability about the outcome. This is borne out by the experience of other wars, for example Vietnam in the 1960s, where a smaller population and industrially inferior economy defeated its much more powerful American opponent. In the latter case, the general property of America's larger population and industrial sector was insufficient to produce victory. Though historians may explain event E as the outcome of its antecedents, there is never anything necessary or law-given about this. Any variant on E that arose from a different combination of antecedents (say, a southern victory in the Civil War) would have been just as explicable, even though radically different.

The impossibility of prediction does not, however, rule out the possibility of comprehension. What happens in history is by no means random or chaotic. Any major change in history is dependent on, that is, contingent upon, everything that came before. Contingency, Gould contends, is the central principle of all historical explanations. The modern order of animal life, he says, was not guaranteed by underlying laws such as natural selection nor by any mechanical superiority in the anatomical design of those animal types that have survived the evolutionary process. Gould uses the evidence from the Burgess Shale to show that, over the last 570 million years, the number of different animal phyla (the fundamental divisions among animals based on anatomical design) has greatly reduced, not expanded as older theorists of evolution thought. Dramatic changes in climate and geography in the ensuing period have eliminated many more species than now exist. The rule that determined which would survive was not that of 'the fittest' in absolute terms but merely that of the species that happened to be better adapted to the quirks of local environmental change. Often, relatively insignificant creatures—such as mammals were sixty million years ago—withstood drastic changes that eliminated creatures such as dinosaurs—that had been supremely well-adapted to the previous environment. The fact that one of the phyla that survived the Cambrian era, the chordates, should have eventually evolved into human beings was, Gould argues, an 'awesome improbability'. Although this outcome was rooted in contingency, the historical method of evolutionary biologists can explain it in terms that are just as intellectually respectable as those of more conventional science. 'Our own evolution is a joy and a wonder because such a curious chain of events would probably never happen again, but having occurred, makes eminent sense.'[58]

Contingency in history does not mean that explanations are confined to singular statements, with one small event following another without more general phenomena being discernible. Gould points out that life on Earth exhibits a pattern obedient to certain controls: the chemical composition of the planet, the physical principles of self-organising systems and the constraints of design of multicellular organisms as well as the exigencies of the prevailing environment. Similarly, human affairs often conform to processes within which we can discern broad forces to which all persons must bend their will. In human history, it is usually possible to distinguish between wider process and individual agency. In any era, depending on the degree of focus that they choose, historians can describe either the more general social constraints and opportunities or individual actions and their motives. Many, of course, readjust their lens over the course of a work to take in both. The choice faced by historians has been nicely delineated by P. J. Cain and A. G. Hopkins in their recently published history of British imperialism. Explaining their decision to focus more on process than on agency, they write: 'Thus, we are concerned less with anatomising the biographical entrails of a Dilke or a Rhodes than with explaining why Dilke-like or Rhodes-like figures arose in the first place.'[59]

Like other scientific practitioners, historians study their subject by means of a disciplined methodology. This involves adopting practices and standards that are commonly recognised throughout the discipline, especially in their handling of the evidence that goes to make up their explanations. The deployment of evidence within history, however, is one area in which many of those who reject its scientific status believe they have a winning hand. Historical evidence takes the form of the documents that remain from the past, and there are two arguments frequently given about why this is always problematic. First, it is claimed the process is inherently selective. The documents that remain from the past are not a complete record. What has been preserved is often determined by what the historical actors themselves thought desirable to leave to posterity. The evidence available is therefore claimed to be always tainted by subjectivity. Second, it is argued that the process is basically interpretative. Analysing documents is nothing more than interpreting texts and the process of interpretation is, again, always subjective. Hence, on this account, historians are just as far removed from any claim to a scientific method as are literary critics.

Many of those who put one or both of these arguments appear to assume that the evidence upon which historians rely is composed of a fixed and given body of documents. This certainly seems to be behind many of the assumptions of the French author Paul Veyne, whose book *Writing History* mounts a sustained critique of the scientific status of history.[60] The same is true of Michel Foucault who, when interviewed about his history of medicine, *The Birth of the Clinic,* said he had prepared himself by reading *all* the documents on the subject for the period 1780–1820, by which he meant nothing more than the small number of published works written by contemporary health reformers and medical scientists.[61] While this may be acceptable in France, in most other countries historians operate on a different plane. They do not assume there is a given body of specially preserved documents with which they must work. As G. R. Elton has observed, arguments like those above show their authors are not well acquainted with the way historical evidence comes into existence since 'that which is deliberately preserved by observers is a drop in the bucket compared with what is left behind by action and without thought of selection for preservation purposes'.[62]

Rather than 'selecting' from a given body of texts, most historians go in search of evidence to be used to *construct* their own account of what happened. To this extent, those structuralists and poststructuralists who say that history is constructed are correct. However, the historian's construction is not something derived solely from the internal machinations of his or her language and text. Nor is it a mere 'interpretation' of the texts provided by the people of times past. An historical explanation is an inductive argument constructed out of evidence, which is quite a different thing. There is actually a dual process involved: first, determining what evidence exists to address a given issue; second, analysing that evidence, which means testing it for authenticity and then assessing its significance for the case at hand. Although historians construct their case, they do not construct the evidence for that case; rather, they *discover* it. Very few documents left from the past are compiled for the benefit of historians. Probably the biggest single category is made up of the working records that all human institutions—family, workplace, law court, government or military—use to manage their affairs. The archive records of these institutions provide far more historical evidence than the limited range of published essays, books and memoirs consulted by Foucault and Co. . Archival research has to be both painstaking and imaginative—the past does not yield up its secrets willingly—and is never neatly packaged and readily accessible in the way many literary critics and social theorists assume on the basis of their own circumscribed research practices.

It is important to emphasise that those who insist that all historic evidence is inherently subjective are wrong. Archive documents have a reality and objectivity of their own. The names, numbers and expressions on the pages do not change, no matter who is looking at them, and irrespective of the purposes, ideologies and interpretations that might be brought to bear upon them. Historians are not free to interpret evidence according to their theories or prejudices. The evidence itself will restrict the purposes for which it can be used. This is true even of those documents for which all historians agree that varying interpretations are possible. In these cases, the range of possibilities is always finite and can be subject to debate. Ambiguity or lack of clarity do not justify a Derridean dissolution into nullity. Moreover, once it has been deployed, the documentary evidence is there, on the historic record, for anyone else to examine for themselves. Footnoted references and proper documentation are essential to the practise of the discipline. This means that the work of historians, like that of scientists, may be subject to both corroboration and testability by others in their field.

While it is true that historians often come to the task of writing history with the aim of pushing a certain kind of theory, of establishing a certain point, or of solving a certain problem, one of the most common experiences is that the evidence they find leads them to modify their original approach. When they go looking for evidence, they do not simply find the one thing they are looking for. Most will find many others that they had not anticipated. The result, more often than not, is that this unexpected evidence will suggest alternative arguments, interpretations and conclusions, and different problems to pursue. In other words, the evidence often makes historians change their minds, quite contrary to the claims of those who assert that the reverse is true. Although theories or values might inspire the origins of an historic project, in the end it is the evidence itself that determines what case it is possible to make.

Overall, then, historical explanations have a number of characteristics that deserve to be regarded as properly scientific. Although they are narratives of unique, unrepeatable events and are not involved in formulating general laws or making predictions, historical explanations share these characteristics with several other fields of study including evolutionary biology, geology and recent approaches to cosmology. Like these fields, the history of human affairs is defined by its study of the variance over time of its subject matter. Again, like them, its explanations are grounded in contingency. What happens in history is not random but is contingent upon everything that came before. Historical explanations may focus on either general or specific accounts of human affairs, but usually involve the interplay between the two. Historians adhere to a disciplined methodology that involves the construction of explanations from evidence. The evidence they use is not given but is something they must, first, discover and, second, analyse for authenticity and significance for the explanation. Only a minority of the evidence used by historians is that which has been deliberately preserved for posterity. Their biggest single source of evidence comprises the working records of the institutions of the past, records that were created, not for the benefit of future historians, but for contemporary consumption and are thus not tainted by any prescient selectivity. Most of these documents retain an objectivity of their own. Although much historical research may be inspired and initiated by historians' values and theories, the kind of documentation and reference citation used within the discipline means that their explanations can be tested, corroborated or challenged by others. Hence the *findings* made by historical explanations are the product of a properly scientific methodology.

HISTORY AS A DISCIPLINE

The concept of an academic discipline is being assailed these days on a number of fronts. This is especially true in the humanities and social sciences where, as Chapter One recorded, new movements in literary criticism and social theory want either to override the previous boundaries between disciplines or else to subsume some of the older fields within new ones. One of the authors discussed in this chapter, Anthony Giddens, has argued that there is no discernible difference any more between history and sociology and so both should be taken over by a creature of his own invention called 'structuration theory'.[63] From a different perspective, the proponents of cultural studies, as we have seen, believe that they are the ones now best equipped to handle historical issues. What is perhaps of even greater concern is the fact that the major recent champions of traditional academic values and the greatest critics of the new theories have themselves not seen fit to couch their defence within a framework based on the value of academic disciplines. Both Alan Bloom in *The Closing of the American Mind* and Roger Kimball in *Tenured Radicals* have upheld the value of 'the canon' of Western learning; that is, the generally recognised body of 'Great Books' that have stood the test of time and that, until recently, were acknowledged as central to a complete education. But their concept of preserving this canon has not extended to the intellectual disciplines within which most of these books were written. This is not, presumably, because Bloom and Kimball are against this idea. Let me give some reasons why they should have taken their argument one step further.

Rather than the production of a corpus of outstanding works, the basis of Western learning has been the organisation of the pursuit of knowledge into a number of distinct fields called 'disciplines'. Without decrying the stature of the Great Books, it is nonetheless true that their achievements were made possible by the contribution and the example of all those who laboured in the same intellectually coherent field of study. As Edward Gibbon, Isaac Newton and others openly acknowledged, the major figures have always stood on the shoulders of their peers. The history of Western knowledge shows the decisive importance of the structuring of disciplines. This structuring allowed the West to benefit from two key innovations: the systematisation of research methods, which produced an accretion of consistent findings; and the organisation of effective teaching, which permitted a large and accumulating body of knowledge to be transmitted from one generation to the next.

Intellectual disciplines were founded in ancient Greece and gained a considerable impetus from the work of Aristotle who identified and organised a range of subjects into orderly bodies of learning. The next major stimulus to the formation of disciplines was the scientific revolution of the seventeenth century and the Enlightenment of the eighteenth century when new disciplines proliferated and several older fields were revived. However, there had been a long, intervening period, from the early to the late Middle Ages, when the authority of the Christian Church and its sacred texts dominated intellectual life. Although scientific practice did continue through the medieval era and the writings of the ancients became progressively more widely known, theology and revelation nonetheless replaced the secular disciplines as the founts of knowledge. The legacy of having a central authority in this position was that differentiation between subject matter was eroded. There was a lack of criteria for what type of argument or evidence could be counted as relevant in any explanation. Obscurantism and cryptic deliberation flourished. One of the most striking things about the output of late twentieth literary and social theory is how closely it resembles—through its slavish devotion to seminal texts and its unrestrained flight across all subject matter—the theology of the medieval clergy. Today's theorists have substituted French theory for Christian texts but are seeking to break down the disciplines in exactly the same way. They are the most determined advocates for the reorganisation of existing academic fields into multidisciplinary studies. As I argued in Chapter One, their aim is not to merge but to subsume all existing fields in the study of human life under the one central megadiscipline of Cultural Studies. Such a move should be seen for what it is, not a synthesising of intellectual streams but an undermining of the disciplinary traditions that have formed the generative power of Western knowledge for more than two thousand years.

A discipline has a common viewpoint on its subject matter plus a common method of study. Several disciplines can share the same subject matter: human society, for instance, is the subject of history, sociology, anthropology and economics. In this case, the difference between the disciplines is determined by the viewpoint with which the subject is approached and by the methodology used: history has always differentiated itself by its focus on the dimension of time and by an empirical, document-based research process. Disciplines are not fixed or static; they evolve over time, sometimes pursuing the logic of their founding principles into areas not imagined by their initial practitioners. Until recently, history itself was still evolving, as witnessed by the burgeoning of social history and 'history from below' in the 1960s and 1970s which added a valuable new dimension and insight to the field. But disciplines can also arrive at a point of crisis and suffer an irreparable breakdown. One could make a good case, in fact, that this is now the situation facing both sociology and anthropology. They were both founded as time-free studies of society and, now that it has dawned on them that it is impossible to investigate their subjects in this way, the inhabitants of these fields are on a desperate hunt for alternative territory. Hence their interest in occupying the ground that was once the sole province of narrative history.

Overall, it is fair to conclude that, despite all the claims to the contrary, history still retains its credentials as a discipline that demonstrates both the underlying merit of the Western scientific tradition and the fact that this tradition can be properly applied to the study of human affairs. The real test of intellectual value, of course, can only be demonstrated by the output of a discipline. Although they are being assailed on all sides, there is still enough work produced by empirical historians to confirm the worth of what they are doing and to establish that the complete victory of their opponents would amount to a massive net loss for Western scholarship. One of the best expressions of this comes from the now out-of-print and out-of-fashion 1960s manual by G. R. Elton cited earlier. Elton is one of the few commentators to have defended the discipline as a discipline, that is, as a joint effort by its practitioners who, through a process of research, dispute, claim and counterclaim, have made genuine advances in humanity's understanding of itself.

Anyone doubting this might care to take any sizeable historical problem—the decline of the Roman Empire, or the rise of industrial England—and study its discussion in the serious literature of the last fifty years. He will encounter a great deal of disagreement, much proven error, and probably a fair amount of plain nonsense; but if he is at all alert he will be astonished by the way in which the body of agreed knowledge has augmented and by the manner in which variations of interpretation come to be first increased and then reduced by this advance. Historians are so fond of parading their disagreements—and the study does, indeed, progress as often as not by the reopening of seemingly settled questions— that the cumulative building up of assured knowledge of both fact and interpretation is easily overlooked. Yet it is indeed impressive, the product of systematic, controlled, imaginatively conducted research.[64]

1 Anthony Giddens, *The Consequences of Modernity*, Polity Press, Cambridge, 1990, p 39

2 Ann Curthoys, 'Unlocking the Academies: Responses and Strategies', *Meanjin*, 50, 2/3, 1991, p 391

3 Harry Oldmeadow, 'The Past Disowned', *Quadrant*, March 1992, p 63

4 Thomas Kuhn, *The Structure of Scientific Revolutions*, 2nd edn, University of Chicago Press, Chicago, 1970

5 Thomas Kuhn, *The Structure of Scientific Revolutions*, p 149

6 Thomas Kuhn, *The Structure of Scientific Revolutions*, p 150

7 Thomas Kuhn, *The Structure of Scientific Revolutions*, p 94

8 David Bloor, *Knowledge and Social Imagery*, Routledge and Kegan Paul, London, 1976

9 H. M. Collins, *Changing Order: Replication and Induction in Scientific Practice*, Sage, London, 1985, p 148

10 Karl Popper, *Conjectures and Refutations: The Growth of Scientific Knowledge*, (1st edn 1963), 5th edn, Routledge, London, 1989. Popper's other major work on the subject is *The Logic of Scientific Discovery*, Hutchinson, London, 1959

11 Alan Chalmers, *What Is This Thing Called Science?* 2nd edn, University of Queensland Press, St Lucia, 1982, p 28

12 Anthony Giddens, *The Consequences of Modernity*, p 39

13 Thomas Kuhn, *The Structure of Scientific Revolutions*, pp 146-7

14 Alan Chalmers, *What Is This Thing Called Science?* p 61

15 Imre Lakatos, 'Falsificationism and the Methodology of Scientific Research Programs', in I. Lakatos and A. Musgrave (eds), *Criticism and the Growth of Knowledge*, Cambridge University Press, Cambridge, 1970

16 Thomas Kuhn, *The Structure of Scientific Revolutions*, p 156

17 Thomas Kuhn, *The Structure of Scientific Revolutions*, pp 94, 153

18 Imre Lakatos, 'Falsificationism and the Methodology of Scientific Research Programs', pp 93, 178

19 Paul Feyerabend, *Against Method: Outline of an Anarchistic Theory of Knowledge*, New Left Books, London, 1975

20 Paul Feyerabend, *Against Method*, p 275, his italics

21 Paul Feyerabend, *Against Method*, pp 285, 301-2, his italics

22 Paul Feyerabend, *Against Method*, p 299

23 Paul Feyerabend, *Against Method*, p 308

24 'The Worst Enemy of Science', *Scientific American*, May 1993, pp 16-17

25 Paul Feyerabend, *Against Method*, Chapter 16

26 Thomas Kuhn, 'Logic of Discovery or Psychology of Research' and 'Reflections on My Critics', in I. Lakatos and A. Musgrave (eds), *Criticism and the Growth of Knowledge*

27 Karl Popper, *Unended Quest: An Intellectual Autobiography*, Flamingo edn, Fontana Books, London, 1986, pp 128-32

28 Karl Popper, *Conjectures and Refutations*, pp 22-3

29 Karl Popper, *Conjectures and Refutations*, pp 23-5, his italics

30 Karl Popper, *The Logic of Scientific Discovery*, Hutchinson, London, 1959, pp 191, 204, 190

31 David Stove, *Popper and After: Four Modern Irrationalists*, Pergamon Press, London, 1982, p 30

32 Both examples are cited by David Stove, *Popper and After*, p 32. They are from Thomas Kuhn, *The Structure of Scientific Revolutions*, p 156; and I. Lakatos and A. Musgrave (eds), *Criticism and the Growth of Knowledge*, p 158

33 David Stove, *Popper and After*, p 41

34 This is a point that is exclusive neither to hermeneutics nor to the twentieth century. It was first made by the eighteenth century Italian historical theorist, Giambattista Vico, and is one of the theoretical mainstays of the early-twentieth-century movement in sociology known as symbolic interactionism.

35 Hugh J. Silverman (ed.), *Gadamer and Hermeneutics*, Routledge, New York, 1991

36 Anthony Giddens, 'Nine theses on the future of sociology', in his *Social Theory and Modern Sociology*, Polity Press, Cambridge, 1987, pp 30-1. Giddens first advanced the concept of the double hermeneutic in *The Constitution of Society*, Polity Press, Cambridge, 1984, p 284

37 Anthony Giddens, *Social Theory and Modern Sociology*, pp 21, 198

38 Anthony Giddens, *The Consequences of Modernity*, pp 38-9

39 Anthony Giddens, *The Consequences of Modernity*, p 54

40 Anthony Giddens, *The Consequences of Modernity*, p 39

41 Anthony Giddens, *The Consequences of Modernity*, p 53

42 Anthony Giddens, 'What do sociologists do?', inaugural lecture, University of Cambridge, January 1986, published in his *Social Theory and Modern Sociology*, p 20, my italics

43 Anthony Giddens, *The Consequences of Modernity*, pp 39, 54, my italics

44 David Stove, 'Cole Porter and Karl Popper: the Jazz Age in the Philosophy of Science' in his *The Plato Cult and Other Philosophical Follies*, Basil Blackwell, Oxford, 1991, p 19; see also his *Popper and After*, p 51

45 David Stove, *The Plato Cult*, pp 12-18; see also his *Popper and After*, Chapter One

46 I. Lakatos and A. Musgrave (eds.), *Criticism and the Growth of Knowledge*, p 164n, cited by Stove, *Popper and After*, p 10

47 David Stove, *Popper and After*, pp 11, 14

48 Anthony Giddens, *The Consequences of Modernity*, pp 46-7, 39

49 Karl Popper, *Conjectures and Refutations*, p 42, my italics

50 David Stove, *Popper and After*, pp 50-5

51 David Stove, *Popper and After*, p 101

52 Rudolf Carnap, *Logical Foundations of Probability*, University of Chicago Press, Chicago, 1950; Carl Hempel, *Aspects of Scientific Explanation*, Free Press, New York, 1965

53 Cited by David Stove, *Popper and After*, p 102

54 Carl Hempel, 'The Function of General Laws in History', and Alan Donagan 'Explanation in History', both in Patrick Gardiner (ed.), *Theories of History*, Free Press, New York, 1959. Other contributors to the debate collected in the Gardiner volume were Morton White, Ernest Nagel, W. B. Gallie, William Dray, Charles Frankel and Michael Scriven

55 Stephen Jay Gould, *Wonderful Life: The Burgess Shale and the Nature of History*, Penguin, London, 1989, pp 277-91. For current approaches to the history of the universe, see George Smoot and Keay Davidson, *Wrinkles in Time: The Imprint of Creation*, Little, Brown and Co, London, 1993

56 Stephen Jay Gould, *Wonderful Life*, p 283

57 P. Coveney and R. Highfield, *The Arrow of Time*, Flamingo, London, 1990

58 Stephen Jay Gould, *Wonderful Life*, p 285. Though Gould's work reappraises some interpretations of Darwin's maxim of 'survival of the fittest', Gould argues that his own view of post-Cambrian evolution is quite consistent with Darwin's account

59 P. G. Cain and A. G. Hopkins, *British Imperialism: Innovation and Expansion 1688–1914*, Longman, London, 1993, p 49

60 Paul Veyne, *Writing History: Essay on Epistemology*, (1971), trans. Mina Moore-Rinvolucri, Wesleyan University Press, Middletown, 1984

61 Michel Foucault, *Foucault Live: Interviews 1966–1984*, ed. Sylvere Lotringer, Semiotext(e), Columbia University, New York, 1989, p 3

62 G. R. Elton, *The Practice of History*, p 91

63 Anthony Giddens, *The Constitution of Society*; Christopher Bryant and David Jary (eds), *Giddens' Theory of Structuration*, Routledge, London, 1991

64 G. R. Elton, *The Practice of History*, pp 63-4

8

HISTORY AS LITERATURE

FICTION, POETICS AND CRITICISM

NO ONE has ever provoked an objection by claiming history is a form of literature. The literary status of a number of the great practitioners of the discipline has long been beyond dispute. In the academic environment of today, however, this argument is frequently extended into the far more provocative proposition that history is *nothing more* than a form of literature. This latter position is now insisted upon so frequently that it has been accepted by a number of reputable and influential practitioners of the discipline. As a result, some have adopted practices that, a decade ago, they would not have countenanced. Within an environment where the distinction between fact and fiction is under siege, one of the most disturbing developments is that some historians have thought it is now permissible to invent some of their 'facts' and to introduce into their works passages that they acknowledge are fiction. The most publicised author of the latter kind is Professor Simon Schama of Harvard University. In the 1980s, Schama was the author of two highly acclaimed, grand-scale studies of the Dutch mercantile era and the French Revolution. However, a more recent and more modest collection of his essays has attracted even greater attention.

In 1991, Schama published *Dead Certainties*,[1] a book that quickly gained a great deal of publicity and became a big seller in the United States. The essays centre around two events in quite distinct periods of time, but they contain an intriguing linking thread. Schama begins with a reconstruction of the death of General Wolfe at the Battle of Quebec in 1759 in which the British wrested

Canada from the French. This leads on to a piece on Francis Parkman, the nineteenth century Harvard biographer of Wolfe. From Francis Parkman, the essays move on to his uncle, George Parkman, a Boston doctor who in 1849 was murdered by James Webster, Professor of Medicine at Harvard. Webster cut up the body of Parkman Senior and burned the pieces in the university's chemical laboratory. His trial was one of the great scandals of the era and the guilty verdict was controversial. There was no eye witness to the crime, no remains except for the charred dentures, and Webster never confessed. Schama uses the trial to reconstruct the evidence and to examine the basis of the verdict. It becomes clear in the essay, however, that what is really on trial is the process of drawing absolute conclusions from the tiny, highly selective fragments of evidence that remain. In other words, the trial is a parable of the process of historical reconstruction itself, and the verdict an analogy of the historian's claim to produce the truth about the past. Schama's subtitle, '(Unwarranted Speculations)', cleverly mocks the book's main title to question the status of much of what we believe about the past.

The most controversial aspect of *Dead Certainties* was Schama's decision to write some of the book as fiction, and his admission in the Afterword that he had invented some material presented in the essays as factual. He describes the essays as 'works of the imagination, not scholarship' and says that some passages are 'pure inventions'.

Two kinds of passages are purely imagined fiction. In the first kind (as in the soldier's witness of the Battle of Quebec) the narrative has been constructed from a number of contemporary documents. The more purely fictitious dialogues (such as Marshal Tukey's conversation with Ephraim Littlefield) are worked up from my own understanding of the sources as to how such a scene might have taken place.[2]

As might be expected, the book generated some reviews from fellow historians that were highly critical of this innovation. Schama's supporters replied by accusing them of putting on a 'tired and predictable show'. All he had done, the supportive reviewers claimed, was 'simply what, in truth, most historians are doing most of the time, though, unlike Schama, without coming clean'.[3] His publishers, however, were concerned enough to change the cover blurb on the second, paperback edition to describe the essays not as history proper but as 'imaginative reconstructions' and 'a history of stories'.

The author himself has provided a rationale for his position that, in many ways, is an attractive one. Schama is no subscriber to the doctrines of structuralism with its anti-humanist denial of the role of individuals. Instead of arcane jargon, Schama prefers the dramatic clash of real human beings. He is, in fact, a champion of the revival of history as narrative storytelling and of what he calls the 'thrilling, beautiful prose' of the great nineteenth century historians, such as Jules Michelet and T. B. Macaulay. He is also a scathing critic of the dull, fact-grubbing pedantry that he regards as dominating academic history writing today. He sees this in both the university environment—where articles such as 'Labour Relations in the Dutch Margarine Industry 1870–1934', *History Workshop Journal*, 1990, have no difficulty finding a publisher—and in the secondary education system where 'students sit stupefied over world history textbooks the size of telephone directories and about as thrilling to read'.

Entirely missing from these productions are the great narratives of history, written by a single hand or at most a pair, capable of stirring the imagination, feeding the immense hunger for historical drama latent in nearly every young mind.[4]

Schama believes the enemies of this approach are academic empiricists who insist on the professional decorum that writing should strive to be objective and that all evidence should be sourced in footnotes. He says too many historians eschew the subjective and the interpretative. The advice given by the previous generation of professors produced an atmosphere that bordered on the lifeless. According to this advice: 'The road to the truth is the hard and stony way of cumulative empiricism, the holy grail at the trail's end, a chill, limpid objectivity. The face of the historian should not betray the storyteller's animation; it should be a mask of dispassion.'

In the third quarter of the nineteenth century, the free companionship between literature and history was deemed by newly founded university departments to be fundamentally unserious. The storytellers were shoved aside by scientists intent on reconstructing from fragments and clues what they insisted would be an empirical, verifiable, objectively grounded version of an event, its causes and consequences precisely delineated... Storytellers not only lost ground, they became aggressively despised.[5]

Now, much of this is well said. It is perfectly true that too much academic history is composed of soporific volumes meant only to fill in some small gap in the accumulation of detail about topics that few people outside the academy would ever find of interest. Grand, dramatic narrative is decidedly out of fashion, at great cost to history's reputation as literature and to its ability to fire the imagination of the reading public.

However, to respond by abandoning truth and adopting fiction is hardly the way to redress the situation. Readers who come looking for history and find they are offered 'imaginative reconstructions' will inevitably feel cheated. The first seven pages of *Dead Certainties* are presented as if they are an eyewitness account from a soldier of the opening action of the Battle of Quebec. Schama maintains this apparent authenticity even to the extent of using eighteenth century spelling conventions. When the book's readers arrive at the Afterword, they find that this and other passages were not authentic but were merely what Schama admits are composite assemblies from several different documents. However, once some of a book of history is discovered to be fabricated, the reader can never be sure that it is not *all* made up. Under these conditions, how could we have any confidence that the composite version itself is at all accurate or authentic? When a writer presents what he or she says is history, then the reader takes it on faith that the writer is at least trying to tell the truth. Once the writer admits that some of what he or she has written is fiction, the reader not only feels a justified sense of betrayal but is bound to suspend judgement about the credibility of everything the writer has written. Schama's approach, moreover, is a slight on the integrity of the great dramatic historians of the past whom he says he wants to revive. Michelet, Macaulay and Gibbon never made things up. We might today feel that some of their judgements were wrong, that their perspectives were biased, and that they sometimes drew conclusions from insufficient or misleading evidence, but being mistaken is a world away from deliberately inventing fictionalised passages.

The argument that Schama believes justifies his position is that a story will inevitably be biased, because historians must select only a minute fragment of the events that occurred in the past, and must put these together in their own way to create their own story.

Even in the most austere scholarly report from the archives, the inventive faculty—selecting, pruning, editing, commenting, interpreting, delivering judgements—is in full play. This is not a naively relativist position that insists that the lived past is *nothing* more than an artificially designed text... But it does accept the rather banal axiom that claims for historical knowledge must always be fatally circumscribed by the character and prejudices of its narrator.[6]

Now, of course history is highly selective. It is clearly impossible for it to ever be an attempt to re-create on paper, or any other medium, the whole of the past. But the practice of selectivity does not justify the resort to fiction. We always retain the right to distinguish between stories that are true and stories that are invented. There is nothing inconsistent in using selected evidence to establish the truth; it is one of the most common things that human beings do. Every time we work out the cause of an action or indeed come to any conclusion at all about the behaviour of an individual or group of people, we are forced to be selective, for we can never know everything about even the smallest event. Nonetheless, the point Schama makes here is so commonplace in historical discussion today that it is worth dwelling upon. Let me quote another historian, Peter Burke of Cambridge University, who makes the same point as Schama but puts it in a way that exposes the logic of the position a little more clearly.

All historians have to select from the evidence surviving from the past before they can write, and they make their selection according to what they consider important, in other words, according to their values, the values of the group to which they belong.[7]

The argument is: selection is determined by importance and importance is determined by values; hence, selection must be determined by values. The crucial but unsupported premise of this argument is the claim that what historians consider important is determined by their values. While in many cases, this may happen to be true, it is not necessarily so. It is a contingent matter. As I noted in the last chapter, one of the most common experiences of historians is that the evidence they find forces them, often reluctantly, to change the position they originally intended to take. In other words, the evidence itself can often determine what is 'important'. Hence, what historians consider important may be determined either by their values *or* by the historical evidence itself. In other cases, importance may be determined by the nature of the current historical debate on the topic concerned, that is, determined on grounds related more to reason than values. So, while selection *may* be determined by values it is never necessarily so. Unless one takes the hard-line, anti-empirical position that the past is nothing but an artificially designed text, a view that Schama himself repudiates as 'naively relativist', there can be no automatic objection to using selective evidence to discover truths in works of non-fiction. The obligation historians have is to try to shake off their own values and pursue the truth. This may be difficult but there is no reason for it to be impossible.

One of the useful tasks performed by the 'fatally circumscribed' historical knowledge about which Schama expresses such doubt, is to point out when a story has moved from the realm of truth into that of myth. In fact, Schama does precisely this kind of job himself in *Dead Certainties* in an essay that reveals the myth-making behind the famous painting by Benjamin West of the death of General Wolfe. Schama shows that the composition and detail of the painting had very little to do with the battlefield of Quebec and derived more from the conventions of lighting and staging that were popular in the historical dramas performed in the theatre in eighteenth century London. Exposing like this the reality behind some of the legends of our culture is one of the legitimate tasks of the historian. But this role can only be performed by historians who have some faith in the ability of their profession to get to the truth by shaking off the ideological garb in which an individual or an event has been previously clothed, that is, by seeing it objectively. For his argument about the Wolfe painting to be convincing, Schama has to establish that what he tells us about the eighteenth century London stage is true in itself and not simply a reflection of his own, late twentieth century values. In other words,

Schama's own practice in his essay on the artist Benjamin West belies the very argument he adopts himself in the same book to justify his resort to fiction.

Despite all this, Schama is right to endorse the quality of writing that can capture the imagination through the colour of its drama and the ardour of its prose. I want to discuss this issue in more detail, but first there is another aspect of the debate over history as literature that needs to be got out of the way.

THE POETICS OF HISTORY

One of the most ambitious aims of literary critics in the twentieth century has been to develop a theory of literature. Theorising about literature is different from criticism. Rather than explaining what individual works mean, literary theory attempts to analyse the figures and conventions that enable works to have the forms and meanings they do. The pursuit of this goal is behind much of the attraction that littérateurs find in structuralist and poststructuralist philosophy, which both focus intensely on the forms of language. Literary theory is an attempt to establish a 'poetics' that stands to literature as linguistics stands to language. Systematic efforts in this direction were first made in the 1920s by members of the Russian formalist school, who applied their methods to folk tales and to nineteenth century novels. It was not until the 1960s, however, that the movement took off in English-speaking literary circles.

In the 1970s, the American academic Hayden White hit upon the idea of trying to do the same to history. Since works of history were, in his view, nothing but literary texts, it seemed that it might be possible to develop a poetics of history. In his book, *Metahistory*,[8] White became the first to provide a comprehensive argument that history was ultimately a literary or poetic construct. For his efforts, White was appointed Presidential Professor of Historical Studies at the University of California, Santa Cruz. He has since become one of the leading figures in American cultural studies. *Metahistory* is a study of four of the leading European historians of the nineteenth century, Jules Michelet, Leopold von Ranke, Alexis de Tocqueville and Jacob Burckhardt, plus four of the period's most influential philosophers of history, G. W. H. Hegel, Karl Marx, Friedrich Nietzsche and Benedetto Croce. White's book remains the most elaborate attempt to apply analysis derived from literary theory to such a range of major works of history.

The possible forms that any kind of history writing can take, White claims, are based on 'poetic insights that analytically precede them'. He says there are four fundamental types of poetic language or tropes—metaphor, metonymy, synecdoche and irony—and it is these tropes that determine the kinds of interpretations that historians make. Whether they realise it or not, historians are locked into, or 'indentured to', these forms of language, which explains why different historians can reach different conclusions about the same set of events. 'As a result', White says, 'historiography has remained prey to the creation of mutually exclusive, though equally legitimate, interpretations of the same set of historical events or the same segment of the historical process'.[9] When it comes to choosing between different interpretations, he says the grounds of choice cannot be based on who has the strongest evidence, but must be made on grounds that are ultimately moral or aesthetic.

Placed before the alternative visions that history's interpreters offer for our consideration, and without any apodictically provided theoretical grounds for preferring one over another, we are driven back to moral and aesthetic reasons for the choice of one vision over another as the more 'realistic'. The aged Kant was right, in short: we are free to conceive 'history' as we please, just as we are free to make of it what we will.[10]

White contends that the text of every work of history operates at two separate levels. The first is the 'surface level', which consists of both the writer's account of what happened in history and the theoretical concepts that the writer uses to provide explanations for what happened. The second is at a 'deep level of consciousness', where the historian chooses the conceptual strategies within which his or her explanations will be framed. This deep level is a poetic level, and in adopting a mode of operation, the historian performs 'an essentially poetic act'.[11]

In his discussion of the surface level, White is most interested to give an account of the theoretical concepts that historians use for their explanations. For all his emphasis on the literary nature of history, White offers a very clerical framework within which he says historical explanations can be categorised. He starts by saying that there are three principal types of explanations: (1) explanation by emplotment, in which a sequence of events is gradually revealed to be a story of a particular kind; (2) explanation by argument, which explains what happened by invoking laws of historical development; and (3) explanation by ideology, where implications are drawn from the study of past events in terms of political positions. Each of these three types of explanation contains within itself four different styles of history writing. (In preparing this summary, I was initially inclined on grounds of reader fatigue to omit a description of each of the following twelve classifications and, instead, to focus only on White's account of the four major tropes. I decided, however, to include them all as a depressing omen of what is in store when the theorists of cultural studies gain a majority on the committees that decide history curriculum.)

Under White's category of emplotment, there are four archetypal story forms which characterise the different kinds of explanatory effects for which an historian can strive.

Romantic emplotment: This refers to a dramatic story that describes the triumph of good over evil, of virtue over vice and of light over darkness, and tells of the ultimate transcendence of man over the world.

Tragic emplotment: Here White means a story that intimates terrible states of division among men, which lead those who survive the ensuing conflicts to become resigned to the conditions in which they must labour in the world.

Comic emplotment: In this story form hope for the temporary triumph of man over his world is offered by the prospect of reconciliations of the forces at play in the social and natural worlds. These reconciliations are symbolised by the festive occasions that the comic writer describes in terminating his account.

Satirical emplotment: This refers to a drama that is dominated by the apprehension that man is ultimately a captive of the world, rather than its master, and that human consciousness and will are always inadequate to the task of overcoming man's enemy, death.

According to White, different conceptions of what constitutes proper historical explanation can also be categorised into four types:

Formist argument: This is a type of argument that, White says, is complete when a given set of objects has been properly identified, its class, generic and specific attributes assigned, and labels attesting its particularity attached. Formist historians are less inclined to make generalisations about the nature of the historical process and instead emphasise the uniqueness of the different agents, agencies and acts that make up the events to be explained. Examples: Herder, Carlyle, Michelet, Trevelyan.

Mechanistic argument: This is a theory of explanation that searches for causal laws that determine the outcomes of the historical processes uncovered by the historian. A work of history is an attempt to divine the laws that govern its operation and to display in narrative form the effects of those laws. Examples: Buckle, Tocqueville, Marx.

Organicist argument: Those adopting this method tend to construct some integrated entity out of a set of apparently dispersed events. The integrated entity assumes an importance greater than that of any of the individual entities discussed in the narrative. History written in this mode tends to be oriented toward the end or goal in whose direction all aspects of the story are tending. Examples: Hegel, Ranke, Maitland.

Contextualist argument: This form of argument explains why events occurred as they did by revealing the relationship they bear to other events occurring in the same historical dimension. The 'flow' of historical time is envisaged as a wave-like motion in which certain trends are considered to be intrinsically more significant than others. Examples: Herodotus, Burckhardt.

Every historical account of reality, White maintains, contains an irreducible component of ideology, which itself determines the kind of generalisations that historians make. Like emplotment and argument, ideology can be neatly divided into four types.

Anarchist ideology: This is committed to structural transformation of society in the interest of abolishing 'society' and substituting for it a 'community' of individuals.

Radical ideology: This is committed to structural transformation of society in the interest of reconstituting society on a new basis.

Conservative ideology: This is committed to the view that existing social structure is sound but that some change is inevitable. Social change should take a biological form of plant-like gradualisations.

Liberal ideology: This is committed to the view that existing social structure is sound but that some change is inevitable. Social change should take a mechanical form of adjustment or fine tuning of the machine.

Overall, then, White's account of the categories of explanation at the surface level of history can be represented by the following grid:[12]

Type of explanation	Emplotment	Argument	Ideology
Style of history writing	Romantic	Formist	Anarchist
	Tragic	Mechanistic	Radical
	Comic	Organicist	Conservative
	Satirical	Contextualist	Liberal

White maintains that actual history writing always derives from a combination of the above styles. The combination appropriate to each writer can be drawn from the horizontal plane of the grid. Hence, Michelet combined a romantic emplotment, with a formist argument and a liberal ideology. Burckhardt combined a satirical emplotment with a contextualist argument and a conservative ideology, and so on. In some cases, a writer can combine styles from within the same horizontal plane, for example Hegel whose emplotment operated on two levels, one tragic, the other comic. Marx's ideology was steadfastly radical, but his work oscillated between a tragic and comic emplotment, and between a mechanistic and organicist mode of argument.

Although he devotes a great deal of space in his book to fleshing out the way that his chosen historians fit into these categories, White's major interest is in his second level, or the 'deep level of consciousness'. He maintains that the choices the historian makes at the 'deep level' actually determine the styles of explanation adopted at the surface. Before a historian can start writing, White says, he needs to have three things at hand: (1) the data or evidence he has uncovered about his subject; (2) the concepts and explanations he will use to make sense of the data; and (3) a way of 'prefiguring' the historical field in which the data and explanations will be presented. This act of 'prefiguring' determines the nature of the 'deep level' at which the historian will operate. This is a 'poetic act', which White says is 'indistinguishable from the linguistic act in which the field is made ready for interpretation'.

In short, the historian's problem is to construct a linguistic protocol, complete with lexical, grammatical, syntactical and semantic dimensions, by which to characterise the field and its elements in his own terms (rather than in the terms in which they come labelled in the documents themselves), and thus to prepare them for the explanation and representation he will subsequently offer of them in his narrative.[13]

White says that this prefiguring, or preconceptualising, at the deep level can itself best be explained in terms of the concepts used to analyse poetic language. To do this, he introduces the theory of 'tropes'. The term 'tropes' refers to figures of speech in which the poet modifies or plays upon the literal meaning of language to create an effect. Theories about art and rhetoric that were developed in Ancient Greece, and that were revived in the Renaissance, identified four classifications of tropes: metaphor, metonymy, synecdoche and irony. In the 1950s and 1960s, theorists using the structuralist methodology applied the theory of tropes to both anthropology and literature. The cultural anthropologist Claude Levi-Strauss used it to analyse the naming systems and mythologies of primitive cultures.[14] The literary theorist Roman Jakobson adopted it to argue that the literature of the nineteenth century could be classified into two major stylistic divisions: the romantic–poetic–metaphorical tradition on the one hand; and the realistic–prosaic–metonymical tradition on the other.[15] White maintains that the tropes are actually embedded in human consciousness where they act as 'paradigms, provided by language itself, of the operations by which consciousness can prefigure areas of experience that are cognitively problematic in order subsequently to submit them to analysis and explanation'.[16]

White's thesis is that in the tropes he has found the irreducible nature of each mode of writing history. 'It is my view', he says, 'that the dominant tropological mode and its attendant linguistic protocol comprise the irreducibly "metahistorical" basis of every historical work.'[17] Let me summarise his own meaning for each of the four categories.

METAPHOR: This is a representational figure of speech. The example 'my love, a rose' affirms the adequacy of the rose as a representation of the loved one. The phrase is meant to be taken figuratively, as an indication of the qualities of beauty, preciousness, delicacy and so on possessed by the loved one. Metaphor is representational in the same way as formist arguments are.

METONYMY: This is a reductionist figure of speech. When, for example, 'fifty sail' is used to mean 'fifty ships', it is being suggested that ships are in some sense identifiable with that part of themselves without which they cannot operate. In another metonymical phrase, 'the roar of thunder', there is a cause–effect relationship in which the thunder is reduced to the particular sound, the roar, that it has produced. Metonymy is reductive in the same way as mechanistic arguments are.

SYNECDOCHE: This is an integrative figure of speech. The example 'he is all heart', suggests that a quality with which the individual is identified represents every aspect of his being. Synecdoche is close to metonymy, but instead of reducing an individual to one of its parts, it describes a relationship among the parts. Synecdoche is integrative in the same way as organicist arguments are.

IRONY: This is a negational figure of speech. In this trope, the author signals a real or feigned disbelief in the truth of his own statements. Ironic statements are cast in a self-consciously sceptical tone. As well as pointing to the absurdity of the beliefs it parodies, White says, an ironic statement points to the potential foolishness of all linguistic characterisations of reality. Irony thus represents a stage of consciousness in which the problematical nature of language has become recognised. It is therefore 'dialectical' in its apprehension of the capacity of language to obscure more than it clarifies. The 'ironic apprehension' commits those who adopt it to a world view of the 'irreducible relativism of all knowledge'.

White's work follows that of the eighteenth century Italian writer Giambattista Vico, who used these four tropes to characterise what he saw as the four great stages of human cultural development. According to Vico, the age of metaphor was the first stage of human culture, which he called the Age of the Gods, when people perceived similarities between natural phenomena and human artefacts in a direct way. The age of metonymy was the Age of Heroes, when people perceived differences among themselves and the social structure became feudal, with lords and patricians arrogating to themselves the vision and powers of the deities. The age of synecdoche was the Age of Men, when people perceived the world in terms of interrelated groups and recognised their interdependency. The final age defined by Vico was the Age of Irony, the modern era of decay, when people find that language—which cannot grasp the world as it is—becomes misused by groups consumed by greed and seeking power to further their own ends.

White's book, *Metahistory,* has a parallel structure to Vico's work, except that White applies the four tropes not to a version of universal history but to the development of historical writing in the nineteenth century. White says that at the level of the 'deep structure of the historical imagination', there was a process of evolution in the dominant modes of historical thinking from the Enlightenment of the eighteenth century onwards. Enlightenment writers adopted a pessimistic outlook on the nature of history. This meant, White says, that their works were dominated by the trope of irony. Thinkers such as Voltaire, Gibbon, Hume, Kant and Robertson had come to view history in 'essentially Ironic terms'.[18] However, the nineteenth century dawned with a romantic reaction against this. In the work of Rousseau, Justus Moser, Edmund Burke, Herder and others, there was a common antipathy to Enlightenment rationalism and a romantic belief in 'empathy' as a method of historical enquiry. Their approach was cast in the metaphorical mode. The conflict between the thinking of the Enlightenment and that of the romantics inspired renewed interest in the problem of how to gain historical knowledge. The most profound formulation of this problem was, according to White, the work of Hegel who identified the conflict as, at bottom, one between the ironic and metaphorical modes of apprehending history. Hegel's major book on the subject, *The Philosophy of History* (1830), was itself expressed in the synecdochic mode.

By the 1830s, White says, there were three distinct schools of historical thought: the romantics, the idealists (Hegel and followers) and the positivists (Auguste Comte and followers who emplotted history as comedy). All shared an antipathy to the ironic mode. This constituted the first phase of historiography of the period. The second phase of historiography lasted from 1830 to 1870 and produced four of the masters of the craft: Michelet, Ranke, Tocqueville and Burckhardt. According to White, Michelet presented a view of history written in the metaphorical mode, Ranke's work represented the synecdochic mode, while both Burckhardt and Tocqueville were committed to the trope of irony. The third stage of historiography of the nineteenth century, according to White, was represented not so much by historians as by philosophers of history. The precursor of these, Karl Marx, had 'attempted to combine the synecdochic strategies of Hegel with the metonymical strategies of the political economy of the time'.[19] The major works of the third stage belonged to Nietzsche and Croce. Nietzsche's work was self-consciously metaphorical, while Croce's philosophy represented yet another descent into irony.

For White, the practice of history in the twentieth century has remained dominated by the trope of irony. Academic historiography, the body of history taught in modern universities, has been captured by the ironic perspective, with its 'inherent scepticism, which passes for scholarly caution and empiricism, and its moral agnosticism, which passes for transideological neutrality'.[20] Rather than academic history being objective and neutral, White says that its adoption of the ironic mode means it is actually elitist and is squarely within the camp of the political Right.

Irony tends to dissolve all belief in the possibility of positive political actions. In its apprehension of the essential folly or absurdity of the human condition, it tends to engender belief in the 'madness' of civilisation itself and to inspire a Mandarin-like disdain for those seeking to grasp the nature of social reality in either science or art.[21]

Today, he says, the real opponents of these Mandarins of the academy are the advocates of speculative philosophy of history, that is, the followers of Hegel, Marx and Nietzsche. White then provides a list of writers, most of whom are either Marxists or existentialists, including Martin Heidegger, Jean-Paul Sartre, Walter Benjamin, Michel Foucault and George Lukacs, whom he says provide a contemporary alternative to empirical historians. One of his main aims, the reader finds near the end of his book, has been to redefine how we perceive the discipline of history. Instead of seeing 'history' as being confined to the works of empirical historians, White wants us to regard the philosophy of history as the legitimate alternative to the empirical mainstream. Moreover, he claims that we can have no logical grounds for preferring empirical history over the speculative philosophy of Heidegger, Sartre, Benjamin, Foucault, Lukacs and Co. . The only grounds on which we can choose, White insists, are either moral or aesthetic.

In the human sciences, it is still a matter not only of expressing a preference for one or another way of conceiving the tasks of analysis but also of choosing among contending notions of what an adequate human science might be... When it is a matter of choosing among these alternative visions of history, the only grounds for preferring one over another are *moral* or *aesthetic* ones... And if we wish to transcend the agnosticism which an Ironic perspective on history, passing as the sole possible 'realism' and 'objectivity' to which we can aspire in historical studies, foists upon us, we have only to reject this Ironic perspective and to will to view history from another anti-Ironic perspective.[22]

In other words, we are free to conceive of history as we will, and to adopt any perspective we please. White's thesis demonstrates just how ambitious is the agenda being brought to history by the proponents of cultural studies. What starts out as an exercise in framing history within literary categories, ends up as a redefinition of both the scope and nature of the discipline itself.

THE INCOHERENCE OF TROPE THEORY

Despite the reputation White has earned for his thesis, and despite the obvious success of his book (it is still in print twenty years after it was written), there are serious problems in the way he applies the theory of tropes to history writing. White himself admits that some of the writers he discusses do not fit neatly into the categories of tropes to which he assigns them. He says that Jacob Burckhardt often used synecdochic language in his historical works to describe the relationship between the culture of a society and the power of Church and state. However, the underlying story Burckhardt's writings told about the history of the Renaissance was of a fall from great achievement into decadence and ruin. Burckhardt conceived the reasons for this in the metonymic mode, as the result of a struggle between forces that had their origins in human nature. Yet both the language and the perspective that Burckhardt adopted, and with which he addressed his readers, says White, was that of irony.[23] Similarly, White acknowledges that the writings of Marx contain elements that are ironic, metonymic and synecdochic.[24] The work of Nietzsche is 'metaphorically ironic'.[25] And Tocqueville 'mediates' between two modes of consciousness, metaphorical and metonymical, which are inherent in his subject matter, while the ground of this mediation is irony.[26]

White engages in a great deal of equivocation when he discusses the use of more than one trope by the same writer. In particular, he says that the 'dialectical' approach of Hegel and Marx allows them to transcend the problem of combining two modes within the one body of work. But nothing he says can acquit his whole schema from the charge of incoherence. If the poetic modes at the deep level of the historic consciousness are as fundamental as he claims, it should not be possible for them to allow for any overlaps, mergers, tensions, or any other kind of dual existence. His original claim for these modes was that they constitute an irreducible linguistic protocol that 'prefigures' the framework within which the historian operates. White says the interpretations that derive from each of these frameworks are, as I recorded above, mutually exclusive.[27] The historian undertakes a 'poetic act' in adopting *one* of these frameworks. Hence, if the tropes are to have the analytical power that White accords them, some historians cannot operate in a way that bestrides them, nor can others float between them, and nor can others transcend them. If they can do this then, on his own reasoning, there should be other, even deeper tropes beneath them to provide *their* conceptual strategies.

White demonstrates just how preposterous is his thesis in his claim that, by sometimes adopting one of these figures of speech, a historian is thereby committed to a world view that has that figure of speech at its core. Anyone who adopts an ironic approach, he says, is thereby committed to a belief in the 'irreducible relativism of all knowledge'. In adopting irony a writer adopts a linguistic paradigm that itself rejects the attempt to capture the truth of things in language. 'It [irony] points to the potential foolishness of all linguistic characterisations of reality as much as to the absurdity of the beliefs its parodies.'[28]

Now, to argue that anyone who uses irony or sarcasm as a stylistic device thereby becomes committed to a relativist view of everything and at the same time abandons the belief that language cań describe reality, is to draw the longest and most implausible bow imaginable. The academic historian today who writes within an empirical, realist framework can often be dull and boring, it is true, but it is rare to find one who is so devoid of wit that he or she fails to make one or two ironic observations about his or her historical subjects, especially when, as so often happens in human affairs, actions fail to live up to promises. In the hands of some of the masters of narrative realism, such as Edward Gibbon or A. J. P. Taylor, irony is a constant and entertaining undertone deployed to prick the pomposities of the characters who bestride the historic stage. In none of these cases does the mere adoption of an ironic style determine the author's methodology let alone his belief in reality.

Neither irony, nor any of the other tropes for that matter, constitute deep abstractions that can account for a whole approach to history writing. Historians are free to adopt any of them to colour their language or to dramatise the stories they tell, just as we all do when we use figures of speech in our everyday talk and writing. Tropes are not deep foundations that determine the whole structure. Rather, they are relatively minor stylistic devices used *within* historical accounts. Sometimes they function in the construction of the drama told by the writer, but mostly they operate at no deeper level than that of the sentence. White has mistaken the surface for the substance, the decoration for the edifice.

CRITICISM, STYLE AND COMMITMENT

Despite the recurrent attempts of literary critics to demonstrate the superiority of their judgements over those of the artists they analyse, and despite all the recent talk within English departments about 'the death of the author', criticism is an essentially dependent activity. Critics cannot exist without works to criticise. Critics need novels, poems and plays in a way that novelists, poets and dramatists do not need critics. Historians, however, are the opposite. Most have been attracted to the field by the prospect of writing their own works of history. In an analogy with literature, historians are the novelists and dramatists, not the critics. The few who have written books and essays (as distinct from book reviews) that focus primarily on the criticism of history writing have usually done so as something peripheral to their main concern. Of course, historians have written plenty of biographies that have studied the lives and ideas of their colleagues and there is a vast number of commentaries on the claims made by historians about what happened in history. But historians have done only a small amount of work on historiographic criticism, by which

I mean the analysis of historical writing as a form of writing. One of the reasons that littérateurs are now moving into history is because they perceive a gap in the market. The criticism of history writing appears fair game to outsiders.

One of the most notable exceptions to all this is the American academic John Clive, who until his recent death was Professor of History and Literature at Harvard. While today one might regard such a merging of domains within the one chair as yet another victory for textualism, Clive instead was one of the notable contributors to the traditional discipline of history. Like Simon Schama, Clive was an ardent admirer of the great individual historians of the past. In 1989 a collection was published of the best essays he had written over the previous thirty years. Clive entitled the collection *Not By Fact Alone*, to signal that, though he accepted that historians were obliged to pursue the truth and get their facts right, some had the ability to cast a literary spell over the mind of the reader and to make their work conducive not just to reading but to rereading.[29] He saw history, in other words, as both art and science.

The focus of Clive's work was the critical appreciation of a number of the outstanding historians of the nineteenth century, especially Thomas Babington Macaulay, Thomas Carlyle, Jules Michelet and Alexis de Tocqueville. He has strayed into the eighteenth century to write about Edward Gibbon and into the twentieth century to discuss Elie Halévy. In making a case for reading the great historians of the past, Clive says the reason we should do so is not because of the scientific contribution of their work to the discipline today. The research they did and the information they uncovered has long been absorbed and surpassed. No supervisor would advise a new graduate student to start research into the French Revolution by reading Carlyle, Michelet or Tocqueville, even though each has written a celebrated book on the topic. The great historians are still worth reading, Clive argues, because of their writing style and the way they structure their stories.

Macaulay, for instance, is one of the best writers of prose in the English language. Two qualities that make his *History of England* compelling reading, Clive says, are his strongly developed sense of the concrete in pictorial form and his capacity to animate characters, motives and situations into forward motion in time. Macaulay recorded changes in customs not only by abstract generalisations and statistical extracts but by appropriate visual images presented in every line. For example, he translated the doctrines of the Puritans into concrete and familiar images: 'It was a sin to hang garlands on a Maypole, to drink a friend's health, to fly a hawk, to hunt a stag, to play at chess, to wear lovelocks, to put starch into a ruff, to touch the virginals, to read the *Faerie Queene*.' When the country squires hurried to London in 1690 to oppose the Corporation Bill which they saw was intended to damage the Tory Party: 'A hundred knights and squires left their halls hung with mistletoe and holly, and their boards groaning with brawn and plum porridge, and rode up post to town, cursing the short days, the cold weather, the miry road, and the villainous Whigs.'[30] Clive says Macaulay was master of the art of transition, that of making an orderly linkage between one paragraph or section of writing and the next, in a seemingly ineluctable propulsion. This was more than a stylistic device because it derived from Macaulay's 'propulsive imagination', which was tied to his conviction that the history of England was a history of progress. His prose, in other words, reflected the total story told by his history. Clive argues that the way Macaulay structured the transitions in his prose remains a model for history writing today. On his famous Chapter Three, the social history chapter, Clive comments:

We move naturally from the subject of the difficulty of travelling in late-seventeenth-century England, which resulted in making the fusion of the different elements in society so imperfect, to the subject of the badness of the roads. For it was, of course, by road that both travelers and goods generally passed from place to place. Why were the roads in such a wretched condition? One major reason was the defective state of the law. And that brings Macaulay to the first of the turnpike acts and its results.[31]

Clive argues that there are similar strategies at work in Edward Gibbon's *Decline and Fall of the Roman Empire*. In an essay on Gibbon's use of humour, Clive shows him mocking earlier authors of his subject, making sexual innuendos, ridiculing many of the claims of the Church and its saints, and infusing his entire voluminous work with a sense of playfulness and vivacity. One of the aims of *Decline and Fall* was to capture the territory of the early history of Christianity for the secular historian. To do this Gibbon sought not only to establish the factual record against the devotional, but to use humour to deride many of the miraculous claims made by later clerical authors. In an account of the monastic saints, Gibbon writes: 'They familiarly accosted, or imperiously commanded, the lions and serpents of the desert; infused vegetation into a sapless trunk; suspended iron on the surface of the water; passed the Nile on the back of a crocodile; and refreshed themselves in a fiery furnace.'[32] He mocks what he calls a frank confession of a Benedictine abbot: 'My vow of poverty has given me an hundred thousand crowns a year; my vow of obedience has raised me to the rank of a sovereign prince', and adds, 'I forget the consequences of his vow of chastity'. Clive argues that Gibbon's irony served a number of purposes: as a weapon against intellectual opponents; as a means of sometimes distancing himself from his subject matter to lend the appearance of Olympian detachment; as a protective device in an age when explicit attacks on Christianity were dangerous; and as a means of mediating an amused and objective view of human nature in all its variety.

Clive uses the work of the French historian Elie Halévy to show one way to structure a work of history that will hold a reader's attention: the creation of suspense and curiosity through a narrative structure that, like a detective story, does not reveal its solution until its tale is told. This is the structure of Halévy's *England in 1815*, the first volume of his *History of the English People in the Nineteenth Century*. The puzzle Halévy poses is: why did England have no 'French' revolution? Why was the country able to preserve political and social continuity without major violence? To answer his question, the author goes through the economic organisation of the country, then examines its political institutions, then considers some other explanatory factors. He does not reveal his answer in his Preface but instead leads the reader through the range of political and economic variables operating at the start of the nineteenth century. It is only after he has concluded that none of these areas possessed the stability needed to prevent revolution, that he turns to religion and culture and finds the answer there. The Halévy thesis was that Methodism and Evangelicalism were the chief stabilising forces in English society at the time. Clive's aim in tracing this story is not to argue in favour of the thesis, which itself remains a controversial one, but to praise the benefits of basing a narrative structure on the lure of mystery and suspense.[33]

Apart from prose style and narrative structure, Clive has his own thesis about what makes a work of history striking and what makes its writing compelling. The great historians, he writes, all create their own mental and moral universes. Reading their work is a matter of entering their worlds and experiencing their perspectives and values. Clive argues:

> the quality of their writing, which turns out to exert the greatest power over us (and that may be an unexpected quality), is intimately related to each historian's chief intellectual or personal concerns. It is never merely stylistic, merely methodological, or merely didactic. Marx's use of literary devices reflected his view of history as class struggle; Tocqueville's quest for the laws of social life derived in great part from his French and American political experience; Carlyle's obsession with a new method of writing history was closely related to his metaphysics; Burckhardt's view of the moral ambivalence to be found in fifteenth century Italy was coloured by his own pessimism about the fate of nineteenth century Europe.[34]

All great historians, from the Greeks to the present, he argues, exude the same quality. Hence, from this perspective, historical scholarship and literature are both compatible with the capacity of an individual author to take a stand. We might term this the 'Clive thesis'. The enduring appeal of the 'thrilling, beautiful prose' championed by Simon Schama derives from what Clive sanctions as 'the encounter between personal commitment and scholarly curiosity which lies at the heart of all great history'.[35]

There is nothing incompatible, we might note, between the Clive thesis and the scientific status of history discussed in the previous chapter. No two historians could ever write about the same topic in exactly the same way, so, of necessity, every work of history has to represent some kind of individual expression by its author. The important issue is that, in creating their individual expressions, historians should adhere to the research methodology of the discipline and should present their evidence in ways that can be corroborated, confirmed or challenged by others. Hence, there is no contradiction between, on the one hand, a work of history that presents an individual author's world view and, on the other hand, one that adopts a properly scientific methodology.

While the publication of Clive's essays has done more for the practice of historiographic criticism than any other recent development, he insists himself that the field is still largely underdeveloped. There are a whole range of questions about historians' use of language, especially image and metaphor, that need to be analysed. To say this is not, of course, to endorse promoters of literary theory such as Hayden White who have adopted this question in a way that undermines history's credentials rather than contributes to something illuminating or constructively critical. Some of the questions that need to be asked, Clive says, are best answered in a biographical context. For instance, do historians, especially those who deal with abstract entities such as groups, or classes or movements, need a special capacity in the use of metaphors? In what ways are the sorts of imagery chosen by any great historian related to his or her personality and general outlook on the world? Do historians, consciously or otherwise, derive inspiration not merely from contemplation of their sources but from extraneous experiences?

Constructive though these issues may be, their focus on language and style still leaves a yawning crevasse in the total agenda of the analysis of history as a form of literature. This chasm is the artistry involved in historical *research*. The next section takes up this issue.

RESEARCH, SCHOLARSHIP AND POPULARITY

The questions about history as literature are far from confined to those about writing. The greatest quantity of effort that a real historian puts into any project is in the research phase. It is the quality of this research that, more often than not, determines the quality of the work as a whole. The art of history thus lies as much in the archival research and in the marshalling of evidence as it does in the writing of the explanation and the way the story is told. Hence, the art of history goes far beyond any of the criteria that might be suggested by literary criticism or biographical analysis.

Probably the greatest claim to artistry that research and evidence can make occurs when they allow us to see things from a new, unexpected and illuminating perspective. For my money, the most outstanding example of this in Australian historiography is Charles Rowley's 1970 publication *The Destruction of Aboriginal Society* which, for reasons I gave in Chapter Four, threw the history of European settlement since 1788 into a vivid new relief that has since been impossible not to recognise. John Clive cites the example of the nineteenth century English medievalist Frederick William Maitland. Maitland's conclusion that in the thirteenth century the English parliament was not primarily a national assembly or legislature but rather a session of the king's council whose function was chiefly judicial and administrative, was called by the late Helen Maud Cam 'a magnificent attack on after-mindedness'. The essence of Maitland's original insight was the ability to see the past not through the distorting medium of what followed, but in its own terms.[36] Though he is now out of fashion and often cited as one of those dead white males whose interests and emphases most need overturning, Lewis Namier's work on English politics in the Georgian era had a similar impact to that of Maitland's work. In the 1930s, Namier demolished the Whig interpretation that eighteenth century politics had been a story of enlightenment and progress. By looking for political motives beyond those expressed in parliamentary papers and public speeches, and by adopting the then-innovative approach of scrutinising politicians' personal letters and diaries, Namier not only rewrote the politics of the period but established new grounds in research methodology as well. The same can be said of the work of Edward Thompson who, in *The Making of the English Working Class,* published in 1964, almost single-handedly established the viability of 'history from below' and created a whole new movement in social history. Eschewing official labour movement sources such as trade union and political party records, Thompson proved that a wealth of archival data existed that recorded the aspirations of the vast ranks of the lower orders of society whose uneducated and often illiterate condition had been assumed by other historians to have obliterated them from the historic record. Even if we put aside his magnificent prose style, Thompson's research stands on its own as a work of consummate artistry.

One of the difficulties in appreciating this kind of artistry lies in recognising its originality. Unless you are steeped in the same field yourself, or at least very well read, you need someone who *is* to explain the significance of a particular research achievement. In other words, most readers can appreciate the artistry of research only with the aid of scholarly commentary and critique. The big problem here is that for the last thirty years at least, too many publishers of history books have not appreciated this and have encouraged their authors to get on with telling the story and to leave out all the scholarly stuff. The publishers' actions have been based on what they perceive as the dictates of the market. In the case of books that they hope will sell beyond the academic trade, authors have been advised to exclude their disputes with other historians, to omit their analyses of how their own work fits into the current debate on the topic, and even to transfer footnotes from the bottom of the page to the end of the book. For instance, in the English-language abridged edition of Fernand Braudel's *The Mediterranean,* the abridger Richard Ollard says that his decision to cut out all the footnotes was made to seize a 'golden opportunity' to bring new readers to the work. 'Such readers, unlike the professed student of history, might be deterred by the magisterial citation of authorities which the notes contain, or by the learned and leisurely debate with other scholars, for the terms of which antecedent knowledge is often needed.'[37] For the Australian Bicentenary in 1988, the large team of historians that was assembled to write the popularly oriented fourteen-volume series, *Australians: A Historical Library,* decided to omit all footnotes and eliminate the scholarly debate in all but a handful of reference works.

Most of these decisions underestimate both the intelligence and the taste of readers. It is a mistake to equate the typical general reader of a history book with the consumers of tabloid newspapers or glossy magazines. The market for history is far more refined than the readership of the press. Anyone who buys a history book to read (rather than decorate the bookshelf) is making a commitment to a long and sustained engagement with it. Publishers and editors who assume that these readers cannot handle or do not want to know about the writer's sources, or the status of the work in relation to others in the field, are both patronising and mistaken. One of the characteristics of modern readers is that none of them take anything on trust simply because someone in authority has told them so. The purchasers of history books are generally well educated and epistemologically sophisticated enough to know that claims to knowledge need to be properly established. Modern readers expect to be far more than passive observers of a work. They continually read between the lines and are constantly making a series of fine judgements about whether the claims made by an author are worth believing or not. An appropriate analogy here is the detective novel. The main interest in these stories is not who done it but the methodology of the detective in solving the crime. The methodology of the historian, similarly, is of considerable interest to the modern reader. It is true, as Richard Ollard says above, that some academic debate assumes more esoteric knowledge than the average reader possesses, but this is something that authors should learn to correct, not a justification for abandoning discussion of method altogether.

The proof of the case argued here lies in the success of some notable works that have made no concessions at all to what is mistaken for popular taste.

Since it was published in paperback as the one thousandth Pelican book in 1968, Edward Thompson's *The Making of the English Working Class* almost certainly ranks as one of the world's biggest selling history books of the last fifty years. It made its author an academic celebrity in almost every English-speaking country. Yet it is an unabridged 958 pages long, has detailed and often annotated footnotes at the bottom of almost every page, and is peppered throughout with discussions about the strengths and weaknesses of its sources, about problems in interpreting evidence and about the perception or blindness of other historians who have previously traversed the same field. Manning Clark's *History of Australia* is a massive six volumes in length and, though it lacks the kind of spirited engagement with other authors that characterises Thompson's book, it still sources its evidence in full and provides proper footnotes at the bottom of its pages. Yet it is far and away the biggest selling work of Australian history published since the Second World War.

The conclusion to draw from all this is that, since the research is part of the artistry of history, practices that hide the research process also hide some of this artistry. These practices do not make a work more popular; they diminish its appeal. To underline this point, let me turn once again to John Clive and his discussion of the great nineteenth century historians. Clive cites some examples from the *Old Regime and the French Revolution* where Alexis de Tocqueville takes the reader into his confidence as he discusses his encounters with archival sources. Tocqueville makes a point of discussing those encounters that overturned his preconceptions. 'I well remember my surprise', he reports, 'when I was for the first time examining the records of an intendancy with a view to finding out how a parish was administered under the old order'. Tocqueville was surprised because he had until then thought that the local government of American rural towns was unique to the New World. However, he found the same features in the French parishes of the pre-revolutionary regime; for good reason, since the original model for both had been the rural parish of the Middle Ages. Similarly, Tocqueville writes 'I was almost startled' to find eighteenth century bishops and abbots planning the construction of roads and canals, and that, in studying the *cahiers* drawn up before the meeting of the revolutionary Estates General, 'I realised with something like consternation that what was being asked for was nothing short of the systematic, simultaneous abolition of *all* existing French laws and customs'.[38] These passages are very good illustrations of the integration of scholarly method with the main narrative. Beneath the drama of the genesis of the revolution itself, Tocqueville injects a sub plot of the drama of his own research investigations.

LET ME FINISH this chapter with a qualified endorsement of Alan Bloom's call for a return to teaching from the canon of the great works of Western learning as an answer to the relativism and incoherence cultivated by late twentieth century intellectual fashion. As I argued in the last chapter, the teaching of a canon can only be useful within the framework of an intellectual discipline. Within a discipline, it is more valuable to know all that current scholars are saying about a particular subject area than to know how the same topic was treated one or two centuries ago, largely because the canonical works on that subject have usually been absorbed within the perspectives that are now being debated. From the point of view of the content of knowledge, the great works of history are of value primarily because of the way they defined their subjects and resolved the debates over the issues within those topics. G. R. Elton's point in the last chapter is an accurate description of what normally occurs: on most historical topics, there are often a variety of interpretations that, in the early phases of scholarship, typically increase in number but, as investigation and debate proceed, gradually reduce as they become resolved and assimilated into the body of knowledge. If we accept that knowledge accumulates and that disciplines evolve, the great works do not have any special claim on our attention apart from the contribution they made in the past to solving historical problems and developing the discipline. To base education *exclusively* on a canon, as Bloom advised, would diminish the work of the other contributors to the discipline and, if taken seriously, would mean that each generation would have to engage in the equivalent of reinventing the wheel. This, anyway, would be the outcome in history—though maybe not in philosophy, which was Bloom's main concern.

On the other hand, an education in history that omits the great works is clearly incomplete, even though this is the fate of most undergraduates who actually major in the discipline today. I still count myself fortunate to have been forced to read Gibbon, Macaulay, Carlyle, Maitland and Tocqueville for an undergraduate course on historical method at the University of Sydney in 1966. The students who today attend compulsory seminars on Foucault, Heidegger and poststructuralism are grossly underprivileged by comparison. The best reasons for studying the works of the historical canon are those given by John Clive: the great writers show us how history can be a literature that attains the highest form of art. Reading their works provides not only lessons in the form and structure of writing and research but inspiration to ignite the ardour of both readers and writers. Moreover, in showing us what we stand to lose if this endangered discipline is hunted to extinction, the great works give us not only the grounds to truly value history but the determination needed to hold off all the theoretical and literary interlopers who are now so hungrily stalking the corridors.

1   Simon Schama, *Dead Certainties (Unwarranted Speculations)*, Granta Books/Penguin, London, 1991

2   Simon Schama, *Dead Certainties*, p 327

3   Roy Porter, 'The history man', *New Statesman and Society*, London, 7 June 1991, p 43

4   Simon Schama, 'No future for history without its stories', *Sydney Morning Herald*, 18 November 1991, p 13

5   Simon Schama, 'No future for history without its stories'

6   Simon Schama, *Dead Certainties*, p 322

7   Peter Burke, 'People's History or Total History', in Raphael Samuel (ed.), *People's History and Socialist Theory*, History Workshop Series, Routledge and Kegan Paul, London, 1981, p 7

8   Hayden White, *Metahistory: The Historical Imagination in Nineteenth Century Europe*, Johns Hopkins University Press, Baltimore, 1973

9   Hayden White, *Metahistory*, p 428

10 Hayden White, *Metahistory*, p 433

11 Hayden White, *Metahistory*, p 12

12 Hayden White, *Metahistory*, p 29

13 Hayden White, *Metahistory*, p 30

14 Claude Levi-Strauss, *The Savage Mind*, Weidenfeld and Nicholson, London, 1966, pp 205-44

15 Roman Jakobson, 'Linguistics and Poetics', in Thomas Sebeok (ed.), *Style in Language*, Technology Press/John Wiley, New York, 1960

16 Hayden White, *Metahistory*, p 36

17 Hayden White, *Metahistory*, p xi

18 Hayden White, *Metahistory*, p 38

19 Hayden White, *Metahistory*, p 40

20 Hayden White, *Metahistory*, p 433

21 Hayden White, *Metahistory*, p 38

22 Hayden White, *Metahistory*, p 433, his italics

23 For Burckhardt in both synecdochic and metonymic modes, see Hayden White, *Metahistory*, p 262; for Burckhardt's use of ironic language, see p 250

24 For Marx in ironic mode, see Hayden White, *Metahistory*, pp 296, 315-16, 324-5; in metonymic mode, pp 281, 285-6, 315, 377-8; in synecdochic mode, pp 282, 285-6, 315-16

25 Hayden White, *Metahistory*, p 41

26 Hayden White, *Metahistory*, p 203

27 In a later essay, White has realised the inconsistency to which he has committed himself by describing interpretations this way and so specifically denies the phrase 'mutually exclusive' to describe the different interpretations of the French Revolution offered by Michelet and Tocqueville. See 'The Historical Text as a Literary Artifact', in Hayden White, *Tropics of Discourse: Essays in Cultural Criticism*, Johns Hopkins University Press, Baltimore, 1985, p 85

28 Hayden White, *Metahistory*, p 37

29 John Clive, *Not By Fact Alone: Essays on the Writing and Reading of History*, Collins Harvill, London, 1990, p xiv

30 John Clive, *Not By Fact Alone*, p 70

31 John Clive, *Not By Fact Alone*, p 20

32 John Clive, *Not By Fact Alone*, p 58

33 John Clive, *Not By Fact Alone*, pp 21-4

34 John Clive, *Not By Fact Alone,* p 39

35 John Clive, *Not By Fact Alone,* p 47

36 John Clive, *Not By Fact Alone,* p 200

37 Richard Ollard, Preface to Fernand Braudel, *The Mediterranean,* trans. Siân Reynolds, Harper Collins Publishers, 1992, pp ix-x

38 John Clive, *Not By Fact Alone,* p 30

9

THE RETURN OF TRIBALISM

CULTURAL RELATIVISM, STRUCTURALISM AND
THE DEATH OF COOK

IN THE PREFACE to his book *The Order of Things*, Michel Foucault opens with a paragraph that has since become one of his most famous. Foucault describes a passage from 'a certain Chinese encyclopedia' that, he claims, breaks up all the ordered surfaces of our thoughts. By 'our' thoughts, he means Western thought in the modern era. The encyclopedia divides animals into the following categories: '(a) belonging to the Emperor, (b) embalmed, (c) tame, (d) sucking pigs, (e) sirens, (f) fabulous, (g) stray dogs, (h) included in the present classification, (i) frenzied, (j) innumerable, (k) drawn with a very fine camelhair brush, (l) *et cetera*, (m) having just broken the water picture, (n) that from a long way off look like flies.' Foucault writes that, thanks to 'the wonderment of this taxonomy', we can apprehend not only 'the exotic charm of another system of thought' but also 'the limitation of our own'. What the taxonomy or form of classification reveals, says Foucault, is that 'there would appear to be, then, at the other extremity of the earth we inhabit, a culture ... that does not distribute the multiplicity of existing things into any of the categories that make it possible for us to name, speak and think'.[1] The Chinese taxonomy does not simply represent an earlier, mistaken view of how to classify animals, which Western thought has since improved upon. Rather, Foucault says, the stark impossibility of our thinking in this way demonstrates the existence of an entirely different system of rationality.

The American ethnographer Marshall Sahlins cites Foucault and the Chinese taxonomy as part of his case against his opponent Gananath Obeyesekere, in what has now developed into the most publicly contested debate in anthropology of recent times. In 1992 Obeyesekere had denied the thesis of

Sahlins that the natives of Hawaii in 1779 had regarded Captain James Cook as their returned god Lono. Obeyesekere had claimed that the Hawaiians had too much 'practical rationality' to mistake an Englishman, who wore strange clothes, spoke no Hawaiian and knew nothing of their religious beliefs or practices, for one of their gods. In his 1995 book *How "Natives" Think*, Sahlins replies that Obeyesekere, though a Sri Lankan, is a captive of Western concepts, a man who cannot think outside this form of rationality and who imagines that Western thought constitutes the universal mind of humanity. However, says Sahlins, the existence of radically different systems of classification like that of the Chinese encyclopedia is evidence that different cultures both perceive the world and order their perceptions in radically different ways. 'If the classifications of the same sets of organisms by different peoples so vary', Sahlins argues, 'it must mean that objectivity itself is a variable social value.'[2] Hence, Westerners should not impose their own perceptions and ideas of what is logical upon other cultures. Obeyesekere cannot assume that the Hawaiians would have had more sense than to have mistaken Cook for Lono, Sahlins says. Rather, we have to appreciate that what might make 'sense' to those who share a Western frame of thought can be seen in a totally different perspective by people from non-Western cultures. Obeyesekere's notion that there is some kind of 'practical rationality', or basic psychology that all people share because of their humanity, is a mistaken attempt to universalise what Sahlins dismisses as 'commonsense bourgeois realism'. It is, he claims, to do 'a kind of symbolic violence' to other times and other customs. 'I want to suggest', Sahlins says, 'that one cannot do good history, nor even contemporary history, without regard for ideas, actions, and ontologies that are not and never were our own. Different cultures, different rationalities'.[3]

In May 1995 I gave a paper on the themes and debates in *The Killing of History* to a staff and graduate student seminar in the Department of History at the University of Sydney. Although most of the postmodernists in the department declined to attend, they deputised a colleague, Alastair MacLachlan, to reply to my talk and, hopefully, to tear me apart. My respondent opened his remarks by citing Foucault and the Chinese taxonomy. Didn't I realise, he chided me, that other cultures have such dramatically different conceptual schemes that the traditional assumptions of Western historiography are inadequate for the task of understanding them? Foucault and his followers, I was told, have been sources of genuine enlightenment because they have lifted the veil of Western arrogance from our eyes, allowing us to see that Western thought is but one form among many. Other cultures have their own rationality and their own legitimacy which, I was assured, we should respect in their own right.

There is, however, a problem rarely mentioned by those who cite the Chi-

nese taxonomy as evidence for these claims. There is no Chinese encyclopedia that has ever described animals under the classifications listed by Foucault.
In fact, there is no evidence that any Chinese person has ever thought about
animals in this way. The taxonomy is fictitious. It is the invention of the
Argentinian short story writer and poet Jorge Luis Borges. This revelation, of
course, would in no way disturb the assumptions of the typical postmodernist
thinker who believes that the distinction between fact and fiction is arbitrary
anyway. Foucault himself openly cites Borges as his source and has no problem in using the mere fictional possibility of such a radically different taxonomy as grounds for his belief that Western forms of classification are themselves nothing but the arbitrary products of our own time and space. The
example, however, is now so frequently cited in academic texts and debates,
such as the University of Sydney history seminar, that it is taken as a piece of
credible evidence about the state of mind of non-Western cultures. It deserves to be seen, rather, as evidence of the degeneration of standards of
argument in the contemporary academy. That a piece of fiction can be seriously deployed to make a case in history or anthropology indicates how low
debate has sunk in the postmodern era.

It should be said that Sahlins does not rely entirely on fictional evidence to
argue his case about taxonomies but also cites some findings by anthropologists. He gives the example of the Chewa people of Malawi who classify
certain mushrooms in the same group with game animals, rather than with
plants, on the basis of the similarities of their flesh. For the Chewa, domestic
ducks are not classified with birds, nor with wild ducks. Sahlins also describes
the Kalam people of the New Guinea highlands who classify animals and
plants not by visual qualities such as size or colour but by their smell, based on
whether they 'smell', 'stink' or 'decay'. Hence, according to Sahlins, the
Kalam are 'giving the lie to the Western perceptual economy which accords
affect to olfactory sensations and intellect to visual sensations'. [4]

Unfortunately for Sahlins, it is not difficult to show that this more empirical
type of evidence still provides no support for his claim that different taxonomies
demonstrate different rationalities. Let me give one simple example to put the
issue into perspective. I have in front of me a recent document from the
National Heart Foundation of Australia. It contains a table classifying plant
and animal products. It puts the following items into one group: skim milk,
lean red meat, skinless chicken, fresh fish, egg whites, bread, pasta, all fruit
and vegetables, legumes, water, tea, coffee, fruit juices. And it links the following together into another, different group: coconut oil, butter, full cream
milk, fried meat, bacon, sausages, egg yolks, croissants, toasted breakfast ce-
real, coconut, milkshakes, coffee whiteners. According to the Sahlins view of
the power of taxonomies, this table should be a demonstration of the mental-

ity of a radically different culture. What else should we think when the Foundation groups together such apparently unrelated items as coconuts, egg yolks and milkshakes, thereby, like the Chewa, putting plant and animal products into the one category? If we accept the logic of Sahlins's position, we should argue that only a non-Western mind would want to classify skinless chicken in the same group with bread and coffee. Should we thus assume from this taxonomy that the National Heart Foundation has become possessed of some unfathomably different rationality? Sadly, the answer is more mundane. The first category comprises foods that the Foundation recommends as being low in cholesterol and saturated fat. The second group comprises those that are high in cholesterol or saturated fat and which should be avoided by people to reduce the risk of heart disease.

Surely it is obvious that within any one culture and between any two or more cultures, human beings who share the same rationality are quite capable of adopting a variety of methods for classifying the same things and a variety of ways of looking at things depending on how they intend to use them. Different uses generate different classifications. There is nothing surprising about a Malawi tribe that puts domestic ducks and wild ducks into different categories. We make exactly the same distinction in Western culture ourselves, else we would have little use for the words 'domestic' and 'wild'. Under Western legal systems, the gross taxonomy of domestic and wild animals has been unchanged since Roman law.[5] Indeed, when we classify animals and plants for our own consumption we use groupings not dissimilar to those of the Chewa. The big difference between our culture and theirs is that we *also* have a method of classification derived from the science of biology. In this case we classify creatures not from our own interest but from the relations we find in nature. In fact, biology is the most obvious example of a science that adopts classifications that derive objectively from nature, despite the claims of postmodernists that such a thing is impossible. Our scientific taxonomies of species are in no way human-inspired or arbitrary but, rather, correspond precisely to the patterns of reproduction we find in nature. If animals or plants do not reproduce with each other they do not constitute a species. This is a taxonomy that exists in nature and did so eons before the emergence of Western science; indeed, it would still have existed even if human beings had never evolved to discover it.

STRUCTURALISM AND THE DEATH OF COOK

Marshall Sahlins's insistence that different cultures house radically different rationalities is the principal point he makes against his critic Gananath Obeyesekere. As I discussed in Chapter Three, Obeyesekere's book *The*

Apotheosis of Captain Cook is a critique, in specific terms, of Sahlins's interpretation of the death of Cook in Hawaii in 1779 and, in more general terms, of the attempt to use structuralist theory in the writing of history. I argued in that chapter that Obeyesekere's critique of Sahlins could be extended to include the work of the Australian academic Greg Dening and his structuralist interpretation of native responses to the first European contact with both Hawaii and Tahiti. Sahlins's reply was made in his 1995 book *How "Natives" Think: About Captain Cook, For Example.* The subsequent debate has had a very high profile, generating lead articles in the *Times Literary Supplement* and the *New York Review of Books* as well as book reviews in newspapers and journals around the world. It is full of acrimony, personal abuse and *ad hominem* argument. Sahlins, for example, accuses Obeyesekere of assuming 'a kind of pop nativism' and of practising 'pidgin anthropology'. In short, it is one of the most enjoyable academic fights in a decade and the best in anthropology since Derek Freeman demolished Margaret Mead in the early 1980s.

Although his reply covers a very broad front, Sahlins places his biggest single emphasis on the question of the 'different rationality' of the Hawaiians. He does this because of the nature of the charge made against him by Obeyesekere. The Sri Lankan had accused the American not only of not properly understanding the Hawaiian mind but also of perpetuating European myths. As a non-European, Obeyesekere said he was able to spot a European myth when he saw one, and the belief that the natives mistook the white explorers for gods is in this category. Obeyesekere said that rather than being a Hawaiian concept, the idea of apotheosis—that a mortal could become a god—is part of the traditions of Indo-European religion, including the Christian cult of sainthood and its ancient Roman predecessors.[6] The idea that Cook was taken for a god first appeared in print in the oral histories of Hawaiian beliefs recorded and collected in book form by American missionary schools in the 1830s. Obeyesekere argued that since some of these texts contain a number of decidedly non-Polynesian concepts—for instance, that before the Europeans arrived the natives were led by Satan and 'living in sin'—the Hawaiians' oral histories had obviously been contaminated by their subsequent conversion to Christianity. The claim that they first thought the explorers were gods has to be read in this light.

From Obeyesekere's perspective, two issues are raised. First, Sahlins's reputation as an ethnographer and relativist who can read a culture of 'the other' in its own terms is seriously cast into question. Like the missionaries, he seems to be just another American with a low opinion of the gullibility of the native mind. Second, there is the broader issue of the theoretical consequences of the interpretation. The theoretical framework in which Sahlins is operating derives from the French structuralist Claude Levi-Strauss, who proposed that tribal native mentalities are locked within the cultures that determine their cosmos or world view. Events that European 'common sense' might suggest would explode that cosmos—such as the arrival of English sailors with vastly superior technology and with tales of other countries and peoples far beyond the limits of the world previously imagined by the natives—do not have this shattering effect, since people cannot take off their culture as they take off their clothes. Sahlins himself is more of an evolutionary structuralist than an ahistorical structuralist like Levi-Strauss. Part of his interest in Cook's visit is to show that, given certain 'conjunctures' such as the meeting of English and Hawaiian culture in 1779, while each culture remained intact it nonetheless made some adaptations as a result of contact with the other. Obeyesekere, on the other hand, says that Cook's visit had a profoundly disruptive impact on Hawaiian culture, all in a matter of weeks. Hence, major events can change people's ideas and cultures rapidly, and so structuralist theory does not provide a good account of native mentalities in the post-contact period.

The reason there can be such divergent opinions on this issue is that, apart from Hawaiian memories of their former religion recalled fifty years later, the principal evidence about native beliefs in 1779 comes from the diaries and journals kept by officers and sailors during the relatively brief visits by the English ships. These men had only a smattering of the local language (gained from previous English contact with the Polynesian culture of Tahiti) and gleaned what they could of native religious beliefs from observation of their ceremonies. The debate within anthropology arises out of differing interpretations of these fragments of evidence.

It is perhaps inevitable in an academic contest of this kind that others will be dragged in. However, some of those whom Sahlins has chosen for his side seem to be strange selections. His most curious choice is Stephen Greenblatt, the postmodernist literary critic, whom Sahlins persuaded to write an endorsement for his dust jacket. Apart from being the self-proclaimed founder of the movement in literary theory and criticism called 'new historicism' (which I discussed in Chapter One), Greenblatt has no credentials as either an anthropologist or an historian. It is not so strange, though, that the other dust jacket endorsement comes from Greg Dening, since the latter's own work depends so heavily on the credibility of Sahlins's texts. Dening is, without a doubt, Sahlins's most enthusiastic follower, describing him as a 'world master' and 'genius'.

Most of the recent academic reviews of this debate have declared that Sahlins is the victor. This is partly an effect of his having had, so far, the last word. (When Obeyesekere's book first appeared in 1992 he himself had had the last word at the time and was then generally regarded as winner, being awarded, for example, the Louis Gottschalk prize by the American Society for Eighteenth Century Studies.) However, few of the reviews of Sahlins's book have gone very far into the detail of the debate or examined much of the evidence deployed by each protagonist. Few, moreover, with the notable exception of the American anthropologist Clifford Geertz,[7] have demonstrated more than a passing familiarity with Obeyesekere's original case. So, to assess both theses, it is worth first restating their main points.

Sahlins's thesis is that the Hawaiians believed the god Lono arrived by sea as an invisible presence during the period of the Makahiki festival and circled the island as part of a native procession in his honour. Lono was a god associated with peace, games and agricultural fertility. When Cook landed on Hawaii in January 1779 he landed at Kealakekua Bay, close to the site where the Makahiki procession began and ended. He was greeted by the natives as the manifestation of Lono and worshipped by both commoners and priests as the god. The priests took him to their temples for the appropriate ceremonies. Cook departed the island in February but returned ten days later to repair a sprung mast. His return, however, now coincided with the period dominated by the warlike god Ku. There were no welcomes this time; rather, the people and their chiefs were sullen and insolent. After an attempt to take the high chief Kalani'opu'u hostage for the return of a stolen cutter, Cook was turned upon by the natives and killed. According to Sahlins, the Hawaiians assaulted Cook because, in the season of Ku, their warrior leader Kalani'opu'u eclipsed the authority of Lono and killed his embodiment to usurp his godly powers.

Obeyesekere's counter claim is that, instead of treating Cook as a god, the Hawaiians treated him as a chief, most probably to enlist his support in the interminable warfare with the chiefs of other islands in the group. Cook was an obvious foreigner who did not speak the Hawaiian language and knew nothing of their religion—unlikely behaviour for an Hawaiian god. Instead of conforming to Lono's mythical procession around the island by land, Cook circled the islands by sea. The rituals the islanders performed on Cook's arrival show he was not regarded as a god. For example, he was made to genuflect in a temple before an image of the god Ku. This was something a chief could do but a god could not. At the same ceremony, Cook was wrapped in red tapa cloth, a garment that other chiefs wore. The Hawaiian chiefs and priests did not prostrate themselves before Cook as they would before a god. Only the common people prostrated themselves, as they normally did for their chiefs. While Cook was certainly given the name Lono, it was not unusual for chiefs and priests to be given divine names. One of the priests who greeted Cook in Kealakekua Bay was also named Lono. It is unlikely that Cook arrived in Hawaii during the Makahiki festival since none of the journal writers on Cook's ships mention the term 'Makahiki'. Given the great interest the English had in ethnographic detail of this kind, it is improbable that they arrived during Makahiki without being aware of it. Cook's death did not conform to Hawaiian beliefs about the legendary clash between Lono and the chief and, moreover, Sahlins's claim that the natives would have read the events 'in reverse' is implausible. The only sense in which Cook might have been deified was when his bones became objects of worship in subsequent Makahiki festivals. This is further evidence of the strategy of the Hawaiian king to make a military alliance with the English by installing their leader as a sacred Hawaiian chief, since such a chief was entitled to deification after his death.

What follows is an attempt to assess both sides of this debate. Readers will hardly need reminding that, since I committed myself to Obeyesekere's side in Chapter Three, I am not a disinterested observer. There are four issues in the debate that pose major difficulties for one or other of the protagonists.

HAWAIIAN CONCEPTS OF 'GODS': Sahlins argues that the indigenous Hawaiian concept of 'gods' was radically different from that of Western religious beliefs. Like all Polynesians, the Hawaiians did not distinguish between the natural and the supernatural as Western religion does. Certain winds, fishes and crops could be manifestations or 'bodies' of Lono.[8] Sahlins says he has never argued, as Obeyesekere claimed, that the Hawaiians had 'made' Cook a god or even 'mistaken' him for a god, since this would be the misapplication of Western euhemeristic concepts to Polynesian understandings. Rather, Sahlins's position is that Cook 'was recognised and honoured as a form of Lono: Father Lono of the Makahiki'.[9] Moreover, the English journal writer David Samwell captured the sense of Hawaiian beliefs when he described Cook being treated by the priests as a character 'partaking something of divinity'. Sahlins says that Hawaiian chiefs were themselves believed to be divine since they were descended from the gods. Lieutenant King wrote that Cook's title of Lono 'belonged to a personage of great rank and power in the island, who resembles pretty much the Delai Lama of the Tartars, and the ecclesiastical emperor of Japan'.[10] Hence, Sahlins argues, Obeyesekere's claim that Cook was invested as a chief not a god is based on a false Western distinction between the natural and supernatural. In Hawaii, as in Tibet and Japan, chiefs were regarded as divine personages and embodiments of the gods.

If Sahlins's account of Hawaiian religion is accurate then he would clearly have a winning argument here. However, one of the problems involved in assessing this debate is that when appeal is made to wider concepts that might resolve an issue, such as the nature of Hawaiian religion, each of the parties draws upon a different body of interpretation. Sahlins's account is framed within the general corpus of work produced by structuralist theorists. His principal support for the idea that Hawaiian chiefs were divine is the structuralist ethnographer Valerio Valeri,[11] a former student of Sahlins and a professor of anthropology in the same faculty and institution as Sahlins himself at the University of Chicago. In his 1985 book on ritual in ancient Hawaii, which is one of the principal authorities cited by Sahlins, Valeri gratefully acknowledges his 'even greater debt' to both the advice and documents provided him by his former teacher, now colleague, in the preparation of the work.[12] On the other hand, Obeyesekere is operating with an alternative set of interpretations of Polynesian and Hawaiian religions provided in the 1940s by Peter Buck and in the 1980s by John Charlot and the Danish scholars Bergendorff, Hasagar and Henriques, all of whom reject the idea that Hawaiian chiefs were regarded as gods in this period.[13] Moreover, not only the general accounts but specific details given of Hawaiian religion rely on interpretations that themselves vary according to particular theoretical dispositions. For instance, as part of the greeting ceremonies, Cook was wrapped by the priests in red tapa cloth. Obeyesekere says this means he was being dressed like the Hawaiian chiefs and thus was being invested as a chief. Sahlins replies that being wrapped in red cloth was a sign of divinity, since the Hawaiian idols of their gods were also wrapped in red cloth. The chiefs were wrapped in red not because they were chiefs but because they were divine. But the source that Sahlins cites as 'proof' of the meaning of being wrapped in red is, once again, Valerio Valeri.[14]

Anyone who thinks this debate might possibly be resolved on the evidence of internal inconsistencies and implausibilities is warned by Sahlins that what might appear implausible to Western eyes can have quite a different appearance to the native. At a number of places, he castigates Obeyesekere for his 'invocation of the common wisdom' and for 'substituting a folkloric sense of "native" beliefs for the relevant Hawaiian ethnography'.[15] Forewarned then, allow me to discuss some parts of Sahlins's case that, to my Western way of thinking, are rather hard to swallow.

On the question of the meaning of being wrapped in red cloth, Sahlins himself records one detail which questions his own interpretation. The other British naval captain on the expedition, Charles Clerke, commander of the *Discovery*, was also wrapped in red cloth on one occasion when he came ashore.[16] Yet Clerke was not named as a god nor made the subject of rituals as Cook was. Hawaiian oral history does not remember him as the embodiment or manifestation of a god. So, clearly, red cloth was not necessarily or always a symbol of divinity. Another part of the greeting ritual concerned Cook's actions in the temple before an image of Ku. Obeyesekere says that if Cook was the god Lono he could not have genuflected to the rival god Ku. Sahlins replies that in the descriptions of the ceremony given by Cook and

King it is unclear whether Cook actually imitated the actions of the priest
Loah who prostrated himself and kissed the image of Ku or whether he simply followed after him. Sahlins acknowledges that three scholars have interpreted the accounts as indicating that Cook only kissed the image of Ku
while three others (including Sahlins himself in a 1985 paper) have thought
they meant that Cook prostrated himself as well. Sahlins says that unless some
new document is discovered, we will never know what actually happened.
He adds that, anyway, 'kissing' in the Hawaiian manner means pressing one's
nose to another's nose or cheek while inhaling. 'For all we know, then, Cook
just sniffed at it.'[17] This is, to say the least, farfetched. The only descriptions
that exist of the ceremony were written in English for an English audience.
When the writers used the word 'kissed' they obviously meant the English
sense of pressing one's lips to something. They would have no reason to use
this word to describe the different Hawaiian practice. Cook, then, most probably kissed the image of Lono's rival Ku, an action that, if Cook was the god
Lono, would have no place in the Hawaiian religious order. Hence, in the
interpretation of two of the crucial events in this one ceremony (which itself
provided the most important single set of observations about Hawaiian religion at the time) the weight of plausibility clearly leans towards Obeyesekere's
side.

Bearing in mind Sahlins's imprecation against applying 'bourgeois rationality' to the native mind, there remains another great implausibility in his account. Obeyesekere says that the Hawaiians would have been highly unlikely
to come to the conclusion that an English sea captain could be a Polynesian
god. His foreignness of dress, colour, language and culture would have ruled
out such a belief. Sahlins replies that foreignness is exactly what Polynesians
expected of their gods who were 'foreign by origin'. 'They are transcendent,
invisible and originate in places beyond the horizon.' It was no surprise that
Cook did not speak the Hawaiian language since, Sahlins says, 'the transcendence of the gods has its counterpart in incommunicability'. The speech of the
gods is incomprehensible to the ears of men. (Valeri is his source here yet
again.[18]) Even if we were to accept all this, however, there are a number of
aspects of Cook's behaviour that are most ungodlike. The principal one is
that he was a god who appeared to know nothing about his own religion. At
the first rituals, as Sahlins himself acknowledges, Cook had to be shown at
every stage what to do. When he was supposed to stand holding his arms
outstretched to make the sign of the Makahiki, a priest had to raise one of his
arms and Lieutenant King had to be shown how to raise Cook's other arm.
Every action Cook was required to undertake was first performed by a priest
whom Cook was then encouraged to imitate. Moreover, there were some
rituals that Cook was requested to perform—such as allowing his clothes to

be anointed with coconut flesh previously chewed by a priest—from which he 'begged to be excused'.[19] On the question of the language of the gods, Sahlins is similarly hard to take. He makes a big play of criticising Obeyesekere for his inconsistency in arguing that Cook could be regarded like the Dalai Lama and the emperor of Japan yet not seen as divine. Both characters, Sahlins argues at length, were held to be men who were gods. Now, it is quite believable that the Dalai Lama, who spoke Tibetan and who understood and presided over his own religious ceremonies, and the emperor of Japan, who did the same in his own country, could both be seen by their subjects as men who were divine. However, it is simply incredible that Cook's lack of all these abilities could have accorded him the same status in Hawaii. Western and bourgeois though this assumption might be, it has logic and probability (two more bourgeois concepts, of course) on its side.

This last point is underlined by Sahlins's own comparisons of other religions of the Pacific region. Even though they have radically different cultures and genetic histories, Sahlins says it is common to find natives in Australia, Melanesia and Micronesia who, like the Polynesians, saw their first contact with Europeans as meetings with gods.[20] He fails to give a source for this supposed belief in Australia—for the very good reason that no one has ever recorded such an assumption being made by Australian Aborigines—but does give some anthropological evidence for New Guinea. Until the 1930s, the three-quarters of a million people who inhabited the fertile valleys of the New Guinea highlands in some of the most densely populated rural areas on earth, were completely unknown to the outside world and vice versa. However, their discovery was not, Sahlins argues, the fateful world-historical irruption of their traditional existence and culture that Europeans like to imagine always accompanies their own appearance. Many of these Melanesian people believed that the handful of gold prospectors who first stumbled across their villages were spirits of their dead. Even when the prospectors shot and killed local tribesmen, he says, the events did not enter 'social memory', being only of consequence to the eyewitnesses and relatives of the dead. Sahlins says he believes it is common for first contacts to be of this kind. The 'collective representations' of the natives explain the contacts in their own religious terms, and their overall culture remains unaffected. It is only after colonisation and political domination, he says, that the native historical consciousness changes. Sahlins's principal source for his account of the New Guinea highlands is the widely acclaimed 1987 book *First Contact* by the Australian anthropologists Bob Connolly and Robin Anderson, which records a number of reminiscences by highland natives of their encounters with the prospectors in the 1930s.[21] Many of these old people did remember quite clearly that they first thought the white men were 'lightning beings from the sky' or the ghosts of dead ancestors. However, whether such thoughts ever represented the 'social memory' or 'collective representations' of the highlanders is another question entirely. Sahlins himself acknowledges that Connolly and Anderson found there were other natives who quickly saw that the white strangers were people like themselves. Warriors of the Asaro Valley decided to observe the visitors closely and used their findings to argue against their tribe's original belief that they were dead people. A number of the highlanders became paid employees of the gold prospectors, operating sluices, living and working in their camps. They not only quickly saw the outsiders as human beings like themselves but just as quickly came to understand their exchange system. In particular, it was the women who saw through the initial spiritual assumptions. 'We had sex together and then we knew they were men.'[22] Sahlins himself admits that, as in New Guinea, it was the women of Hawaii who boarded the English ships and had sex with the sailors who took the lead in demystifying the visitors.[23] In fact, his rather surprising attempt to introduce the events of New Guinea into the debate only serves to diminish his case. In the examples he cites from Connolly and Anderson, as well as from some other anthropologists who have done field work among Melanesian people, all the initial native references to the whites describe them not as gods but as the returned dead, an idea that many of them fairly quickly abandoned. The idea of a *social* memory', which lends support to structuralist assumptions about first contact, is not something concluded by the authors Connolly and Anderson but, rather, is an interpretation made solely by Sahlins himself from his reading of their book. When he strays off his own turf, the special pleading involved in his predilection to make the facts fit the theory becomes only too apparent.

THE TIMING OF HAWAIIAN FESTIVALS: Another critical dispute between Obeyesekere and Sahlins is over the timing of the Makahiki—the season of Lono—and the timing of the following season—that of the war god Ku. Obeyesekere doubts whether Cook's landing coincided with Makahiki since none of the English journal writers mention the season's name. In his reply, Sahlins provides details that, on the one hand, are rather open-ended about the timing of the festival and, on the other hand, are very precise. The Makahiki festival was abandoned in 1819, more than a decade before the native oral histories were recorded, so there is no exact European record of its normal date. Moreover, it underwent dramatic changes between 1795 and 1810 under the reign of Kamehameha I who conquered the chiefs of the other islands. So there is a distinction to be made within the oral histories between the Makahiki of Kamehameha and the Makahiki of the time of Cook. Sahlins makes three further distinctions: the term 'Makahiki' can mean 'year'; it can refer to a four-month cycle beginning in October–November; and it can also refer to the specific twenty-three days of the Lono procession and celebrations.[24] Moreover, priests and chiefs had the power to change the dates of the Makahiki rituals. This could be done by the priests to rectify the regular differences that arose between the Hawaiian lunar notion of calendar and the solar-related timing of seasonal and diurnal changes (since a lunar year is only 354 days). The timing could also be changed by chiefs for political reasons. In 1794 Kamehameha postponed the rituals for one month during the visit of the English explorer Vancouver. Within the limits of these historical variations, Sahlins estimates that there are at least two 'reasonable options' for the dates of the rituals during Cook's visit: one beginning on 22 September 1778 and ending on 3 January 1779; the other beginning on 21 October 1778 and ending on 2 February 1779.[25] Since Cook landed on 17 January, only the second option fits his thesis. Despite all this potential for variability and reliance on probability, Sahlins claims throughout the rest of the book that Cook landed at Kealakekua Bay precisely thirteen days after the Lono procession was completed. The date of Cook's departure is even more propitious for his thesis. On the night of 3 February the *Resolution* weighed anchor and Cook left the islands. If we accept Sahlins's second option for the timing of Makahiki, Cook would have left precisely on the day that the Hawaiian religion expected Lono to depart. On his own evidence about the difficulties involved in calculating the dates of the period, and about the political and religious manipulations that were possible, this claim appears singularly over-confident— but this, of course, does not mean it could not be true.

Nonetheless, there is one piece of evidence Sahlins offers that does show that, in all probability, there was a Makahiki season in progress during the time of Cook's landing. This is a drawing by John Webber done on 2 February showing a boxing match in progress. To the left of the drawing is an image of the Makahiki representing gods at play (an elevated wooden cross-piece about three metres high from which white tapa cloth and birdskins hang). If we accept the oral history evidence that this image was only used during the Makahiki rituals then there was, indeed, a Makahiki in progress at some time during Cook's visit. Sahlins claims that boxing matches, as well as wrestling and other amusements, were traditionally staged at the end of the Makahiki to mark the passage of Lono. Overall, the weight of evidence about the timing of the Makahiki favours Sahlins's interpretation.

When Cook returned to Hawaii with a sprung mast on 13 February he was, according to Sahlins, 'out of season'. Some of the English journal writers recorded that the Hawaiian chiefs appeared 'dissatisfied' with their return and that 'our former friendship was at an end'. Sahlins argues that this was be-cause, by returning in the time of Ku, the English 'presented a mirror image of Makahiki politics' in which the Hawaiian warrior king challenges the god. Despite the considerable detail he offers for the timing of the Makahiki, Sahlins does not offer any argument about the precise position in the Hawaiian calendar of the time of Ku. He assumes it follows immediately upon the end of the Makahiki, without any break or intermission. The closest he comes to specifying the date is to say that it occurred 'soon after' the first full moon that followed the closure of the Hawaiian New Year ceremonies. Since the timing of the Hawaiian religious seasons is so crucial to his argument—he must be correct about the dates to within a handful of days—this is an odd omission. Again, it does not mean he is wrong but, when considered in conjunction with the problems for his thesis raised by the details of the fatal assault on Cook (discussed in the next section), it leaves a major hole in his argument.

THE DEATH OF COOK: The ancient Hawaiian religion held that at the end of the Makahiki the warrior king took over the powers of Lono, the god of health, wealth and agricultural fertility. 'The politics of the Makahiki', Sahlins assures us, 'was all about the aggressive seizure of Lono's gifts by the warrior chief'. The new season saw a 'transfer of rule' in which the king played the role of the upstart and humanised warrior (Ku aspect) capturing the reproductive powers of the god (Lono aspect). This happened during the Kal'i ritual in which the king comes ashore with his warriors to confront the god who stands before his temple. A warrior of the god attacks the king with spears. One of these touches the king and he dies a symbolic death as a foreign being but at the same time is reborn as an Hawaiian sovereign. A sham battle ensues in which the king emerges as conqueror.[26] Sahlins argues that Cook met his death because the Hawaiian warriors of the king Kalani'opu'u were re-enacting the Kali'i ritual. He also acknowledges, however, that the events on the fateful day, 14 February 1779, diverged in a number of ways from the detail of the ritual.

Cook had gone ashore after the theft of his ship's cutter during the night. He decided to retaliate with force, to take the Hawaiian high chief or king Kalani'opu'u captive and hold him to ransom for the return of the cutter. Cook landed with a company of marines at Kealakekua Bay and then walked the considerable distance to Kalani'opu'u's home. The king was an old man and was asleep when Cook arrived. The Englishman waited for Kalani'opu'u to waken. Cook then took him by the hand and both walked, apparently quite amicably, back to the beach. This all took several hours. Meanwhile, as part of the operation, Lieutenant Rickman had set up a blockading party at the other end of the bay. At some stage he was involved in a skirmish with the Hawaiians and shot and killed a chief named Kalimu. By the time Cook reached the beach with Kalani'opu'u, news of Kalimu's death had reached the king's wife. In company with two other chiefs, she hurried to her husband, threw her arms around him, told him of the killing of Kalimu and persuaded him not to go on board the English boats. The old man then sat down on the beach, looking 'dejected and frightened', and refused to move. By this time, more than a thousand Hawaiians had gathered to watch the affair. As the old king began to show distress, they crowded around. The English then tried to escape. The natives struck several of them, including Cook, with stones and clubs. A native drew a knife and gave Cook a fatal wound. Others then joined in stabbing him. Sahlins acknowledges that, before the intervention of Kalani'opu'u's wife, nothing had evoked the king's suspicions. 'The transition comes suddenly, at the moment the king is made to perceive Cook as his mortal enemy', he writes. 'This is the structural crisis, when all the social relations begin to change their signs.'[27]

This is also the point where Sahlins loses the argument. There is so much discrepancy between his own account of what Hawaiian religion expects to occur between Lono and the warrior king, and what actually happened between Cook and Kalani'opu'u, that his attempt to sort out what he calls this 'melee of meanings' through 'an anthropological reading of the historical texts'[28] would be found convincing by only his most charitable supporter. There are at least three major discrepancies.

First, despite the misgivings the chiefs might have had about the return of the English sailors, when Cook went to Kalani'opu'u's house he was not treated as some kind of hostile god who had returned 'out of season'. He was still regarded highly by the Hawaiians who prostrated themselves before him and, while he waited for Kalani'opu'u to waken, presented him once again with gifts of pigs and red tapa cloth. Second, in the Kali'i ritual, it is not the god who comes in from the sea but the king. He then confronts the god on shore. Sahlins acknowledges this but still insists that the scene was 'reminiscent of the climactic ritual battle, the kali'i, but played in reverse. The god Lono (Cook) was wading ashore with his warriors to confront the king'.[29] However, even in this 'mirror image' version, the 'cosmic confrontation' did not occur in the way Sahlins says it did. Cook was not killed while wading ashore but had been on land for hours. When the attack occurred, the English were running through the water, away from the beach, trying to get to their boats. Third, the king himself did not initiate any confrontation with Cook. He was initially compliant and demure. Until the fatal moment there had been nothing 'aggressive' about the actions of the king or his retinue; in fact, quite the opposite. If he was the 'upstart' representative of Ku, he appeared completely unaware of it himself until his wife persuaded him that Cook threatened his life. In direct opposition to the ritual, it was Cook, the supposed manifestation of Lono, who was the aggressor.

The credibility of Sahlins's account thus depends on his readers accepting the notion that so many aspects of the ritual could actually be 'played in reverse' and that the ancient Hawaiians would see it that way, despite their religious traditions. On the other hand, a 'Western bourgeois' interpretation would read the events in far more prosaic fashion. Kalani'opu'u's wife was worried that if he went with Cook he would suffer the same fate as Kalimu. So the Hawaiians attacked the English to save their king's life. Since the central issue to be explained in this debate comes down to a matter of choice between anthropological 'readings' of the events on the beach that day, and since the 'bourgeois' reading is less inconsistent and inherently more probable, Sahlins's case is fatally flawed. Plainly, it is the reading by Sahlins that imposes its own interpretation on the native mind, not vice versa.

STRUCTURALISM AND THE 'TRUE HETEROLOGY OF THE OTHER': The reason this debate has generated interest well beyond the ranks of scholars of Cook's voyages and ancient Hawaii is because it is the site of a struggle of considerable academic consequence about social theory and methodology. In a postcolonial era, when anthropologists and historians are acutely aware of the undesirability of imposing their own cultural categories on the cultures they are studying, the interpretation of the death of Cook throws this prospect into sharp relief. Traditionally, most heterologies or 'discourses on the other' (in plain English: 'studies of exotic cultures', but let us stick with the jargon for a while) have been made from the perspective of the observer who is a representative of Western culture and rationality. This, argues Sahlins, is 'precisely the opposite of a true heterology or science of the other', which can appreciate the radically different rationality of the other.[30] The way to approach an 'other' culture is to revive its own logic. Sahlins says this involves following Michel de Certeau's advice and taking seriously what appear to us to be incongruities or illogicalities in the behaviour and beliefs of the other. These incongruities, de Certeau assures us, 'resist Occidental specification'; that is, Western logic cannot make sense of them. As I explained in Chapter One, they are the 'shards' that remain following Western attempts to make sense of the other's culture—strange 'resistances' and 'survivals' that disrupt any apparently coherent system of interpretation, and which create a space for the 'return of the repressed'.

Sahlins's own attempt to produce a 'true heterology of the other' combines ethnography with structuralist theory. Ethnography, he argues, should resist the attempt 'to substitute our good sense for theirs, more precisely our rationality for their culture'.[31] While structuralism under previous practitioners might have been guilty of being ahistorical and unable to account for social change, Sahlins claims to have overcome this defect. In fact, his main claim to academic prominence has been the amendments he has proposed to structuralism on these grounds. He has been a critic of the concept of 'stereotypical reproduction', the idea that a culture has a propensity to replicate its structures continually no matter how dramatic the impact of particular historic events. He has argued that, in a cultural theory of history, the process 'is as much reconstruction as reproduction'. He complains with some justice that Obeyesekere misunderstands him as a supporter of the concept of stereotypical reproduction when he has in fact cited it as a defect of classical structuralist theory since 1977.[32] In *Historical Metaphors* in 1981, Sahlins explained his theory of social change, arguing that the situations encountered in practice had their own dynamic—a 'structure of the conjuncture'; that is, a set of historical relationships that both reproduce the traditional cultural categories and give them new values out of the pragmatic context. In the structure of the conjuncture, the values that are present in real events are always the product of traditional values but their modifications in practice 'have the capacity then of working back on the conventional values'.[33]

So, then, does this combination of culturally relative ethnography and evolutionary structuralism count as a 'true heterology of the other'? One only has to ask the question to see it is absurd. Every one of these concepts—'cultural relativism', 'ethnography', 'evolution' and 'structuralism', not to mention 'heterology' itself—is a product of the Western bourgeois culture that Sahlins so disparages. To follow de Certeau's advice, a 'true heterology' should take seriously all those 'shards', incongruities and apparent illogicalities that constitute the remnants of the culture of the other. The shards represent, as it were, the tip of the other's suppressed cultural iceberg and to recover them fully means rescuing the logic of the culture as well as its content. This could only be done if one adopted the basic concepts, assumptions and methodologies of the other. In other words, it is a self-contradiction to claim to study a non-Western culture in its own terms if the conceptual framework employed is entirely Western in origin. (This last statement, by the way, should not be read as a roundabout concession that all Western concepts are themselves limited to Western culture. As I argue below, the Western empirical approach is not bound by culture but is, rather, a universal scientific method.)

Structuralism, on the other hand, is neither a 'true heterology' nor a value-free methodology. Instead, it is an ideology in the same way that Marxism is an ideology. As I noted in Chapter One, it is a form of linguistic idealism. Anyone who adopts a structuralist approach has already decided a great deal about how the story of what happened in history will be told. Structuralism imposes the primacy of culture onto history in the same way that Marxism imposes the primacy of the class struggle. It believes the world is made of language and culture in the way that Marxism believes the basis of society is the means of production. Structuralism diminishes the force of economics and politics in history to the same extent that Marxism diminishes the force of religion, art and ideas. Structuralism assumes a consensus social model; that is, culture is relatively stable and not inherently riven with internal contradictions. Marxism assumes a conflict model; that is, the inevitable contest between social classes is the dynamic of history. In postmodernist jargon, both structuralism and Marxism 'decentre the subject'—they reduce or omit the impact of the individual on history. Every one of these concepts and assumptions is a product of Western social theory and, from the perspective of 'the other'—such as the ancient Hawaiians who believed that the gods were immanent in animate and inanimate objects alike—makes no sense at all.

The only way to fulfil de Certeau in a consistent way is to completely throw off Western cultural assumptions and simply record native stories and religious beliefs as they are told and reproduce them verbatim. (The reproduction would obviously be in the form of some type of Western technology, such as a book or recording, but apart from this could, in principle, remain culturally 'pure'.) To be faithful to such an account, the compiler should omit any introduction or preface, which would inevitably contaminate the native culture by rendering it all within symbolic inverted commas. The compiler should not even say 'this is what the natives believe'; he would only be able to record them saying 'this is how it is'. Sahlins might not be able to see that this is the logical consequence of the demand for a 'true heterology' but others can. In recent years a number of academics in Australia have published anthologies of Aboriginal visual, oral and written works without any apparent editorial intervention. Ironically, this has since become a successful career path for a number of non-Aboriginal academics in cultural studies.[34] In the next section I look in more detail at this approach and its problems through one similar, highly celebrated, but ultimately unsatisfactory attempt in New Zealand to reproduce the perspective of the Maori.

CULTURAL RELATIVISM AND THE RETURN OF TRIBALISM

Michel Foucault's argument that the Western sciences have no universal validity, but are merely expressions of those in authority within Western culture, has been enormously influential. It complemented the relativist conclusions about science drawn by Thomas Kuhn and Paul Feyerabend discussed in Chapter Seven. And it supported the aims of those anthropologists who in the 1970s and 1980s were seeking to establish the rational legitimacy of the native cultures they were studying. From three different directions thus emerged an intellectual impetus that has persuaded many people in the humanities and social sciences of the efficacy of cultural relativism.

Those who accept cultural relativism argue that Western ways of knowing do not deserve any privileged status. Western epistemologies should be judged as simply different from, not superior to, those of other cultures. The claim that Western science has found the path to objectivity is nothing but a cultural conceit. 'Every civilisation tends to overestimate the objectivity of its thought', the French structuralist Claude Levi-Strauss has observed, 'and this tendency is never absent.' Citing this remark, Marshall Sahlins goes on to argue that the very perceptions upon which Western scientific empiricism are based can themselves never be free of cultural conditioning. Sahlins claims that, while all human beings share the same biological mechanisms of perception, people from different cultures actually see things in different ways because their experience, including the training of their senses, is organised 'according to social canons of relevance'. Hence, he argues, 'people who are perceiving the same objects are not necessarily perceiving the same *kinds* of things... And conversely, people may agree about what certain images are, while perceiving them in entirely different ways—as happens to the red-green colour blind'.[35] According to this view, the human baby is born with an inbuilt capacity for learning but no 'hard-wired' perception, behaviour or social dispositions of any kind. Sahlins has long been an advocate of the notion that biological or evolutionary patterning of human behaviour is mistaken. Causality does not flow outward from the individual's psychology, he has argued, but inward from the social world.[36] In short, culture determines our being and, since cultures vary, there can be no such thing as a common human perception, a common human nature or what Obeyesekere calls a common human 'practical rationality'.

Not only do cultural relativists reject the notion that Western ideas provide greater insights than those of other cultures but, as I showed Foucault arguing in Chapter Five, the empiricist epistemology that provided the methodology for Western science from the seventeenth to the twentieth century is now said to have run its course. According to Foucault, it is being replaced by a new discursive formation drawn from hermeneutics and Nietzschean philosophy. So cultural relativism regards what is usually called 'Western knowledge' as an intellectual phenomenon with strict limitations in terms of both geographic space and historic time.

Cultural relativism's attitude both to morals and to politics is similar to its views on epistemology. There can be no universals in either. While those of us brought up with Western concepts of morality might find the practices of some non-Western people abhorrent—such as the ritual execution and cannibalisation of thousands of people a year practised by the Aztecs of Mexico, which I documented in Chapter Two—cultural relativism holds that we should recognise such feelings as the product of our own cultural confines. We have no right either to judge or to act, as the Spaniards of the sixteenth century did, against the practices of such other cultures. The political perspective of cultural relativism regards each culture as free to pursue its own ends within its own traditions and rationalities. Western concepts such as democracy, free speech and human rights are not universal principles but merely the products of specific times and places—the Enlightenment of eighteenth century Europe and its Western successors—which should not be imposed on other times and places. Hence, Foucault, though a citizen of republican, democratic France, found no inconsistency in publicly endorsing the bloody and authoritarian religious state of the Ayatollah Khomeini in Iran.

The late Ernest Gellner pointed out the basic logical flaws in cultural relativism. In his book *Postmodernism, Reason and Religion*, Gellner showed that relativists are saddled with two unresolvable dilemmas. They endorse as legitimate other cultures that do not return the compliment. Some other cultures, of which one of the best known is Islam, will have no truck with relativism of any kind. The devout are totally confident of the universalism of their own beliefs which derive from the dictates of God, an absolute authority who is external to the world and its cultures. They regard a position such as postmodern cultural relativism as profoundly mistaken and, moreover, debasing. Relativism devalues their faith because it reduces it to merely one of many equally valid systems of meaning. So, entailed within cultural relativism is, first, an endorsement of absolutisms that deny it, and, second, a demeaning attitude to cultures it claims to respect.[37]

The very existence of the discipline of anthropology itself provides another kind of dilemma. If other cultures were really so alien that there was no common human perception or underlying human nature, their meanings systems would be forever beyond our grasp. We could study their external behaviour but could never pretend to what the German philosophic tradition calls *verstehen*, that is, the ability to think ourselves into their mentalities. Yet *verstehen* is exactly what anthropologists like Sahlins are claiming to offer when they explain the meaning of the religious ceremonies and symbols of other cultures. In a powerful critique of the relativism of what they call the 'standard social science model', the evolutionary psychologists John Tooby and Leda Cosmides have argued that without the existence of a universal human 'metaculture' it would be impossible for us to understand the meanings of other cultures. The best refutation of cultural relativism, they argue, is the activity of anthropologists themselves—who could not understand or live within other human groups unless the inhabitants of those groups shared assumptions that were, in fact, similar to those of the ethnographer.[38] One good example of this truism, we might note, is the anthropology of ancient Hawaii. This is confirmed by nothing less than Marshall Sahlins's own account of that society. In terms of underlying social structure, the Hawaiians of 1779 shared with their English visitors similar forms of organisation. Both had political and religious hierarchies, the separation of church and state, plus all the paraphenalia these two institutions have generated wherever they have been found: meetings, rituals, ceremonies, festivals, temples, icons, warriors and warfare. We could add to the list the familiar activities of everyday life shared by native and visitor cultures alike—boating, fishing, agriculture, animal husbandry, cooking, clothing and sport, not to mention their own versions of astronomy and the calendar. In short, the evidence of Sahlins's own ethnography refutes the relativism he wants to impose upon it.

Dilemmas of this kind, however, have so far remained largely unrecognised or ignored because cultural relativism has one great appeal. The acknowledged superiority of Western technical methods can no longer be taken to extend to non-technical areas such as religion, culture or politics. Other cultures are thus freed from Western intellectual hegemony and can revive their own beliefs and traditions without fear of being contradicted or ridiculed. At a time when many people in postcolonial countries and the West itself are arguing from various perspectives for a revival of cultural autonomy, this is a powerful attraction. The logical consequences, however, go much further than many Western intellectuals who have endorsed the concept might reasonably have expected. Let me give two recent examples of such extensions, one from North America, the other from Australia.

In recent years, some textbook committees of secondary school authorities in Berkeley, California, have been trying to ban history and social science textbooks that assert that native American populations arrived on the North American continent from Asia towards the end of the last Ice Age. These origins, confirmed by generations of archaeologists, anthropologists and prehistorians, run counter to the myths of the native Americans themselves. Academic supporters of the native Americans are now arguing that there is no reason why the findings of non-indigenous scientists should be privileged over the narratives that the indigenes tell about themselves.[39]

This American example has inspired imitators around the globe. One prominent Australian black activist and academic, Roberta Sykes, has recently argued in print that the claim by white scholars that Aborigines arrived in this country by way of the Indonesian archipelago is a 'myth' that 'is contradicted by the Australian Aborigines' own mythology'.[40] Sykes, who holds a PhD from Harvard, is thus arguing that Aboriginal myth has the same status as, and can be used to refute the claims of, Western science. The Aboriginal poet Ken Canning also disputes the claims by scientists that Aborigines migrated to Australia. These assertions are wrong according to indigenous oral history and are at variance with the intense belief of many Aborigines that they are descended from the spirit creators of this land, he says. Canning, an academic employed by the University of Technology, Sydney, argues that by thus continuing to assert the supremacy of their world view, Western scientists and social scientists clash directly with indigenous beliefs in a 'racist' way.[41]

If we accepted this logic, only the relativist could avoid the charge of racism. However, anyone who takes the above beliefs seriously is also committed to the position that the Aborigines did not evolve in Africa along with the rest of us and must therefore belong to a different species. Here we can see not only the disastrous intellectual consequences of this position but also political perspectives that are the opposite of what they claim to be. It is the universalism of Western science that recognises all human beings as the same people with the same origins. In opposition to this, cultural relativism supports the view that each native group is different and unique and that those who think they are biologically distinct are entitled to their belief. It is Western universalism that is anti-racist, not relativism.

One of the seminal texts of the relativist movement is the literary critic Edward Said's 1978 book *Orientalism*. Said argues that Western imperialism's racism and oppression of the Easterner was not just the result of mistaken policies or authoritarian regimes. Rather it was rooted in the Western Enlightenment's self-aggrandising delusion that it had the key to a universally valid knowledge.[42] One of these delusions in the writing of the history of colonialism has been the imposition of what the French postmodernist thinker Jean François Lyotard calls 'metanarratives'. By this he means historical accounts that claim to see meaning in events beyond those apparent to the view of the participants. Edward Said argues that the metanarrative arises out of the perspective provided by imperialism. For instance, in his 1993 book *Culture and Imperialism*, Said claims that the boy hero of Rudyard Kipling's novel *Kim* 'is able to see all India from the vantage point of controlled observation'. This was never a perspective adopted by the people of India themselves, Said says, but was part of the 'microphysics' of power through which the British controlled India.[43]

In particular, both Said and Lyotard reject the attempts by Western historiography to see beyond the judgements of the indigenous peoples who became the subjects of the European imperial powers in the eighteenth and nineteenth centuries. In the countries of North America and the Pacific where the indigenous inhabitants were conquered by Europeans in this period, it is now common to find the views of Lyotard, Said, Foucault and other postmodernists influencing the rewriting of history from a native perspective. In his recent book on the politics and culture of indigenous Australians, *Us Mob*, the Aboriginal author Mudrooroo argues that a proper history of Australia would need to incorporate indigenous culture on indigenous terms. He says this means structuring history around place and family and basing the time sequence on genealogy in the way that Aboriginal oral histories do.[44] Mudrooroo is simply recommending this, rather than actually writing any history this way. However, there is an example from New Zealand of what such a history would be like.

Anne Salmond's 1991 prize-winning work of history and anthropology, *Two Worlds: First Meetings Between Maori and Europeans 1642-1772*, argues that if history is to be faithful to events that involved protagonists from different societies it cannot be fairly interpreted from one point of view. In particular, she wants to give Maori opinions of the meaning of their contact with Dutch and English explorers the same status as those of the European visitors. However, in pursuit of this aim, she reduces the records of both to the level of the stories that each people told themselves about the contacts. For the Maori, the explorers' visits were 'simply puzzling, extraordinary interludes in the life of various tribal communities'.

The ships—floating islands, mythological 'birds' or canoes full of *tupua* or 'goblins'—came into this bay or that, shot local people or presented them with strange gifts, were welcomed or pelted with rocks, and after a short time went away again and were largely forgotten.

For the Europeans, the same encounters 'were simply episodes in the story of Europe's "discovery" of the world—more voyages to add to the great collections of "Voyages" that had already been made'.

The genre of discovery tales was an ancient one in Europe, with a well-worn narrative line—explorers ventured into unknown seas, found new lands and named their coastal features, described exotic plants, animals and inhabitants, and survived attacks by tattooed savages (or worse still, cannibals) with spears. These stories were very popular with ordinary people at the time, for they defined Europeans as 'civilised' in contrast with the 'savages' and 'barbarians' to be found elsewhere ... [45]

The book thus treats both sides of this story as equally interpretable texts. Neither account is shown to be more truthful or penetrating than the other. Salmond tells her readers that she adopted this approach partly through her desire to rescue the Maori side of the story and partly through her reading of European philosophers—'Heidegger, Foucault, Ricoeur, Gadamer, Habermas, Hesse, Derrida, Eco and others who I thought might help me to understand some of the essential questions involved'.[46] At the time of contact with the European explorers, the Maori were engaged in continual tribal warfare. One of the prizes of victory was the killing and eating of opposing warriors. Cannibalism was rife throughout Maori communities and, since they had exterminated all large land animals and birds, human flesh constituted a major source of protein in the Maori diet. To ensure her account is balanced, Salmond also provides an ethnographic sketch of Europe during the seventeenth and eighteenth centuries that focuses largely on the bloody warfare between states, the violent uprisings and revolutions of the period and the cruelty practised towards criminals. To match the distasteful aspects of Maori culture she looks for comparable behaviour in Europe and publishes a number of woodcut illustrations of criminals being subject to 'birching, beheading, hanging, drowning, burning, quartering, eye-gouging and other forms of maiming'.[47] She even reproduces a contemporary artist's drawing of the death of Robert François Damiens whose drawn-out execution for his unsuccessful attempt on the life of Louis XV in 1757 was described in graphic detail in the introduction to Foucault's book *Discipline and Punish*.

What is missing from all this concern with 'balance' is an appropriate sense of the portentous nature of the explorers' contacts. At one stage when discussing her use of the records of Maori oral historians, Salmond writes that 'the European visits were of marginal interest to tribal historians, since the European protagonists were external to the local genealogical networks which provide the key principle for ordering tribal historical accounts'.[48] Another New Zealand historian, Peter Munz, has made a penetrating critique of Salmond's methodology, pointing out that the Maori lack of interest in the strangers and their focus on the bonding effect of the recital of genealogies deprived them of either an historical or sociological perspective that would have served their long-term interests better.

Thus they were not able to take an interest in the Europeans who were coming to threaten and eventually destroy the indigenous style of life. This is a serious matter, for a society in which people are unable to discern and diagnose life-threatening events is lacking in something that is essential.[49]

Similarly, Munz points out, what is omitted from Salmond's account is an historical perspective that transcends parochial Maori culture. Her approach lacks a 'metanarrative' that could put the events into their historical perspective and show that the Maori view of the apparent triviality of the European visits was profoundly mistaken. What her account also does is to considerably reduce the stature of the European side of the story which, rather than simply being one more example of the genre of discovery tales, contained within itself the very metanarrative that the Maori perspective lacked. The Europeans recognised full well the significance of their visit for the Maori. They knew that, once discovered by Europe, the Maori way of life was suddenly vulnerable in a way that no Maori had ever imagined. This was the historical reality whether the Maori historians saw it or not. Munz observes that the European explorers also knew that their visits confirmed many other things they knew but the Maori did not—that the earth was round, that its islands or continents were not yet all known but soon would be, and that they had the expertise in seamanship, astronomy and geography to return to Europe and tell others of their discoveries.

What is really peculiar about the type of history Salmond is trying to write is that her readers know all these things too. With their own hindsight, they cannot help but read into Salmond's account their knowledge that the European discoveries eventually led to white settlement, military conflict and the displacement of the Maori from much of their land. In other words, the attempt to eliminate metanarrative by telling things exclusively from the point of view of the participant is impossible. No matter how pristine the account, readers will always impose their own mental overview onto the story drawn from what they know of the outcome. In short, Salmond's attempt to portray the Maori perspective by replacing one European methodology—empirical historiography—with another—relativist hermeneutics—turns out to be nothing but a futile exercise in political correctness, an attempt to write a euphemistic version of history that offends nobody's racial sensitivity, at the expense of telling what really happened.

Cultural relativism began as an intellectual critique of Western thought but has now become an influential justification for one of the contemporary era's most potent political forces. This is the revival of tribalism in thinking and politics. The demand by representatives of tribal cultures to have the sole governance of their affairs is probably the biggest single cause of bloodshed in the world today. It has produced the charnel house politics of Northern Ireland, Sri Lanka, the Sudan, Central Africa, the Middle East and the Balkans. Postmodernism and cultural relativism are complicit in this—both in their insistence on the integrity of all tribal cultures, no matter what practices or values they perpetuate, and in their denunciation of all imperial cultures. In *Culture and Imperialism*, Edward Said even takes to task the Marxist literary critic Raymond Williams for the 'massive absence' in his work of any condemnation of the English imperialism imposed upon Williams's Welsh ancestors.[50] Rather than an advance in political conceptualisation, however, the politics of relativism should be recognised as simply a mirror image of the racist ideologies that accompanied and justified Western imperialism in the colonial era: once it was the West that imagined it brought civilisation to the heathen; today it is tribal cultures that are revered as humane, and imperial cultures that are condemned as brutish.

This vision, however, is of little assistance for anyone seeking to come to terms with particular political conflicts. How does one differentiate, for instance, between demands for self-determination that appear morally legitimate, such as those made by the people of East Timor against their military annexation by Indonesia, and the barbaric kind of tribalism that committed some of the worst atrocities of recent history in the name of creating a Greater Serbia? How can one define some tribal demands, such as those made by

Armenians against Turks or Kurds against Iraqis, as proper attempts to restore land expropriated only two generations ago, while recognising other ancestral disputes—such as that between Greek and Macedonian based on who occupied territory more than two thousand years ago or on the ethnic identity of Alexander the Great—as political absurdities? We need to be able to make the same kinds of discriminations between imperialisms. As the history of the past millennium clearly demonstrates, imperialism has taken many forms. It has imposed horrors and it has eliminated horrors. Different imperial powers have had different records in these matters and the behaviour of any one imperial power—whether it be English, French, American, Russian, Chinese, Ottoman, Khmer or Mogul—has varied dramatically at different periods of time. How does one judge the difference between the relatively benign imperialism of the Portuguese in Timor and the ruthless oppression imposed by their Indonesian successors, or indeed the great disparity in the treatment by the Portuguese dictator Salazar of his colonial subjects in Timor on the one hand, and war-torn Mozambique on the other?

Relativism is no help in any of these issues. All the relativist can do is either take sides according to ethnic preference or assert that each side has its own legitimate point of view—a position guaranteed to earn contempt from all concerned. The only values that can assist one to sort out these questions are the universal kind, and the only internationally accepted universal values are those based on human rights, that is, those values born and nurtured within the Western tradition. Though they originated in the European Enlightenment and became politically established through their overthrow of the *anciens regimes* of Europe, they have more claim than any others to global acceptance. They form the legal code of virtually all democratic nations and have been sanctioned by international law. One does not have to be a Francis Fukuyama type of historical determinist to recognise that the concepts of human rights and liberal democratic government have swept nearly all before them in the last fifty years and look like continuing the process for the next fifty at least.

In contrast, the values of tribalism, despite their enthusiastic endorsement by the academic left, have much more difficult prospects in the real world. The followers of Michel de Certeau argue that cultural diversity has everywhere proved irrepressible. Wherever an indigenous culture appears to have been wiped out by imperialism, we eventually see 'the return of the repressed'. Today, if proof of the thesis is required, the high profile of indigenous cultural expression in many countries in the form of state-funded artefacts, music and performances can readily be cited. Hence relativists draw the conclusion that, given half a chance, cultural diversity will return to regain its place as the natural condition of humanity. It is this hope that nurtures the multicultural political movement of today.

Unfortunately, the historical record does not support the thesis. For the past ten thousand years at least, indigenous cultures on every continent have been subject to a process of change that has varied from merger and absorption into other cultures to complete obliteration by a conquering power. Every culture that exists today has been subject to either violent or peaceful amalgamation and absorption of earlier smaller communities. The process has occurred just as certainly, if not to the same extent, in the relatively isolated indigenous cultures of New Guinea as it has in the multiracial societies of North America. If this were not true, human beings would still be living in the small family-based clans that constituted hunter-gatherer society. In a striking analysis of the historical logic of cultural change, Peter Munz argues that whether we like it or not, we are all the inheritors of cultures that have been forged out of a long process of suppression and absorption of the cultures that arose before them. [51] Just as inexorably, this has meant that cultures that once were in conflict have ceased their struggle and cultural diversity has diminished. Over time, most of those societies that once housed two or more disparate cultures ceased to be multicultural and became monocultural. This has occurred either by minority cultures succumbing to a dominant culture or through merger and accommodation on terms acceptable to both sides.

Accompanying the long-term tendency to monoculturalism has been a similar change in the degree of openness of communities. The earliest hunter-gatherers formed largely exclusive societies that refused to accept as members, and indeed regarded as enemies, those who did not belong to their descent group. They then developed into societies that admitted outsiders through marriage. With the emergence of large-scale settlement and centralised states came societies that would potentially include anybody who wanted to be included. The difference in these degrees of exclusiveness can be seen plainly today where native communities still exist. In countries like Australia and New Zealand, indigenous people define themselves through ancestry and bloodlines. By contrast, immigrants to these countries, no matter what their ancestry, are accepted by nothing more than declarations of citizenship. As Munz has put it: 'while one cannot "become" a Maori, one can "become" a New Zealander.'[52] Clearly, any attempt at cultural merger and accommodation is made very difficult if one side identifies itself by ancestry and genealogy, thereby defining itself in terms so exclusive that it forever rules out the inclusion of the other side.

Those who are arguing for the revival of tribalism, then, are not only trying to push the barrow of history back up a pretty steep slope but are involved in some expensive political and cultural trade-offs. The return of tribalism would mean a revival of cultural diversity, which might have some value from an aesthetic point of view but would also have its down side. A revival of cultural exclusiveness would mean a return to differentiating between human beings on the basis of genealogical blood lines, in other words, on racial grounds. If the history of the twentieth century has taught anything it is that the attempt to establish societies based on the latter is a sure road to catastrophe. Cultures based on religion, political principles or historical tradition always have the potential for accommodation with others. Cultures based exclusively on race cannot, by their very nature, do this. It is a great irony that the cultural relativist and multicultural movements gain most of their support from those people of European descent who want to avoid derogatory attitudes towards the people and cultures of other races. This is a very decent sentiment and one that derives from the basic principle of Western liberalism that all human beings are equal. These people should be reminded that the first thing to be rejected by cultural exclusiveness, wherever it becomes entrenched, is the very liberal principle that led them to support it in the first place.

Nonetheless, in the postcolonial era it has seemed natural to many brought up on liberal principles to go one step further than simple individual egalitarianism and to argue that it is not just all people that are equal but all cultures or meanings systems as well. This not only puts Western culture in its place but also relativises the whole corpus of Western knowledge. However, this extension of the argument should be recognised as illegitimate. The liberal democratic notion that all people are equal means equal in a legal and political sense. All people should be treated equally before the law and all should have an equal voice in the governance of their society. It has never meant that all people have equality of knowledge, ability or understanding. Similarly, all cultures or meanings systems are demonstrably not equal in terms of knowledge and ability. The inference drawn by ideologues like Edward Said, that the political liberation of colonial peoples should be accompanied by their epistemological liberation, does not follow. Indeed, those former colonies who want to expel Western thought in the way that they expelled Western imperialism should recognise that they would be throwing away the most valuable intellectual tools available to them.

Despite the claims of the relativists, there is one particular style of knowledge that has proven, historically, so overwhelmingly powerful—technologically, economically, militarily and administratively—that all societies have had to make their peace with it and adopt it. Ernest Gellner has argued that, no matter how unfashionable it might be to say it today, there is but one genuinely valid style of knowledge and that the mainstream of the Western scientific tradition has captured it. The epistemological grounds for the empirical methods of science contain some contentious assertions, he acknowledges, and agreement is lacking even among those philosophers who completely endorse the procedures themselves. But this does not constitute a good reason to doubt the efficacy of the methodology. Western science has trumped all other cognitive styles when judged by the pragmatic criterion of technological efficacy, but also when assessed by criteria such as precision, elaboration, elegance and sustained and consensual growth. In other words, Western knowledge works, and none of the others do with remotely the same effectiveness.[53]

In asserting the absolutism and non-relativism of Western scientific method, Gellner says this status is quite separate from any question about the ranking of the inhabitants of Western societies. It has nothing whatever to do with a racist, or any other, glorification of one segment of humanity over another. It is a style of knowledge and its implementation, not any category of personnel, that is being singled out. That style of knowledge did, of course, have to emerge somewhere and at some time, and to this extent it certainly has links with a particular tradition or culture. It emerged in one social context, but it is clearly accessible to all humanity. It endorses no single nation, culture or race. It is not clear which of the conditions surrounding its birth were crucial, and which were merely accidental and irrelevant, and the crucial conditions might well have come together in other places and at other times. Its greatest affinity need not be, and probably no longer is, with its place of origin. Indeed, Gellner observes, the first nation to be both scientific and industrial, Great Britain, is not at present at the top of the 'first industrial division' and in recent years has been struggling in the relegation zone.[54] This powerful form of cognition is not the prerogative of any one human group. So it does not, in this sense, give rise to any ranking of human groups. Far from being bound by Western culture, Western science belongs to the whole of humanity.

The same is true of history. The attempt by cultural relativism and postmodernism to eliminate the metanarrative from history—that is, to eliminate the narrative of what really happened irrespective of whether the participants were aware of it or not—would deprive us all, no matter what culture we inhabit, of genuine knowledge of our past. This attempt is not only a theoretical delusion but is politically inept. Though used most often these days to assert the esteem of indigenous cultures, cultural relativism will never serve the real interests of indigenous peoples if it denies them access to the truth about the past. This book has been designed to demonstrate and to reassert that the best method for gaining this access is through the tools refined by the discipline of history. Just as Western science is open to everyone, Western historical method is available to the people of any culture to understand their past and their relations with other peoples. It is by facing the truth of both our separate and our common histories that we can best learn to live with one another.

1 Michel Foucault, *The Order of Things: An Archaeology of the Human Sciences*, (French edn 1966), Vintage Books, New York, 1994, p xix

2 Marshall Sahlins, *How "Natives" Think: About Captain Cook, For Example*, University of Chicago Press, Chicago, 1995, pp 158, 163

3 Marshall Sahlins, *How "Natives" Think*, p 14

4 Marshall Sahlins, *How "Natives" Think*, pp 157-8

5 James Franklin has drawn my attention to *Stroud's Judicial Dictionary*, 5th edn, London, 1986, and the vagaries of legal definitions of animals (pp 127, 762, 968). Camels, for instance, are domestic animals but performing elephants are wild; a domestic fowl is an animal but a cock kept for cock-fighting is not an animal at all, according to Scottish law. On Sahlins's logic, ethnographers should be flocking to Scotland to study a culture as exotic as anything out of Africa.

6 Gananath Obeyesekere, *The Apotheosis of Captain Cook: European Mythmaking in the Pacific*, Princeton University Press, Princeton, 1992, p 124

7 Clifford Geertz, 'Culture War', *New York Review of Books*, XLII, 19, 30 November 1995, pp 4-6

8 Marshall Sahlins, *How "Natives" Think*, p 167

9 Marshall Sahlins, *How "Natives" Think*, p 144

10 Marshall Sahlins, *How "Natives" Think*, pp 58, 134

11 Marshall Sahlins, *How "Natives" Think*, pp 121, 128-9

12 Valerio Valeri, *Kingship and Sacrifice: Ritual and society in ancient Hawaii*, University of Chicago Press, Chicago, 1985

13 Sir Peter Buck, 'Cook's discovery of the Hawaiian Islands', *Bernice P. Bishop Museum Bulletin*, 157, Honolulu, 1945; John Charlot, 'The use of Akua for living chiefs', in his *The Hawaiian Poetry of Religion and Politics*, Institute of Polynesian Studies, Monograph series no. 5, University of Hawaii Press, Honolulu, 1985, pp 31-5; John Charlot, 'Valerio Valeri, *Kingship and Sacrifice: Ritual and society in ancient Hawaii*, (review) *Pacific Studies*, 10, 2, 1987, pp 107-47; Steen Bergendorff, Ulla Hasagar, Peter Henriques, 'Mythopraxis and History: On the interpretation of the Makahiki', *Journal of the Polynesian Society*, 97, 1988, pp 391-408

14 Marshall Sahlins, *How "Natives" Think*, pp 223-4

15 Marshall Sahlins, *How "Natives" Think*, p 60-1

16 Marshall Sahlins, *How "Natives" Think*, p 224

17 Marshall Sahlins, *How "Natives" Think*, p 55

18 Marshall Sahlins, *How "Natives" Think*, pp 120-1

19 Marshall Sahlins, *How "Natives" Think*, p 59

20 Marshall Sahlins, *How "Natives" Think*, p 178

21 Bob Connolly and Robin Anderson, *First Contact*, Viking Penguin, New York, 1987

22 Connolly and Anderson, *First Contact*, p 140

23 Marshall Sahlins, *How "Natives" Think*, p 185

24 Marshall Sahlins, *How "Natives" Think*, p 27, fn 13

25 Marshall Sahlins, *How "Natives" Think*, p 32

26 Marshall Sahlins, *How "Natives" Think*, pp 69, 70, 81, 82

27 Marshall Sahlins, *How "Natives" Think*, p 84

28 Marshall Sahlins, *How "Natives" Think*, p 83

29 Marshall Sahlins, *How "Natives" Think*, p 82

30 Marshall Sahlins, *How "Natives" Think*, p 118

31 Marshall Sahlins, *How "Natives" Think*, p 118

32 Marshall Sahlins, *How "Natives" Think*, p 246

33 Marshall Sahlins, *Historical Metaphors and Mythical Realities: Studies in the early history of the Sandwich Island kingdom*, University of Michigan Press, Ann Arbor, 1981, p 35

34 Stephen Muecke, Professor of Cultural Studies at the University of Technology, Sydney, is one example, although his anthologies of Aboriginal stories usually include an obligatory essay on Western cultural theory. See Paddy Roe, *Gularabulu* (Stephen Muecke ed.), Fremantle Arts Centre Press, Fremantle, 1983, and Stephen Muecke, (ed.),*Reading the Country: An introduction to nomadology*, Fremantle Arts Centre Press, Fremantle, 1984.

35 Marshall Sahlins, *How "Natives" Think*, p 155

36 Marshall Sahlins, *The Use and Abuse of Biology: An anthropological critique of sociobiology*, University of Michigan Press, Ann Arbor, 1976

37 Ernest Gellner, *Postmodernism, Reason and Religion*, Routledge, London, 1992, p 74

38 John Tooby and Leda Cosmides, 'The Psychological Foundations of Culture', in Jerome H. Barkow, Leda Cosmides and John Tooby, (eds.), *The Adapted Mind: Evolutionary psychology and the generation of culture*, Oxford University Press, New York, 1992, p 92

39 Paul R. Gross and Norman Levitt, *Higher Superstition: The academic left and its quarrels with science*, The Johns Hopkins University Press, Baltimore, 1994, pp 247–8

40 Roberta Sykes, 'History without morality', *Sydney Morning Herald*, 10 December 1994, p 10A.

41 Debra Jopson, 'Racism or just arrogance?', *Sydney Morning Herald*, 14 April 1995, p 11

42 Edward Said, *Orientalism*, (1st edn 1978), Penguin, Harmondsworth, 1985

43 Edward Said, *Culture and Imperialism*, Vintage, London, 1993, pp 162–96

44 Mudrooroo, *Us Mob, History, Culture, Struggle: An introduction to indigenous Australia*, Angus and Robertson, Sydney, 1995, pp 185–6

45 Anne Salmond, *Two Worlds: First Meetings Between Maori and Europeans 1642-1772*, Viking, Auckland, 1991, pp 11–12

46 Anne Salmond, *Two Worlds*, p 15

47 Anne Salmond, *Two Worlds*, p 50

48 Anne Salmond, *Two Worlds*, p 436

49 Peter Munz, 'The Two Worlds of Anne Salmond in Postmodern Fancy Dress', *New Zealand Journal of History*, University of Auckland, 28, 1, April 1994, p 62

50 Edward Said, *Culture and Imperialism*, p 77. Let me play a relativist card here and note that I have the appropriate ethnic credentials to take a position in any debate on Welsh history, unlike Said who should heed his own ethnocentric advice and keep out of our affairs. Rather than being oppressed, my own Welsh ancestors were liberated by English imperialism. My great grandfather, Eleazar Owens, was emancipated from the agricultural labour of his parents and elevated first to the occupation of teacher at one of Her Majesty's Government schools in Aberystwyth and then, happily for his descendants, to the British colony of New South Wales where he became a publican and, in his own words, a gentleman.

51 Peter Munz, 'The Two Worlds of Anne Salmond', pp 71–5

52 Peter Munz, 'The Two Worlds of Anne Salmond', p 75

53 Ernest Gellner, *Postmodernism, Reason and Religion*, pp 61–2

54 Ernest Gellner, *Postmodernism, Reason and Religion*, p 61

ACKNOWLEDGEMENTS

I AM MOST GRATEFUL to the many historians in Australia and New Zealand who have helped to shore up my morale by writing to give me their support for publishing this book. In particular, I would like to thank two philosophers, James Franklin of the University of New South Wales and Robert Nola of the University of Auckland, and the historian Peter Munz of Victoria University of Wellington, for making constructive criticisms of some of my initial points. I have taken advantage of their advice and revised the text for this edition accordingly.

The author and publisher wish to thank the authors and publishers listed below for permission to reprint copyright material.

Perry Anderson, *A Zone of Engagement,* Verso/New Left Books, London
Paul Carter, *The Road to Botany Bay*, Faber and Faber Ltd, London; Alfred A. Knopf Inc, New York
Inga Clendinnen, *Aztecs: An Interpretation*, Cambridge University Press, Oakleigh
Inga Clendinnen, 'Fierce and Unnatural Cruelty: Cortés and the Conquest of Mexico', in Stephen Greenblatt (ed.), *New World Encounters*, University of California Press, Berkeley
Greg Dening, *Mr Bligh's Bad Language: Passion, Power and Theatre on the Bounty*, Cambridge University Press, Oakleigh
Anthony Giddens, *The Consequences of Modernity*, Blackwells Publishers, Oxford
John Keegan, *The History of Warfare*, Hutchinson, London
Thomas Kuhn, *The Structure of Scientific Revolutions*, The University of Chicago Press, Chicago
Hayden White, *Metahistory: The Historical Imagination in Nineteenth Century Europe*, The Johns Hopkins University Press, Baltimore

INDEX

KEITH WINDSCHUTTLE has been a lecturer in history, social policy, sociology, and media studies at a number of Australian academic institutions including the University of New South Wales, the University of Wollongong, the New South Wales Institute of Technology, and Macleay College, Sydney. He is author of five other books on issues in Australian society. He lives in Sydney with his wife and two children.